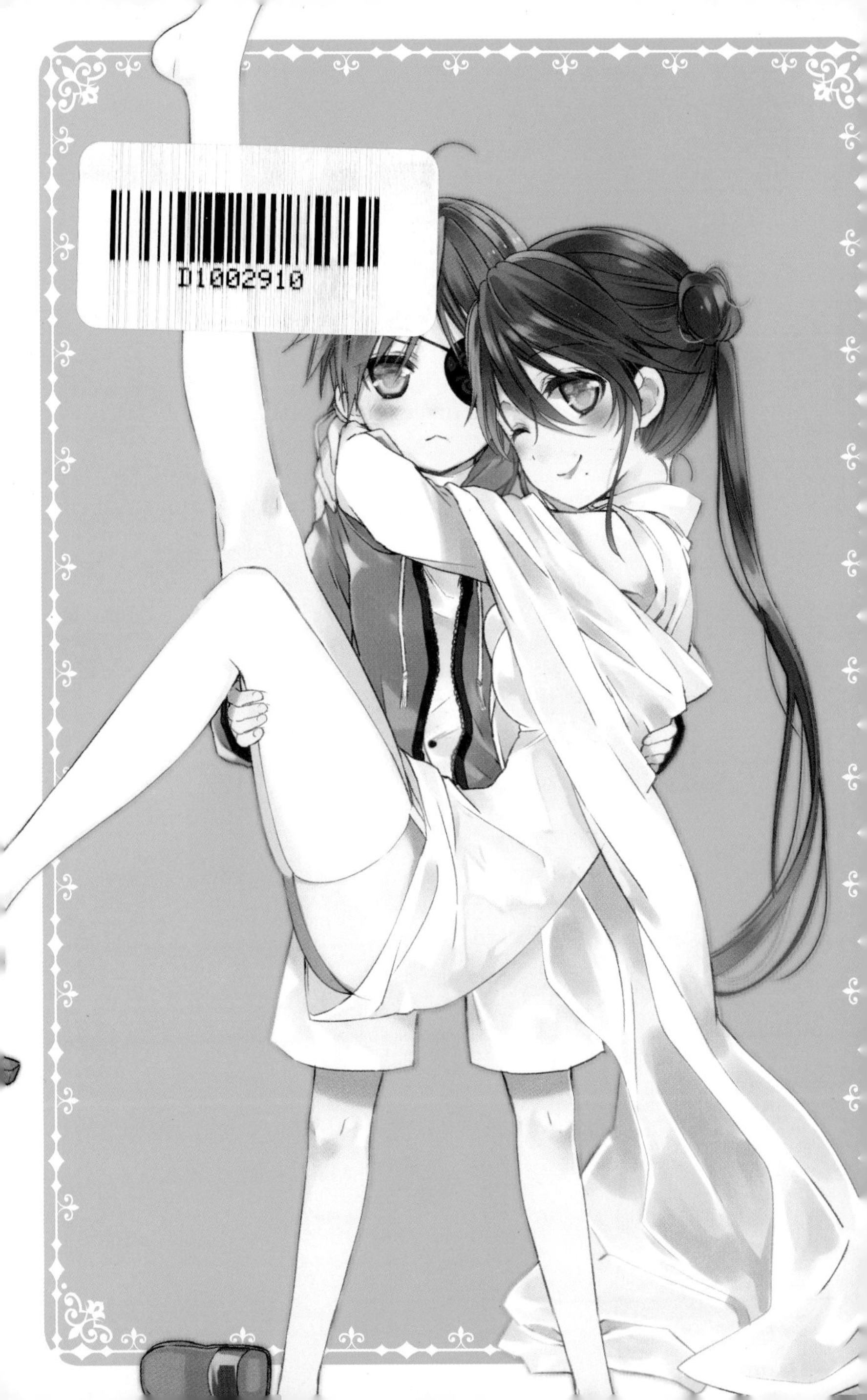

Page 14 ✦ **THE FEELING OF LOVE**........................... 9

Page 15 ✦ **THE DEVOTED DIRECTOR'S DREAM** ... 61

Page 16 ✦ **CHRISTMAS EVE (PART 1)** ..................... 93

Page 17 ✦ **CHRISTMAS EVE (PART 2)** ..................... 125

One Shot 1 ✦ **NOT MY GIRLFRIEND,
MY CHILDHOOD FRIEND** ..................... 169

One Shot 2 ✦ **DEFECTIVE GIRL** ................................... 177

✦ **AFTERWORD** ......................................... 186

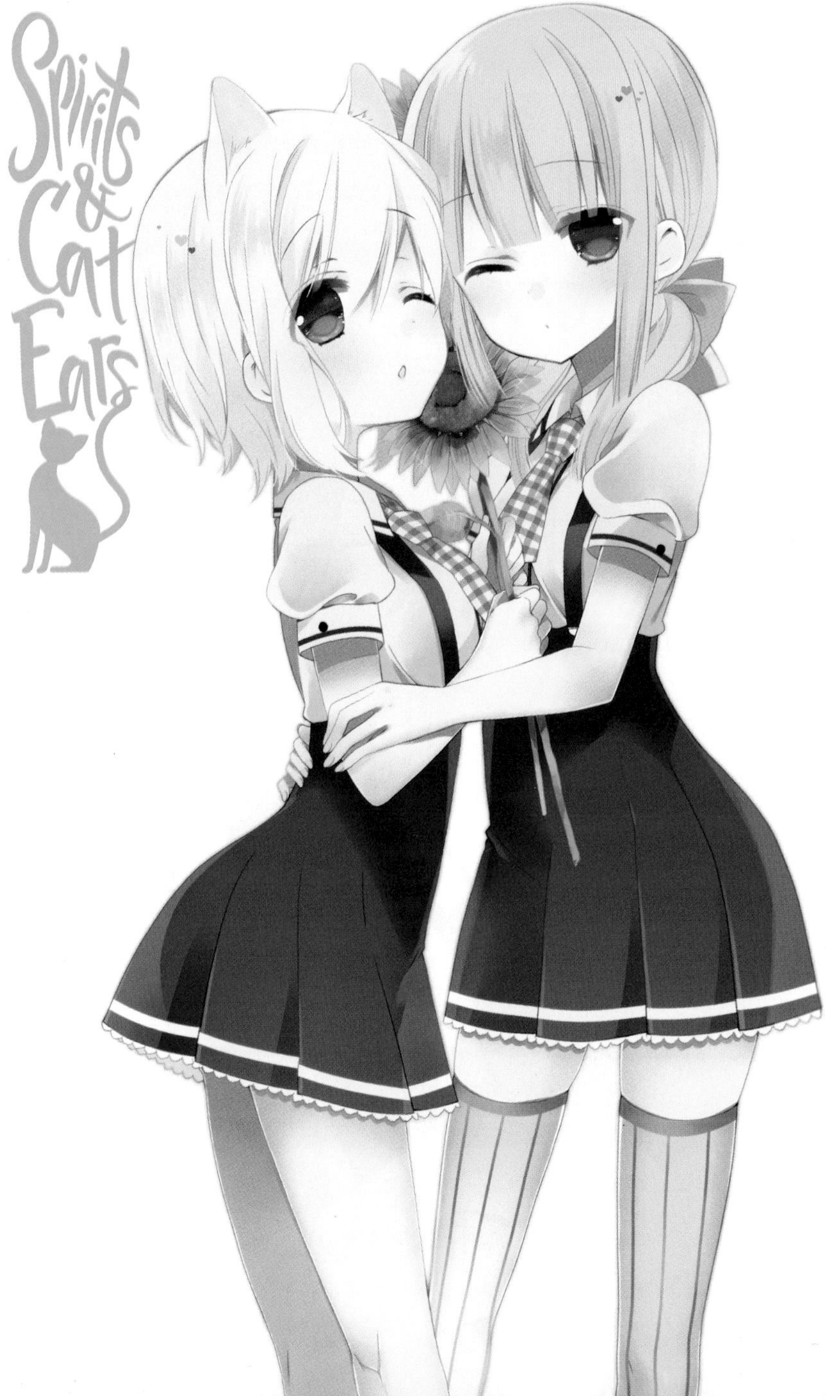
Spirits & Cat Ears

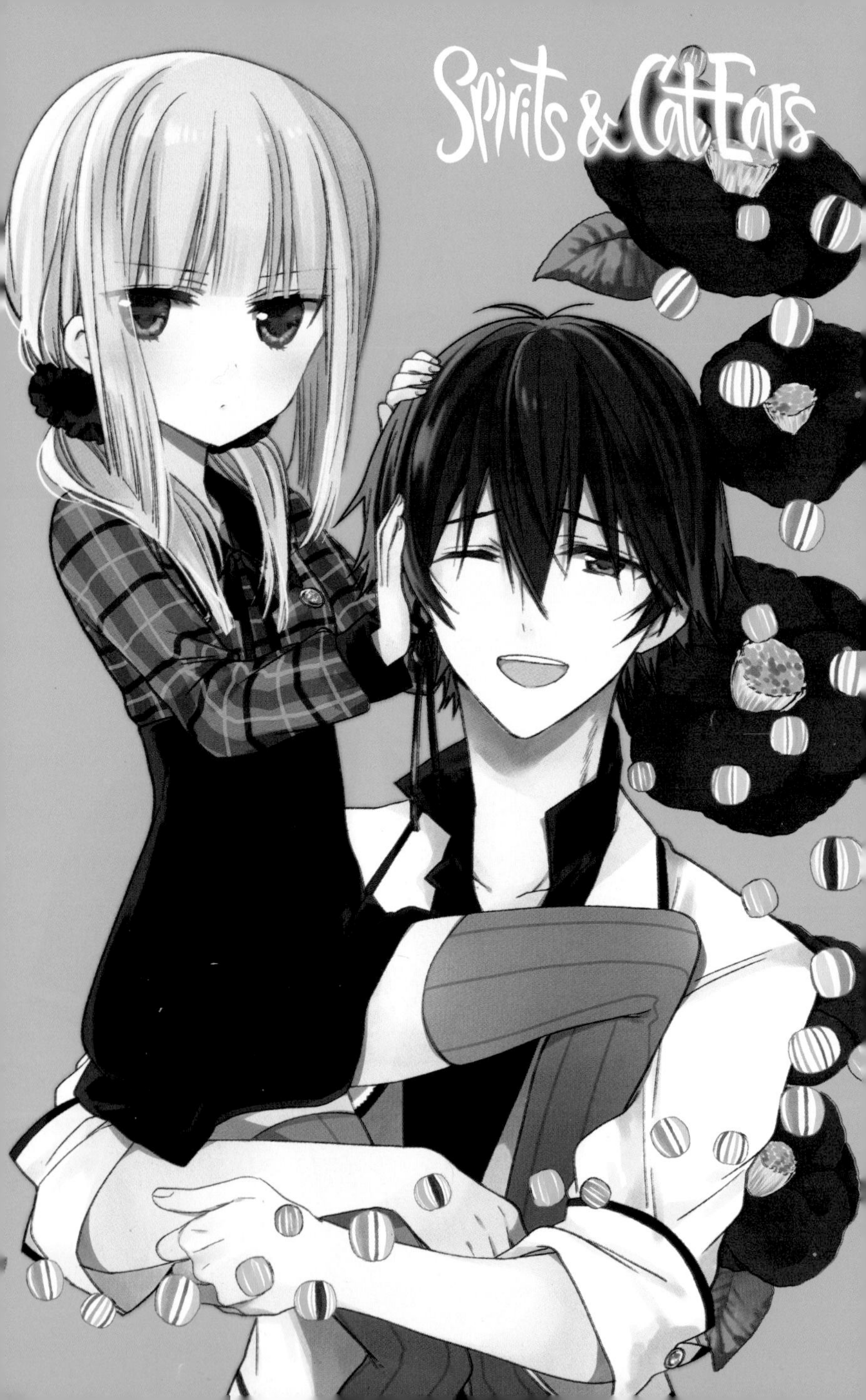
Spirits & Cat Ears

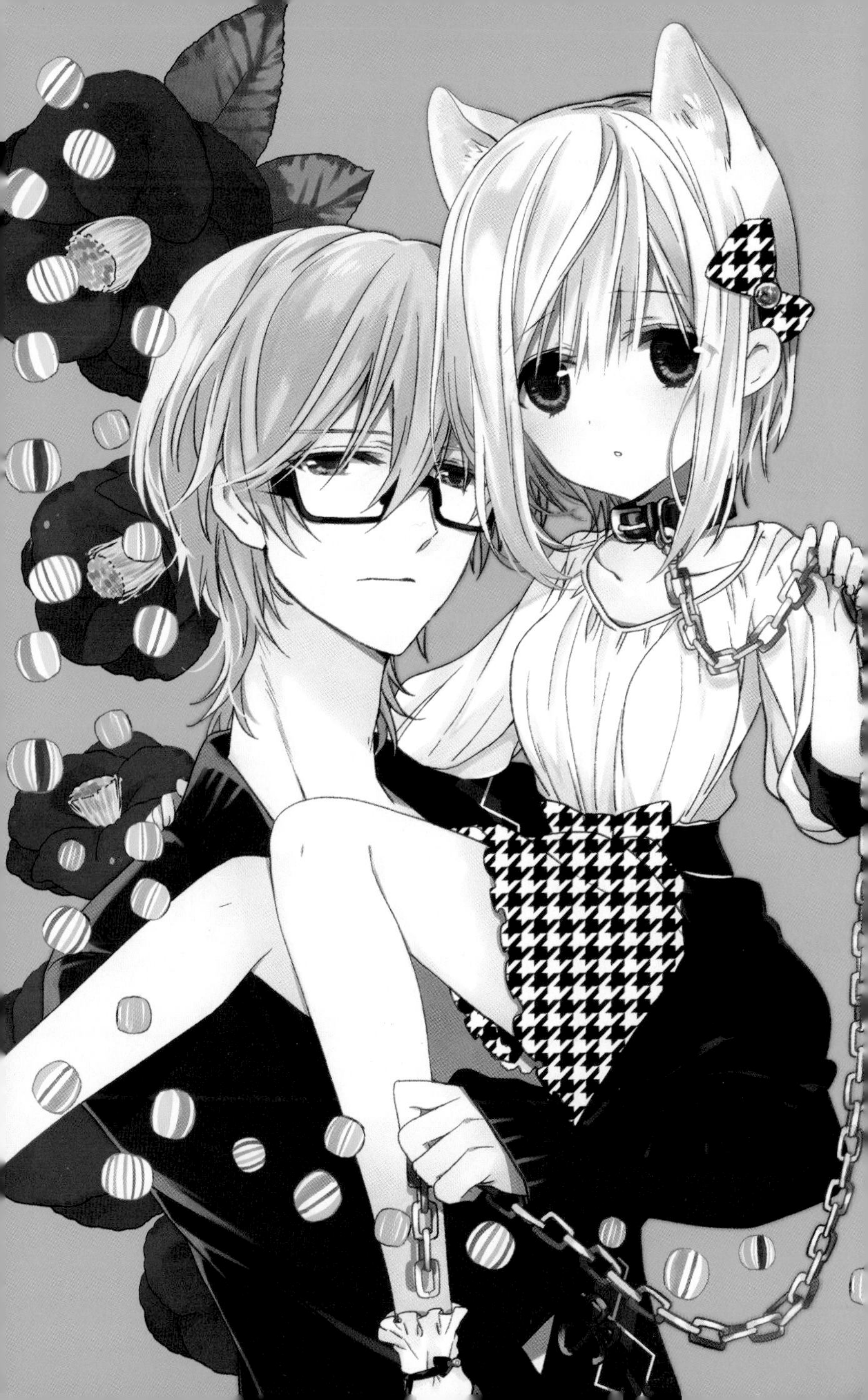

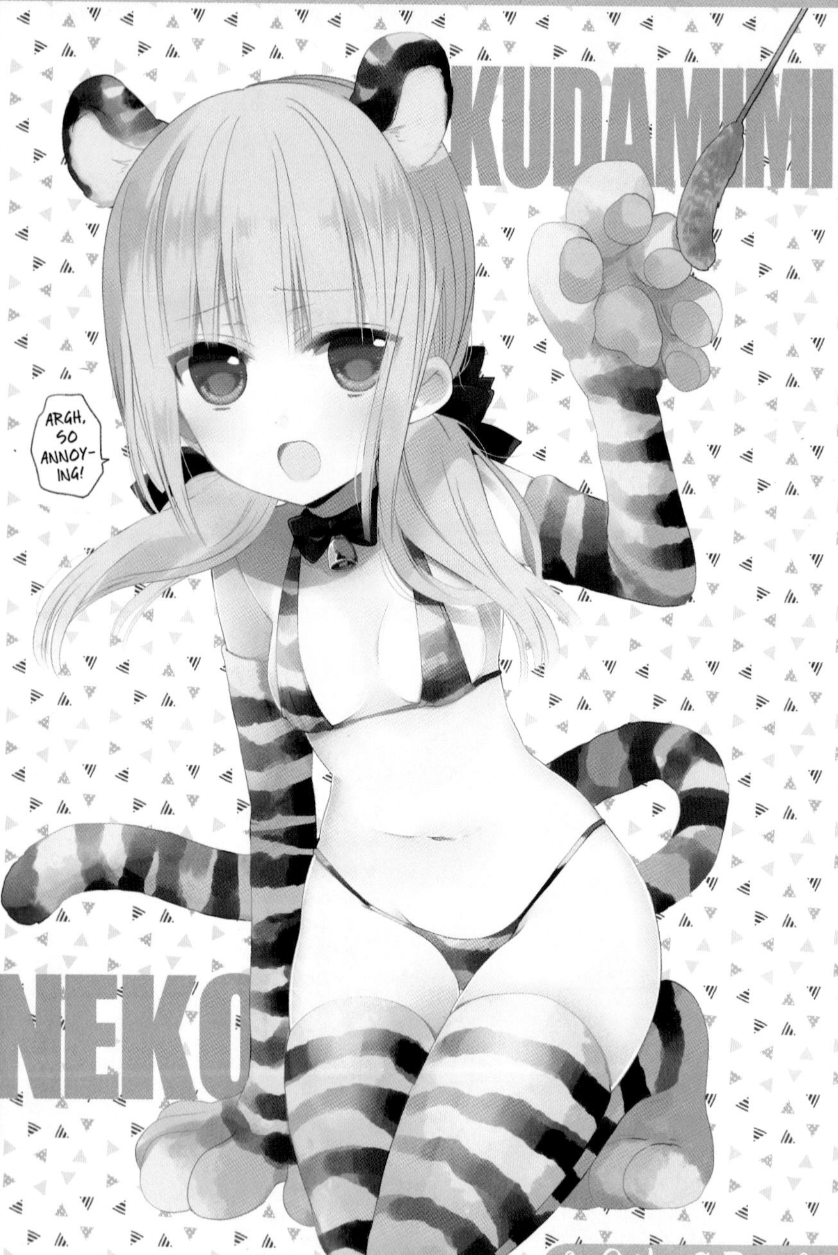
KUDAMIMI
NEKO
ARGH, SO ANNOY-ING!
Spirits & Cat Ears

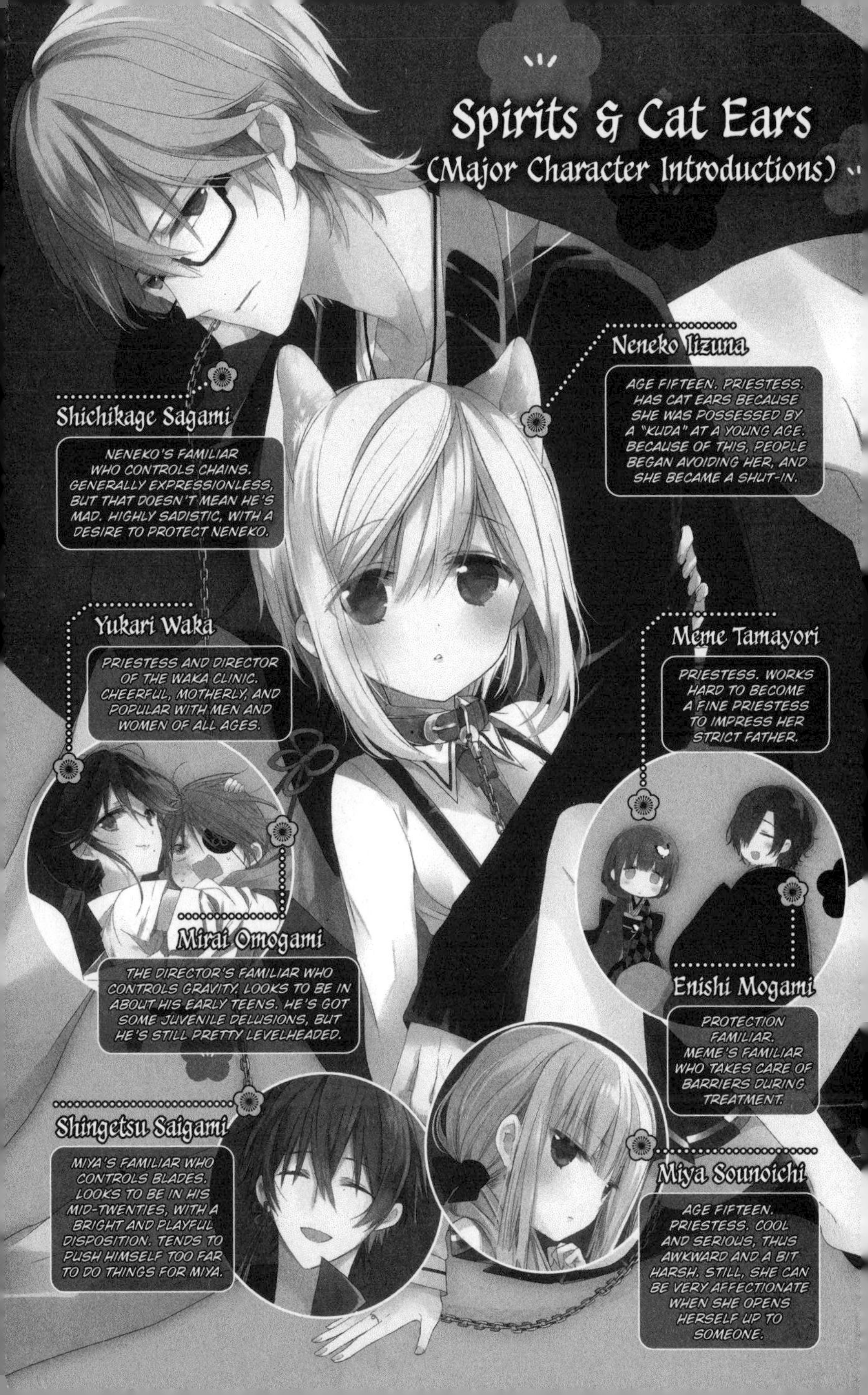
Spirits & Cat Ears
(Major Character Introductions)
Neneko Iizuna
AGE FIFTEEN. PRIESTESS. HAS CAT EARS BECAUSE SHE WAS POSSESSED BY A "KUDA" AT A YOUNG AGE. BECAUSE OF THIS, PEOPLE BEGAN AVOIDING HER, AND SHE BECAME A SHUT-IN.
Shichikage Sagami
NENEKO'S FAMILIAR WHO CONTROLS CHAINS. GENERALLY EXPRESSIONLESS, BUT THAT DOESN'T MEAN HE'S MAD. HIGHLY SADISTIC, WITH A DESIRE TO PROTECT NENEKO.
Yukari Waka
PRIESTESS AND DIRECTOR OF THE WAKA CLINIC. CHEERFUL, MOTHERLY, AND POPULAR WITH MEN AND WOMEN OF ALL AGES.
Meme Tamayori
PRIESTESS. WORKS HARD TO BECOME A FINE PRIESTESS TO IMPRESS HER STRICT FATHER.
Mirai Omogami
THE DIRECTOR'S FAMILIAR WHO CONTROLS GRAVITY. LOOKS TO BE IN ABOUT HIS EARLY TEENS. HE'S GOT SOME JUVENILE DELUSIONS, BUT HE'S STILL PRETTY LEVELHEADED.
Enishi Mogami
PROTECTION FAMILIAR. MEME'S FAMILIAR WHO TAKES CARE OF BARRIERS DURING TREATMENT.
Shingetsu Saigami
MIYA'S FAMILIAR WHO CONTROLS BLADES. LOOKS TO BE IN HIS MID-TWENTIES, WITH A BRIGHT AND PLAYFUL DISPOSITION. TENDS TO PUSH HIMSELF TOO FAR TO DO THINGS FOR MIYA.
Miya Sounoichi
AGE FIFTEEN. PRIESTESS. COOL AND SERIOUS, THUS AWKWARD AND A BIT HARSH. STILL, SHE CAN BE VERY AFFECTIONATE WHEN SHE OPENS HERSELF UP TO SOMEONE.

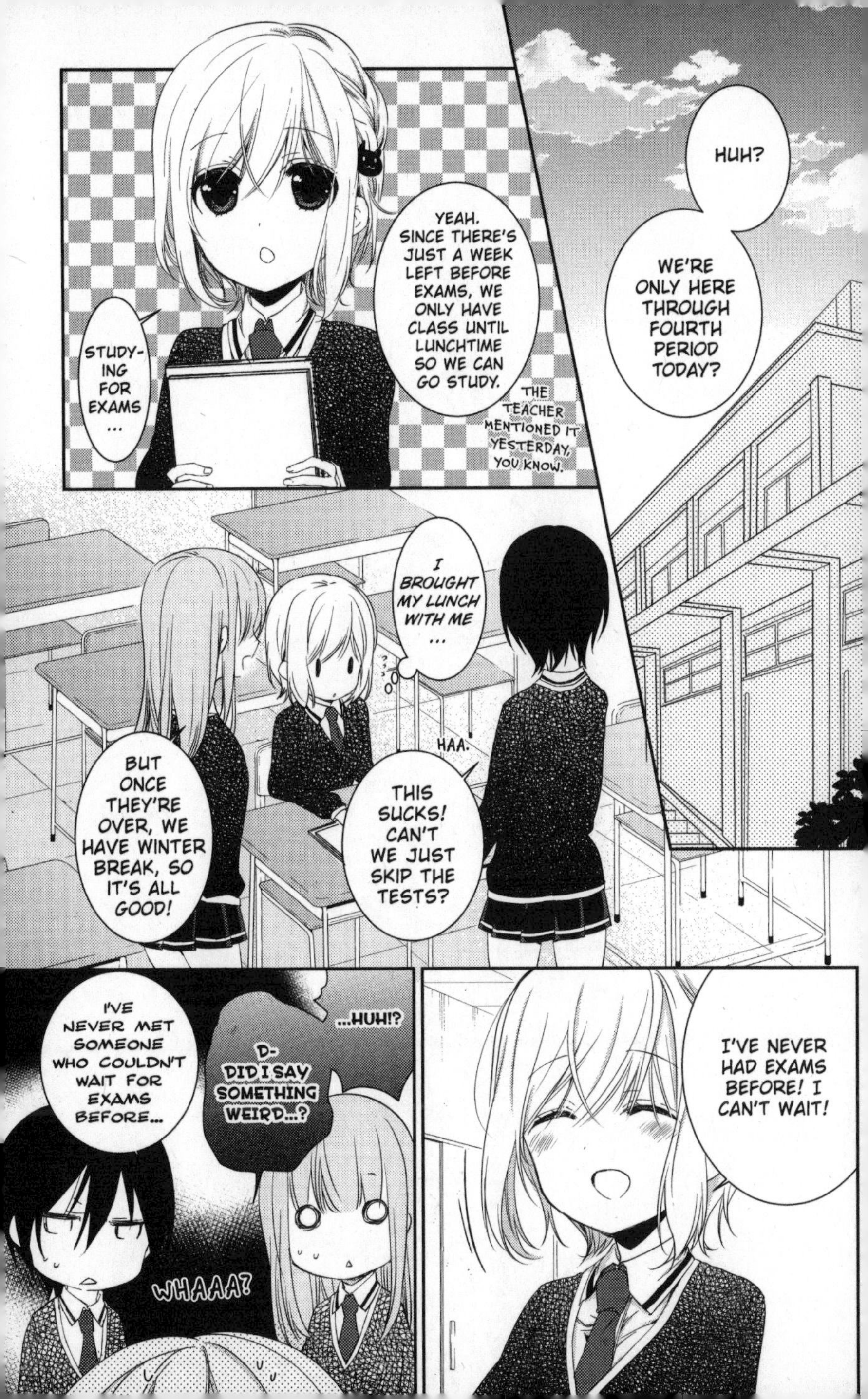
HUH?
WE'RE ONLY HERE THROUGH FOURTH PERIOD TODAY?
YEAH. SINCE THERE'S JUST A WEEK LEFT BEFORE EXAMS, WE ONLY HAVE CLASS UNTIL LUNCHTIME SO WE CAN GO STUDY.
THE TEACHER MENTIONED IT YESTERDAY, YOU KNOW.
STUDYING FOR EXAMS...
I BROUGHT MY LUNCH WITH ME...
HAA.
THIS SUCKS! CAN'T WE JUST SKIP THE TESTS?
BUT ONCE THEY'RE OVER, WE HAVE WINTER BREAK, SO IT'S ALL GOOD!
I'VE NEVER HAD EXAMS BEFORE! I CAN'T WAIT!
...HUH!?
I'VE NEVER MET SOMEONE WHO COULDN'T WAIT FOR EXAMS BEFORE...
D- DID I SAY SOMETHING WEIRD...?
WHAAA?

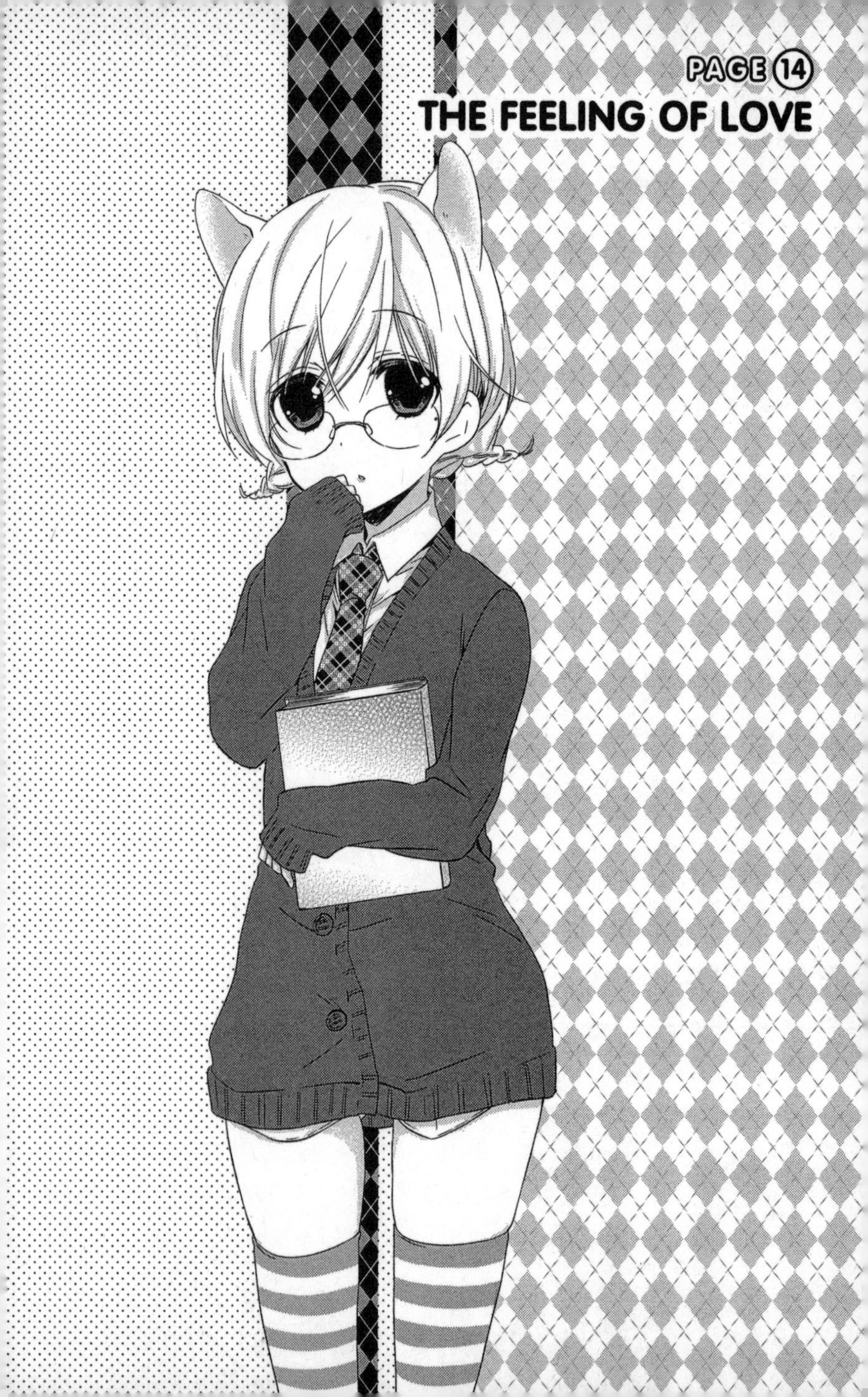
PAGE 14
THE FEELING OF LOVE

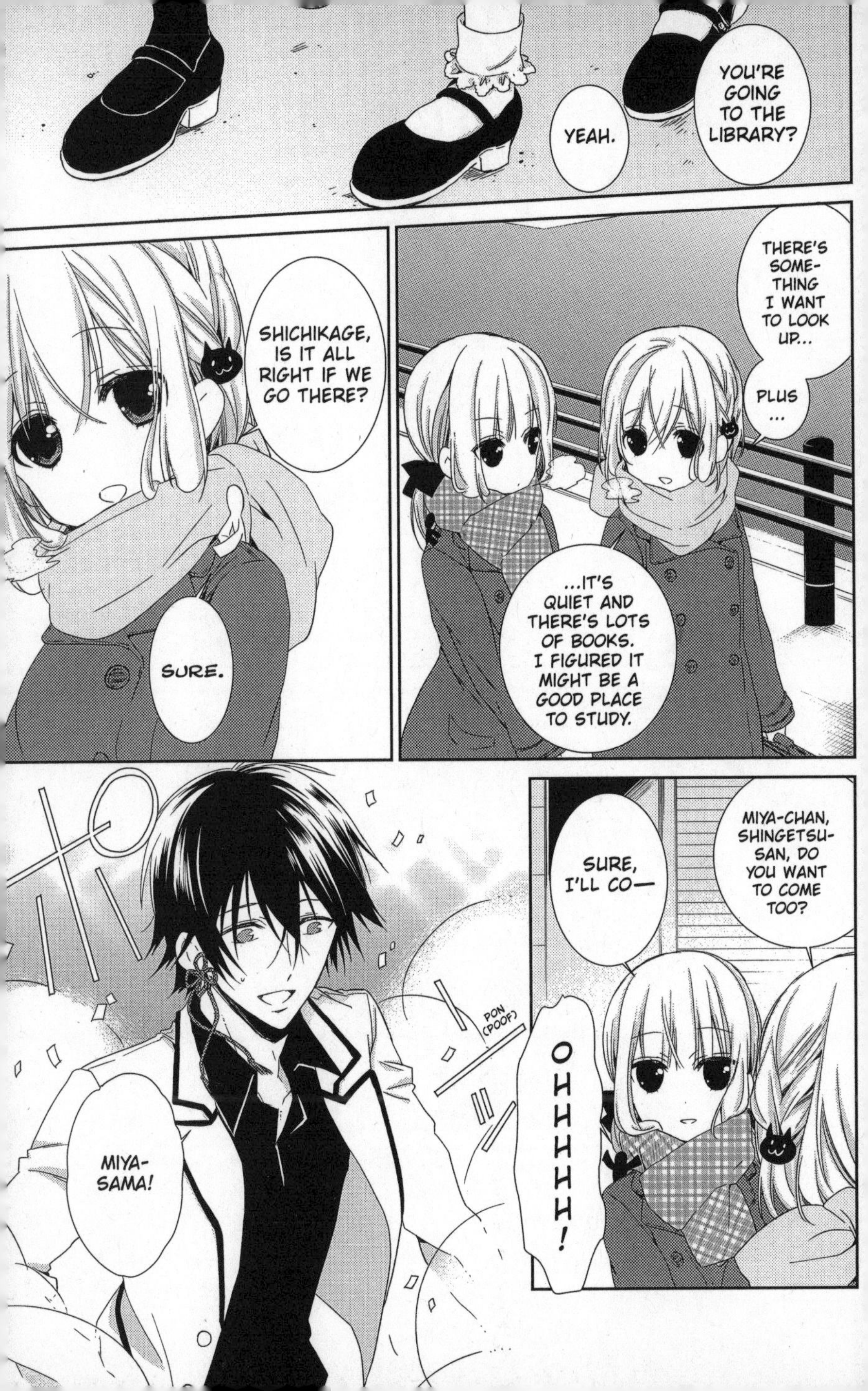
YOU'RE GOING TO THE LIBRARY?
YEAH.
THERE'S SOME-THING I WANT TO LOOK UP...
PLUS ...
...IT'S QUIET AND THERE'S LOTS OF BOOKS. I FIGURED IT MIGHT BE A GOOD PLACE TO STUDY.
SHICHIKAGE, IS IT ALL RIGHT IF WE GO THERE?
SURE.
MIYA-CHAN, SHINGETSU-SAN, DO YOU WANT TO COME TOO?
SURE, I'LL CO—
OHHHHH!
PON (POOF)
MIYA-SAMA!

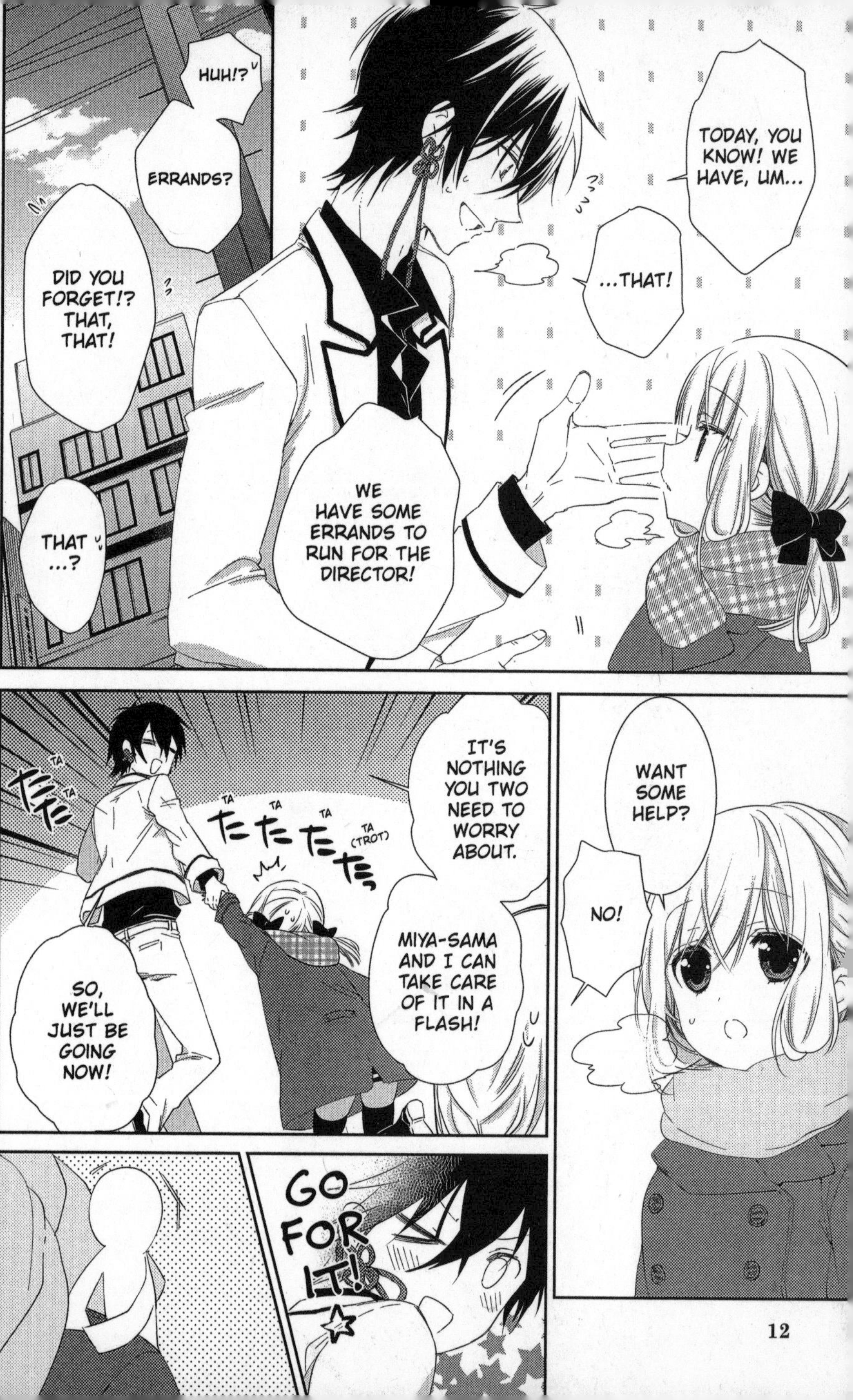
TODAY, YOU KNOW! WE HAVE, UM...
...THAT!
WE HAVE SOME ERRANDS TO RUN FOR THE DIRECTOR!
HUH!?
ERRANDS?
DID YOU FORGET!? THAT, THAT!
THAT ...?
WANT SOME HELP?
NO!
IT'S NOTHING YOU TWO NEED TO WORRY ABOUT.
MIYA-SAMA AND I CAN TAKE CARE OF IT IN A FLASH!
TA TA TA TA (TROT)
TA TA
SO, WE'LL JUST BE GOING NOW!
GO FOR IT!

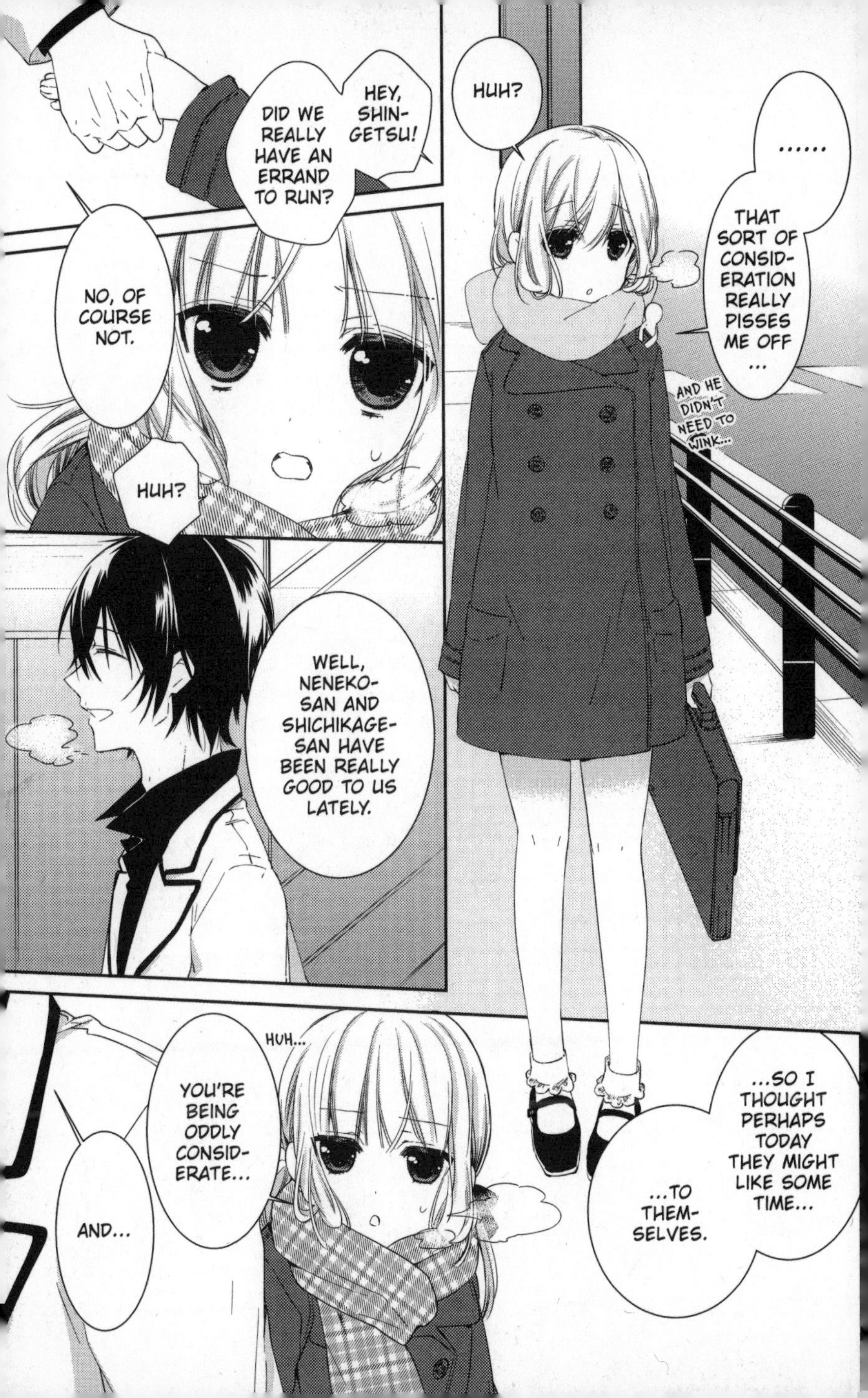
HUH?
......
THAT SORT OF CONSID-ERATION REALLY PISSES ME OFF ...
AND HE DIDN'T NEED TO WINK...
HEY, SHIN-GETSU!
DID WE REALLY HAVE AN ERRAND TO RUN?
NO, OF COURSE NOT.
HUH?
WELL, NENEKO-SAN AND SHICHIKAGE-SAN HAVE BEEN REALLY GOOD TO US LATELY.
...SO I THOUGHT PERHAPS TODAY THEY MIGHT LIKE SOME TIME...
...TO THEM-SELVES.
HUH...
YOU'RE BEING ODDLY CONSID-ERATE...
AND...

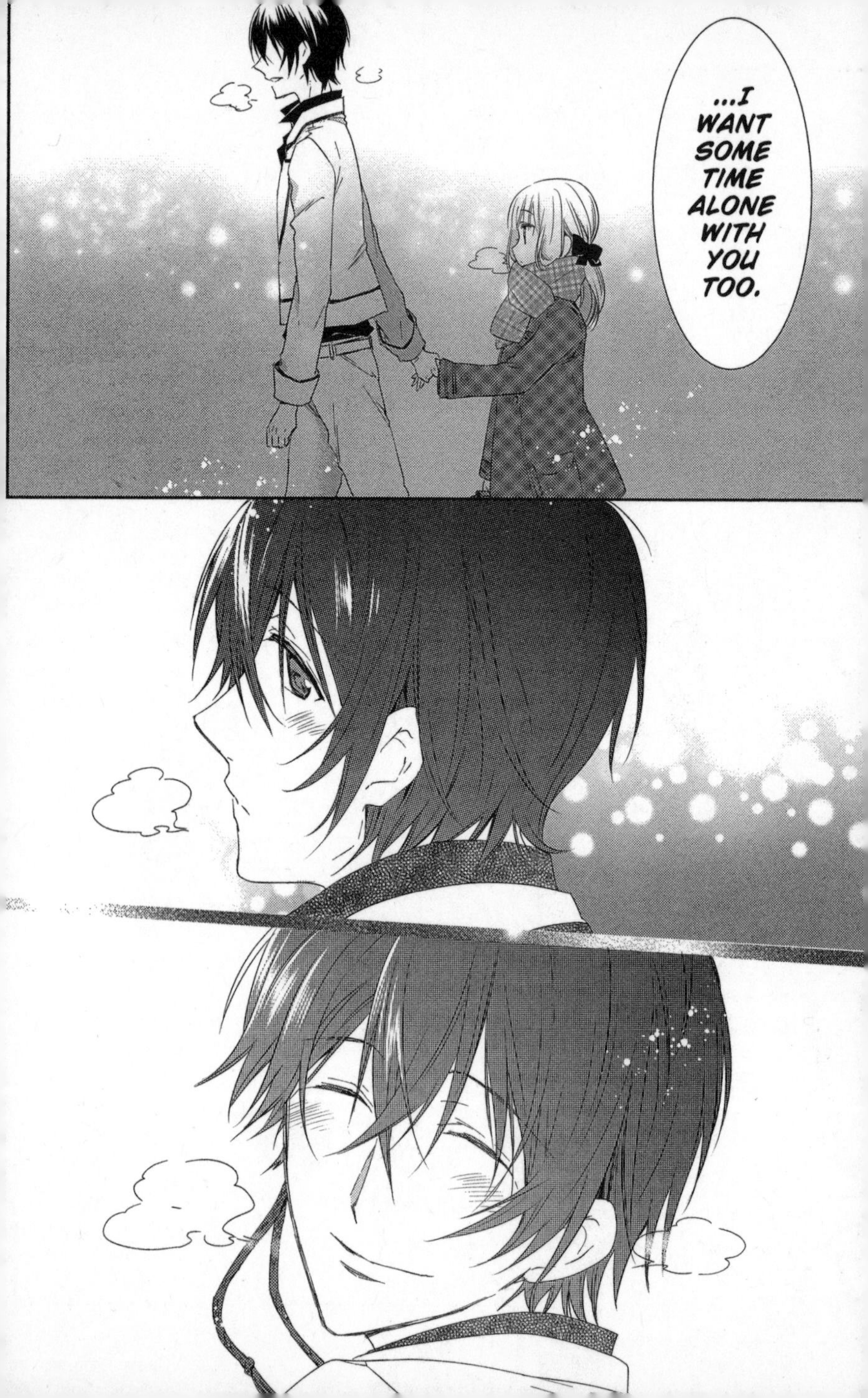
...I WANT SOME TIME ALONE WITH YOU TOO.

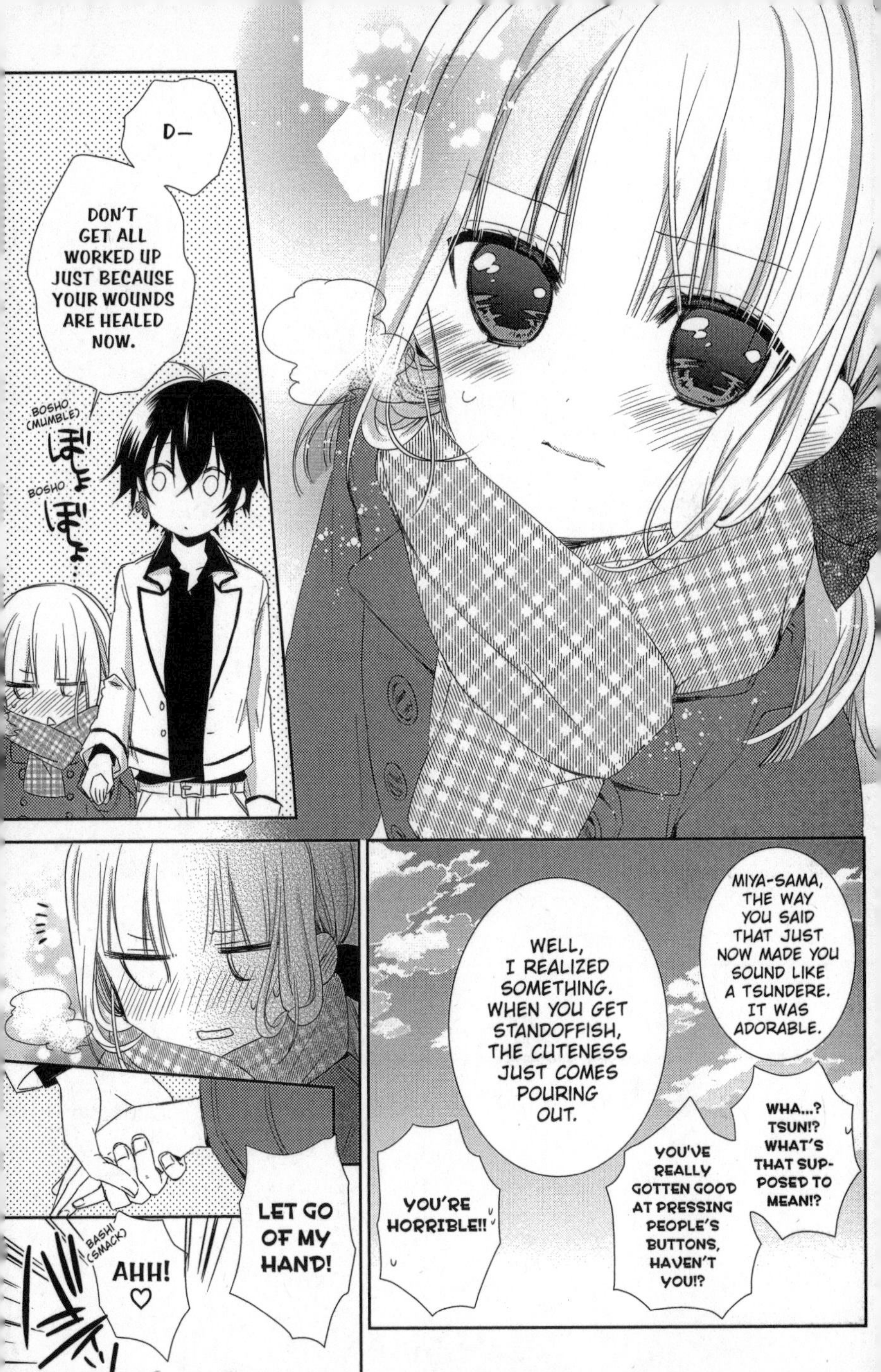
D—
DON'T GET ALL WORKED UP JUST BECAUSE YOUR WOUNDS ARE HEALED NOW.
BOSHO (MUMBLE)
ぼしょ
BOSHO
ぼしょ…
MIYA-SAMA, THE WAY YOU SAID THAT JUST NOW MADE YOU SOUND LIKE A TSUNDERE. IT WAS ADORABLE.
WELL, I REALIZED SOMETHING. WHEN YOU GET STANDOFFISH, THE CUTENESS JUST COMES POURING OUT.
WHA...? TSUN!? WHAT'S THAT SUP-POSED TO MEAN!?
YOU'VE REALLY GOTTEN GOOD AT PRESSING PEOPLE'S BUTTONS, HAVEN'T YOU!?
YOU'RE HORRIBLE!!
LET GO OF MY HAND!
BASHI (SMACK)
AHH! ♡

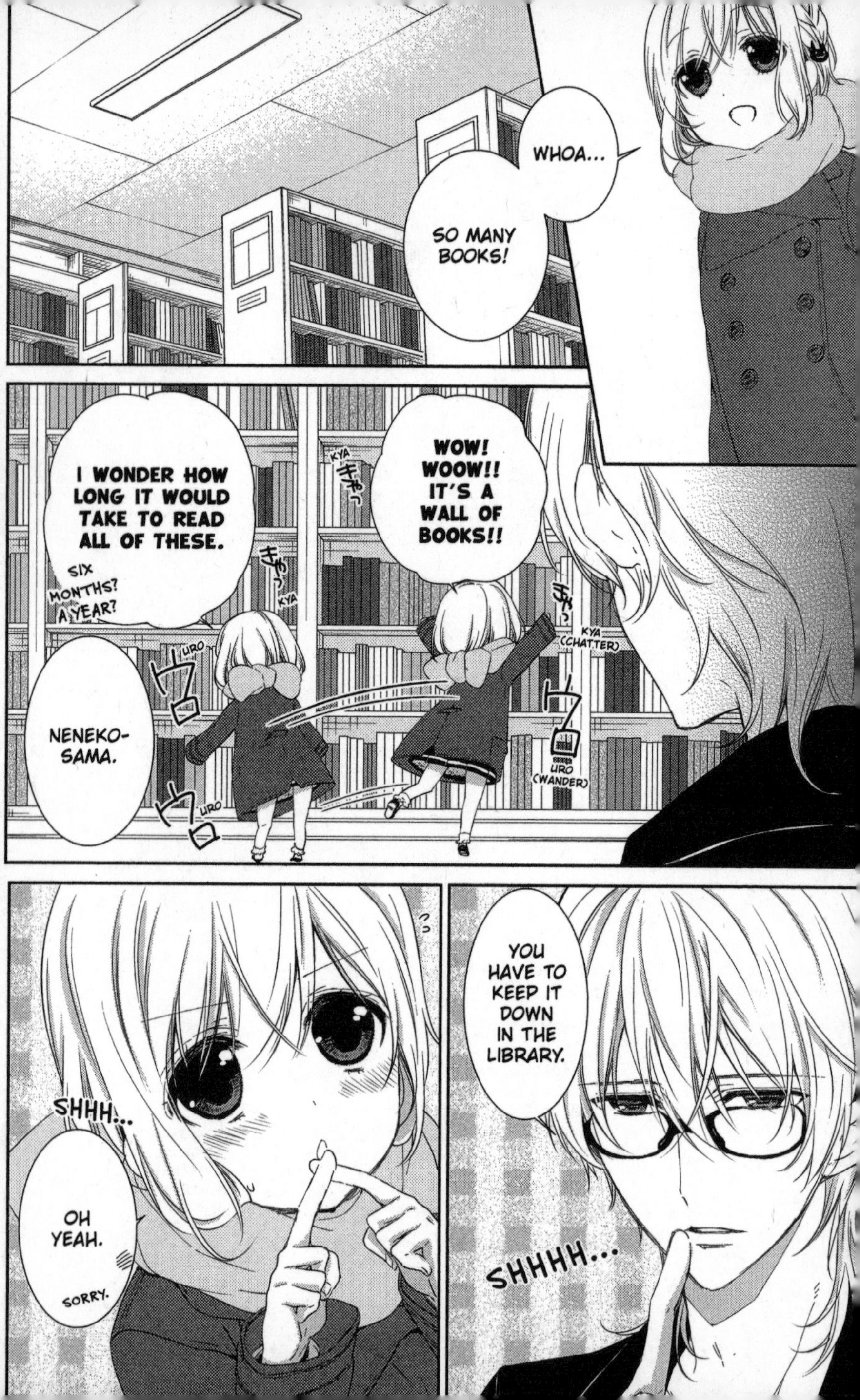
WHOA...
SO MANY BOOKS!
WOW! WOOW!! IT'S A WALL OF BOOKS!!
KYA
KYA (CHATTER)
URO (WANDER)
KYA
I WONDER HOW LONG IT WOULD TAKE TO READ ALL OF THESE.
SIX MONTHS? A YEAR?
URO
NENEKO-SAMA.
URO
YOU HAVE TO KEEP IT DOWN IN THE LIBRARY.
SHHHH...
SHHH...
OH YEAH.
SORRY.

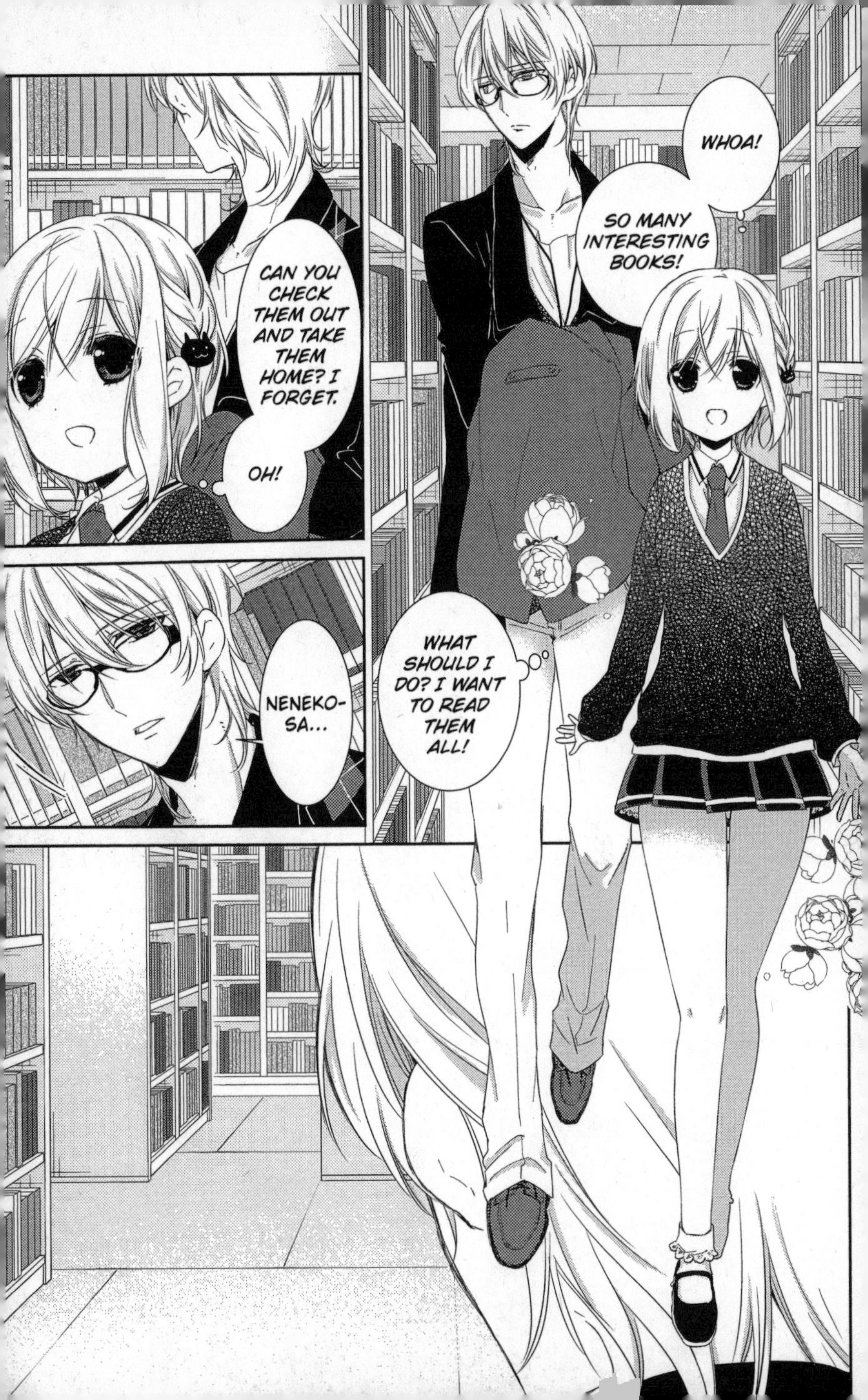
WHOA!
SO MANY INTERESTING BOOKS!
WHAT SHOULD I DO? I WANT TO READ THEM ALL!
CAN YOU CHECK THEM OUT AND TAKE THEM HOME? I FORGET.
OH!
NENEKO-SA...

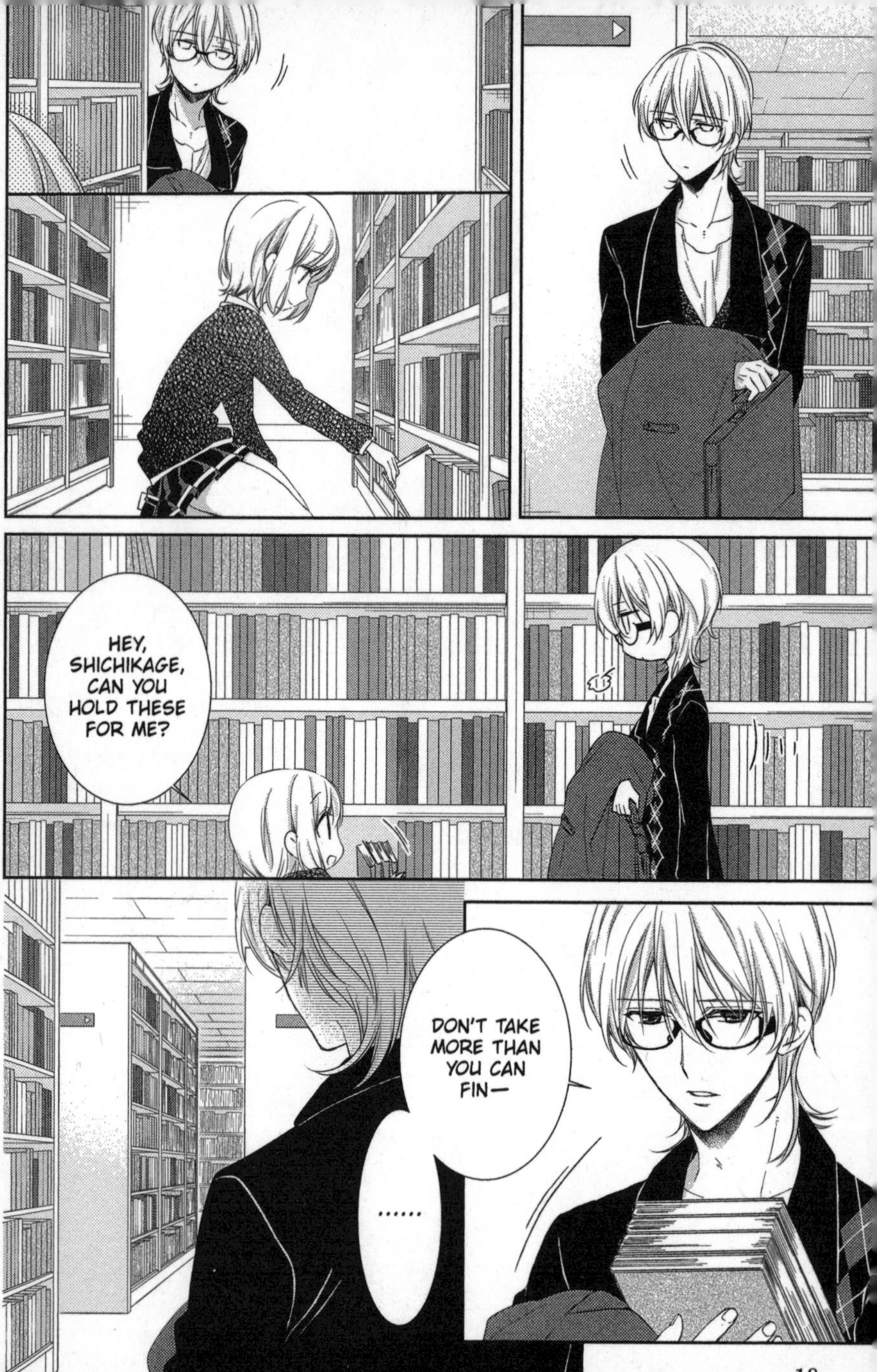
HEY, SHICHIKAGE, CAN YOU HOLD THESE FOR ME?
DON'T TAKE MORE THAN YOU CAN FIN—
......

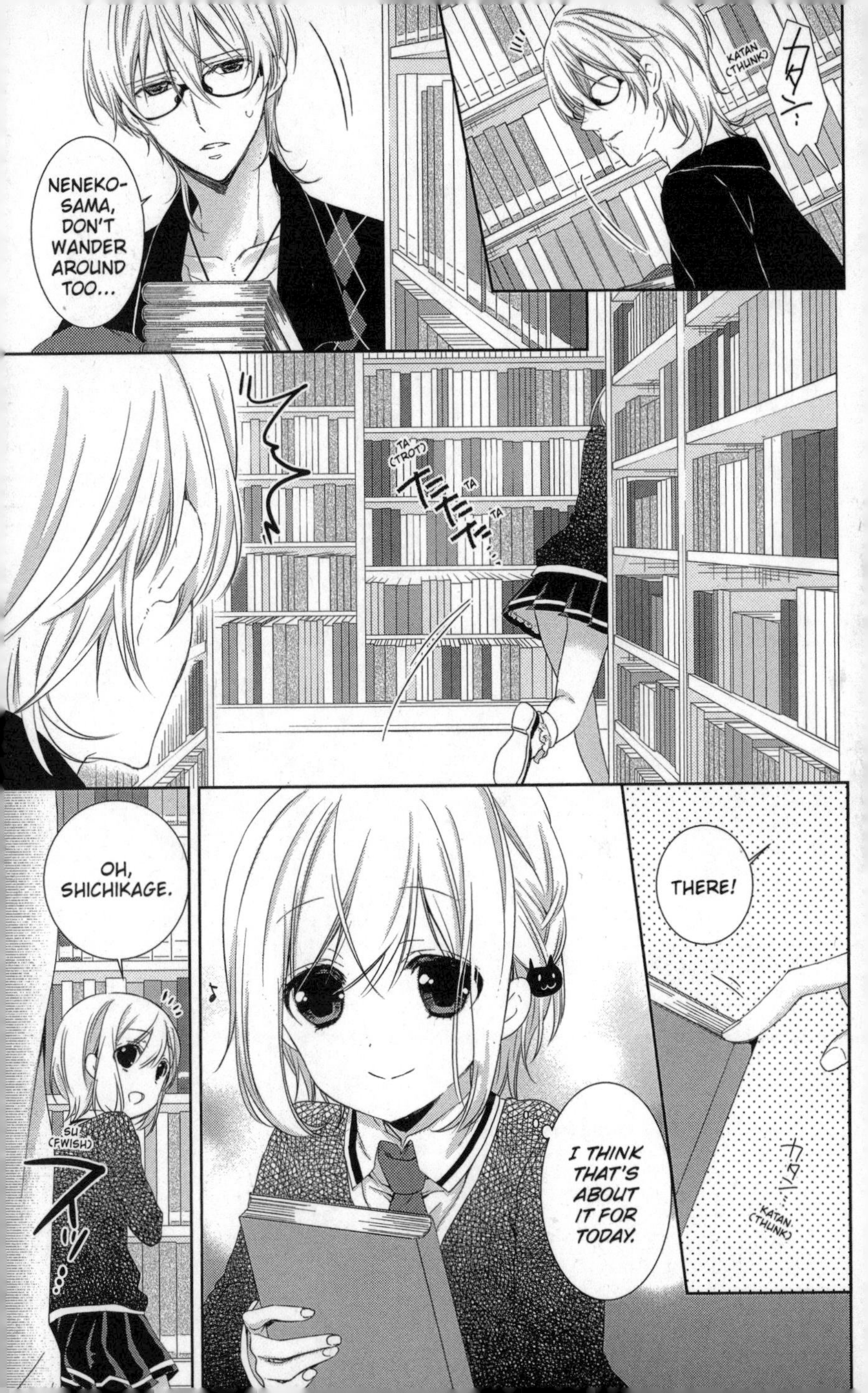
KATAN (THUNK)
NENEKO-SAMA, DON'T WANDER AROUND TOO...
TA (TROT)
TA
TA
THERE!
KATAN (THUNK)
I THINK THAT'S ABOUT IT FOR TODAY.
OH, SHICHIKAGE.
SU (FWISH)

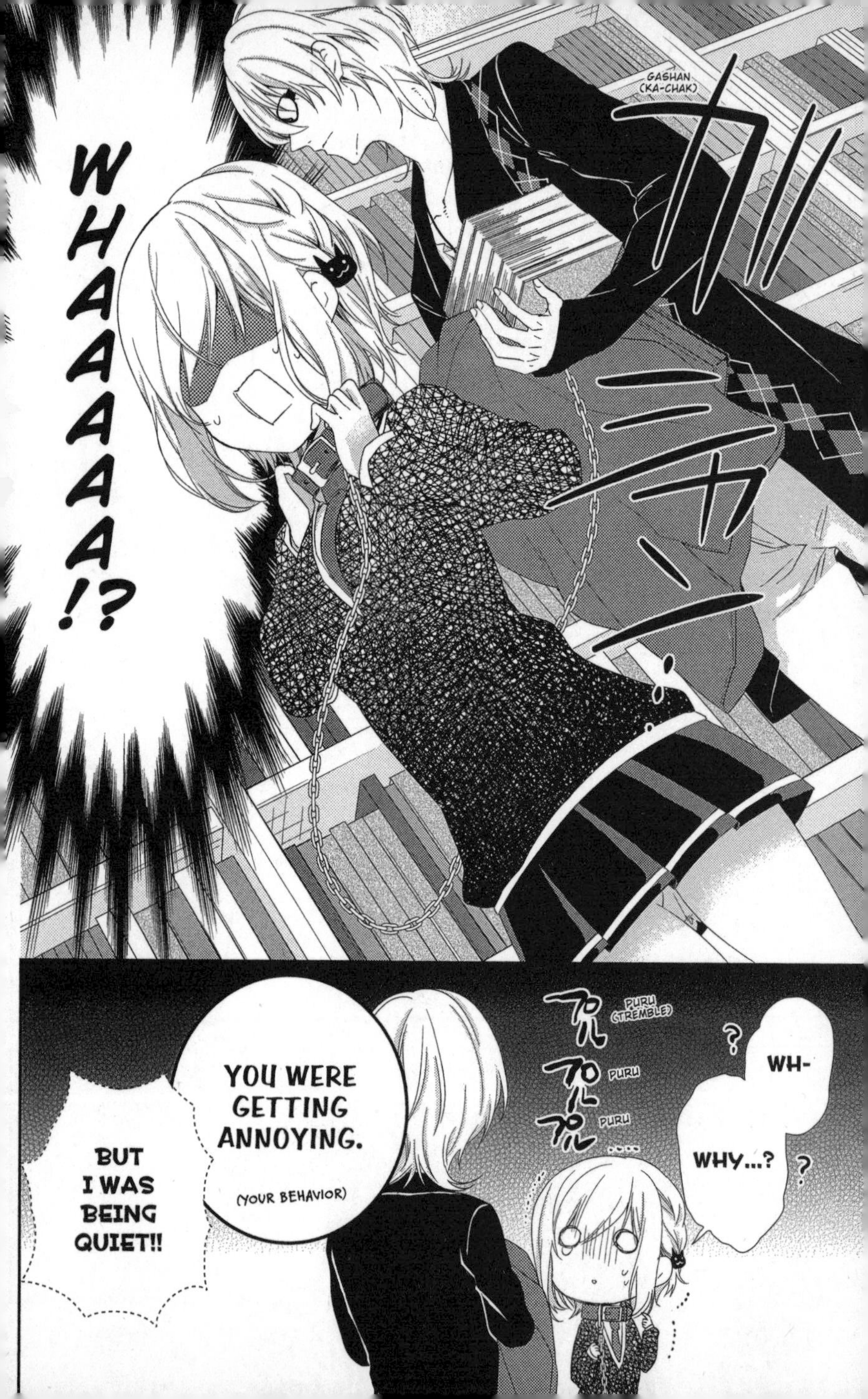
GASHAN (KA-CHAK)
WHAAAAAAA!?
PURU (TREMBLE)
PURU
PURU
WH-
WHY...?
YOU WERE GETTING ANNOYING.
(YOUR BEHAVIOR)
BUT I WAS BEING QUIET!!

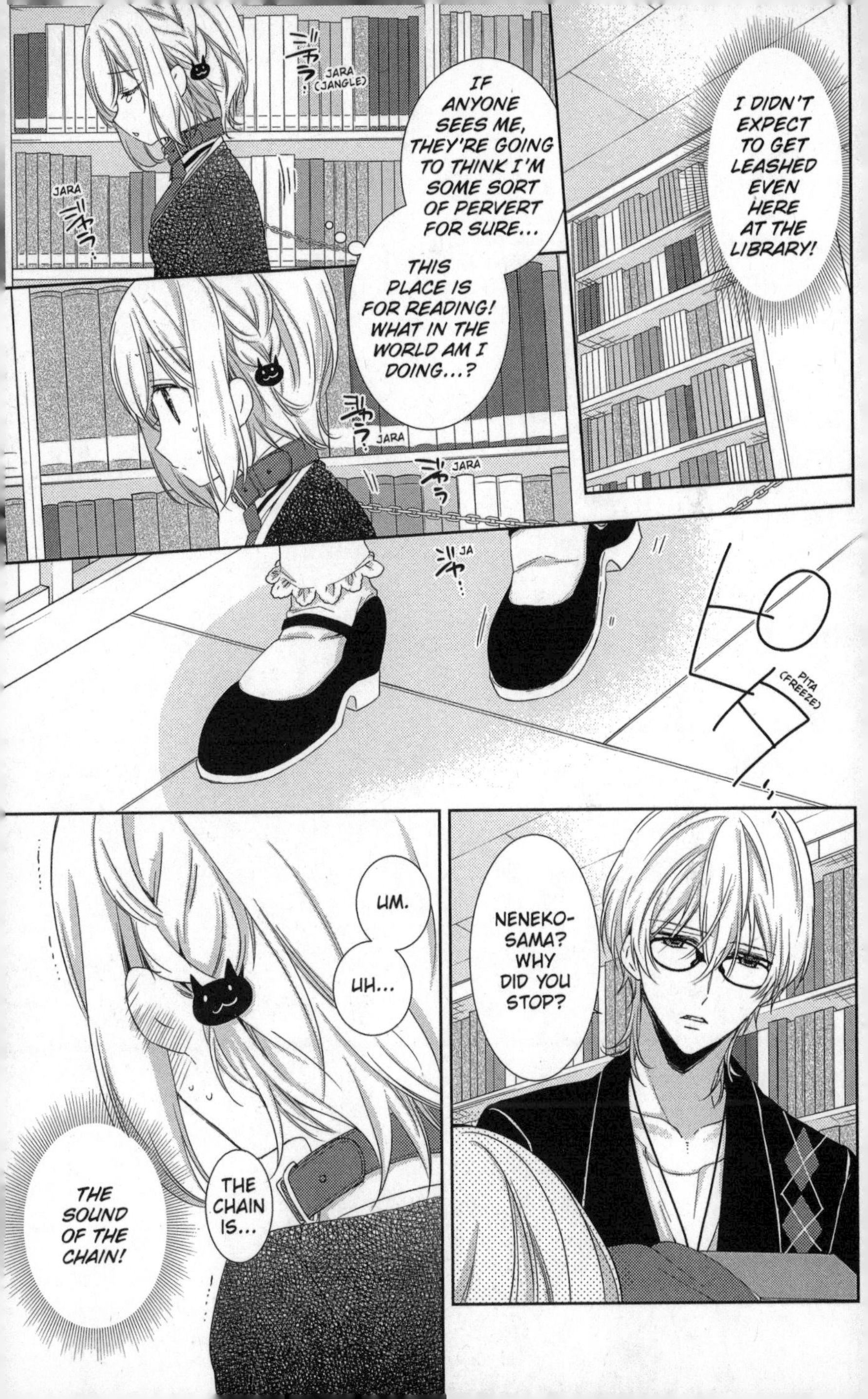
I DIDN'T EXPECT TO GET LEASHED EVEN HERE AT THE LIBRARY!
JARA (JANGLE)
IF ANYONE SEES ME, THEY'RE GOING TO THINK I'M SOME SORT OF PERVERT FOR SURE...
JARA
THIS PLACE IS FOR READING! WHAT IN THE WORLD AM I DOING...?
JARA
JARA
JA
PITA (FREEZE)
NENEKO-SAMA? WHY DID YOU STOP?
UM.
UH...
THE CHAIN IS...
THE SOUND OF THE CHAIN!

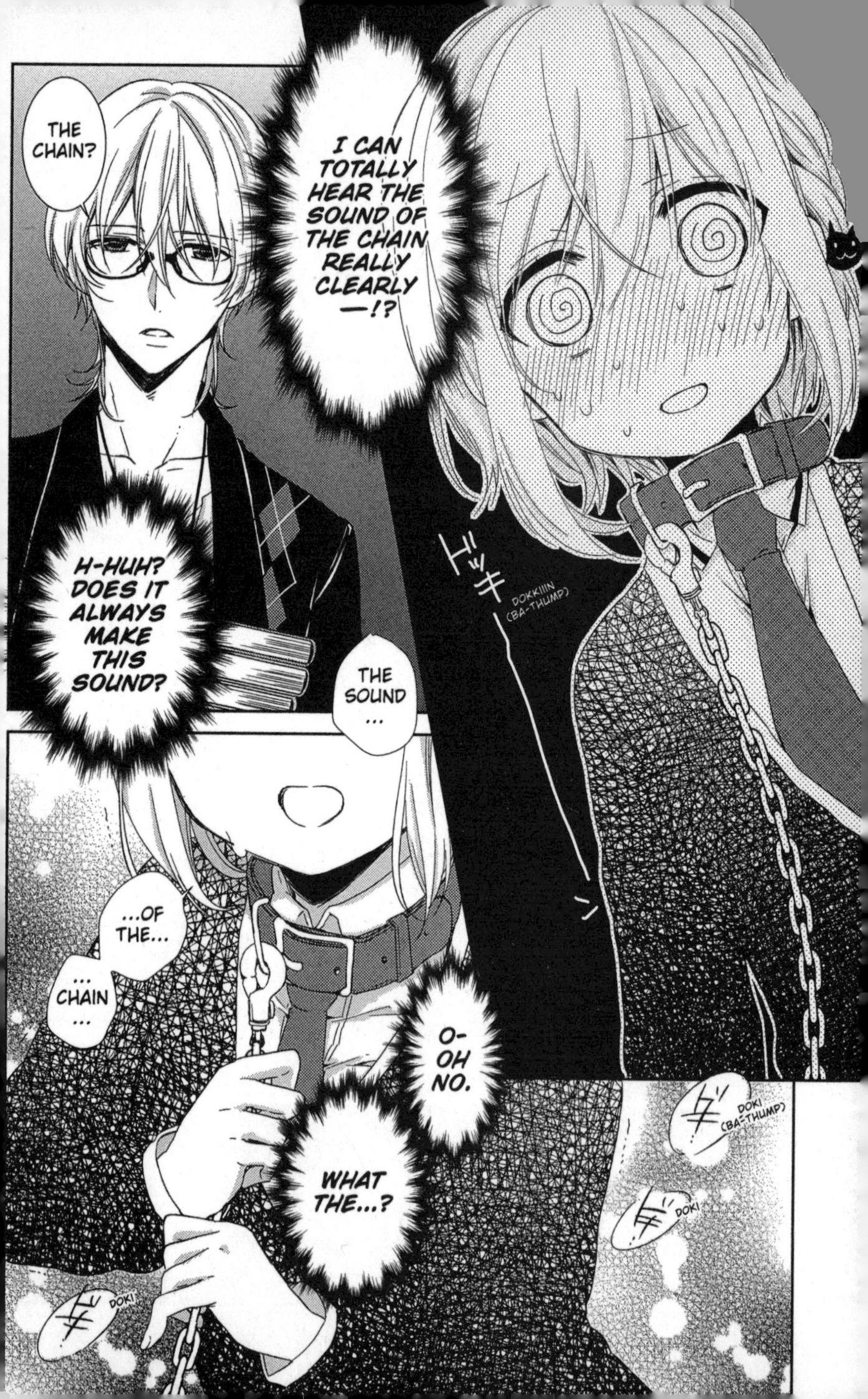
I CAN TOTALLY HEAR THE SOUND OF THE CHAIN REALLY CLEARLY—!?
ドッキーン
DOKKIIN (BA-THUMP)
THE CHAIN?
H-HUH? DOES IT ALWAYS MAKE THIS SOUND?
THE SOUND...
...OF THE...
...CHAIN...
ドキ
DOKI (BA-THUMP)
O-OH NO.
WHAT THE...?
ドキ
DOKI
ドキ
DOKI

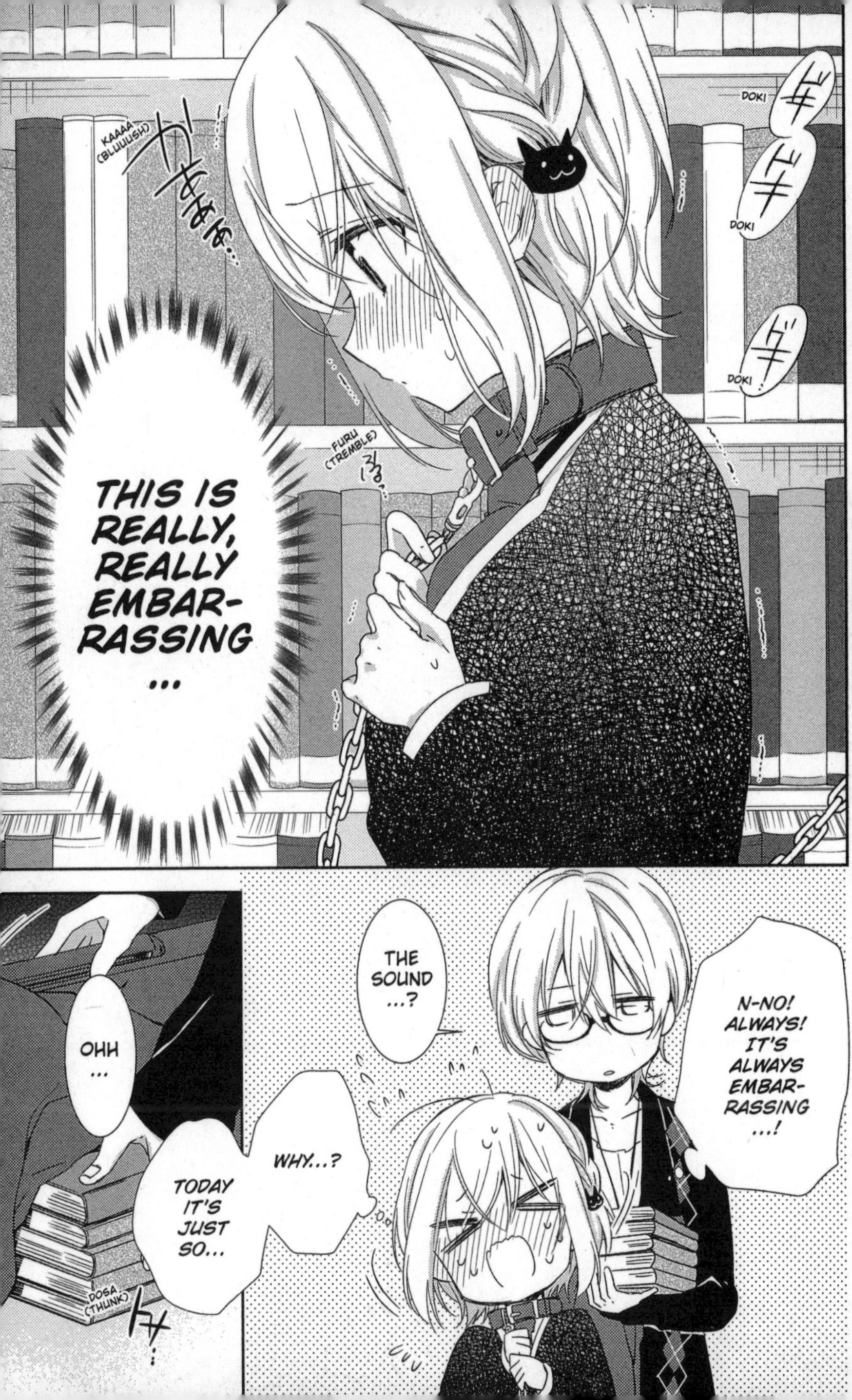
DOKI
DOKI
DOKI
KAAAA (BLUUUSH)
FURU (TREMBLE)
THIS IS REALLY, REALLY EMBARRASSING...
N-NO! ALWAYS! IT'S ALWAYS EMBARRASSING...!
THE SOUND...?
WHY...?
TODAY IT'S JUST SO...
OHH...
DOSA (THUNK)

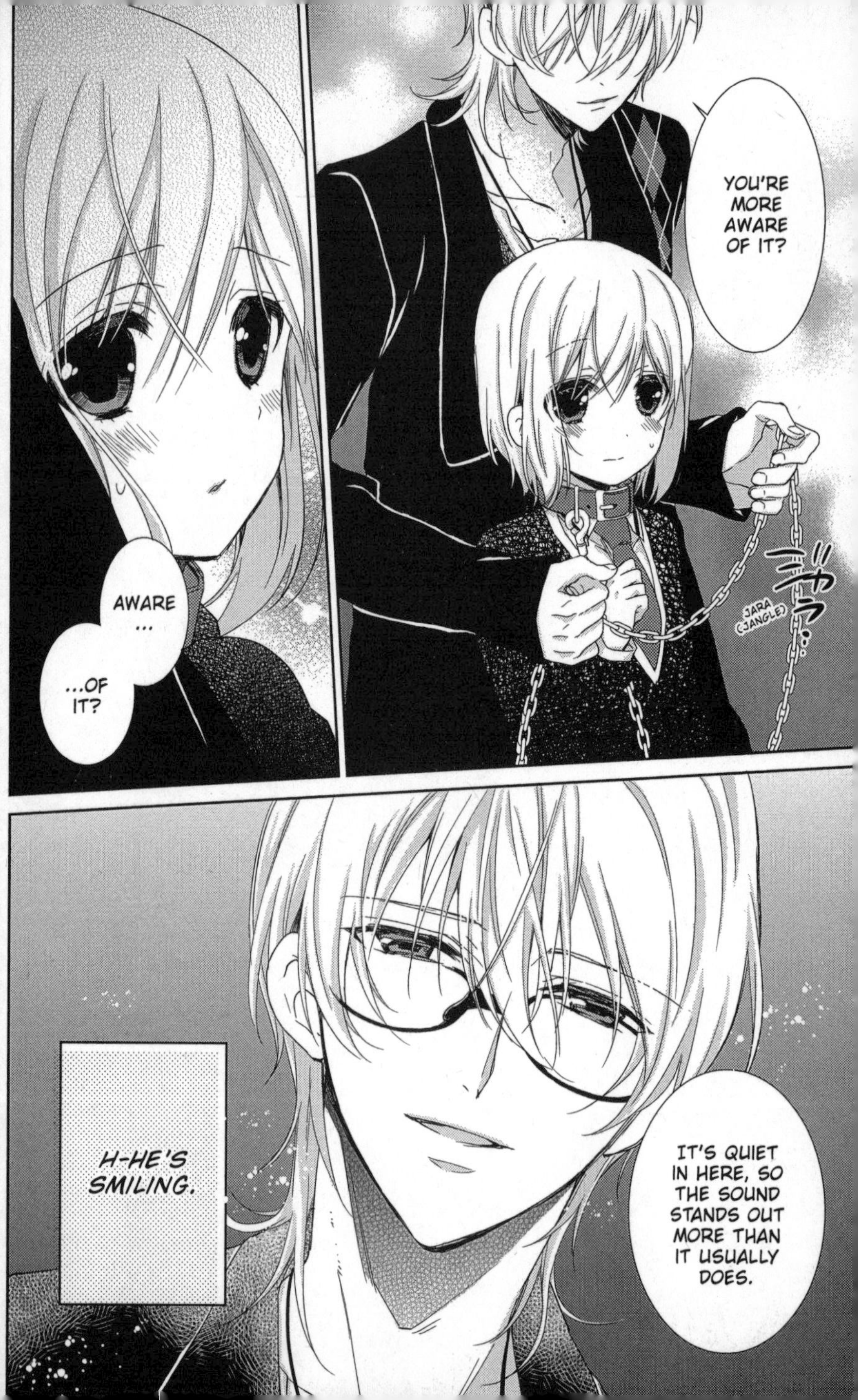
YOU'RE MORE AWARE OF IT?
JARA (JANGLE)
AWARE ...
...OF IT?
IT'S QUIET IN HERE, SO THE SOUND STANDS OUT MORE THAN IT USUALLY DOES.
H-HE'S SMILING.

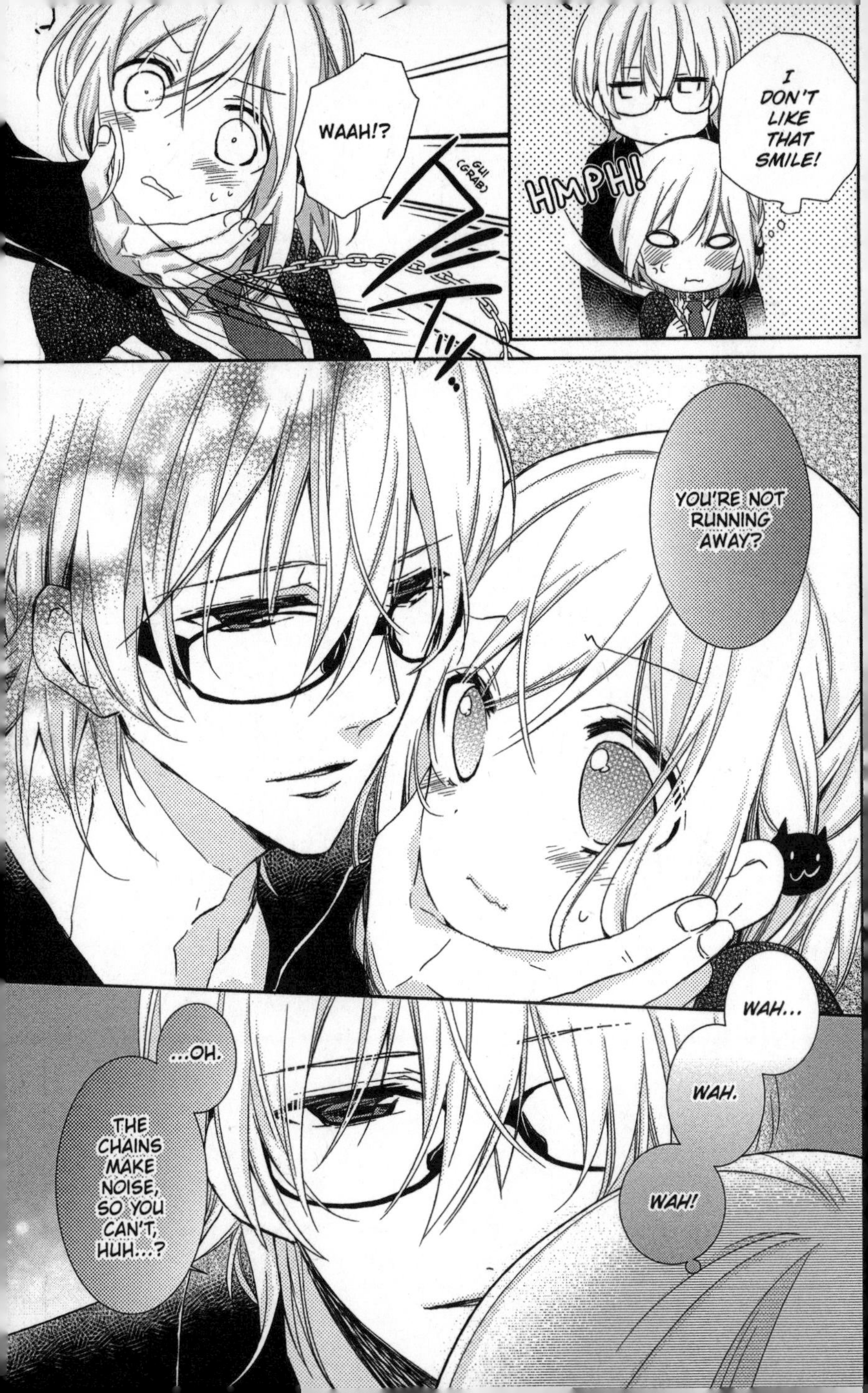
I DON'T LIKE THAT SMILE!
HMPH!
WAAH!?
GUI (GRAB)
YOU'RE NOT RUNNING AWAY?
WAH...
WAH.
WAH!
...OH.
THE CHAINS MAKE NOISE, SO YOU CAN'T, HUH...?

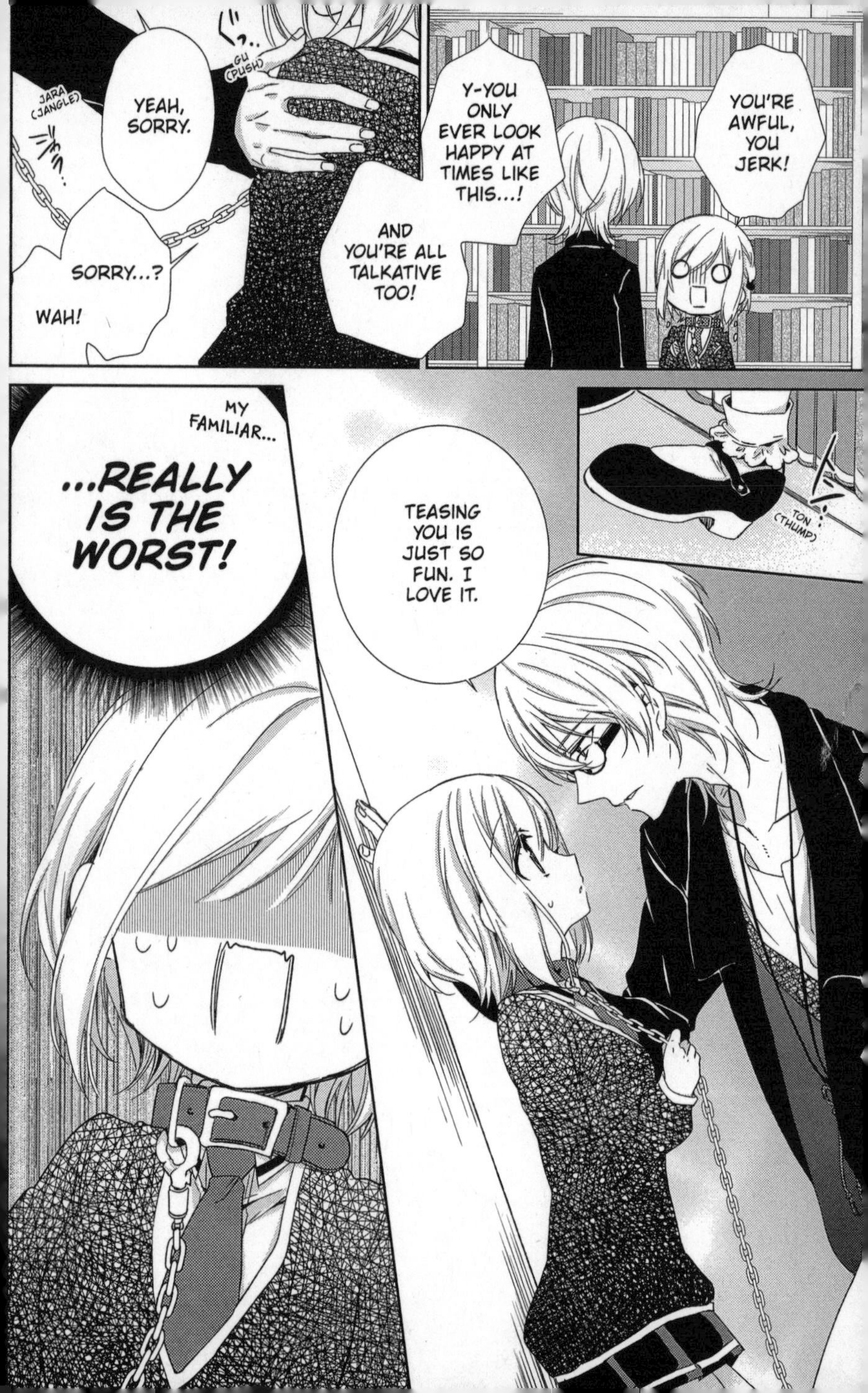

YOU'RE AWFUL, YOU JERK!
Y-YOU ONLY EVER LOOK HAPPY AT TIMES LIKE THIS...!
AND YOU'RE ALL TALKATIVE TOO!
GU (PUSH)
YEAH, SORRY.
JARA (JANGLE)
SORRY...?
WAH!
TON (THUMP)
TEASING YOU IS JUST SO FUN. I LOVE IT.
MY FAMILIAR...
...REALLY IS THE WORST!

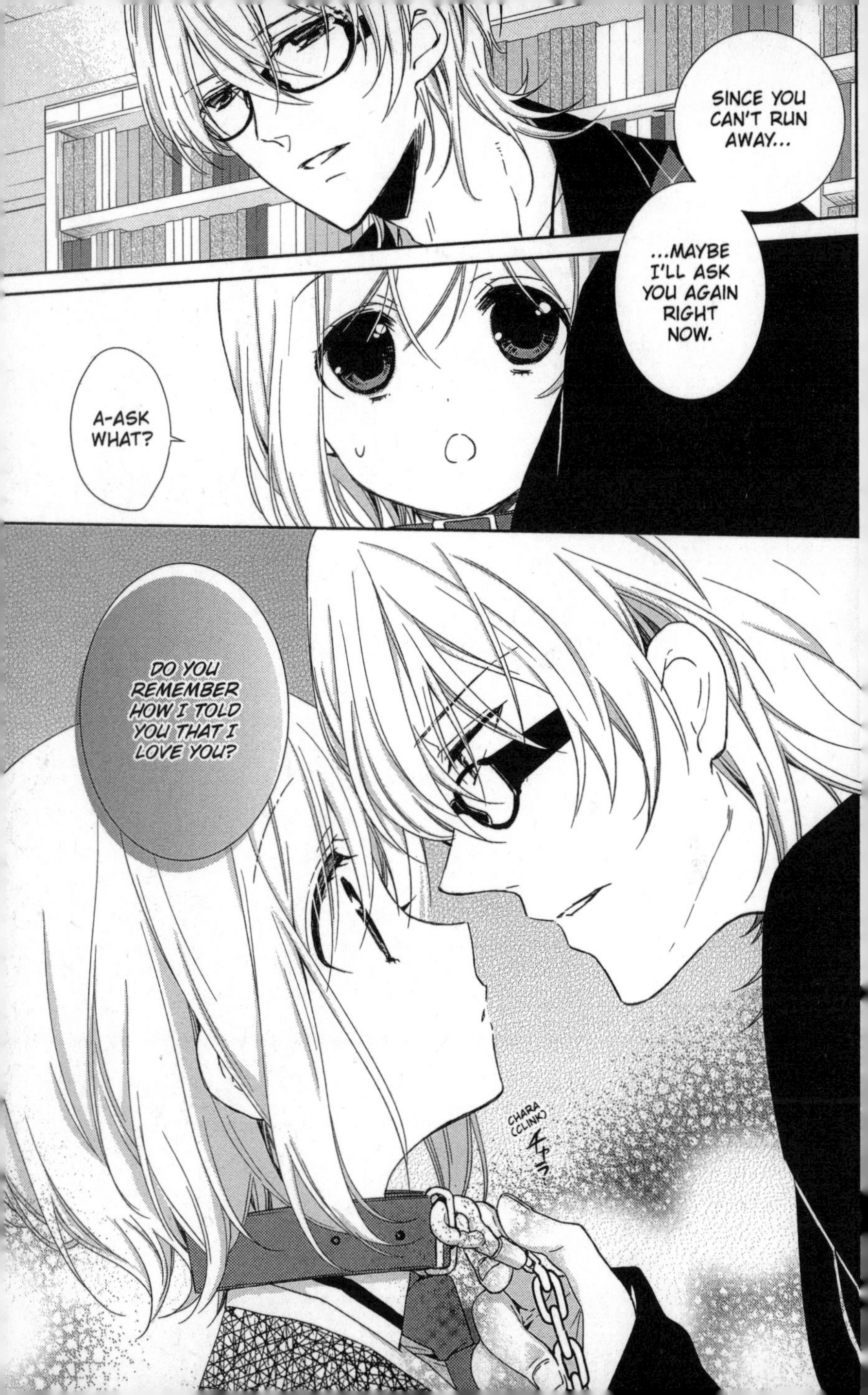
SINCE YOU CAN'T RUN AWAY...
...MAYBE I'LL ASK YOU AGAIN RIGHT NOW.
A-ASK WHAT?
DO YOU REMEMBER HOW I TOLD YOU THAT I LOVE YOU?
CHARA (CLINK)

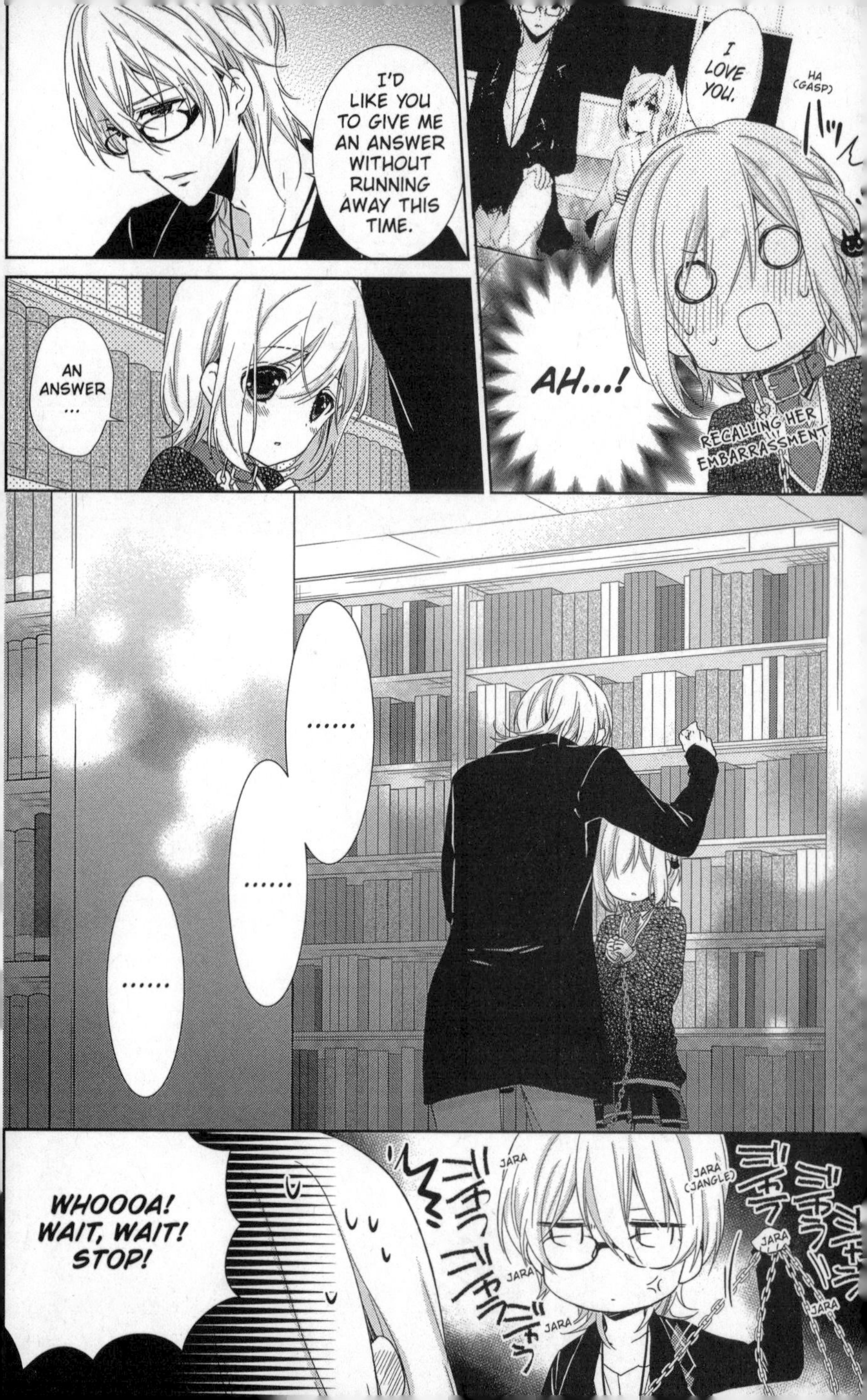
I LOVE YOU.
HA (GASP)
AH...!
RECALLING HER EMBARRASSMENT
I'D LIKE YOU TO GIVE ME AN ANSWER WITHOUT RUNNING AWAY THIS TIME.
AN ANSWER ...
......
......
......
JARA
JARA (JANGLE)
JARA
JARA
JARA
JARA
WHOOOA! WAIT, WAIT! STOP!

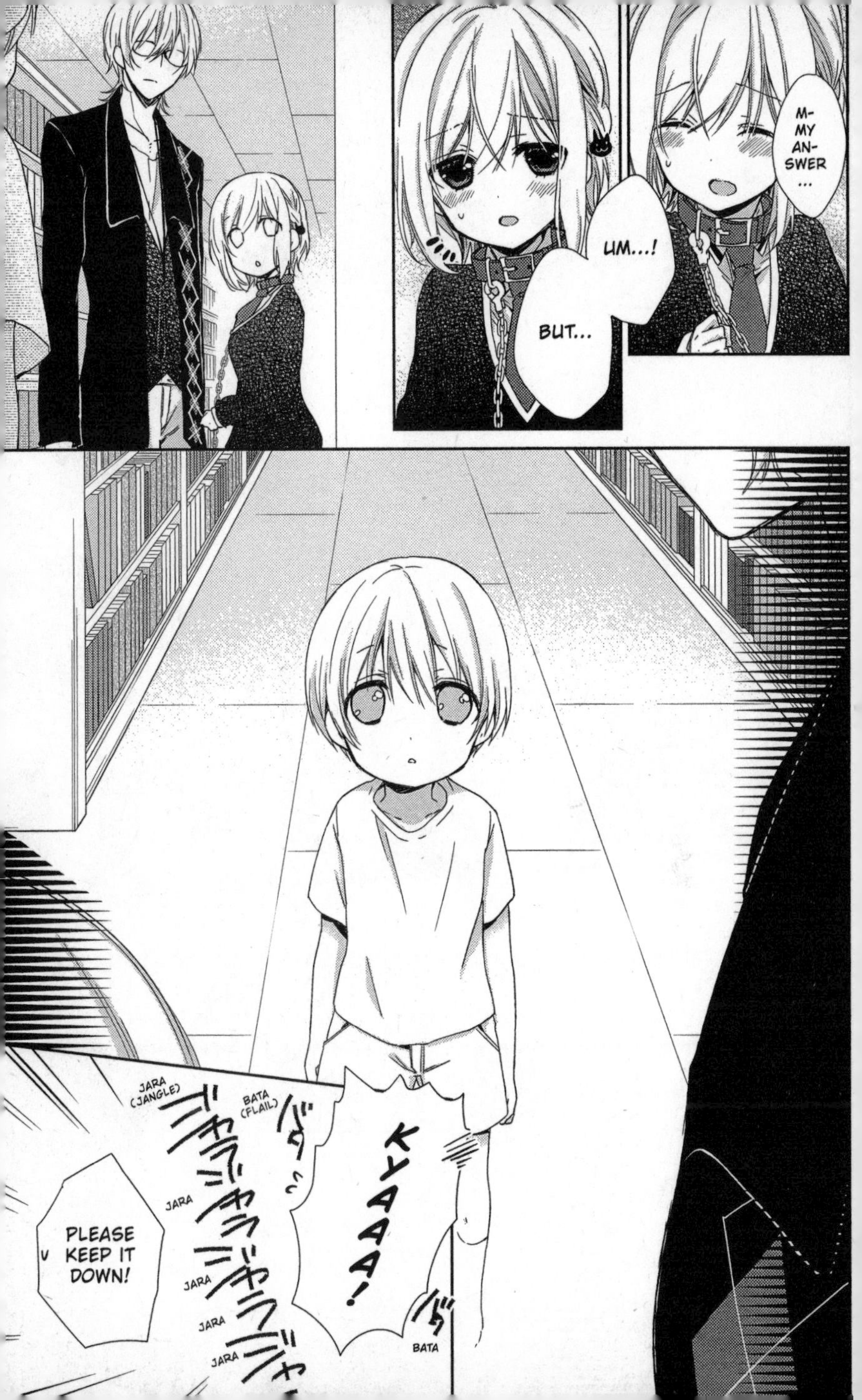
M-MY AN-SWER...
UM...!
BUT...
KYAAAA!
BATA (FLAIL)
JARA (JANGLE)
JARA
JARA
JARA
JARA
BATA
PLEASE KEEP IT DOWN!

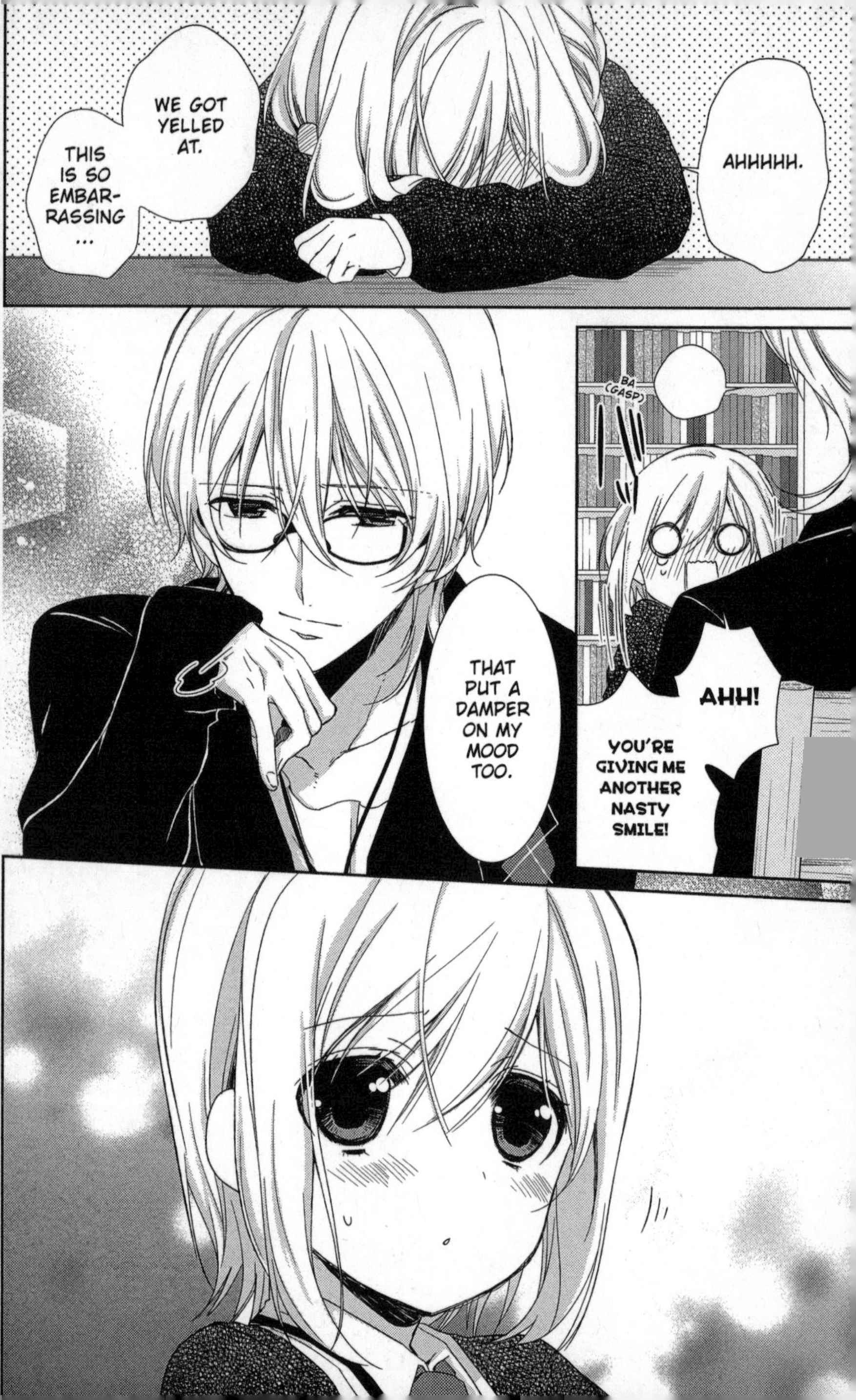
AHHHHH.
WE GOT YELLED AT.
THIS IS SO EMBARRASSING...
BA (GASP)
AHH!
YOU'RE GIVING ME ANOTHER NASTY SMILE!
THAT PUT A DAMPER ON MY MOOD TOO.

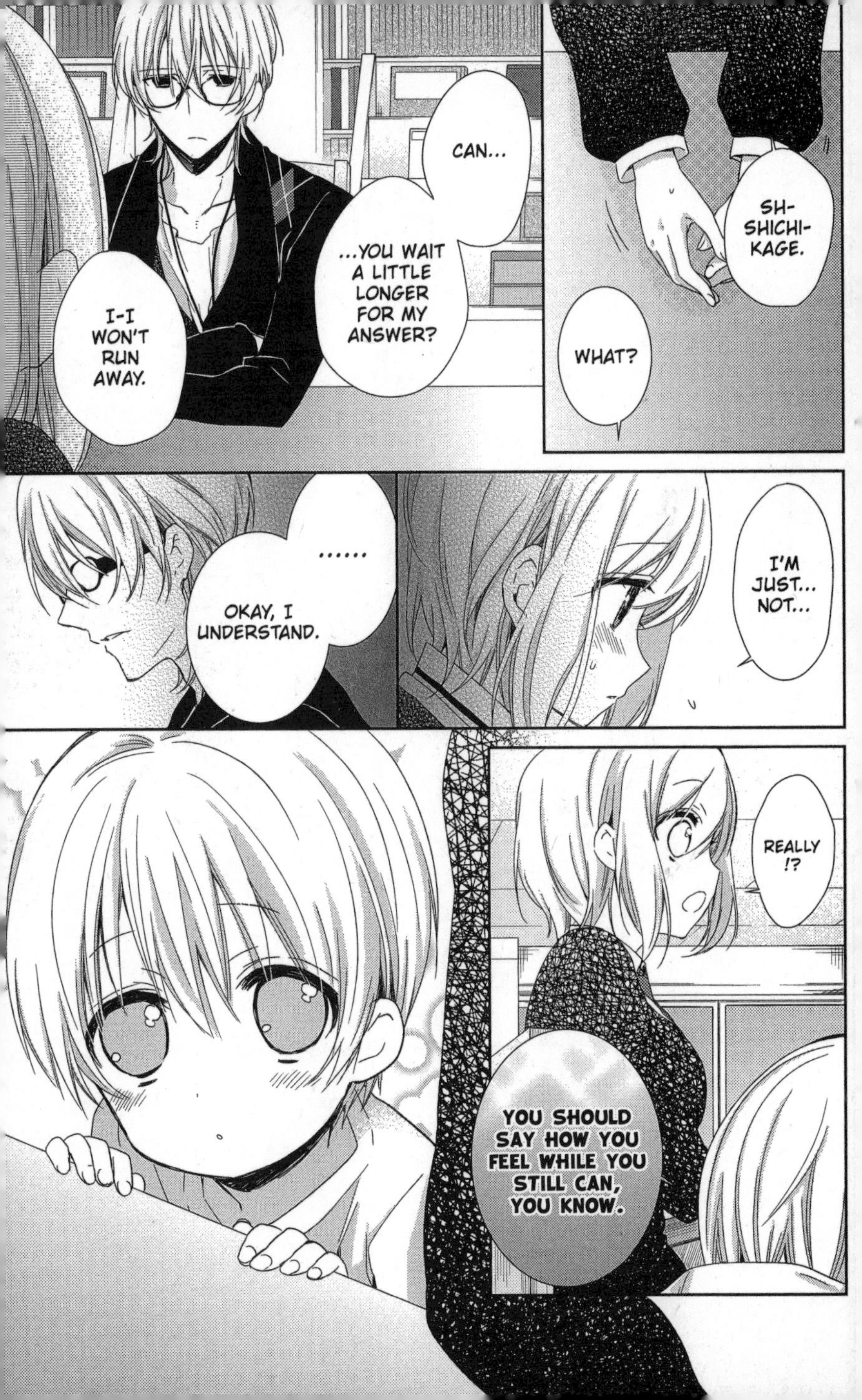
SH-SHICHIKAGE.
WHAT?
CAN...
...YOU WAIT A LITTLE LONGER FOR MY ANSWER?
I-I WON'T RUN AWAY.
I'M JUST... NOT...
......
OKAY, I UNDERSTAND.
REALLY!?
YOU SHOULD SAY HOW YOU FEEL WHILE YOU STILL CAN, YOU KNOW.

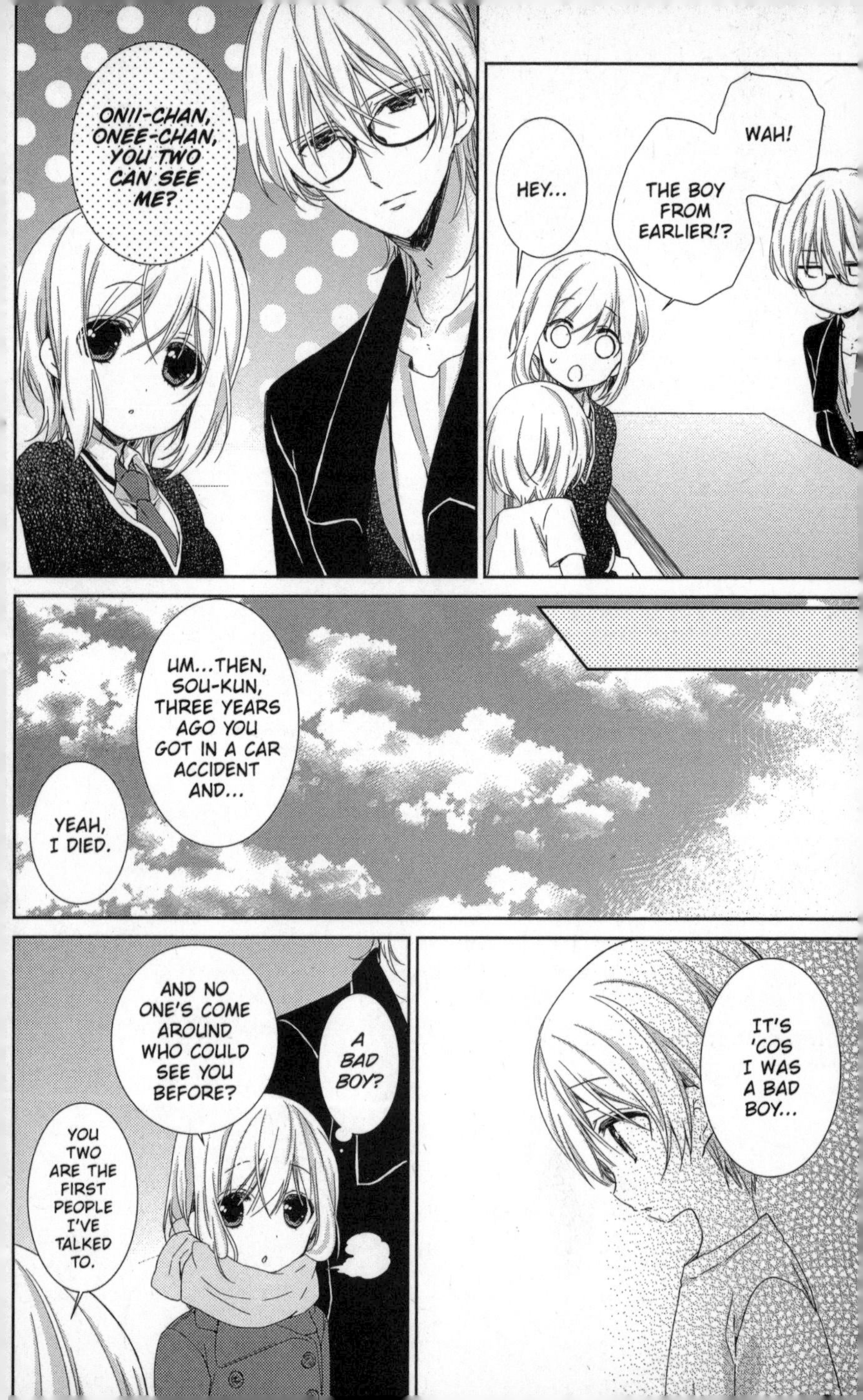
WAH!
THE BOY FROM EARLIER!?
HEY...
ONII-CHAN, ONEE-CHAN, YOU TWO CAN SEE ME?
UM...THEN, SOU-KUN, THREE YEARS AGO YOU GOT IN A CAR ACCIDENT AND...
YEAH, I DIED.
IT'S 'COS I WAS A BAD BOY...
A BAD BOY?
AND NO ONE'S COME AROUND WHO COULD SEE YOU BEFORE?
YOU TWO ARE THE FIRST PEOPLE I'VE TALKED TO.

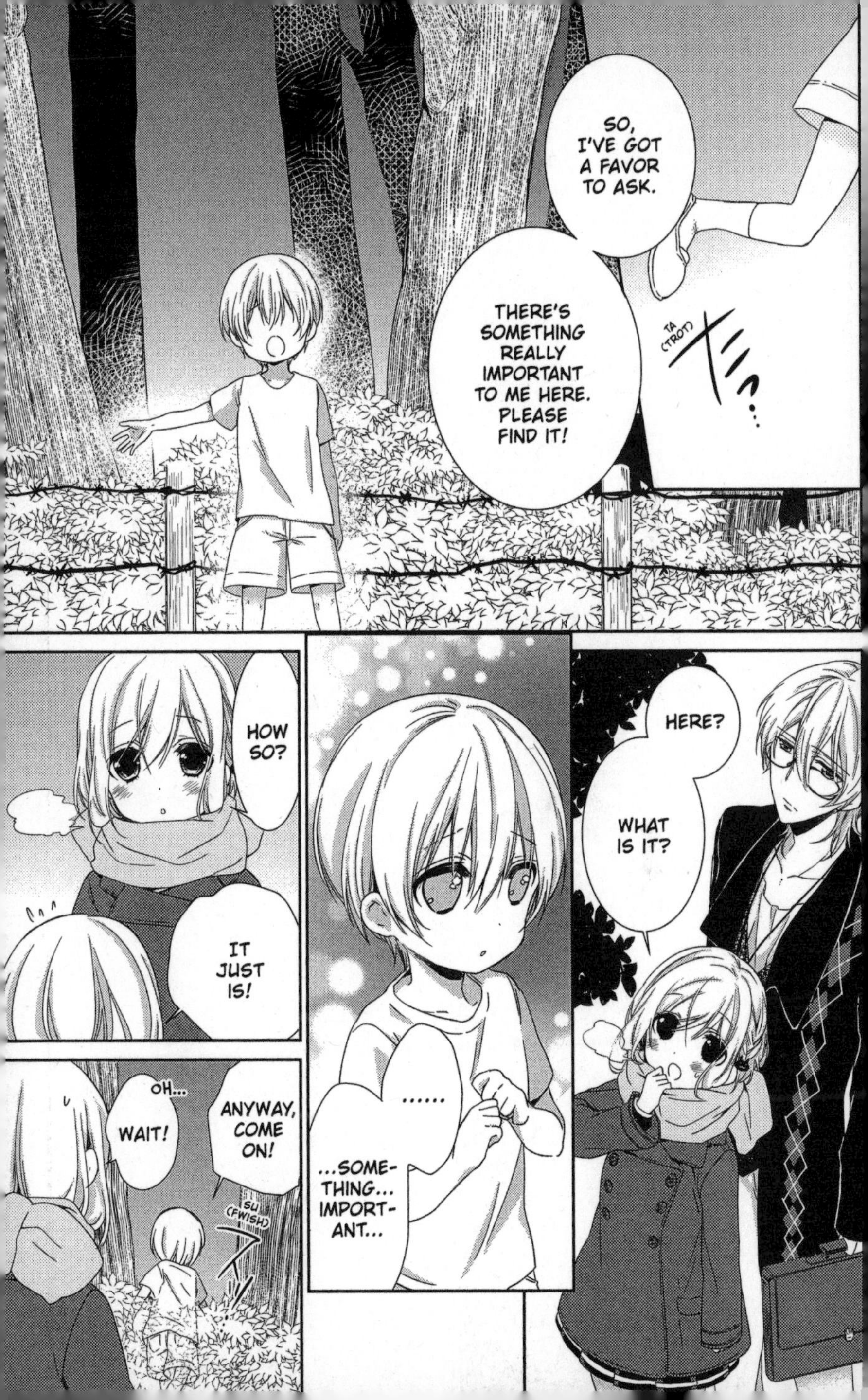
SO, I'VE GOT A FAVOR TO ASK.
TA (TROT)
THERE'S SOMETHING REALLY IMPORTANT TO ME HERE. PLEASE FIND IT!
HERE?
WHAT IS IT?
......
...SOME-THING... IMPORT-ANT...
HOW SO?
IT JUST IS!
ANYWAY, COME ON!
OH...
WAIT!
SU (FWISH)

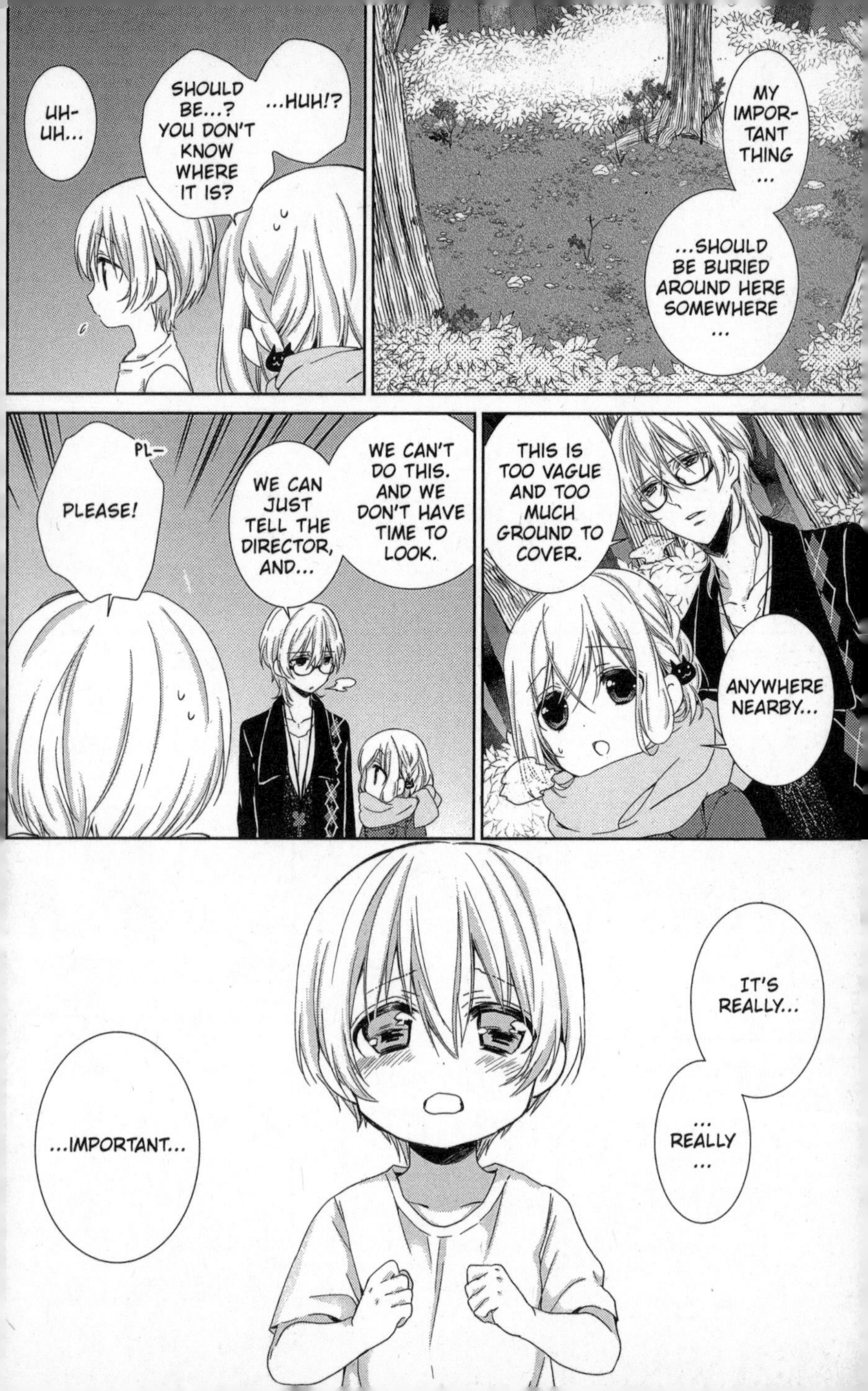
MY IMPORTANT THING...
...SHOULD BE BURIED AROUND HERE SOMEWHERE...
...HUH!?
SHOULD BE...? YOU DON'T KNOW WHERE IT IS?
UH-UH...
THIS IS TOO VAGUE AND TOO MUCH GROUND TO COVER.
ANYWHERE NEARBY...
WE CAN'T DO THIS. AND WE DON'T HAVE TIME TO LOOK.
WE CAN JUST TELL THE DIRECTOR, AND...
PL—
PLEASE!
IT'S REALLY...
...REALLY...
...IMPORTANT...

NENEKO-SA—

GOT IT!

OKAY! WE'LL FIND IT FOR YOU!

REALLY!?

HUH...?

HAA...

HAA...

OKAY THEN, LET'S START DIGGING AT THE EDGES!

MAYBE SHICHI-KAGE WAS RIGHT. THIS IS...

...A BIT TOO MUCH.

ARE WE EVER GOING TO FIND IT...?

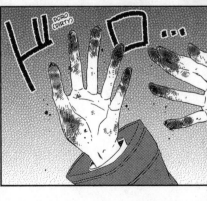

DORO (DIRTY)

...

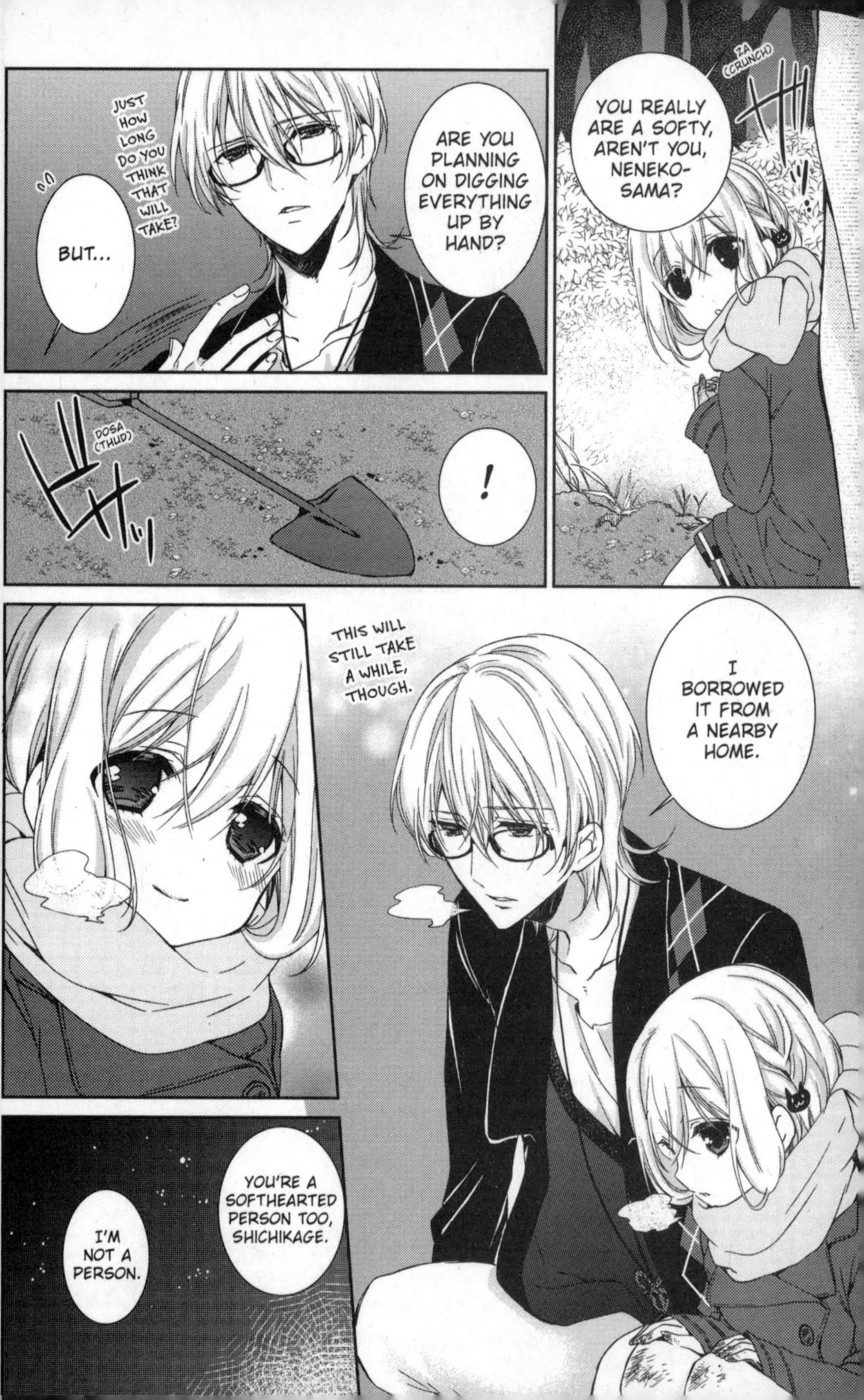ZA (CRUNCH)
YOU REALLY ARE A SOFTY, AREN'T YOU, NENEKO-SAMA?
ARE YOU PLANNING ON DIGGING EVERYTHING UP BY HAND?
JUST HOW LONG DO YOU THINK THAT WILL TAKE?
BUT...
!
DOSA (THUD)
I BORROWED IT FROM A NEARBY HOME.
THIS WILL STILL TAKE A WHILE, THOUGH.
YOU'RE A SOFTHEARTED PERSON TOO, SHICHIKAGE.
I'M NOT A PERSON.

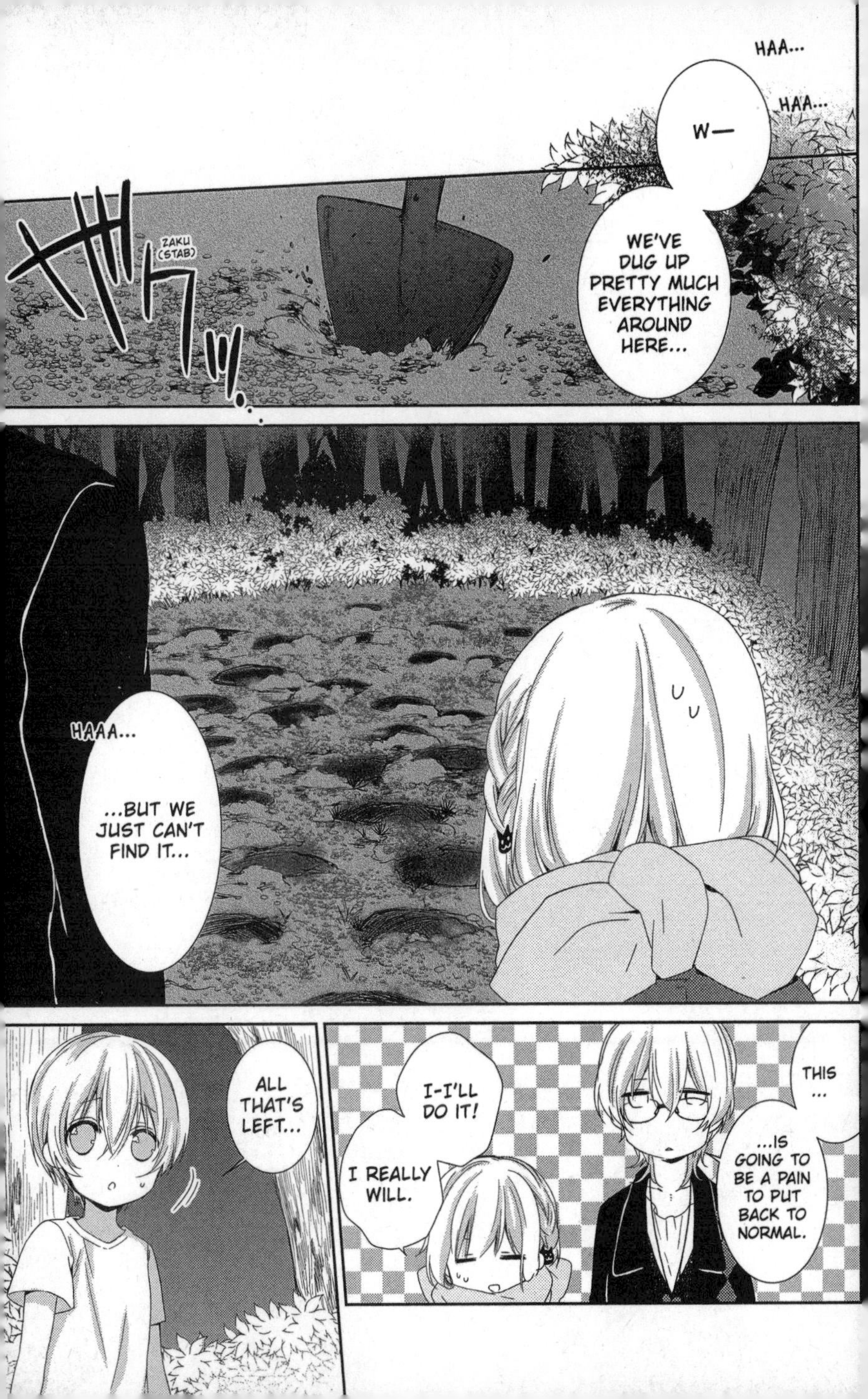
HAA...
HAA...
W—
WE'VE DUG UP PRETTY MUCH EVERYTHING AROUND HERE...
ZAKU (STAB)
HAAA...
...BUT WE JUST CAN'T FIND IT...
THIS...
...IS GOING TO BE A PAIN TO PUT BACK TO NORMAL.
I-I'LL DO IT!
I REALLY WILL.
ALL THAT'S LEFT...

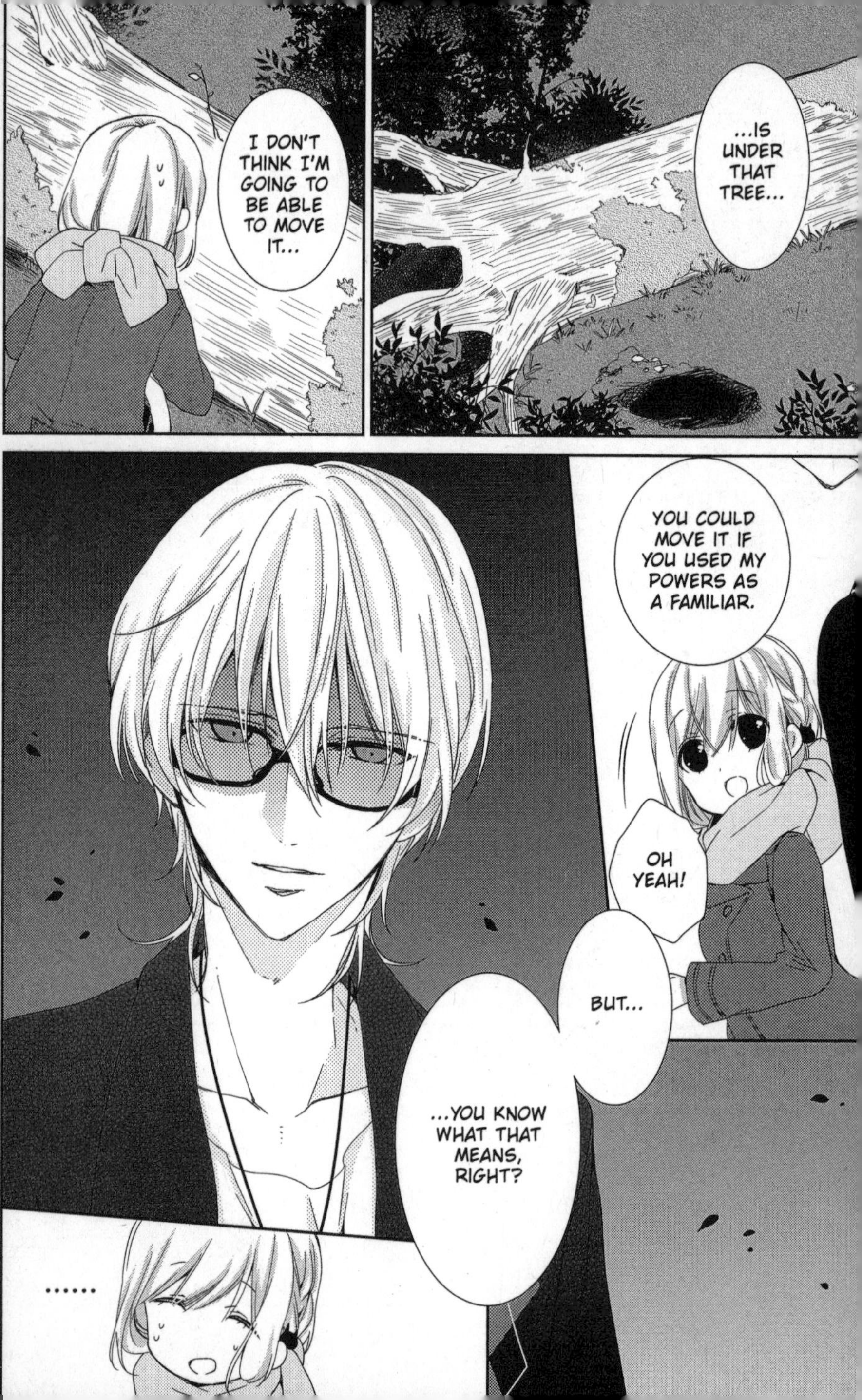
...IS UNDER THAT TREE...
I DON'T THINK I'M GOING TO BE ABLE TO MOVE IT...
YOU COULD MOVE IT IF YOU USED MY POWERS AS A FAMILIAR.
OH YEAH!
BUT...
...YOU KNOW WHAT THAT MEANS, RIGHT?
......

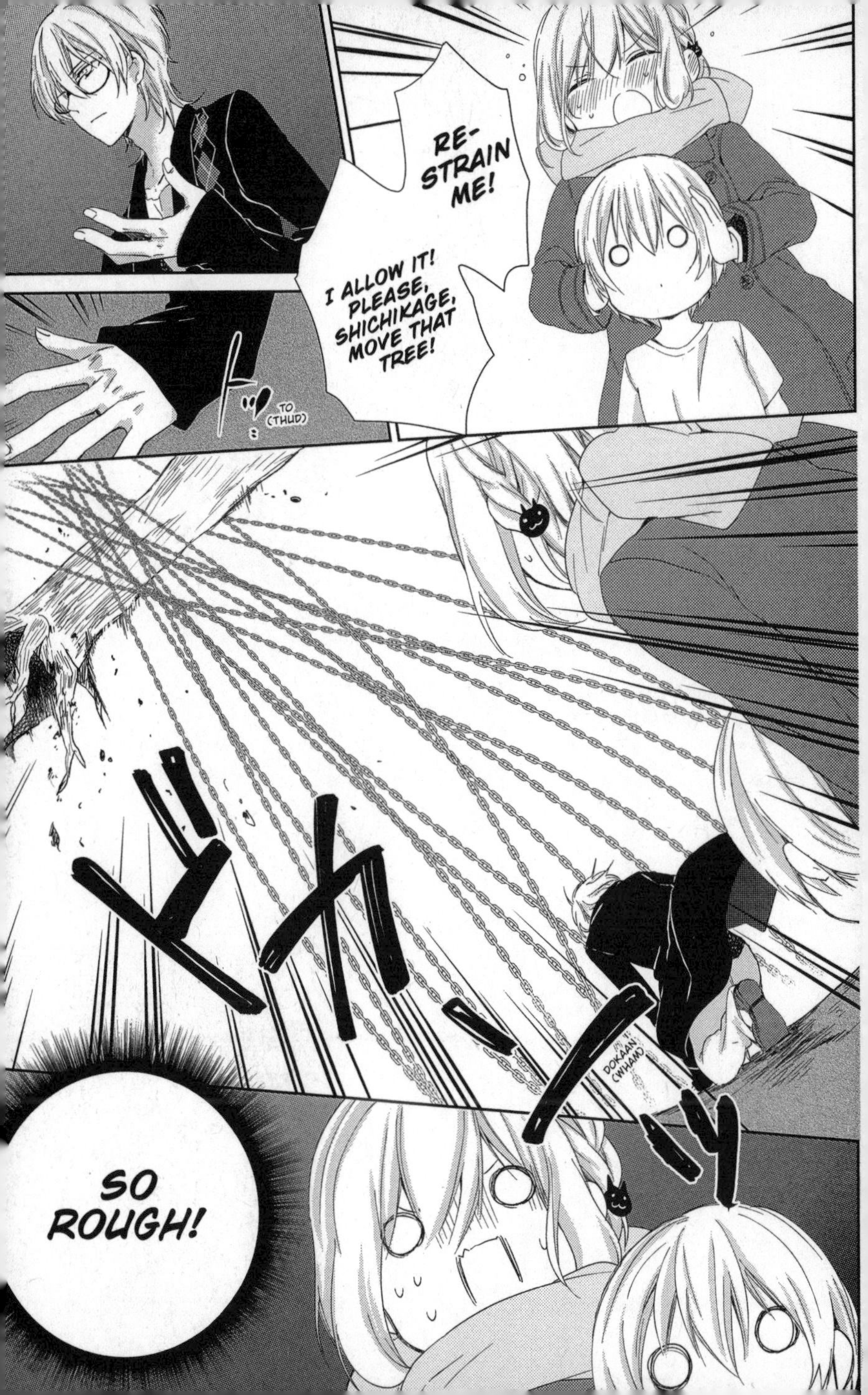
RE-STRAIN ME!
I ALLOW IT! PLEASE, SHICHIKAGE, MOVE THAT TREE!
TO (THUD)
DOKAAN (WHAM)
SO ROUGH!

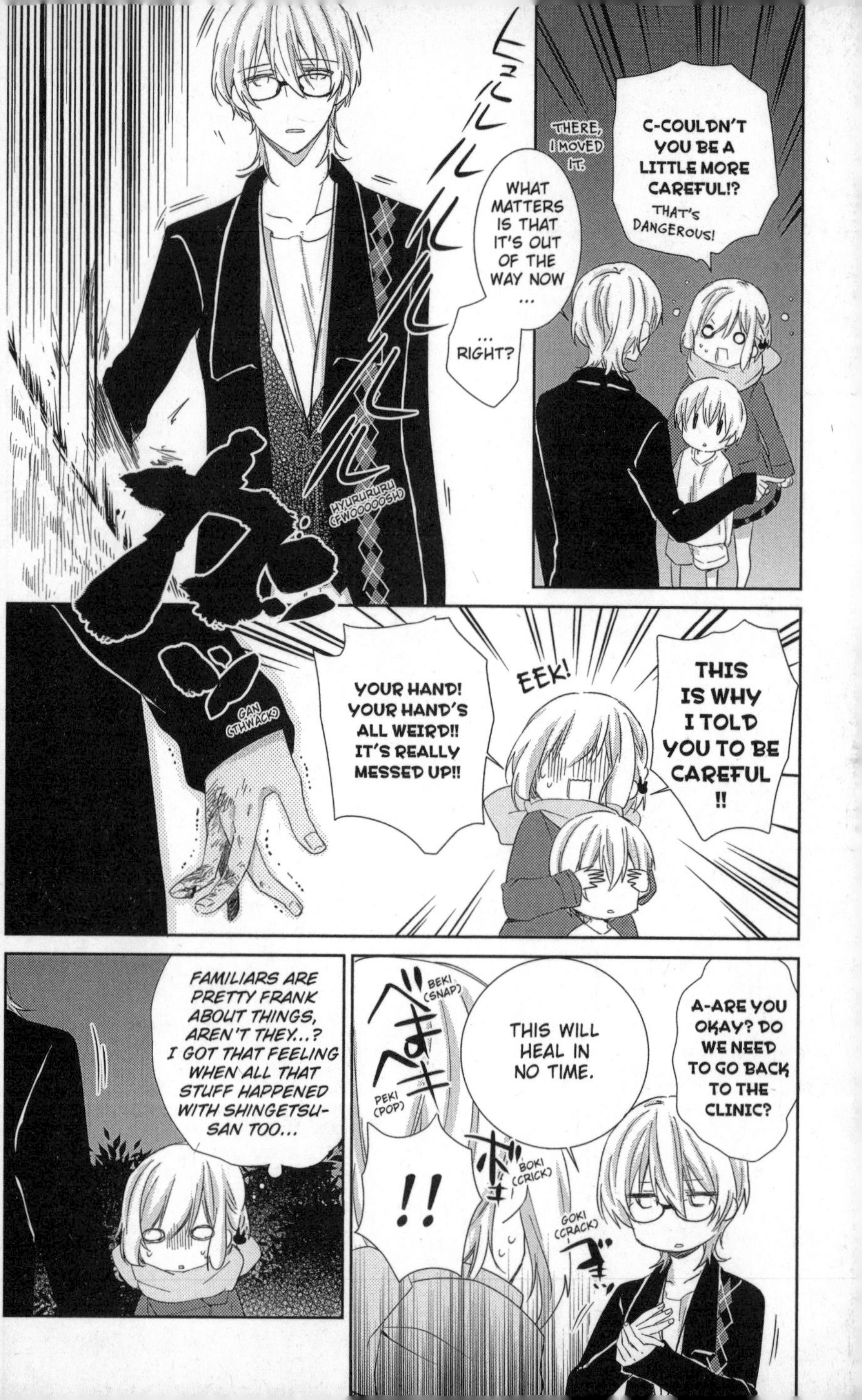
C-COULDN'T YOU BE A LITTLE MORE CAREFUL!?
THAT'S DANGEROUS!
THERE, I MOVED IT.
WHAT MATTERS IS THAT IT'S OUT OF THE WAY NOW ...
... RIGHT?
HYURURURU (FWOOOOOSH)
THIS IS WHY I TOLD YOU TO BE CAREFUL !!
EEK!
YOUR HAND! YOUR HAND'S ALL WEIRD!! IT'S REALLY MESSED UP!!
GAN (THWACK)
A-ARE YOU OKAY? DO WE NEED TO GO BACK TO THE CLINIC?
THIS WILL HEAL IN NO TIME.
BEKI (SNAP)
PEKI (POP)
BOKI (CRICK)
GOKI (CRACK)
!!
FAMILIARS ARE PRETTY FRANK ABOUT THINGS, AREN'T THEY...? I GOT THAT FEELING WHEN ALL THAT STUFF HAPPENED WITH SHINGETSU-SAN TOO...

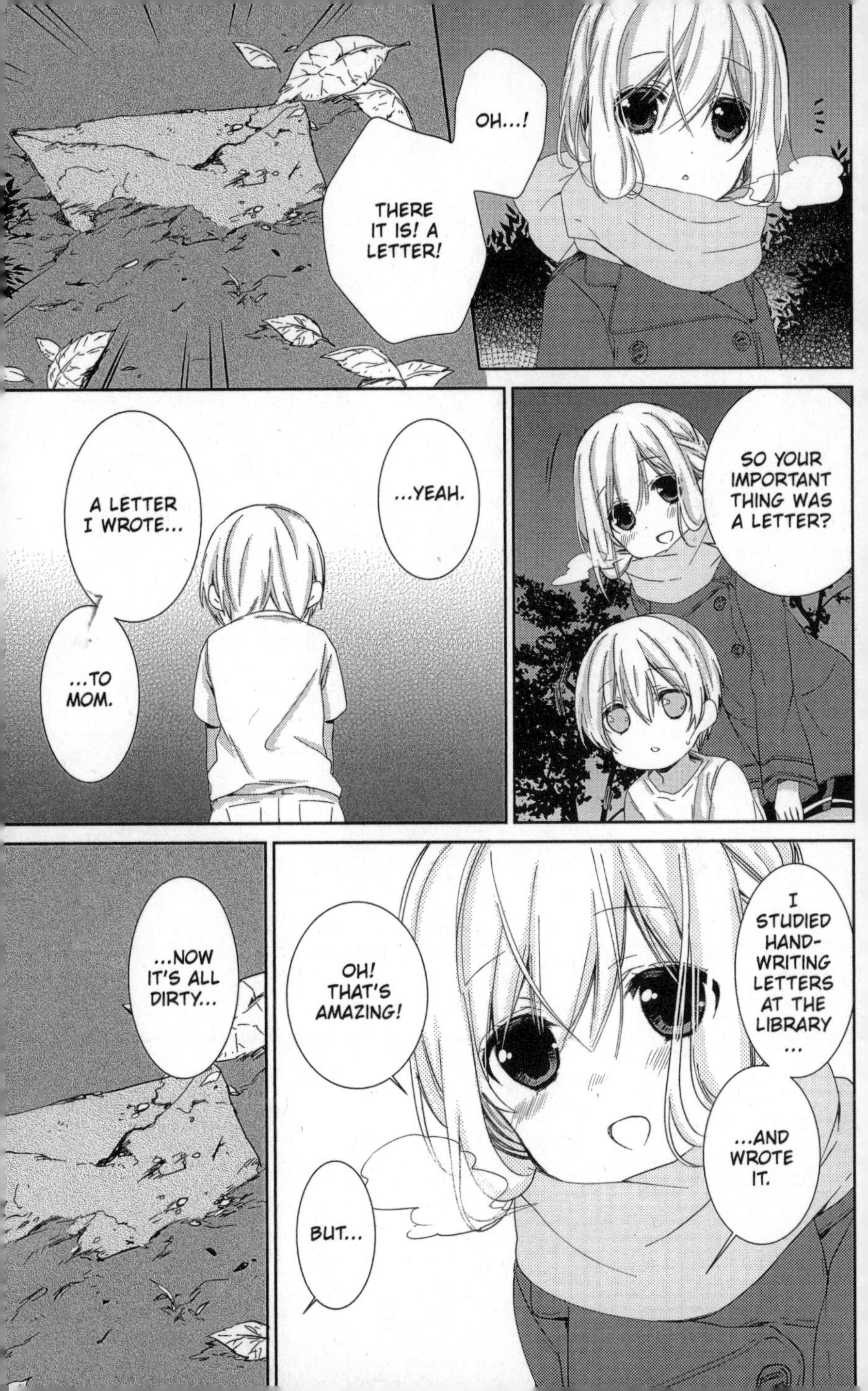
OH...!
THERE IT IS! A LETTER!
SO YOUR IMPORTANT THING WAS A LETTER?
...YEAH.
A LETTER I WROTE...
...TO MOM.
I STUDIED HAND-WRITING LETTERS AT THE LIBRARY...
...AND WROTE IT.
OH! THAT'S AMAZING!
BUT...
...NOW IT'S ALL DIRTY...

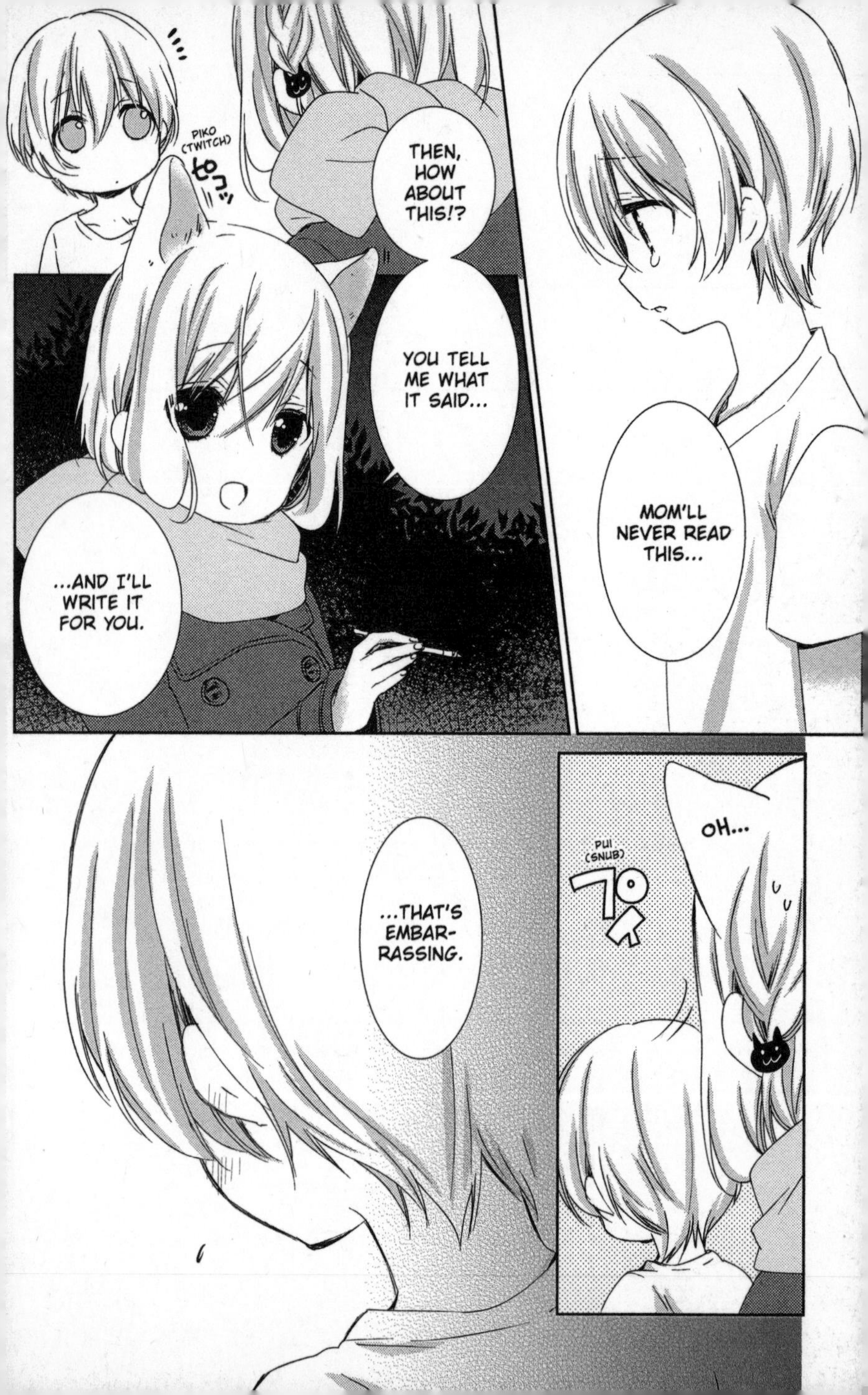
MOM'LL NEVER READ THIS...
PIKO (TWITCH)
ピコッ
THEN, HOW ABOUT THIS!?
YOU TELL ME WHAT IT SAID...
...AND I'LL WRITE IT FOR YOU.
OH...
PUI (SNUB)
プイ
...THAT'S EMBAR-RASSING.

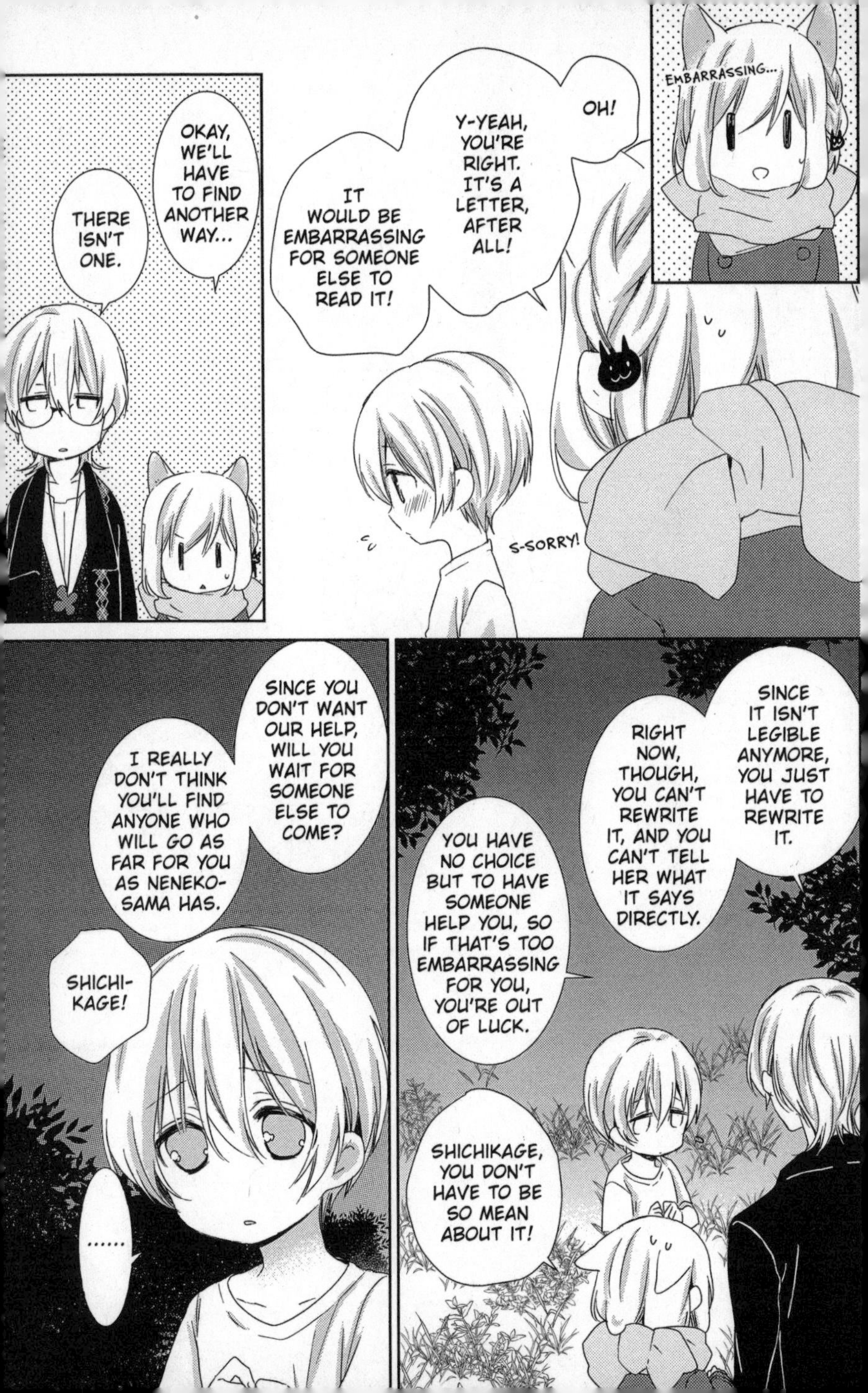
EMBARRASSING...
OH!
Y-YEAH, YOU'RE RIGHT. IT'S A LETTER, AFTER ALL!
IT WOULD BE EMBARRASSING FOR SOMEONE ELSE TO READ IT!
S-SORRY!
OKAY, WE'LL HAVE TO FIND ANOTHER WAY...
THERE ISN'T ONE.
SINCE IT ISN'T LEGIBLE ANYMORE, YOU JUST HAVE TO REWRITE IT.
RIGHT NOW, THOUGH, YOU CAN'T REWRITE IT, AND YOU CAN'T TELL HER WHAT IT SAYS DIRECTLY.
YOU HAVE NO CHOICE BUT TO HAVE SOMEONE HELP YOU, SO IF THAT'S TOO EMBARRASSING FOR YOU, YOU'RE OUT OF LUCK.
SHICHIKAGE, YOU DON'T HAVE TO BE SO MEAN ABOUT IT!
SINCE YOU DON'T WANT OUR HELP, WILL YOU WAIT FOR SOMEONE ELSE TO COME?
I REALLY DON'T THINK YOU'LL FIND ANYONE WHO WILL GO AS FAR FOR YOU AS NENEKO-SAMA HAS.
SHICHI-KAGE!
......

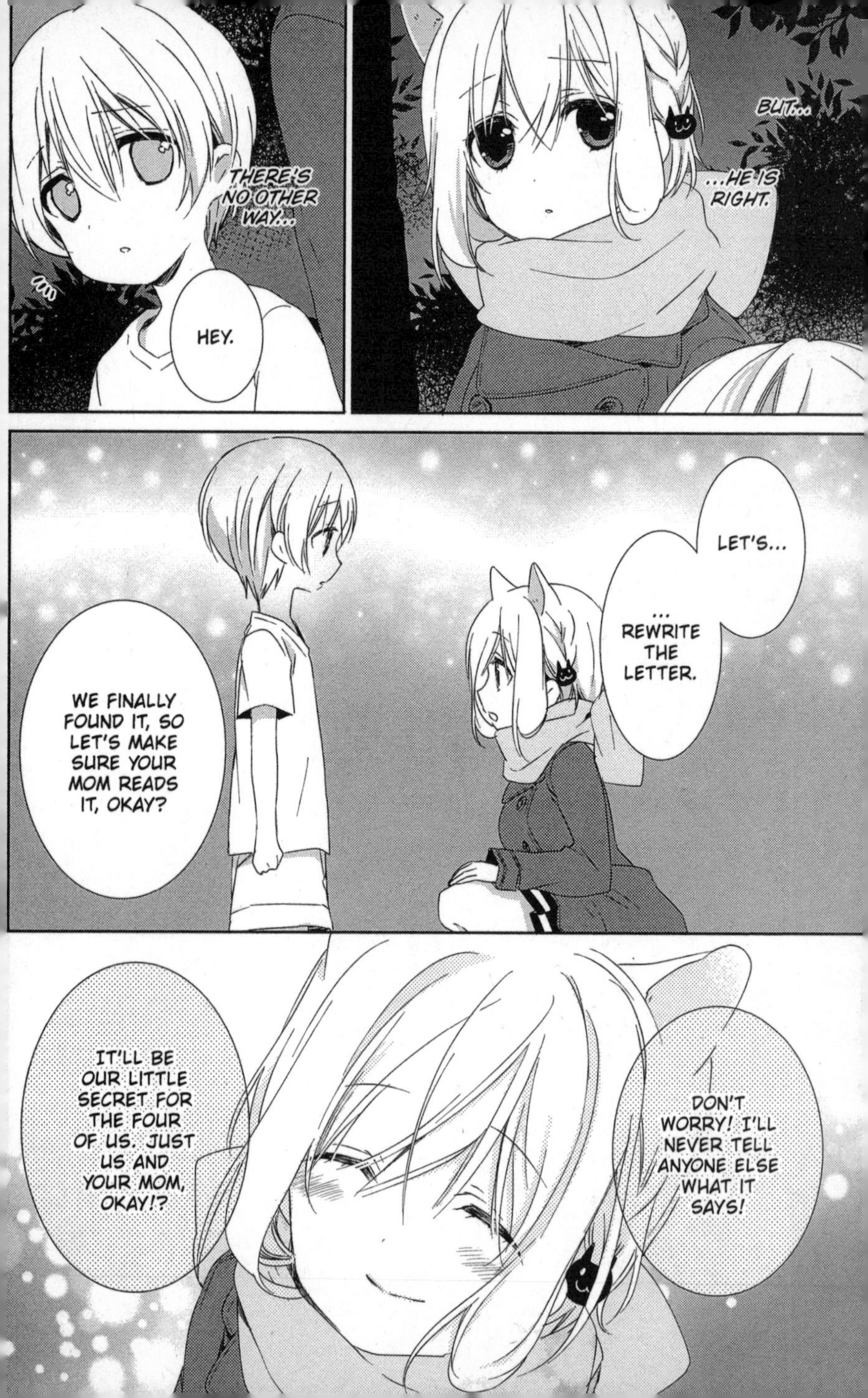
BUT...
...HE IS RIGHT.
THERE'S NO OTHER WAY...
HEY.
LET'S...
... REWRITE THE LETTER.
WE FINALLY FOUND IT, SO LET'S MAKE SURE YOUR MOM READS IT, OKAY?
DON'T WORRY! I'LL NEVER TELL ANYONE ELSE WHAT IT SAYS!
IT'LL BE OUR LITTLE SECRET FOR THE FOUR OF US. JUST US AND YOUR MOM, OKAY!?

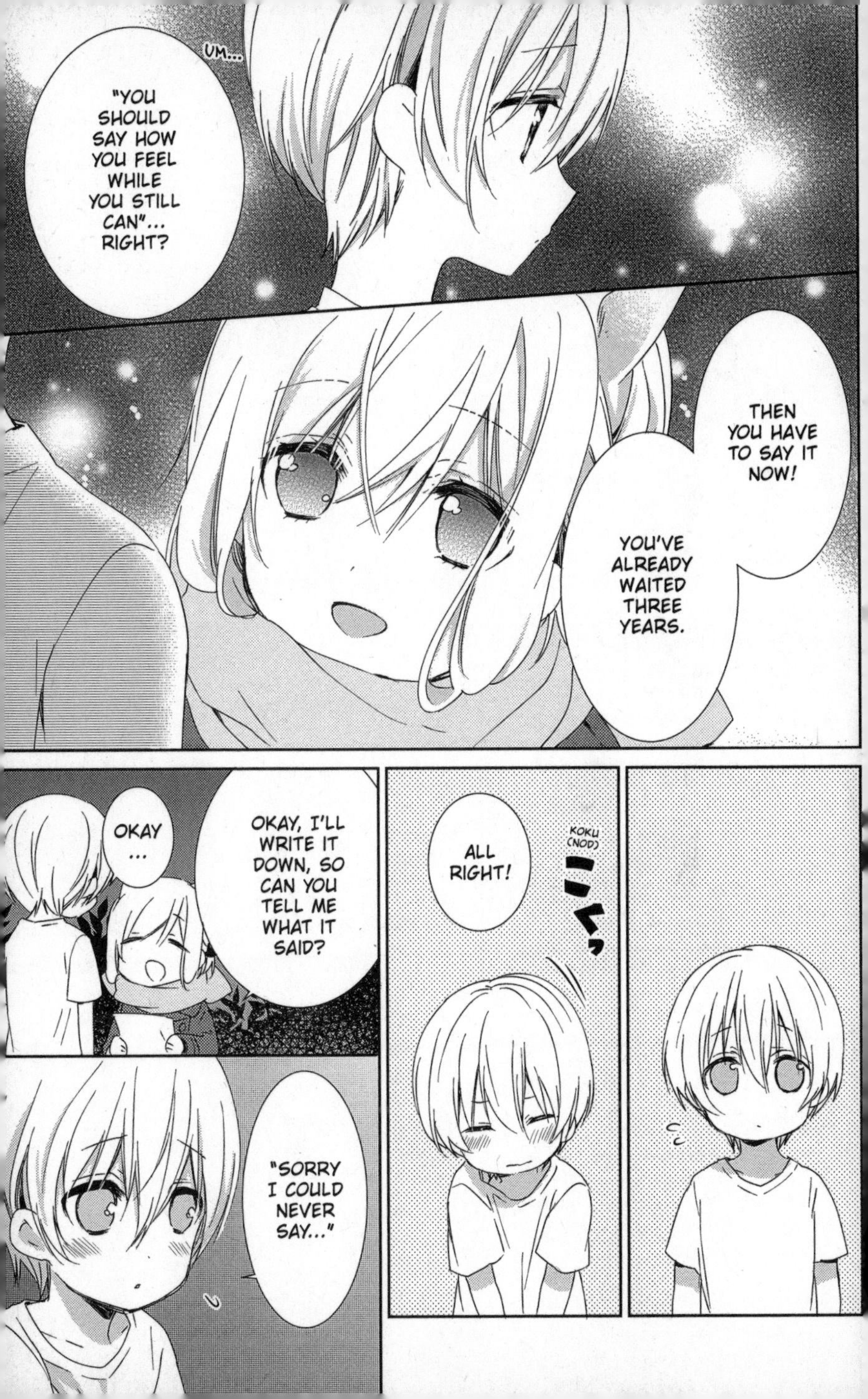
UM...
"YOU SHOULD SAY HOW YOU FEEL WHILE YOU STILL CAN"... RIGHT?
THEN YOU HAVE TO SAY IT NOW!
YOU'VE ALREADY WAITED THREE YEARS.
KOKU (NOD)
ALL RIGHT!
OKAY, I'LL WRITE IT DOWN, SO CAN YOU TELL ME WHAT IT SAID?
OKAY ...
"SORRY I COULD NEVER SAY..."

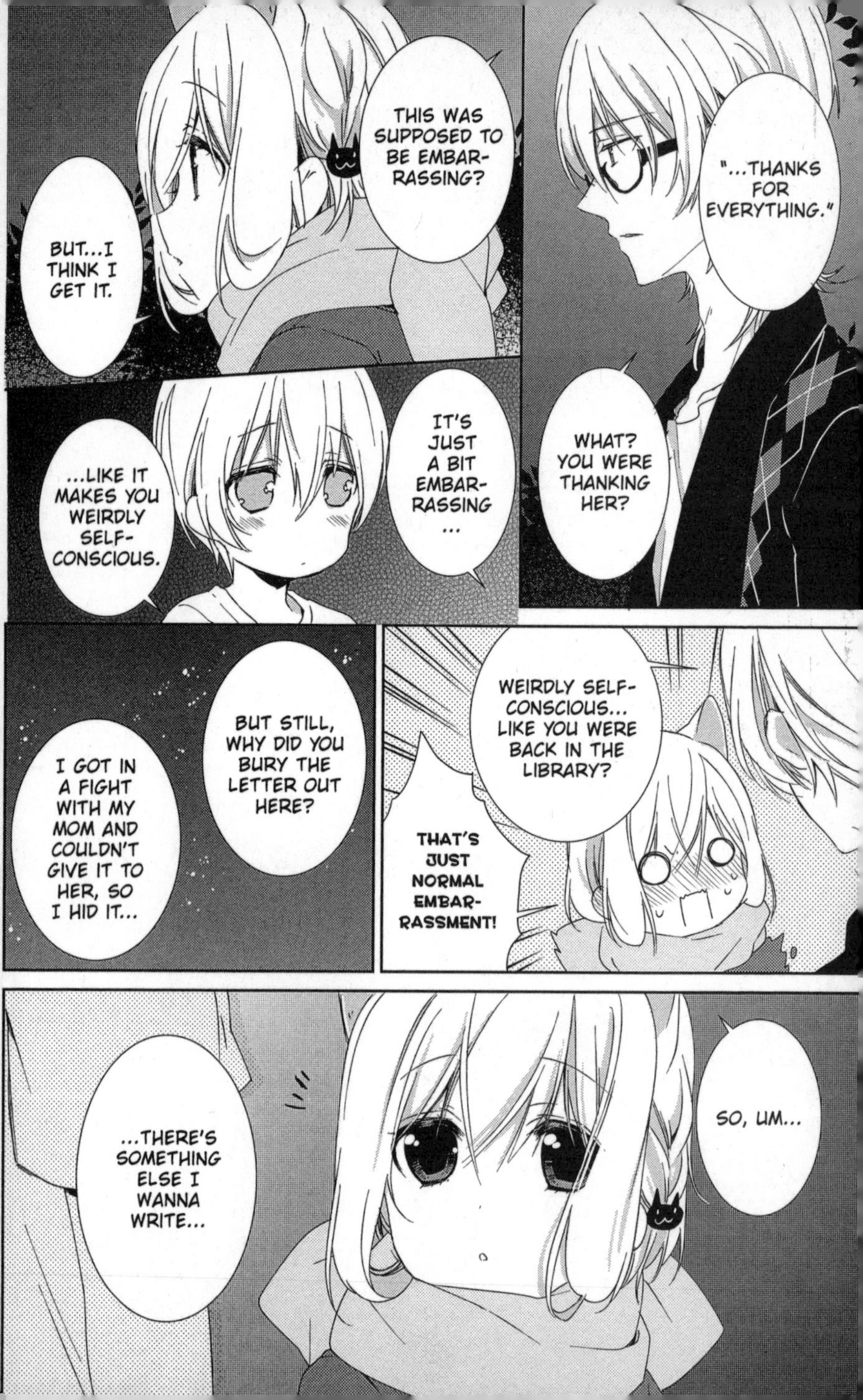
"...THANKS FOR EVERYTHING."
WHAT? YOU WERE THANKING HER?
THIS WAS SUPPOSED TO BE EMBARRASSING?
BUT...I THINK I GET IT.
IT'S JUST A BIT EMBARRASSING...
...LIKE IT MAKES YOU WEIRDLY SELF-CONSCIOUS.
WEIRDLY SELF-CONSCIOUS... LIKE YOU WERE BACK IN THE LIBRARY?
THAT'S JUST NORMAL EMBARRASSMENT!
BUT STILL, WHY DID YOU BURY THE LETTER OUT HERE?
I GOT IN A FIGHT WITH MY MOM AND COULDN'T GIVE IT TO HER, SO I HID IT...
SO, UM...
...THERE'S SOMETHING ELSE I WANNA WRITE...

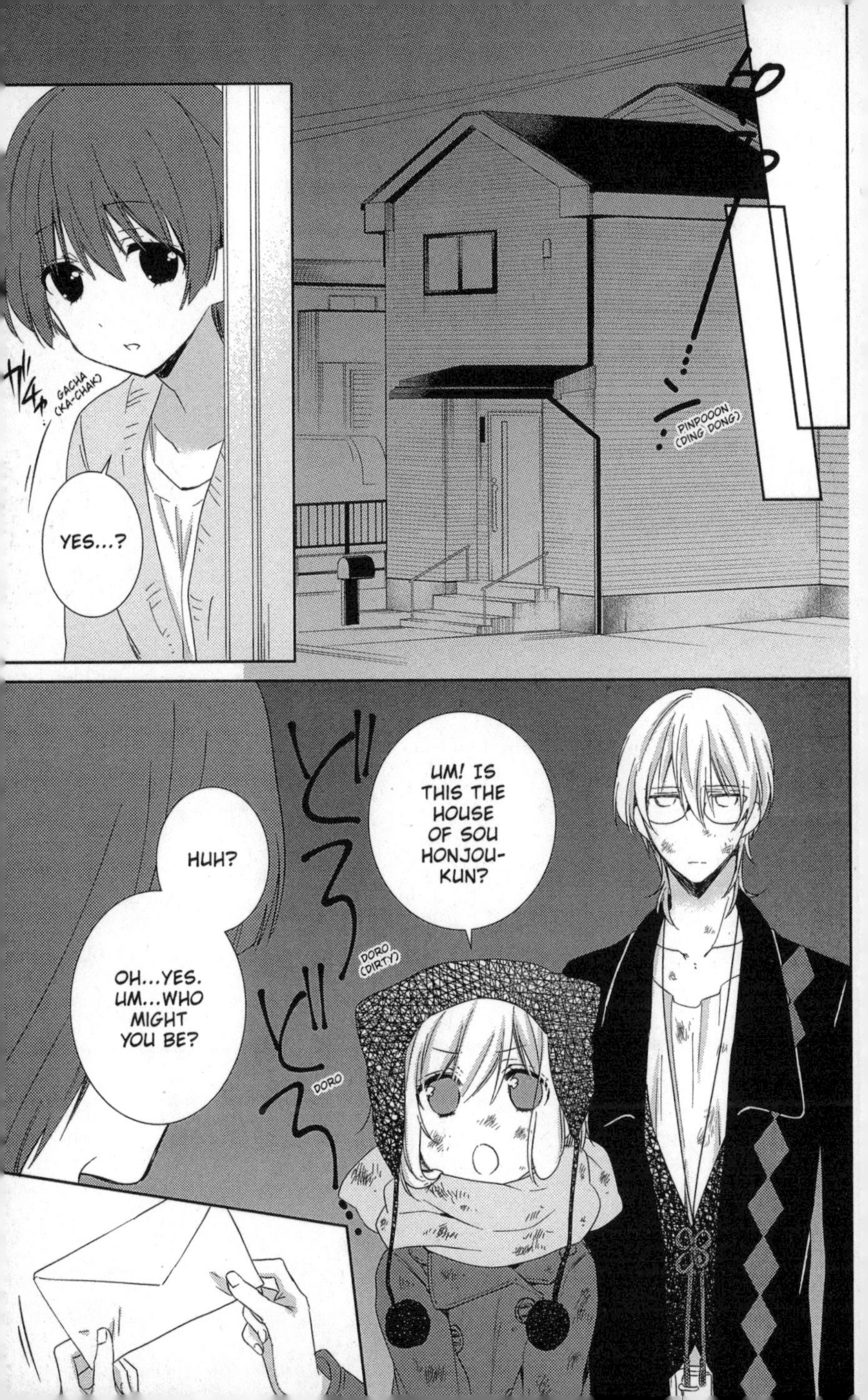
PINPOOON (DING DONG)
GACHA (KA-CHAK)
YES...?
UM! IS THIS THE HOUSE OF SOU HONJOU-KUN?
DORO (DIRTY)
DORO
HUH?
OH...YES. UM...WHO MIGHT YOU BE?

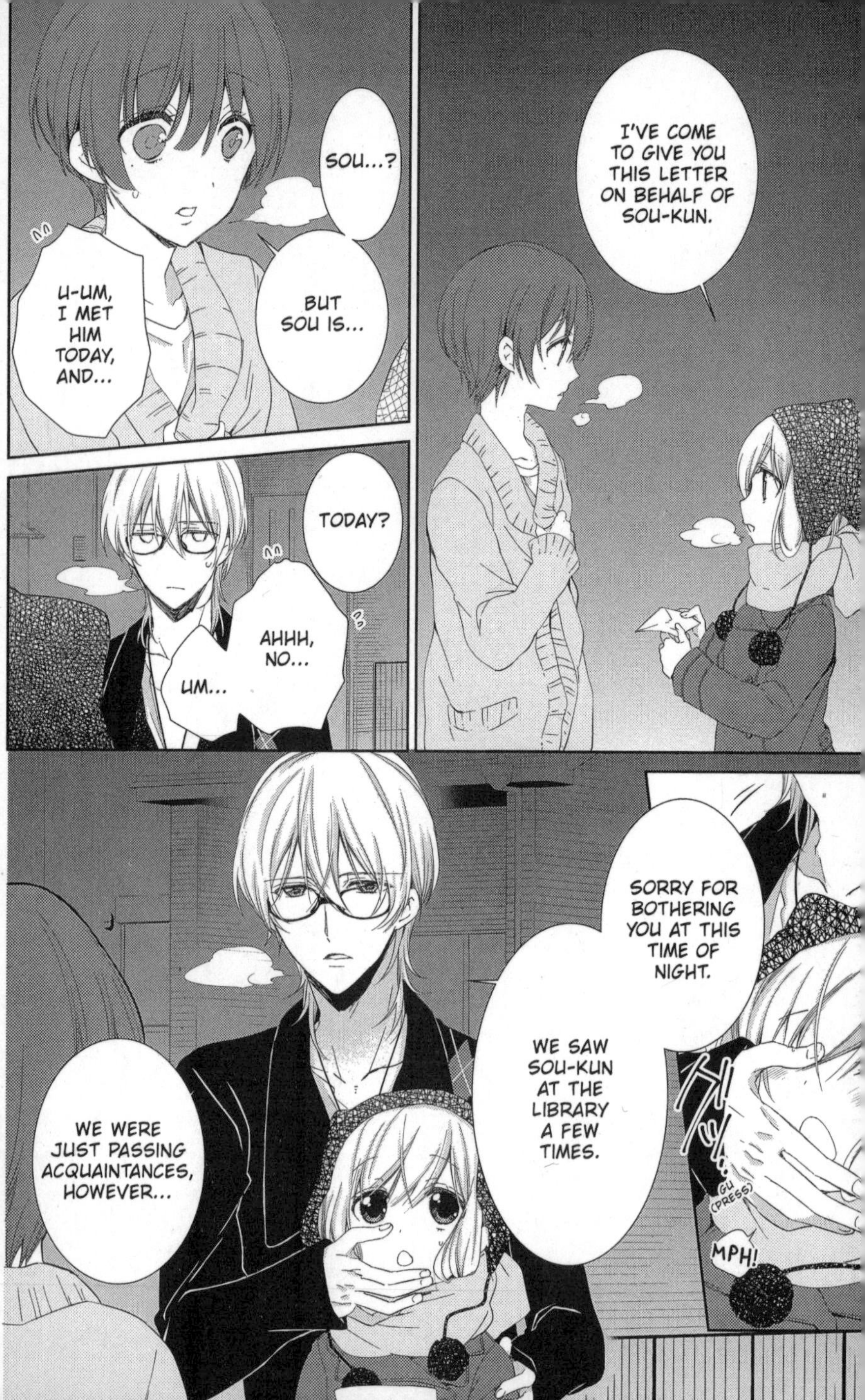
I'VE COME TO GIVE YOU THIS LETTER ON BEHALF OF SOU-KUN.
SOU...?
BUT SOU IS...
U-UM, I MET HIM TODAY, AND...
TODAY?
AHHH, NO...
UM...
GU (PRESS)
MPH!
SORRY FOR BOTHERING YOU AT THIS TIME OF NIGHT.
WE SAW SOU-KUN AT THE LIBRARY A FEW TIMES.
WE WERE JUST PASSING ACQUAINTANCES, HOWEVER...

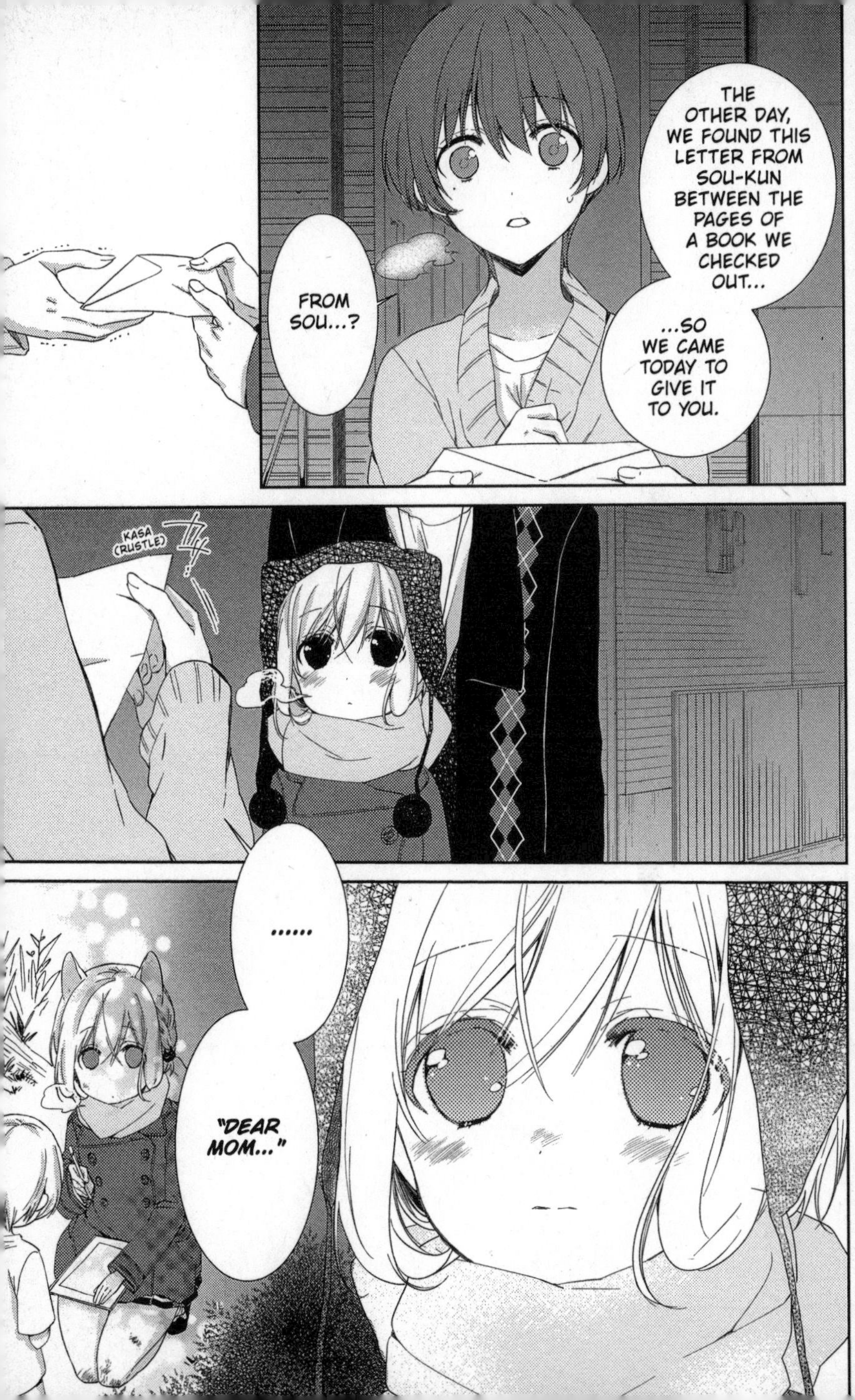
THE OTHER DAY, WE FOUND THIS LETTER FROM SOU-KUN BETWEEN THE PAGES OF A BOOK WE CHECKED OUT...
...SO WE CAME TODAY TO GIVE IT TO YOU.
FROM SOU...?
KASA (RUSTLE)
......
"DEAR MOM..."

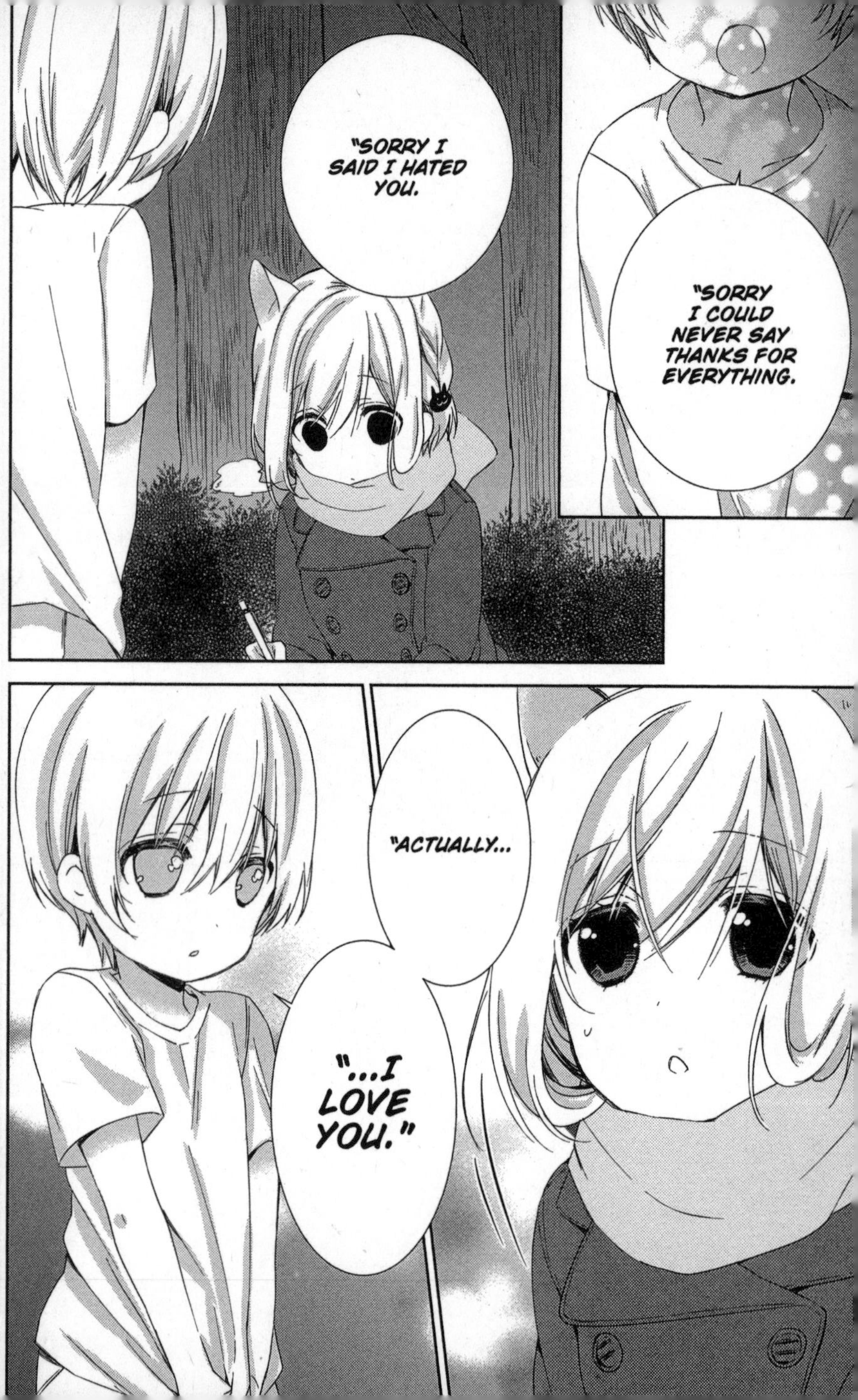
"SORRY I COULD NEVER SAY THANKS FOR EVERYTHING.
"SORRY I SAID I HATED YOU.
"ACTUALLY...
"...I LOVE YOU."

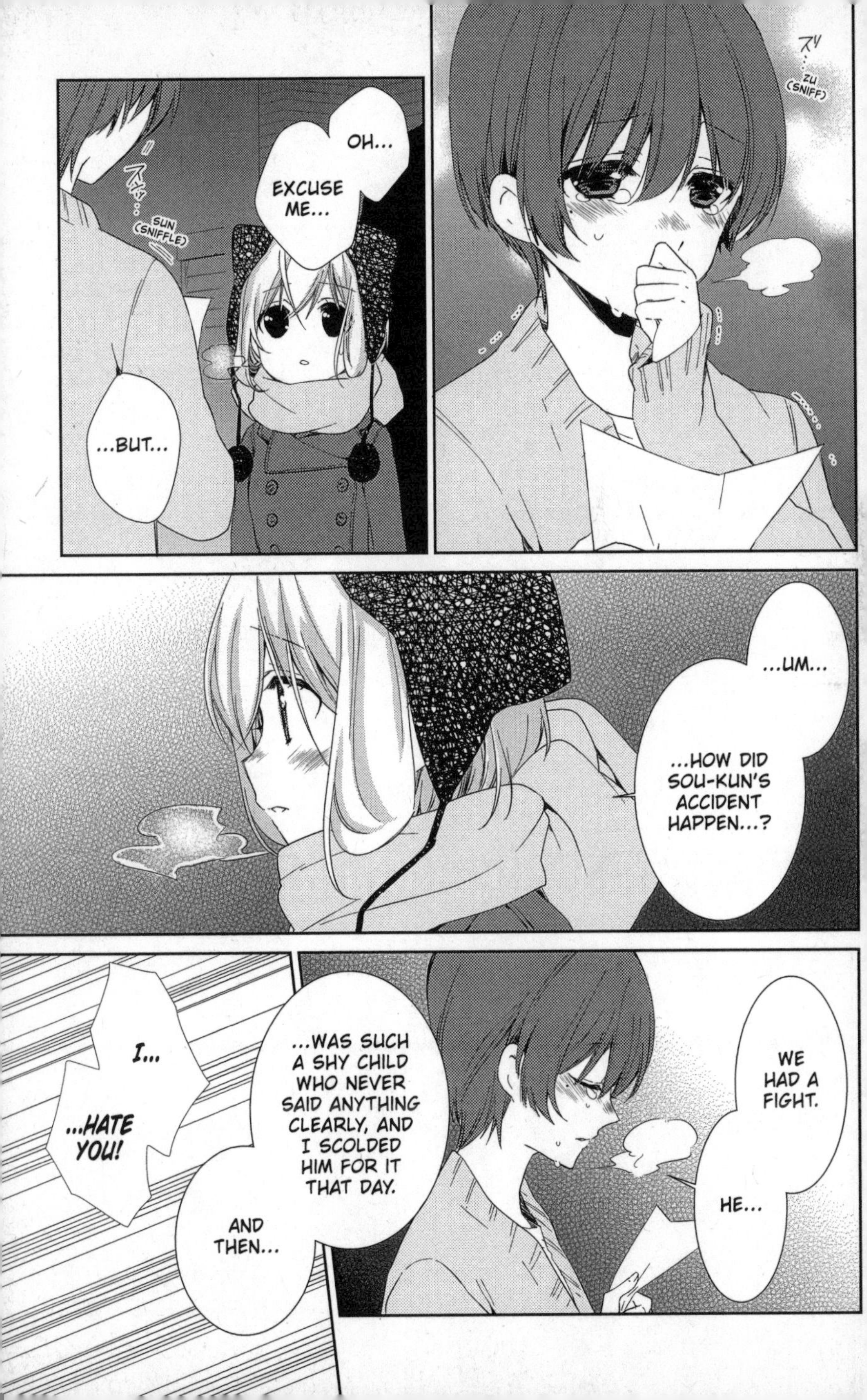
ズ… ZU (SNIFF)
OH… EXCUSE ME…
スン… SUN (SNIFFLE)
…BUT…
…UM…
…HOW DID SOU-KUN'S ACCIDENT HAPPEN…?
WE HAD A FIGHT.
HE…
…WAS SUCH A SHY CHILD WHO NEVER SAID ANYTHING CLEARLY, AND I SCOLDED HIM FOR IT THAT DAY.
AND THEN…
I…
…HATE YOU!

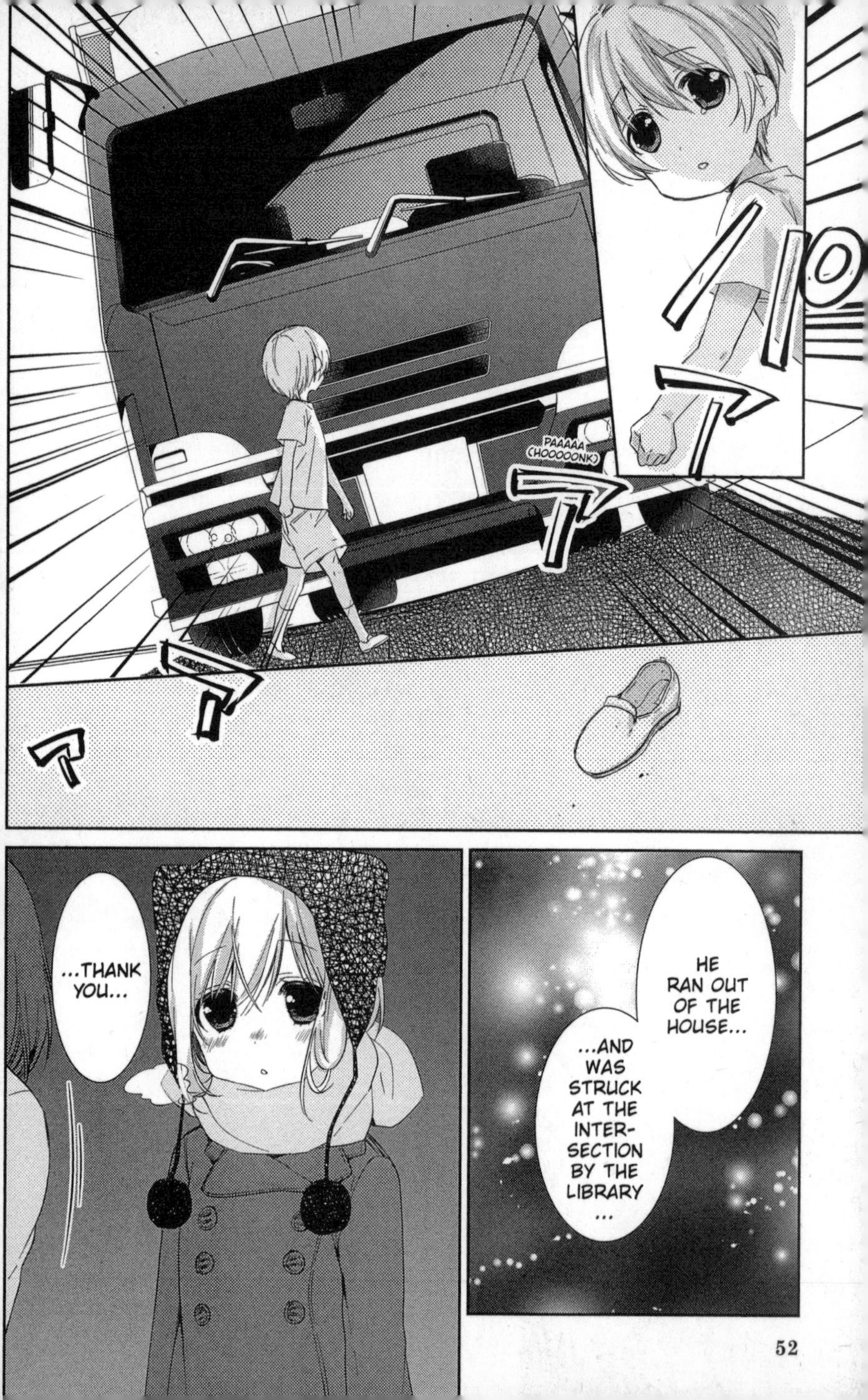
PAAAAA (HOOOOONK)
HE RAN OUT OF THE HOUSE...
...AND WAS STRUCK AT THE INTER-SECTION BY THE LIBRARY ...
...THANK YOU...

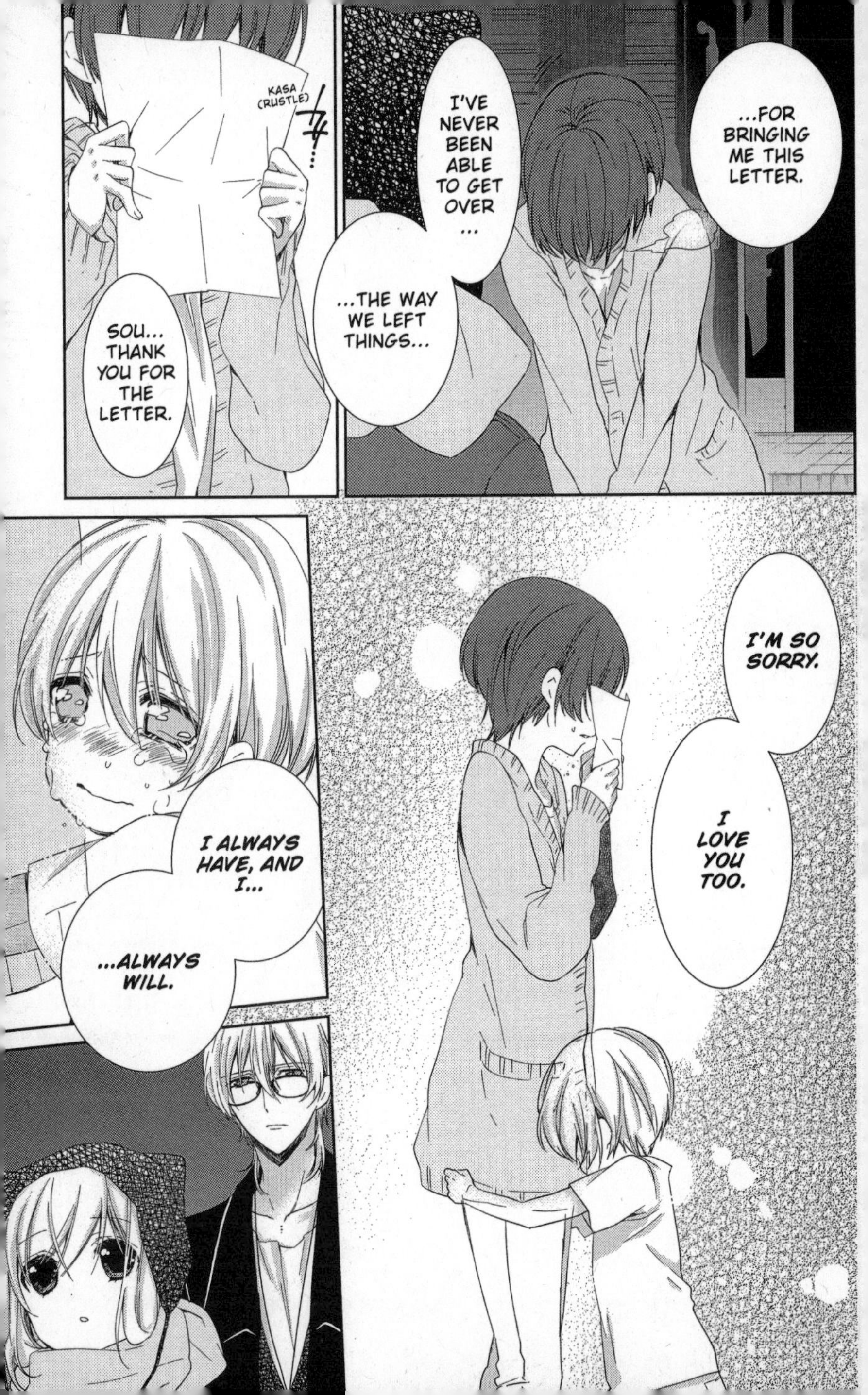
...FOR BRINGING ME THIS LETTER.
I'VE NEVER BEEN ABLE TO GET OVER ...
...THE WAY WE LEFT THINGS...
KASA (RUSTLE)
SOU... THANK YOU FOR THE LETTER.
I'M SO SORRY.
I LOVE YOU TOO.
I ALWAYS HAVE, AND I...
...ALWAYS WILL.

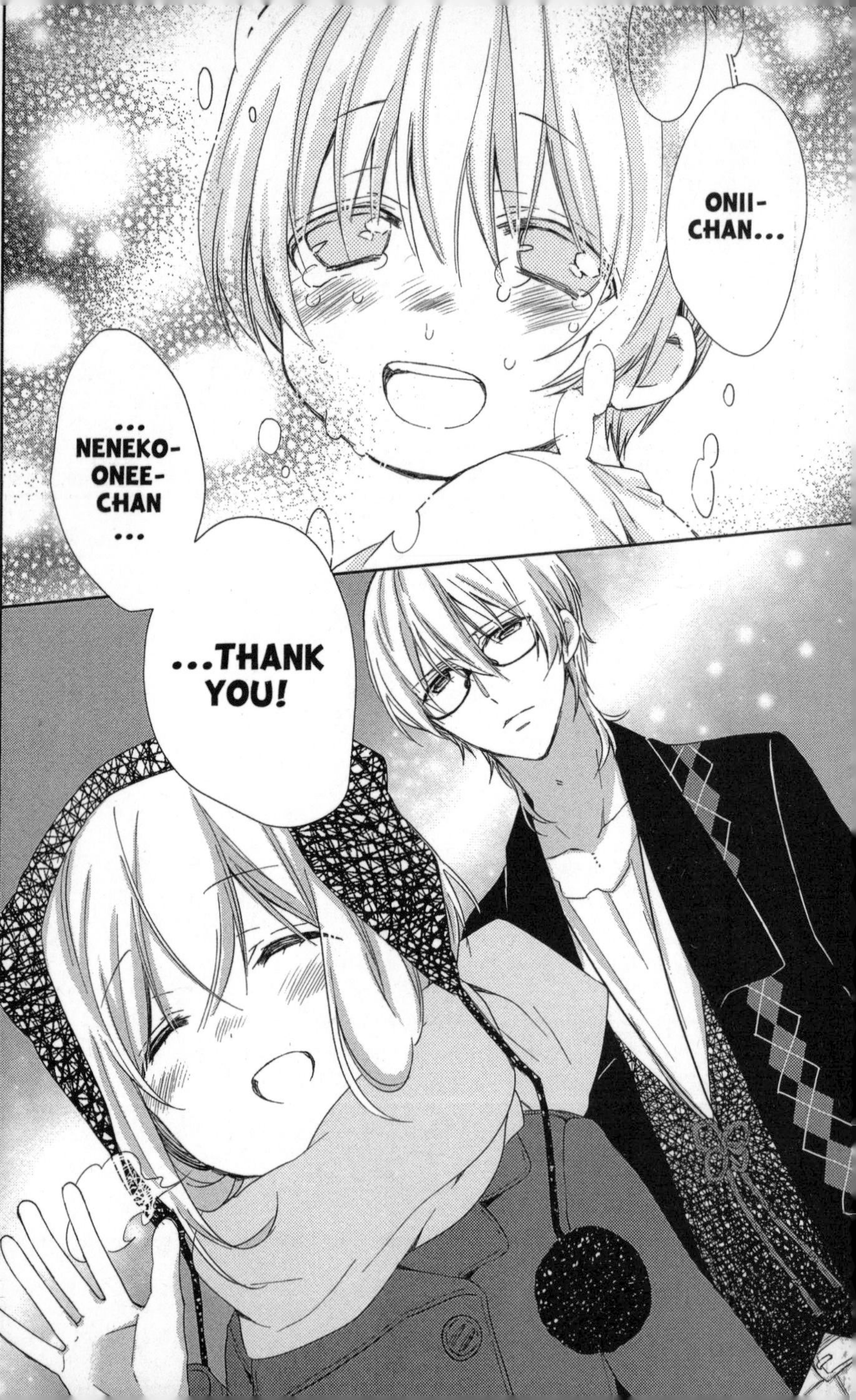
ONII-CHAN...
...NENEKO-ONEE-CHAN...
...THANK YOU!

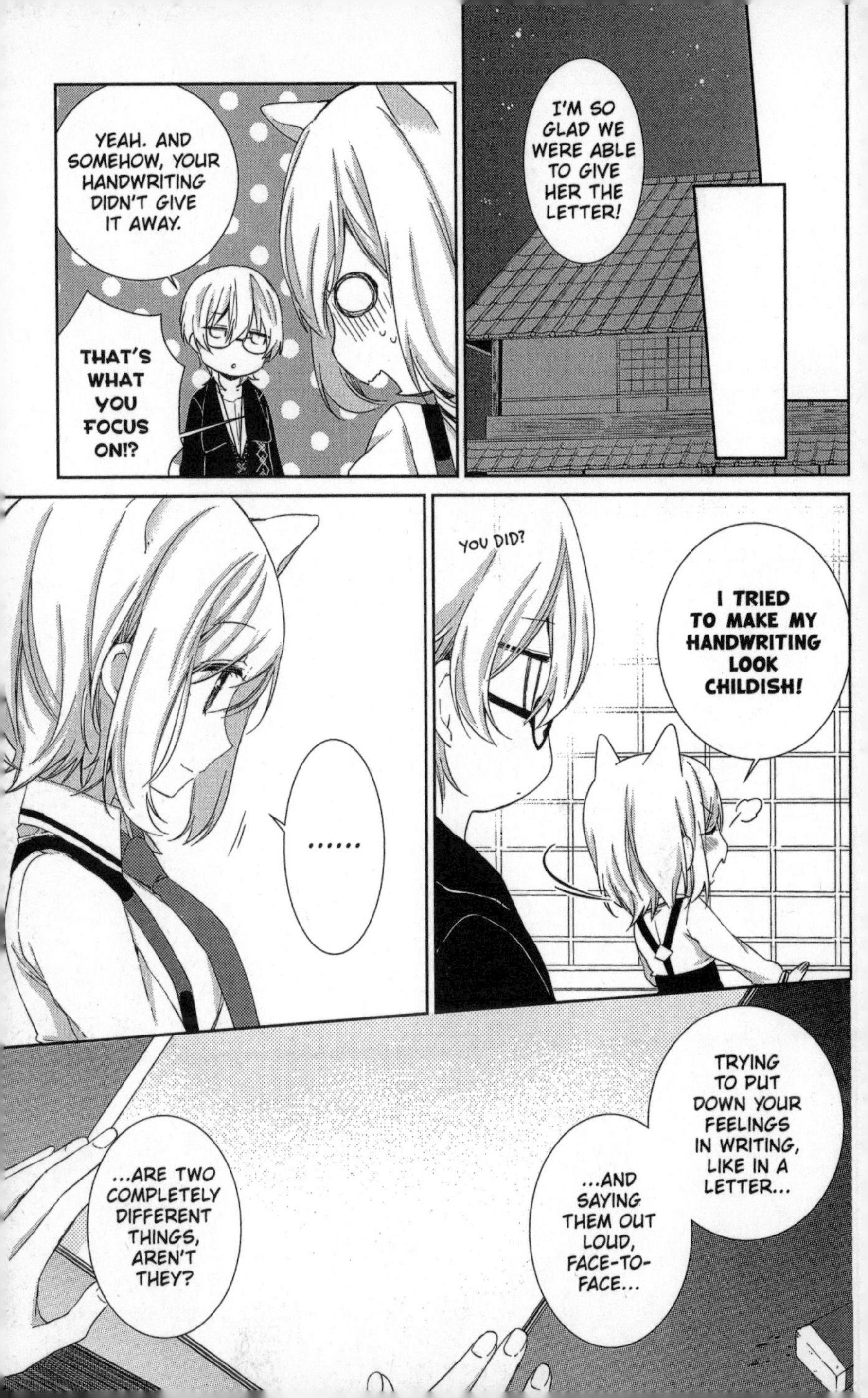
I'M SO GLAD WE WERE ABLE TO GIVE HER THE LETTER!
YEAH. AND SOMEHOW, YOUR HANDWRITING DIDN'T GIVE IT AWAY.
THAT'S WHAT YOU FOCUS ON!?
I TRIED TO MAKE MY HANDWRITING LOOK CHILDISH!
YOU DID?
......
TRYING TO PUT DOWN YOUR FEELINGS IN WRITING, LIKE IN A LETTER...
...AND SAYING THEM OUT LOUD, FACE-TO-FACE...
...ARE TWO COMPLETELY DIFFERENT THINGS, AREN'T THEY?

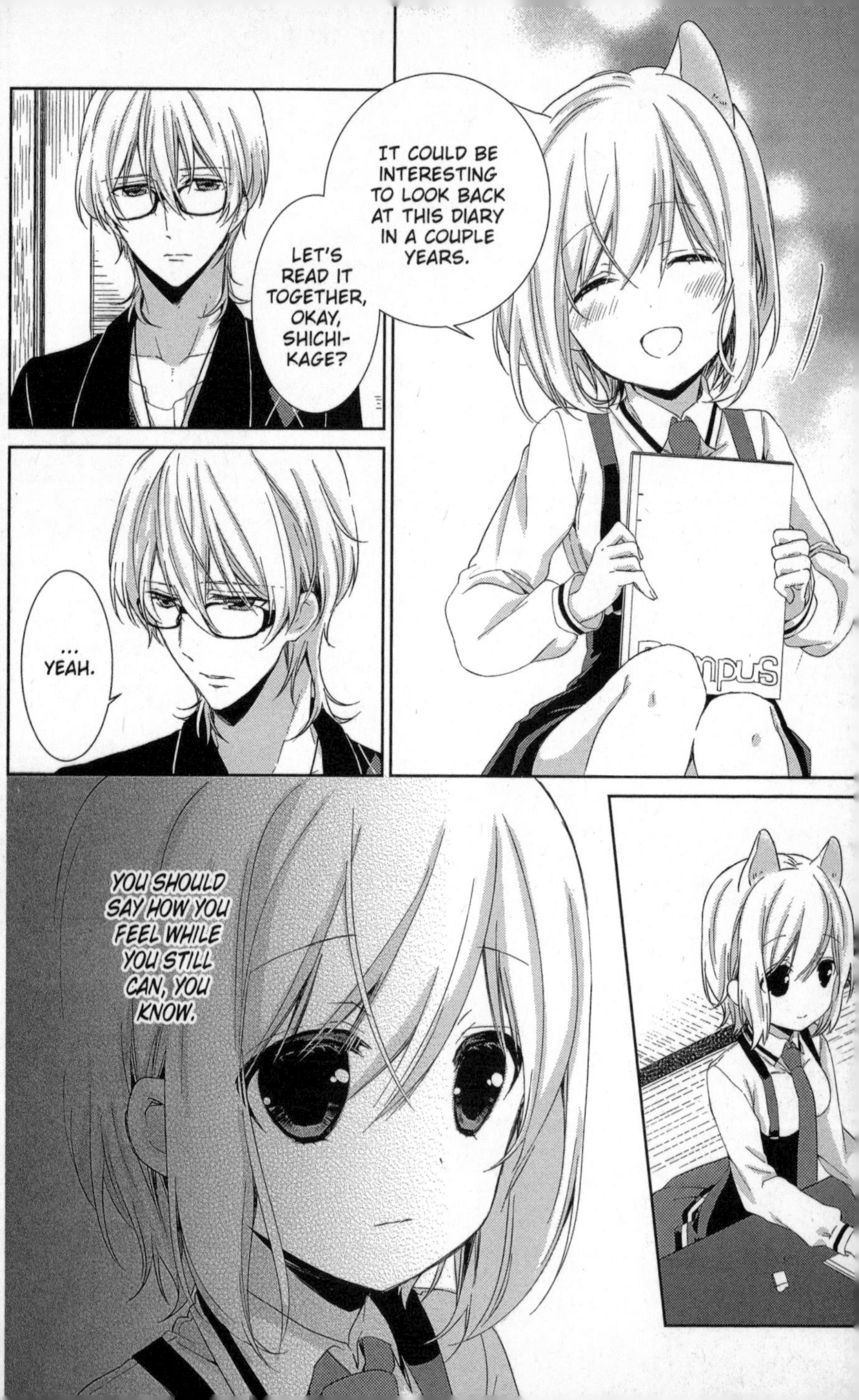
IT COULD BE INTERESTING TO LOOK BACK AT THIS DIARY IN A COUPLE YEARS.
LET'S READ IT TOGETHER, OKAY, SHICHI-KAGE?
... YEAH.
YOU SHOULD SAY HOW YOU FEEL WHILE YOU STILL CAN, YOU KNOW.

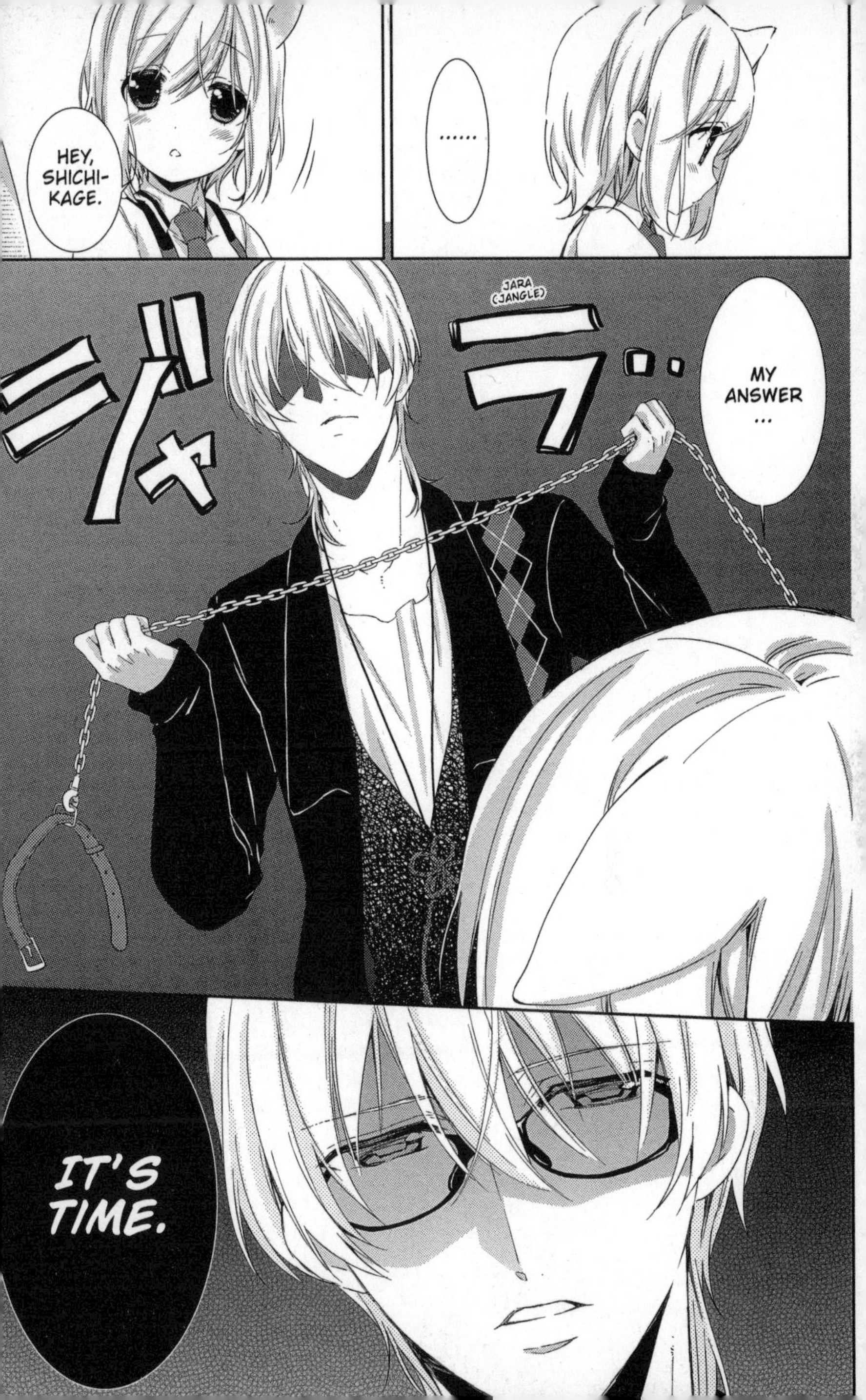
......
HEY, SHICHI-KAGE.
ジャラ
JARA (JANGLE)
MY ANSWER ...
IT'S TIME.

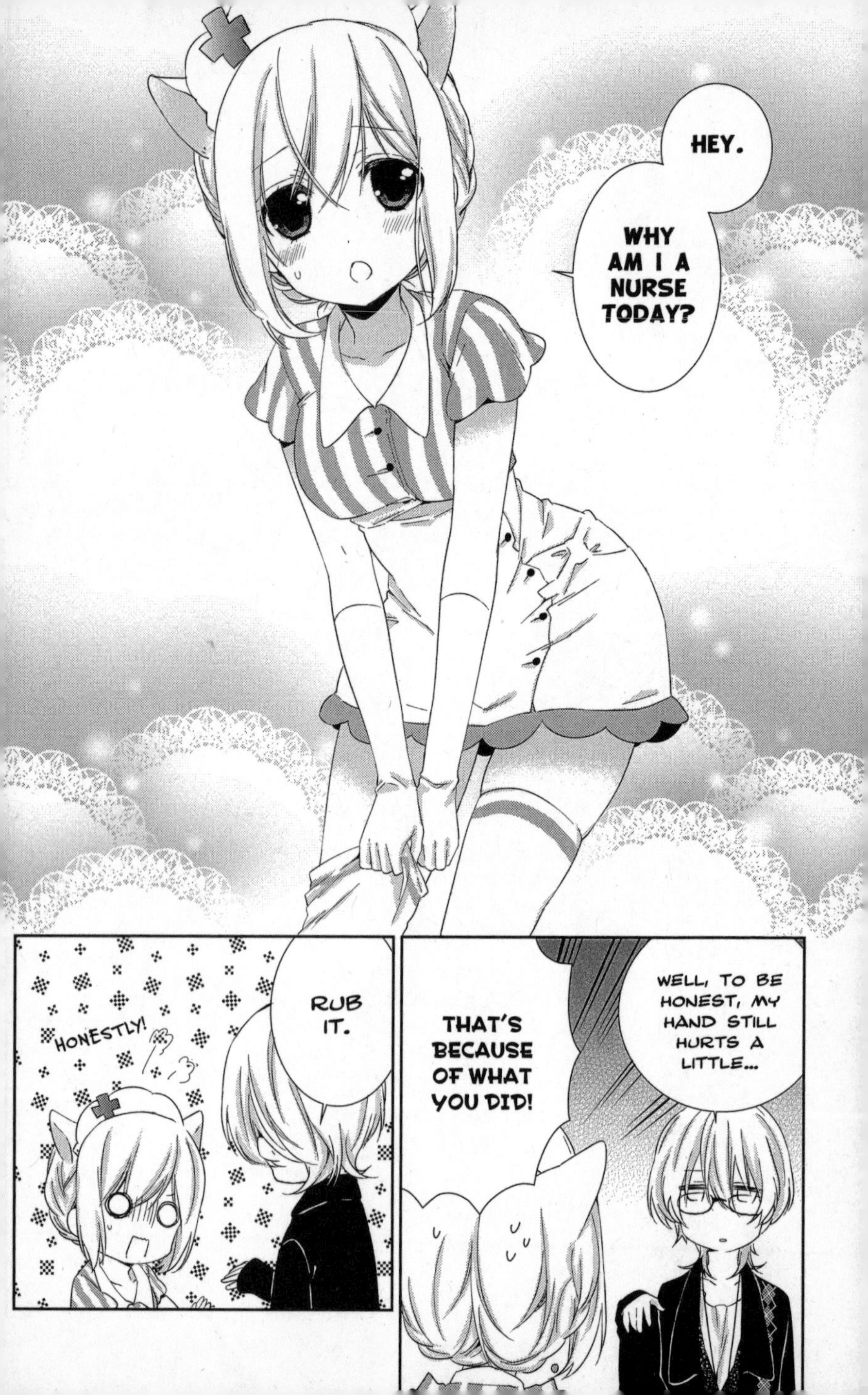
HEY.
WHY AM I A NURSE TODAY?
WELL, TO BE HONEST, MY HAND STILL HURTS A LITTLE...
THAT'S BECAUSE OF WHAT YOU DID!
RUB IT.
HONESTLY!

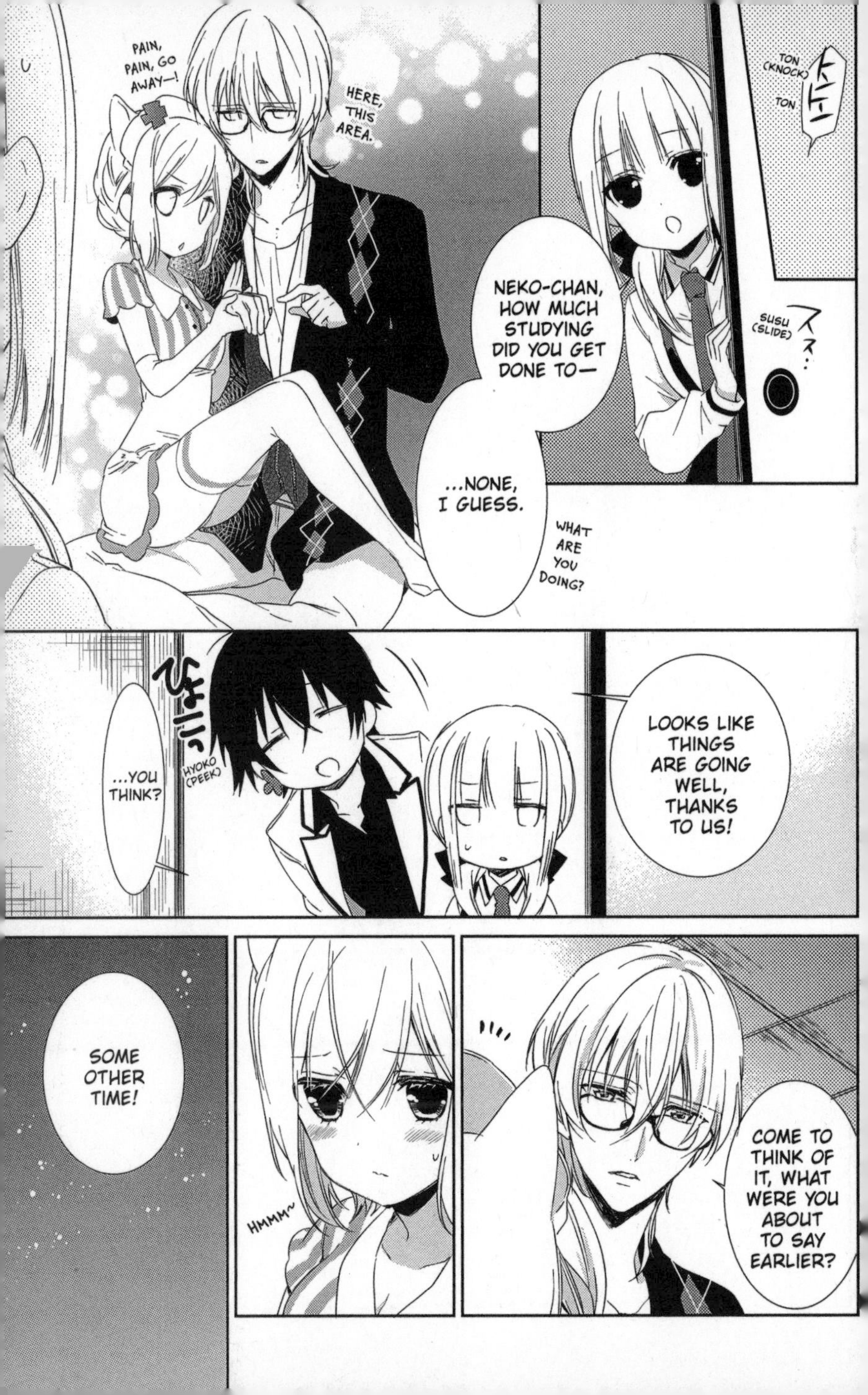
TON (KNOCK)
TON
SUSU (SLIDE)
NEKO-CHAN, HOW MUCH STUDYING DID YOU GET DONE TO—
HERE, THIS AREA.
PAIN, PAIN, GO AWAY—!
...NONE, I GUESS.
WHAT ARE YOU DOING?
LOOKS LIKE THINGS ARE GOING WELL, THANKS TO US!
HYOKO (PEEK)
...YOU THINK?
COME TO THINK OF IT, WHAT WERE YOU ABOUT TO SAY EARLIER?
HMMM~
SOME OTHER TIME!

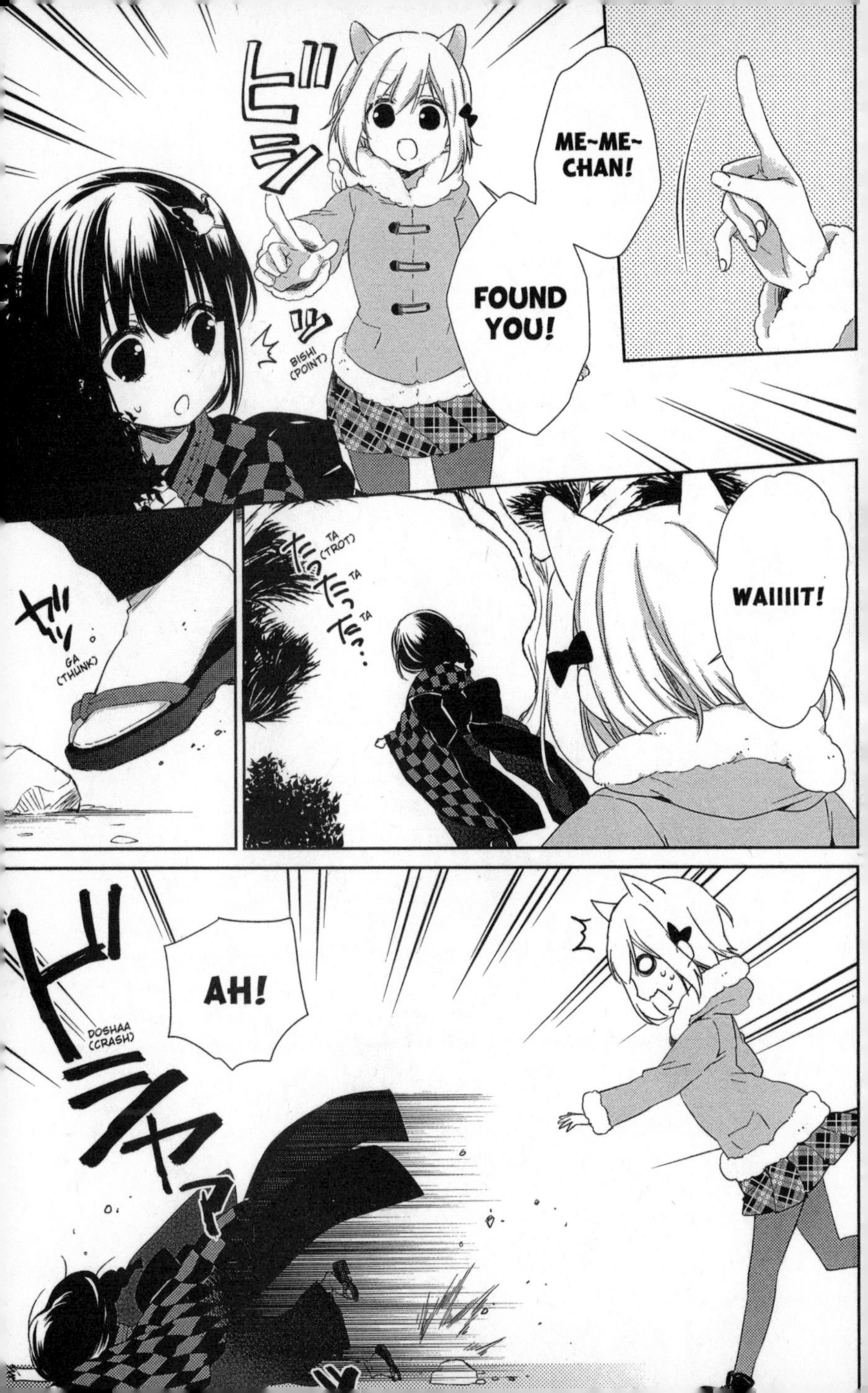
ME~ME~CHAN!
FOUND YOU!
BISHI (POINT)
WAIIIIT!
TA (TROT)
TA
TA
GA (THUNK)
AH!
DOSHAA (CRASH)

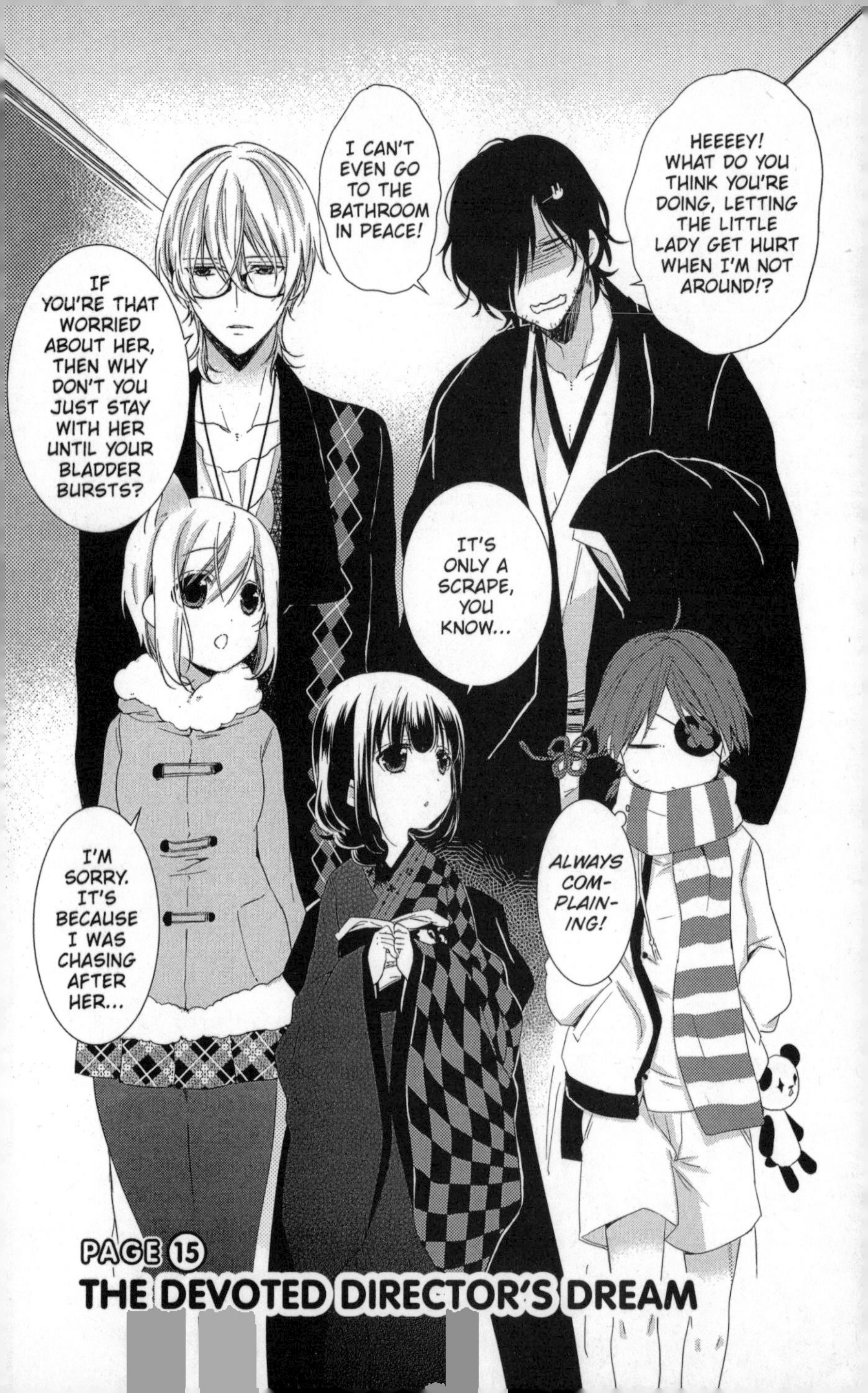
HEEEEY! WHAT DO YOU THINK YOU'RE DOING, LETTING THE LITTLE LADY GET HURT WHEN I'M NOT AROUND!?
I CAN'T EVEN GO TO THE BATHROOM IN PEACE!
IF YOU'RE THAT WORRIED ABOUT HER, THEN WHY DON'T YOU JUST STAY WITH HER UNTIL YOUR BLADDER BURSTS?
IT'S ONLY A SCRAPE, YOU KNOW...
ALWAYS COM-PLAIN-ING!
I'M SORRY. IT'S BECAUSE I WAS CHASING AFTER HER...

# PAGE 15
# THE DEVOTED DIRECTOR'S DREAM

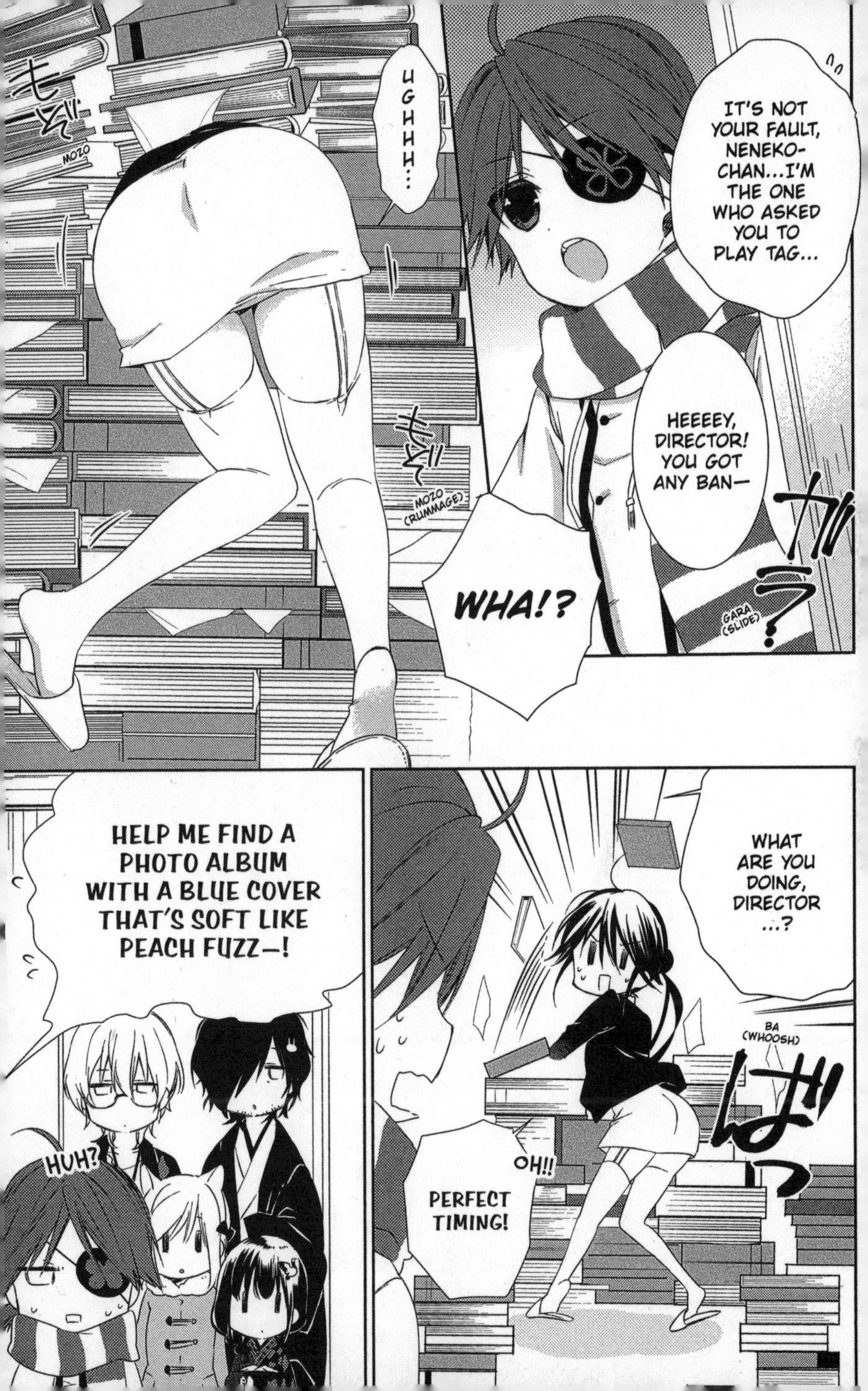

IT'S NOT YOUR FAULT, NENEKO-CHAN...I'M THE ONE WHO ASKED YOU TO PLAY TAG...
GARA (SLIDE)
HEEEEY, DIRECTOR! YOU GOT ANY BAN—
WHA!?
UGHHH...
MOZO (RUMMAGE)
MOZO
WHAT ARE YOU DOING, DIRECTOR ...?
BA (WHOOSH)
OH!!
PERFECT TIMING!
HELP ME FIND A PHOTO ALBUM WITH A BLUE COVER THAT'S SOFT LIKE PEACH FUZZ—!
HUH?

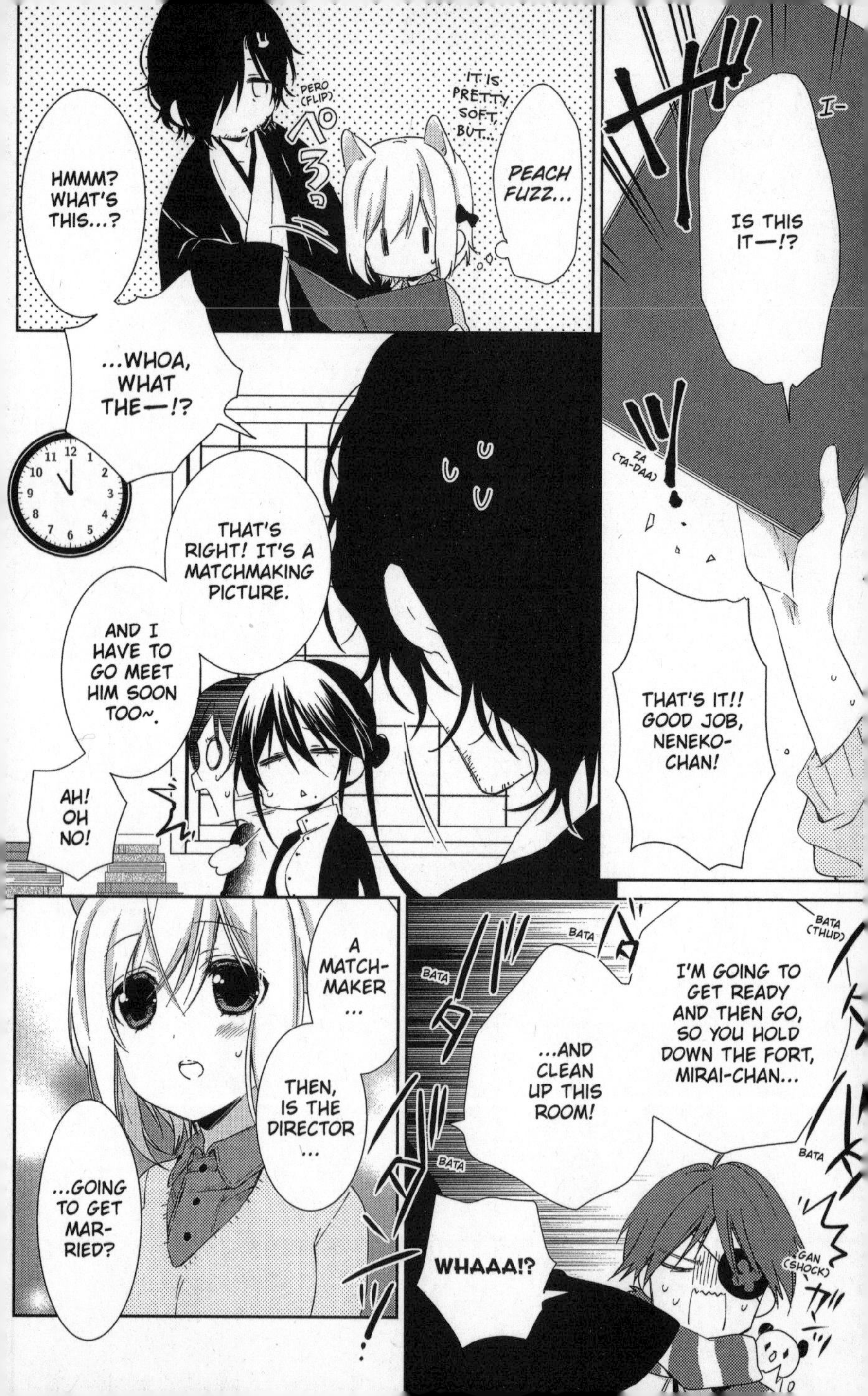
I-
IS THIS IT—!?
ZA (TA-DAA)
THAT'S IT!! GOOD JOB, NENEKO-CHAN!
IT IS PRETTY SOFT, BUT...
PEACH FUZZ...
PERO (FLIP)
HMMM? WHAT'S THIS...?
...WHOA, WHAT THE—!?
THAT'S RIGHT! IT'S A MATCHMAKING PICTURE.
AND I HAVE TO GO MEET HIM SOON TOO~.
AH! OH NO!
BATA (THUD)
I'M GOING TO GET READY AND THEN GO, SO YOU HOLD DOWN THE FORT, MIRAI-CHAN...
BATA
...AND CLEAN UP THIS ROOM!
BATA
BATA
BATA
GAN (SHOCK)
WHAAA!?
A MATCH-MAKER...
THEN, IS THE DIRECTOR...
...GOING TO GET MAR-RIED?

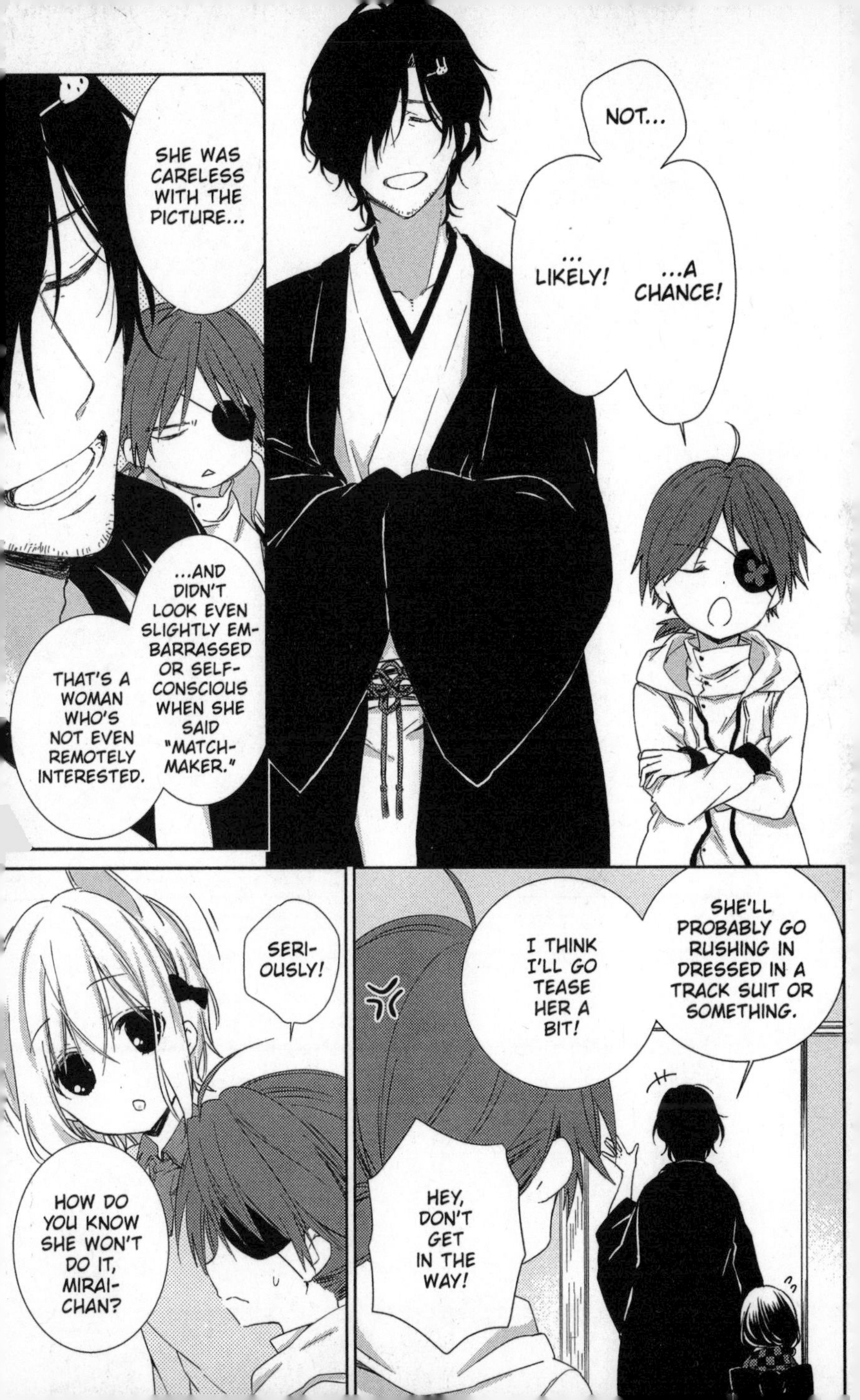
NOT...
...A CHANCE!
... LIKELY!
SHE WAS CARELESS WITH THE PICTURE...
...AND DIDN'T LOOK EVEN SLIGHTLY EM-BARRASSED OR SELF-CONSCIOUS WHEN SHE SAID "MATCH-MAKER."
THAT'S A WOMAN WHO'S NOT EVEN REMOTELY INTERESTED.
SHE'LL PROBABLY GO RUSHING IN DRESSED IN A TRACK SUIT OR SOMETHING.
I THINK I'LL GO TEASE HER A BIT!
HEY, DON'T GET IN THE WAY!
SERI-OUSLY!
HOW DO YOU KNOW SHE WON'T DO IT, MIRAI-CHAN?

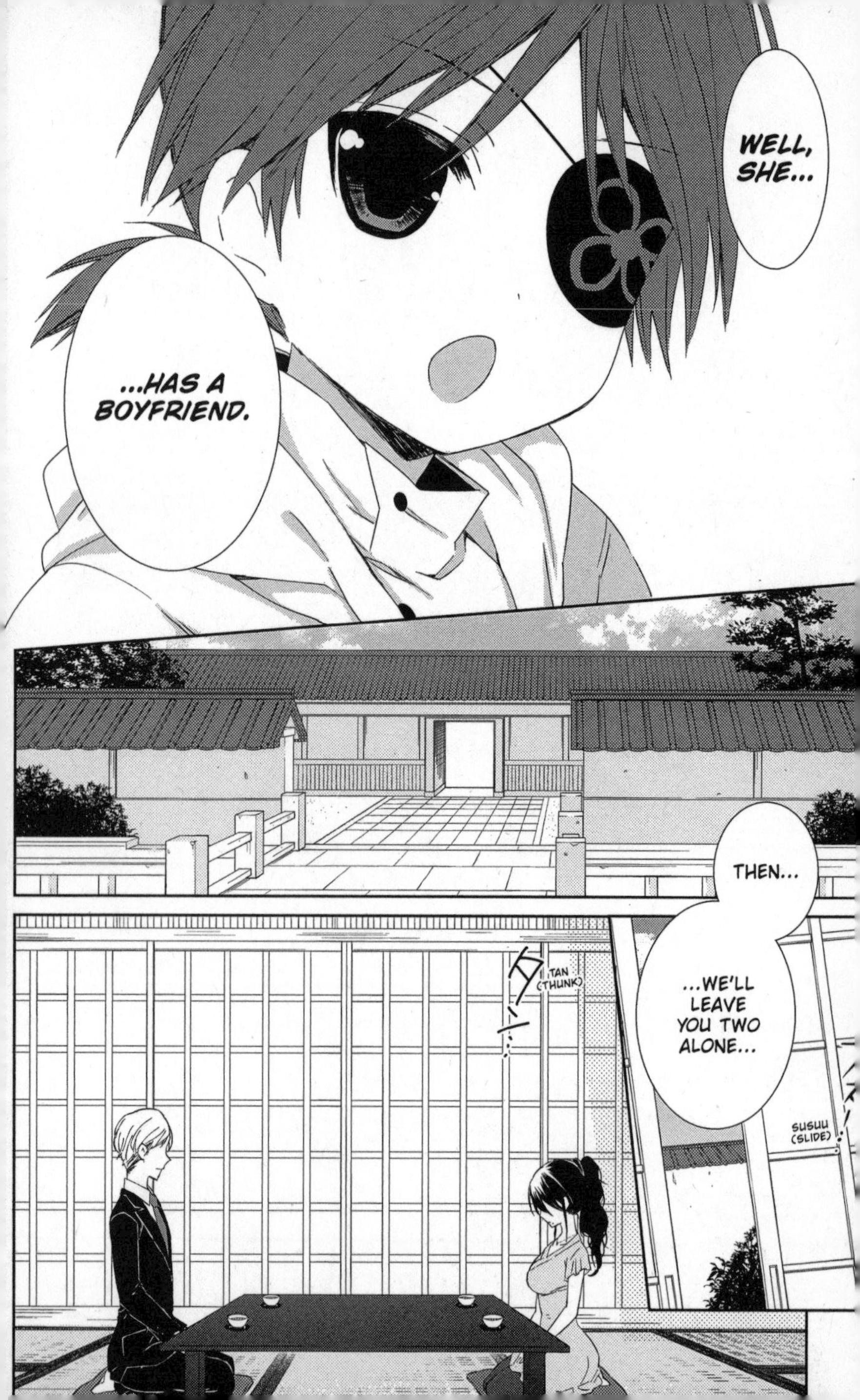
WELL, SHE...
...HAS A BOYFRIEND.
THEN...
...WE'LL LEAVE YOU TWO ALONE...
SUSUU (SLIDE)
TAN (THUNK)

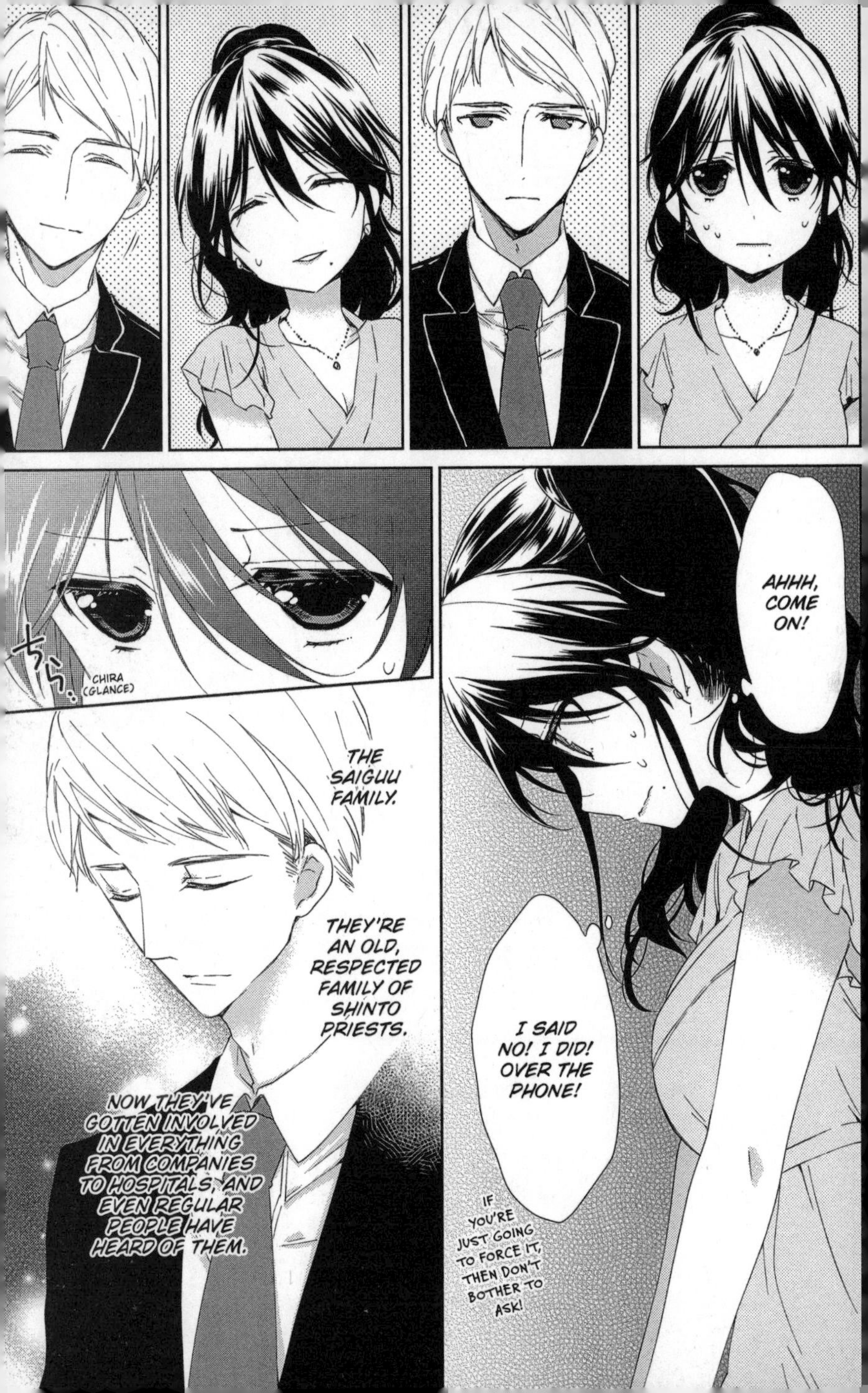
AHHH, COME ON!
I SAID NO! I DID! OVER THE PHONE!
IF YOU'RE JUST GOING TO FORCE IT, THEN DON'T BOTHER TO ASK!
ちら..
CHIRA (GLANCE)
THE SAIGUU FAMILY.
THEY'RE AN OLD, RESPECTED FAMILY OF SHINTO PRIESTS.
NOW THEY'VE GOTTEN INVOLVED IN EVERYTHING FROM COMPANIES TO HOSPITALS, AND EVEN REGULAR PEOPLE HAVE HEARD OF THEM.

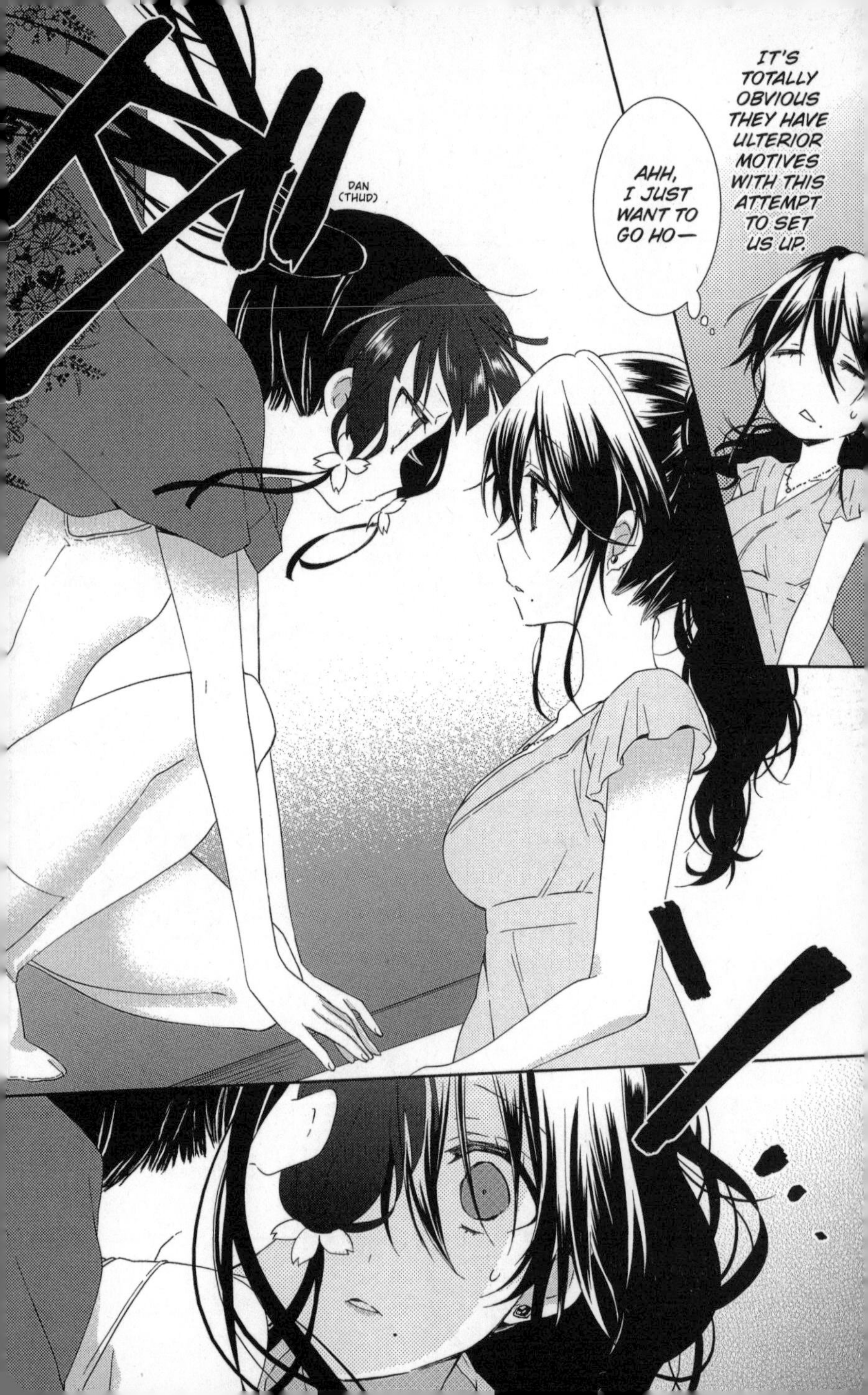
IT'S TOTALLY OBVIOUS THEY HAVE ULTERIOR MOTIVES WITH THIS ATTEMPT TO SET US UP.
AHH, I JUST WANT TO GO HO—
DAN (THUD)

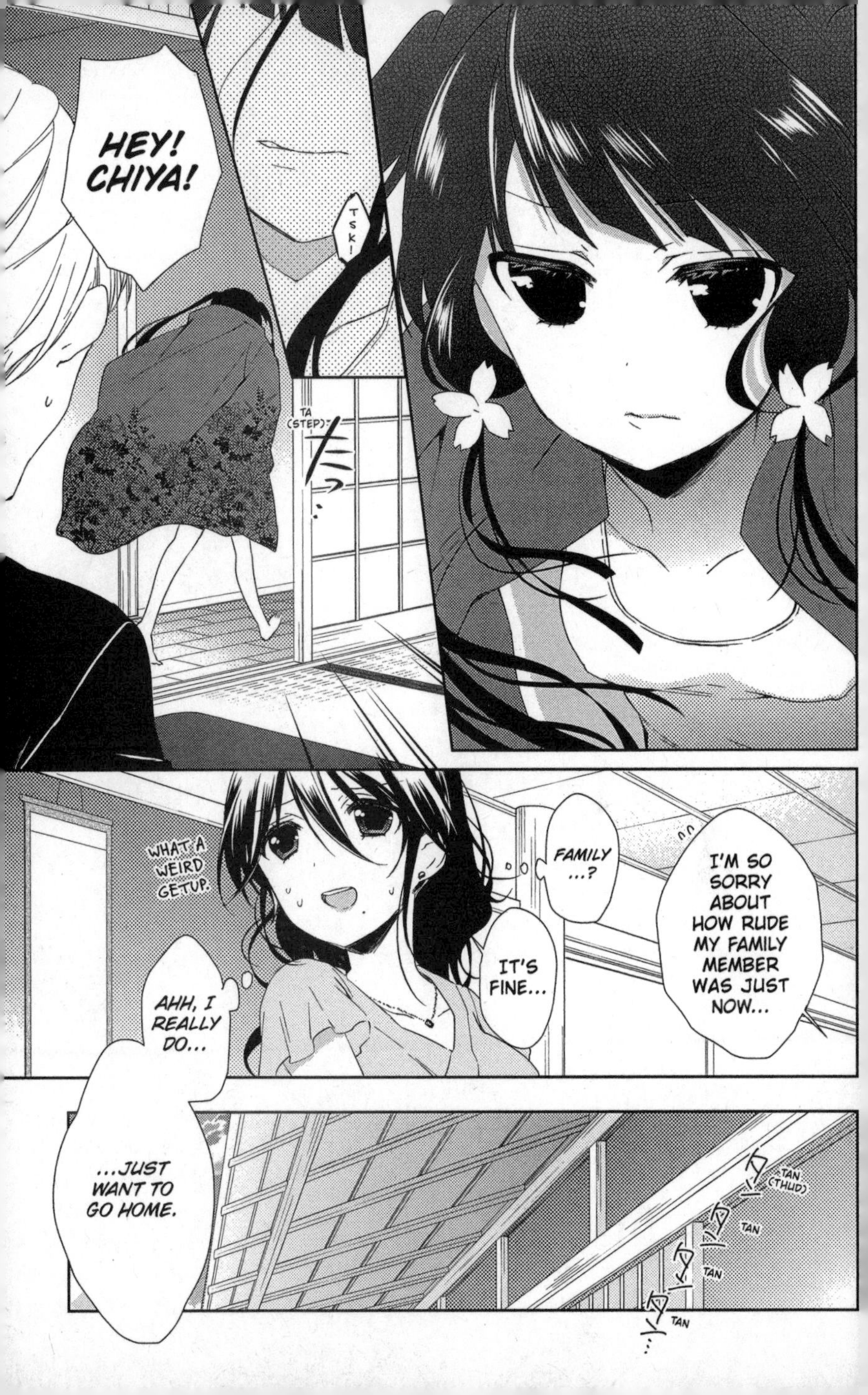
HEY! CHIYA!
TSK!
TA (STEP)
I'M SO SORRY ABOUT HOW RUDE MY FAMILY MEMBER WAS JUST NOW...
FAMILY ...?
IT'S FINE...
WHAT A WEIRD GETUP.
AHH, I REALLY DO...
...JUST WANT TO GO HOME.
TAN (THUD)
TAN
TAN
TAN

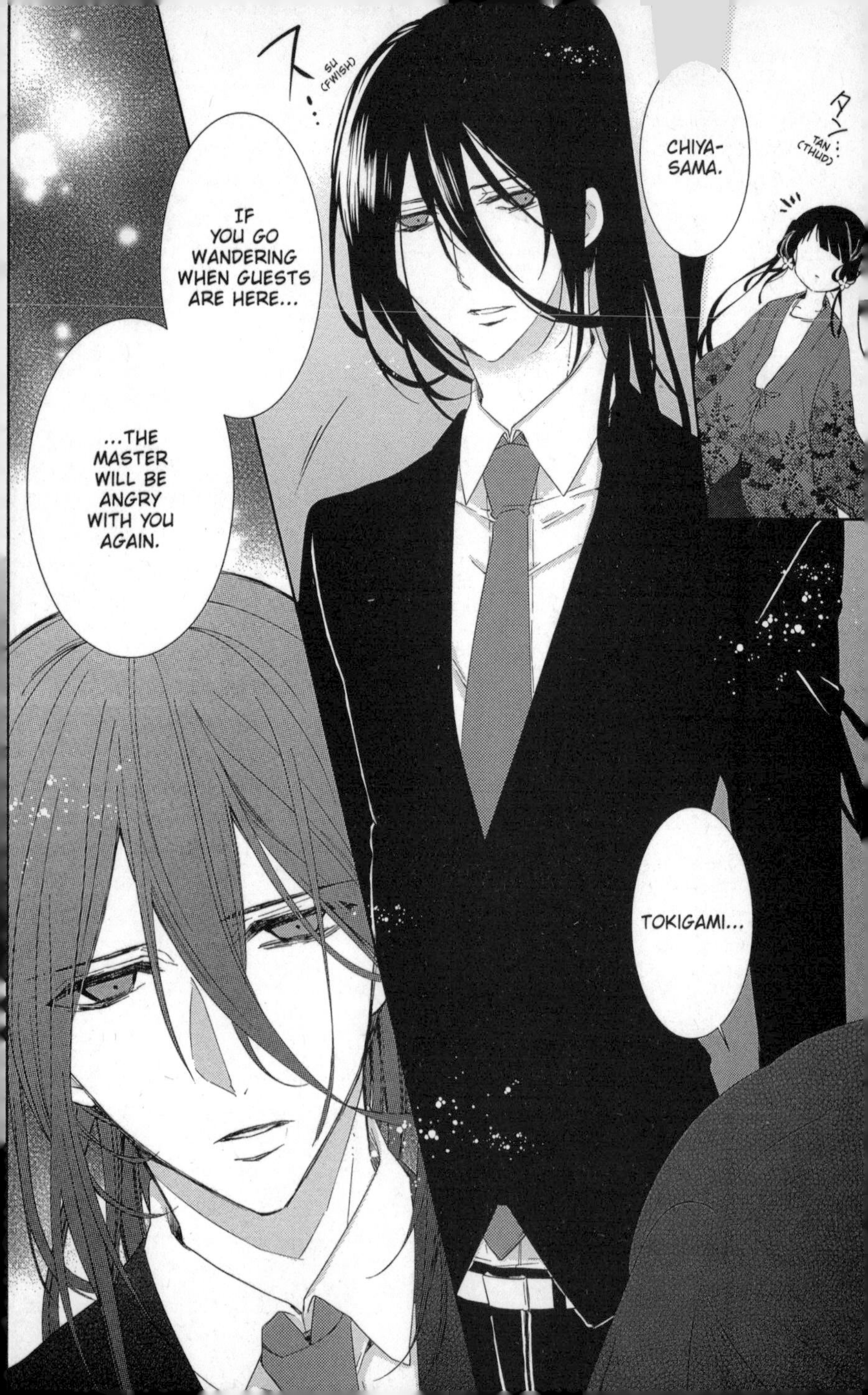
タン…
TAN (THUD)
CHIYA-SAMA.
ス…
SU (FWISH)
IF YOU GO WANDERING WHEN GUESTS ARE HERE...
...THE MASTER WILL BE ANGRY WITH YOU AGAIN.
TOKIGAMI...

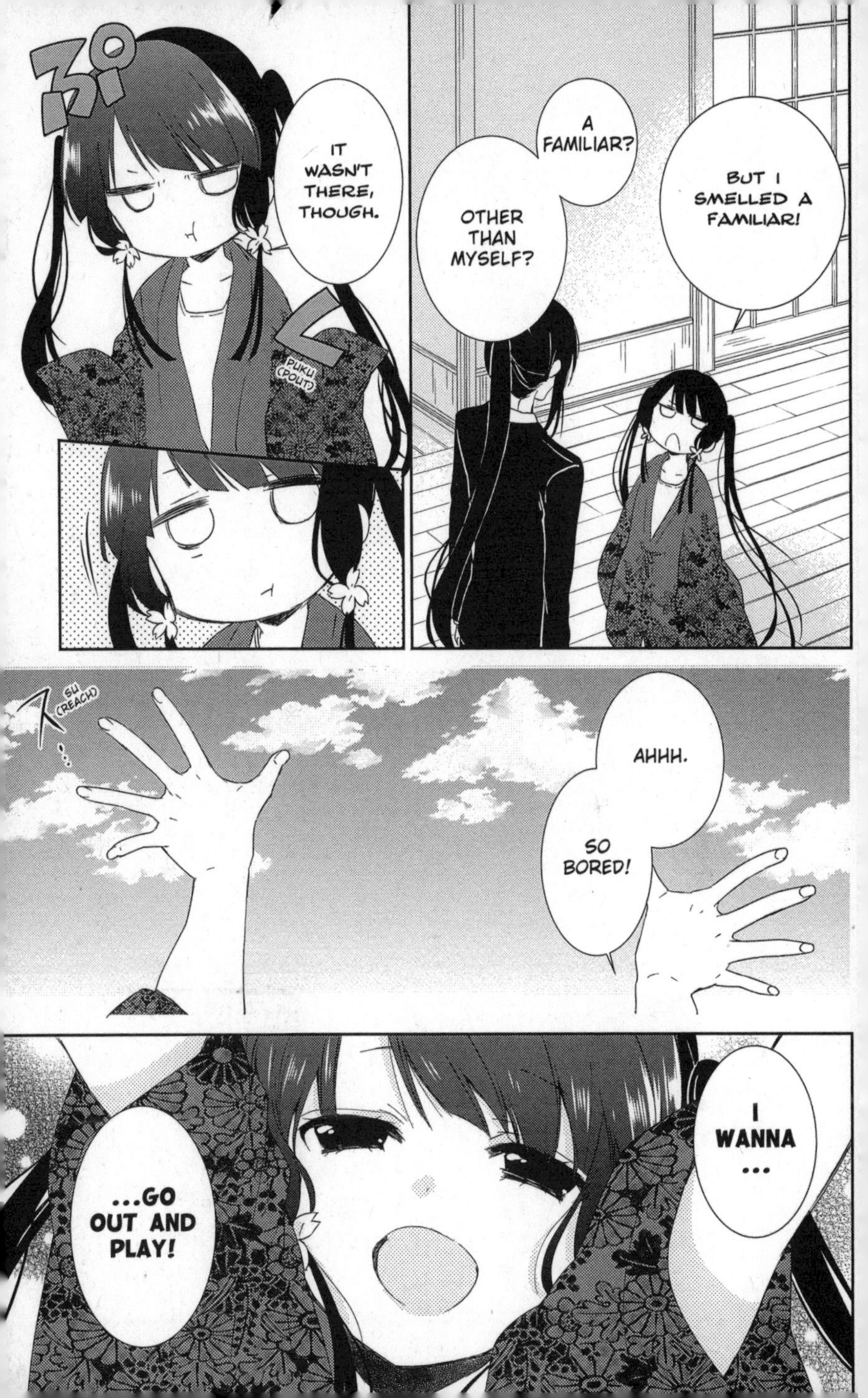
BUT I SMELLED A FAMILIAR!
A FAMILIAR?
OTHER THAN MYSELF?
IT WASN'T THERE, THOUGH.
PUKU (POUT)
SU (REACH)
AHHH.
SO BORED!
I WANNA...
...GO OUT AND PLAY!

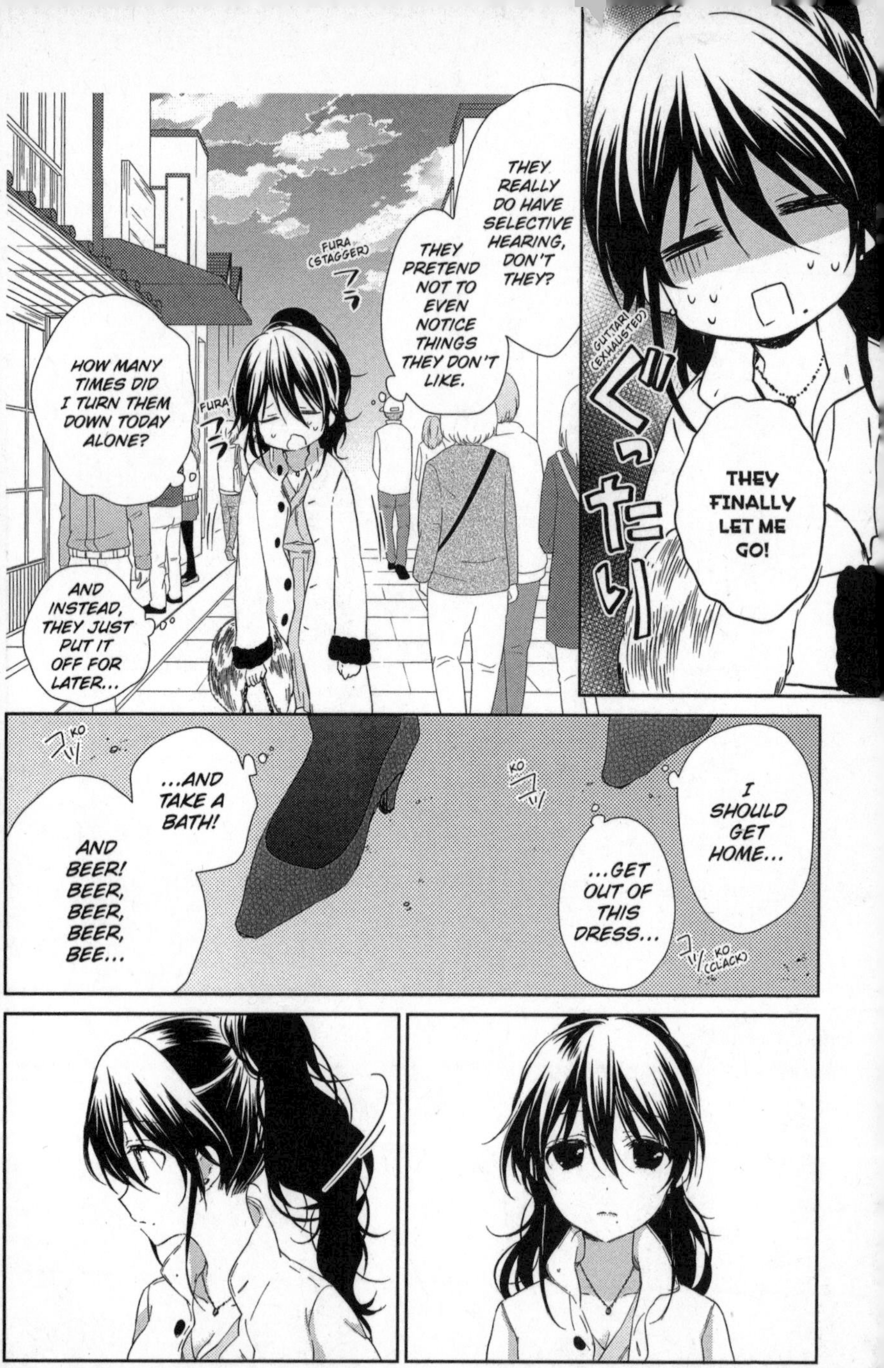
GUTTARI (EXHAUSTED)
THEY FINALLY LET ME GO!
THEY REALLY DO HAVE SELECTIVE HEARING, DON'T THEY?
THEY PRETEND NOT TO EVEN NOTICE THINGS THEY DON'T LIKE.
FURA (STAGGER)
HOW MANY TIMES DID I TURN THEM DOWN TODAY ALONE?
FURA
AND INSTEAD, THEY JUST PUT IT OFF FOR LATER...
I SHOULD GET HOME...
KO
...GET OUT OF THIS DRESS...
KO (CLACK)
...AND TAKE A BATH!
KO
AND BEER! BEER, BEER, BEER, BEE...

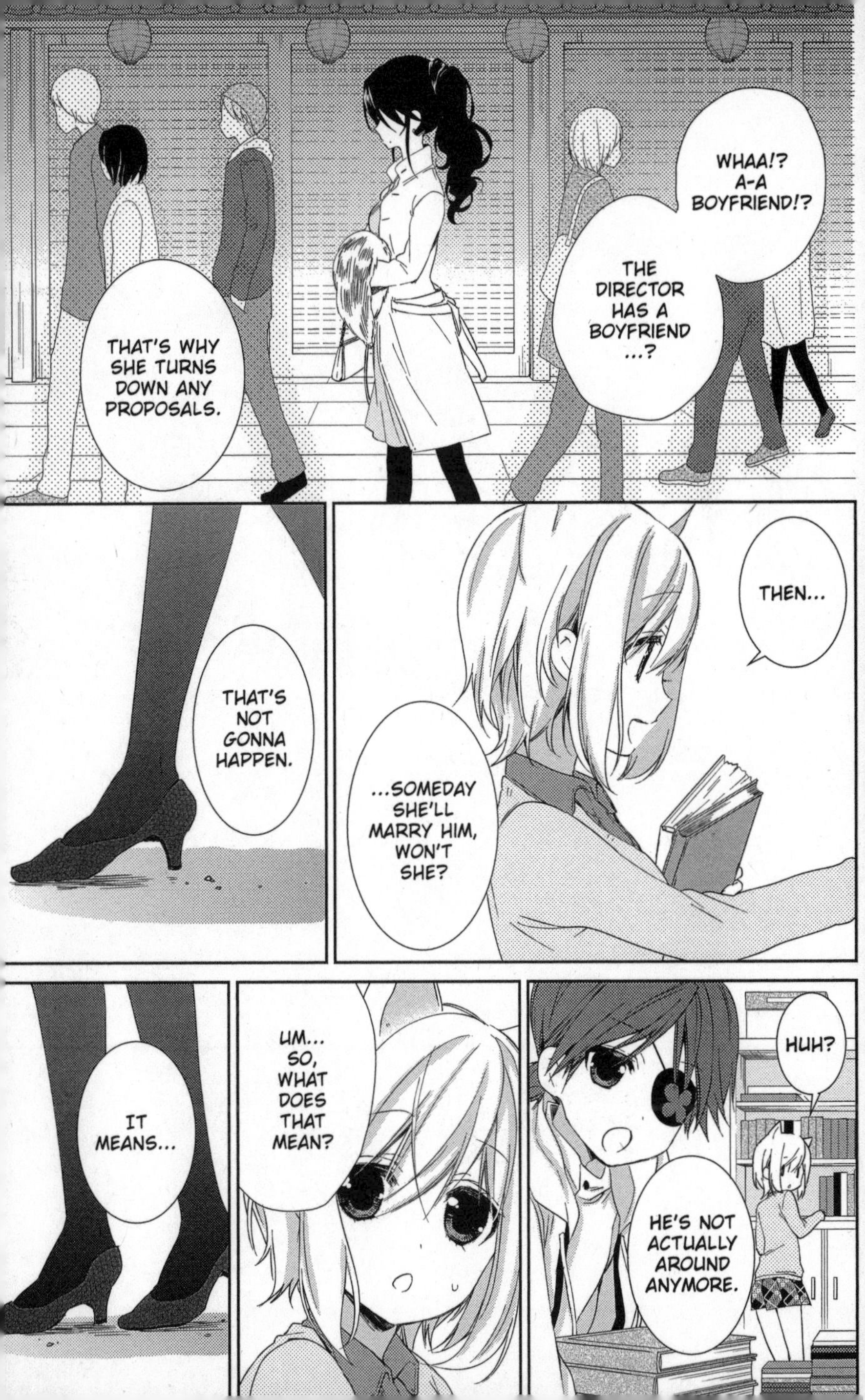
WHAA!? A-A BOYFRIEND!?
THE DIRECTOR HAS A BOYFRIEND ...?
THAT'S WHY SHE TURNS DOWN ANY PROPOSALS.
THEN...
...SOMEDAY SHE'LL MARRY HIM, WON'T SHE?
THAT'S NOT GONNA HAPPEN.
HUH?
HE'S NOT ACTUALLY AROUND ANYMORE.
UM... SO, WHAT DOES THAT MEAN?
IT MEANS...

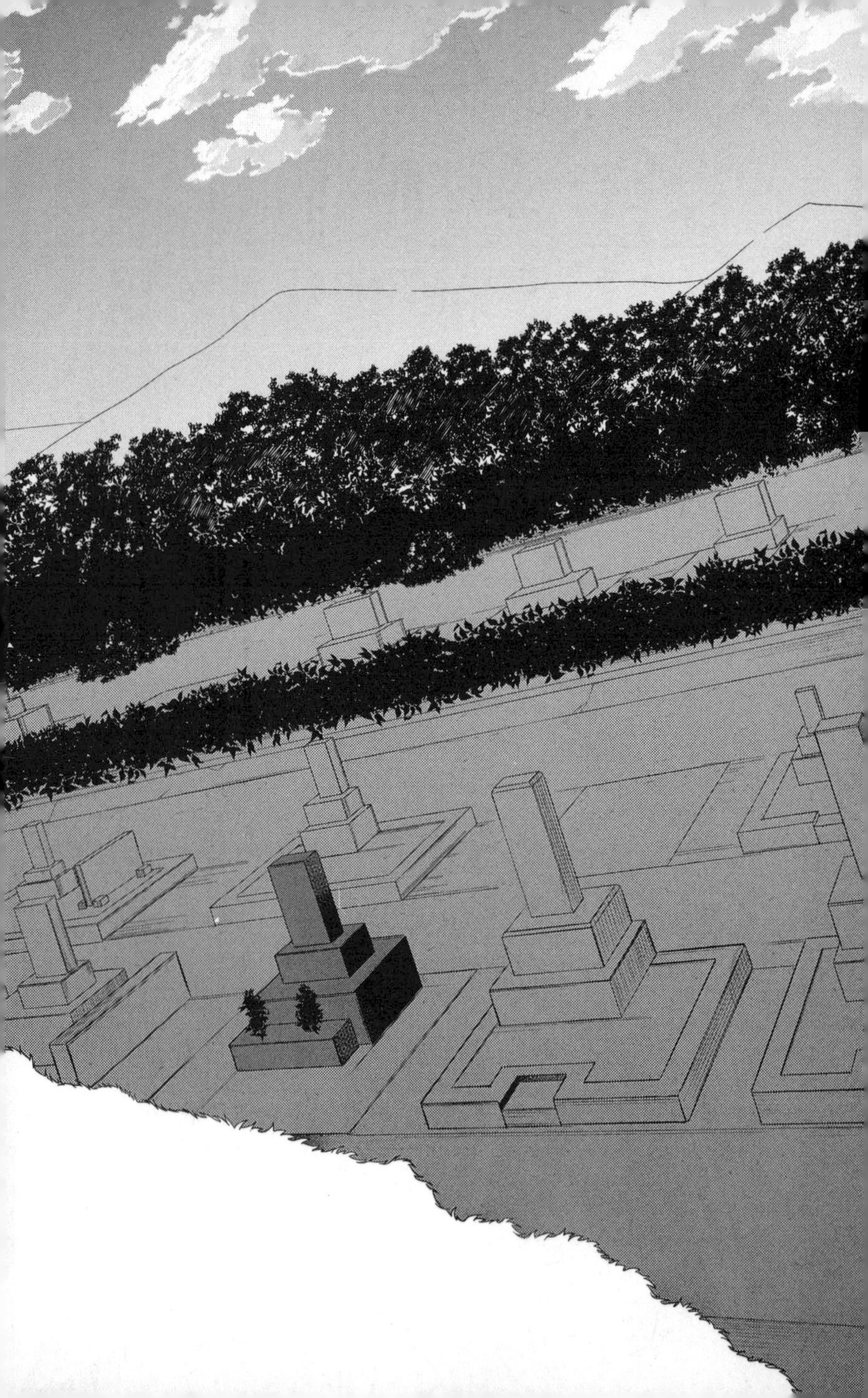

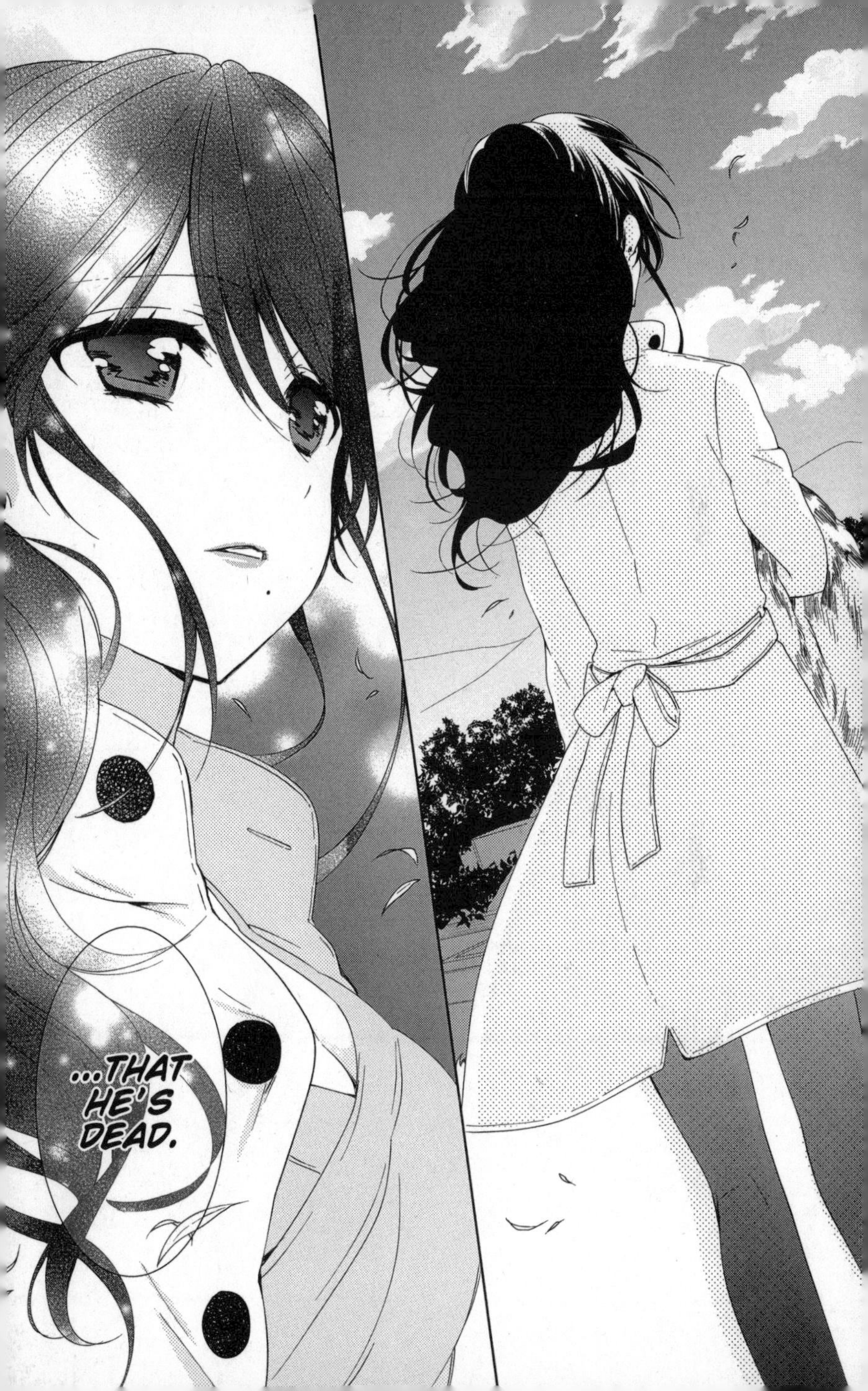
...THAT HE'S DEAD.

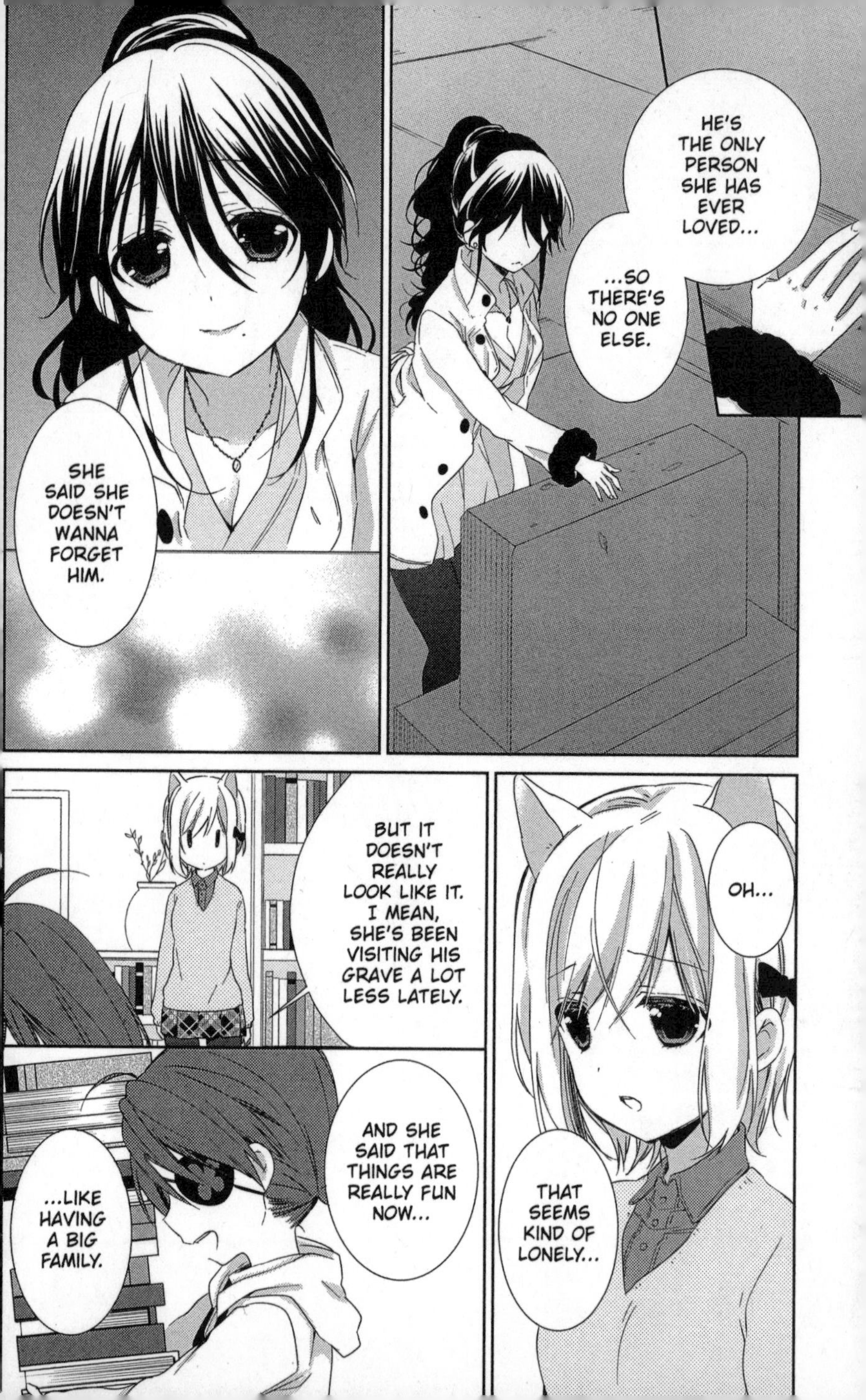
HE'S THE ONLY PERSON SHE HAS EVER LOVED...
...SO THERE'S NO ONE ELSE.
SHE SAID SHE DOESN'T WANNA FORGET HIM.
OH...
THAT SEEMS KIND OF LONELY...
BUT IT DOESN'T REALLY LOOK LIKE IT. I MEAN, SHE'S BEEN VISITING HIS GRAVE A LOT LESS LATELY.
AND SHE SAID THAT THINGS ARE REALLY FUN NOW...
...LIKE HAVING A BIG FAMILY.

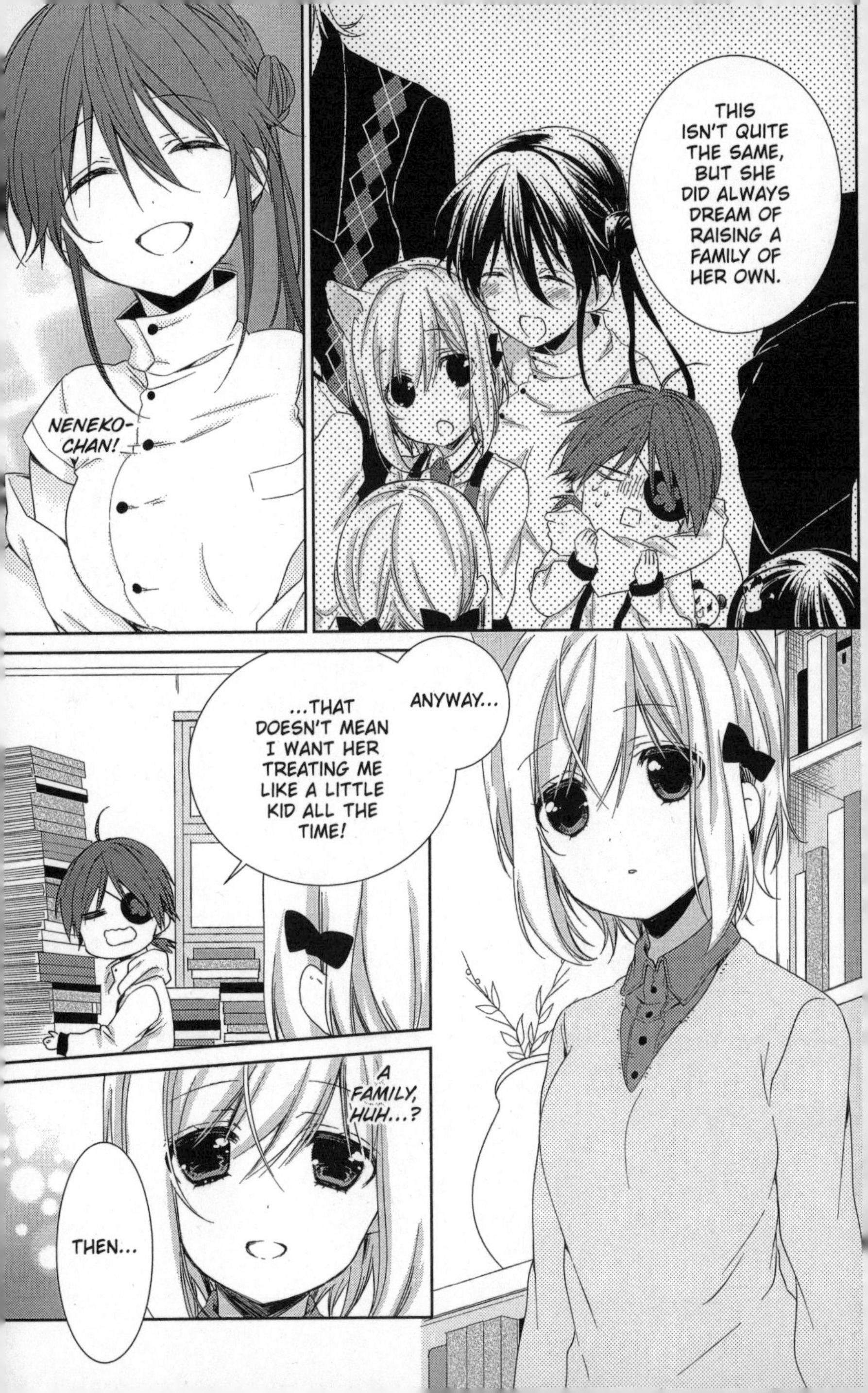
THIS ISN'T QUITE THE SAME, BUT SHE DID ALWAYS DREAM OF RAISING A FAMILY OF HER OWN.
NENEKO-CHAN!
ANYWAY...
...THAT DOESN'T MEAN I WANT HER TREATING ME LIKE A LITTLE KID ALL THE TIME!
A FAMILY, HUH...?
THEN...

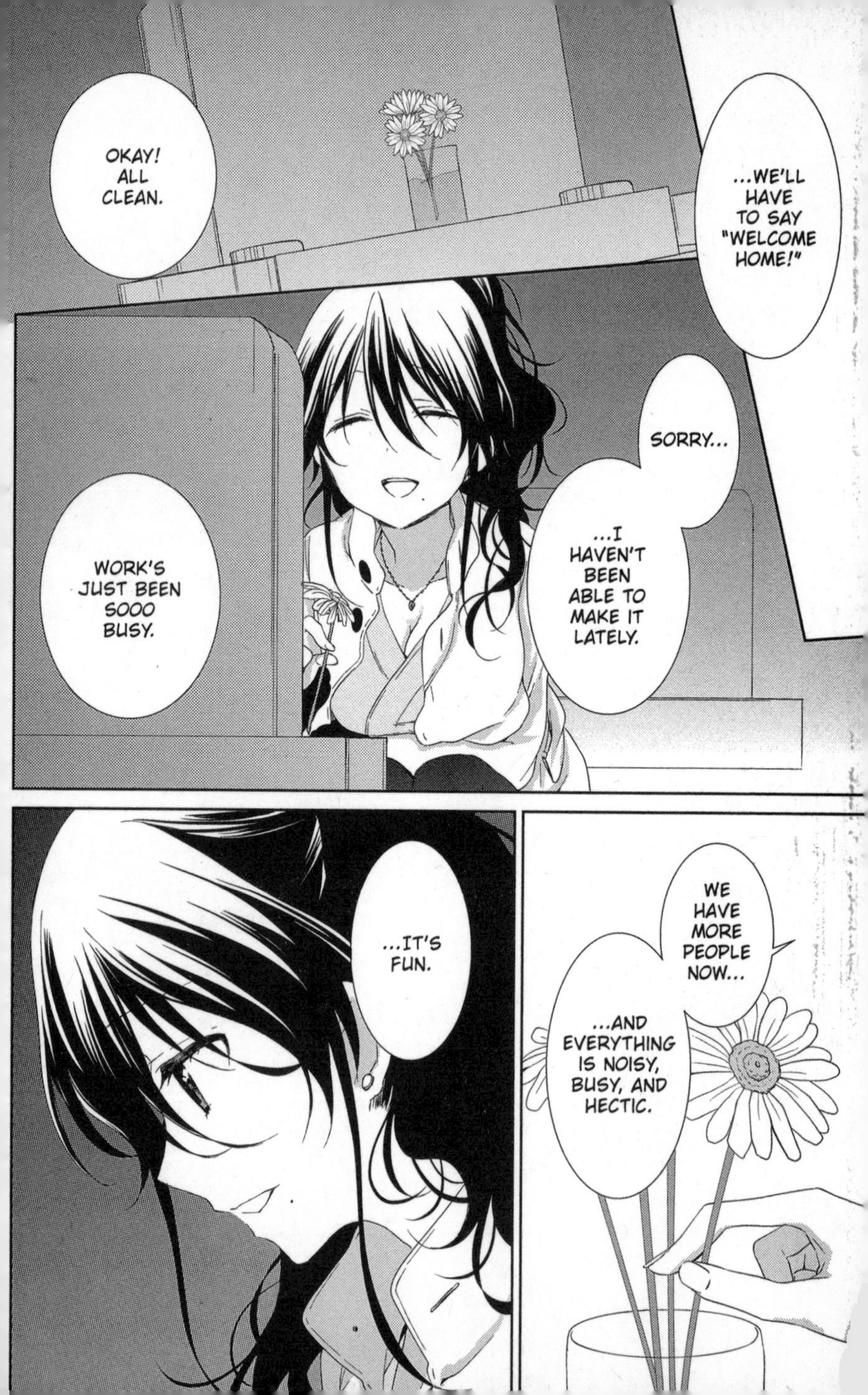
...WE'LL HAVE TO SAY "WELCOME HOME!"
OKAY! ALL CLEAN.
SORRY...
...I HAVEN'T BEEN ABLE TO MAKE IT LATELY.
WORK'S JUST BEEN SOOO BUSY.
WE HAVE MORE PEOPLE NOW...
...AND EVERYTHING IS NOISY, BUSY, AND HECTIC.
...IT'S FUN.

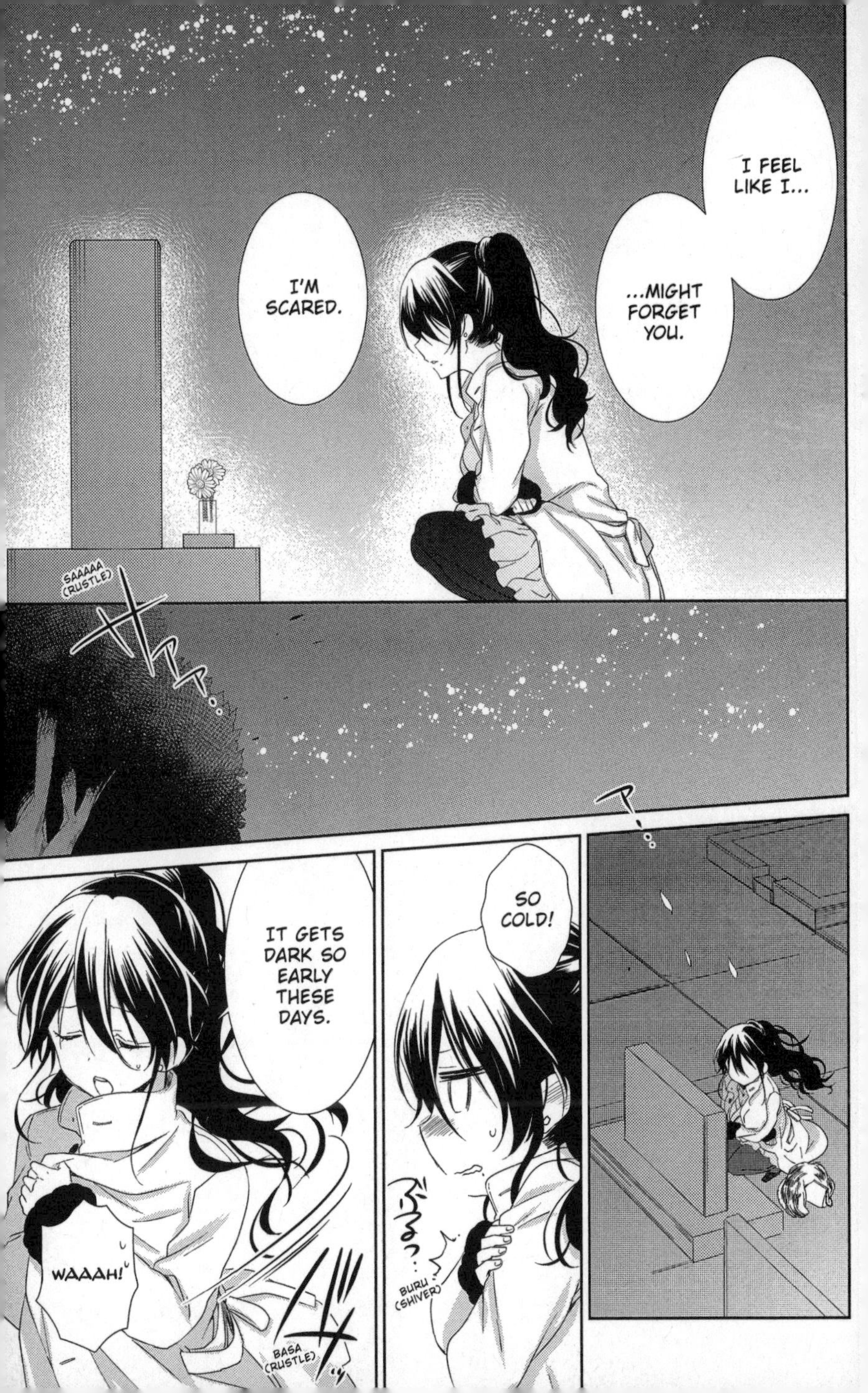
I FEEL LIKE I...
...MIGHT FORGET YOU.
I'M SCARED.
SAAAAA (RUSTLE)
SO COLD!
BURU (SHIVER)
IT GETS DARK SO EARLY THESE DAYS.
WAAAH!
BASA (RUSTLE)

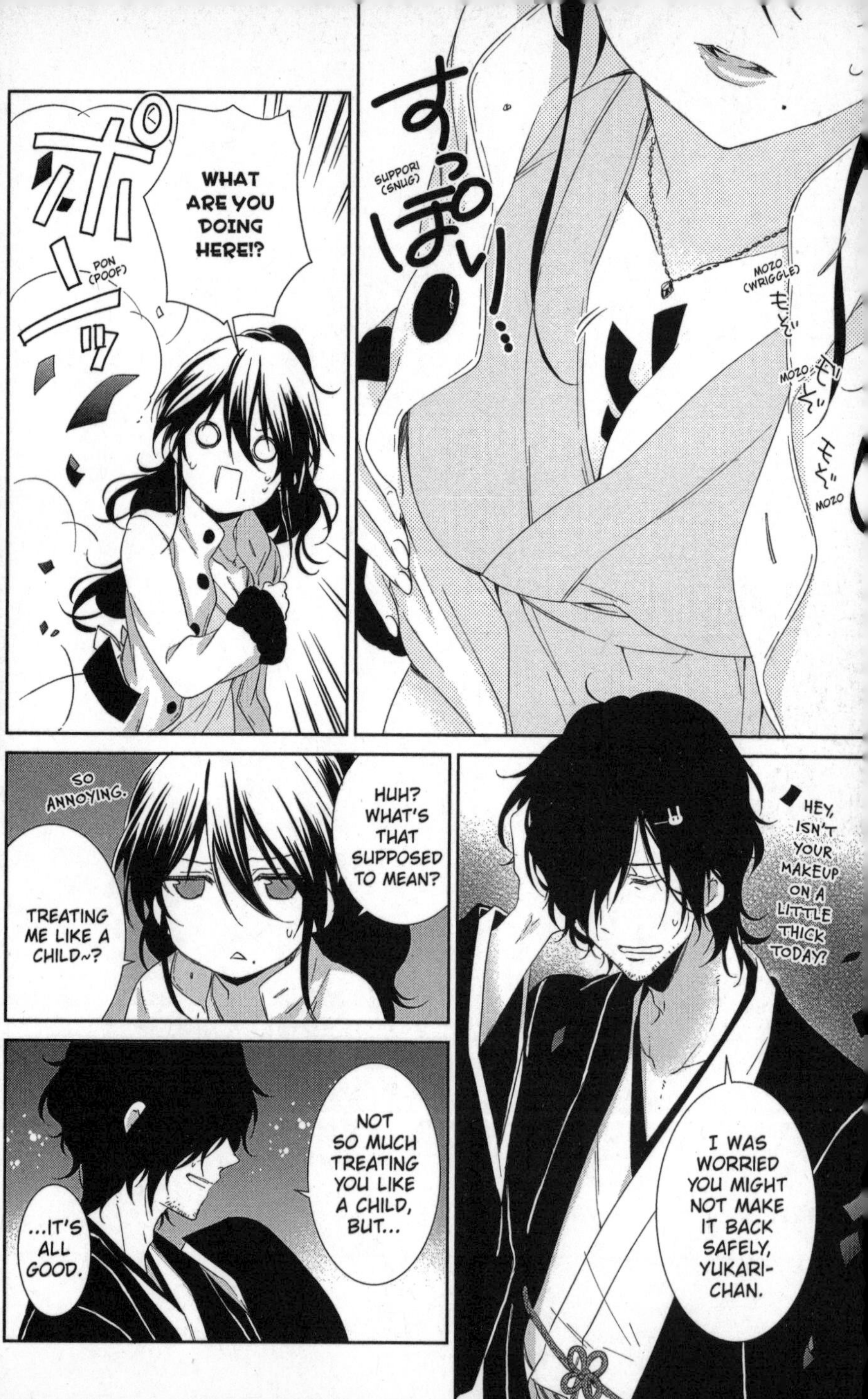
すっぽり…
SUPPORI (SNUG)
もぞ もぞ もぞ
MOZO (WRIGGLE)
MOZO
MOZO
ポンーッ
PON (POOF)
WHAT ARE YOU DOING HERE!?
HEY, ISN'T YOUR MAKEUP ON A LITTLE THICK TODAY?
I WAS WORRIED YOU MIGHT NOT MAKE IT BACK SAFELY, YUKARI-CHAN.
HUH? WHAT'S THAT SUPPOSED TO MEAN?
SO ANNOYING.
TREATING ME LIKE A CHILD~?
NOT SO MUCH TREATING YOU LIKE A CHILD, BUT...
...IT'S ALL GOOD.

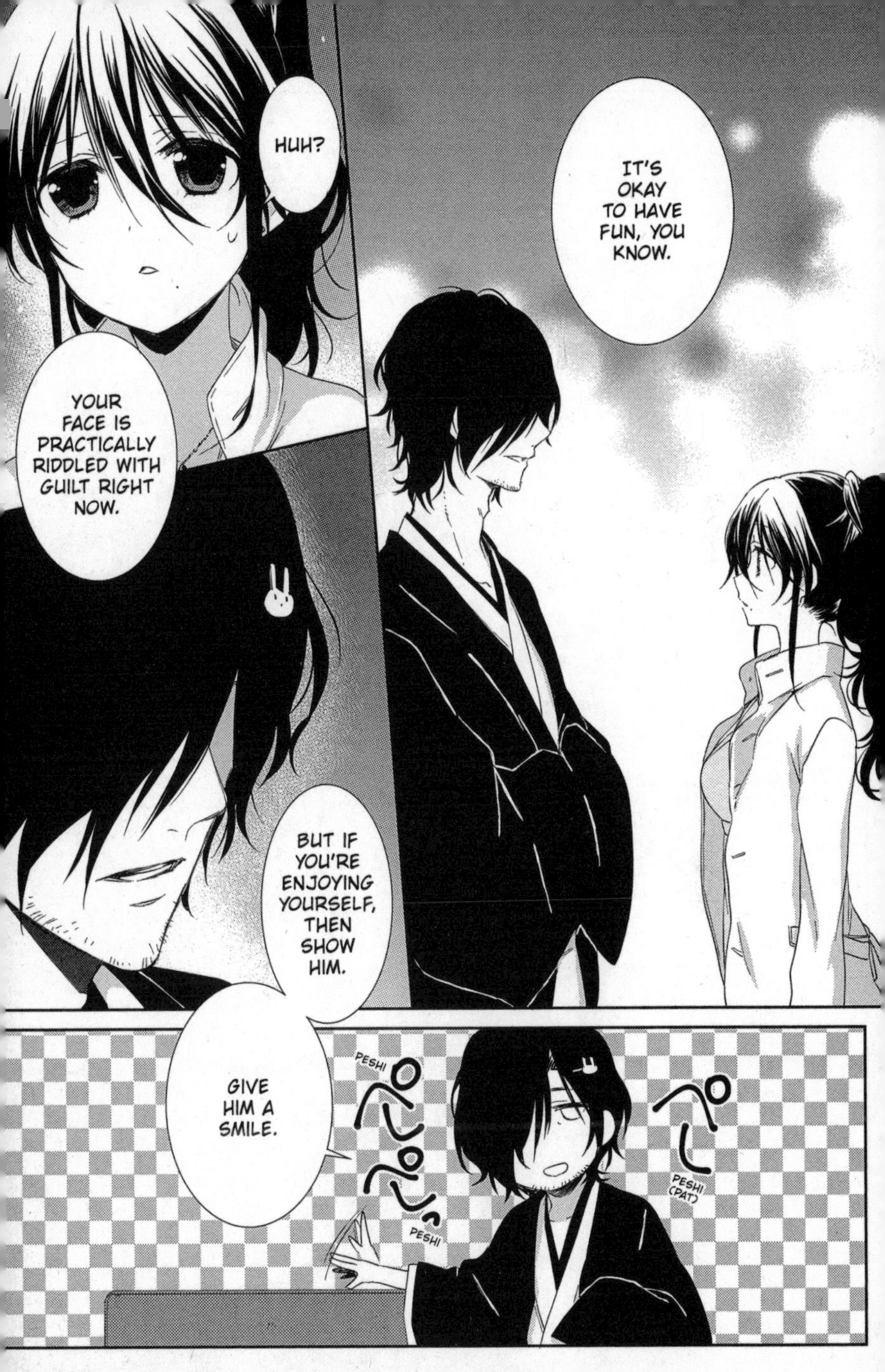
IT'S OKAY TO HAVE FUN, YOU KNOW.
HUH?
YOUR FACE IS PRACTICALLY RIDDLED WITH GUILT RIGHT NOW.
BUT IF YOU'RE ENJOYING YOURSELF, THEN SHOW HIM.
PESHI (PAT)
PESHI
PESHI
GIVE HIM A SMILE.

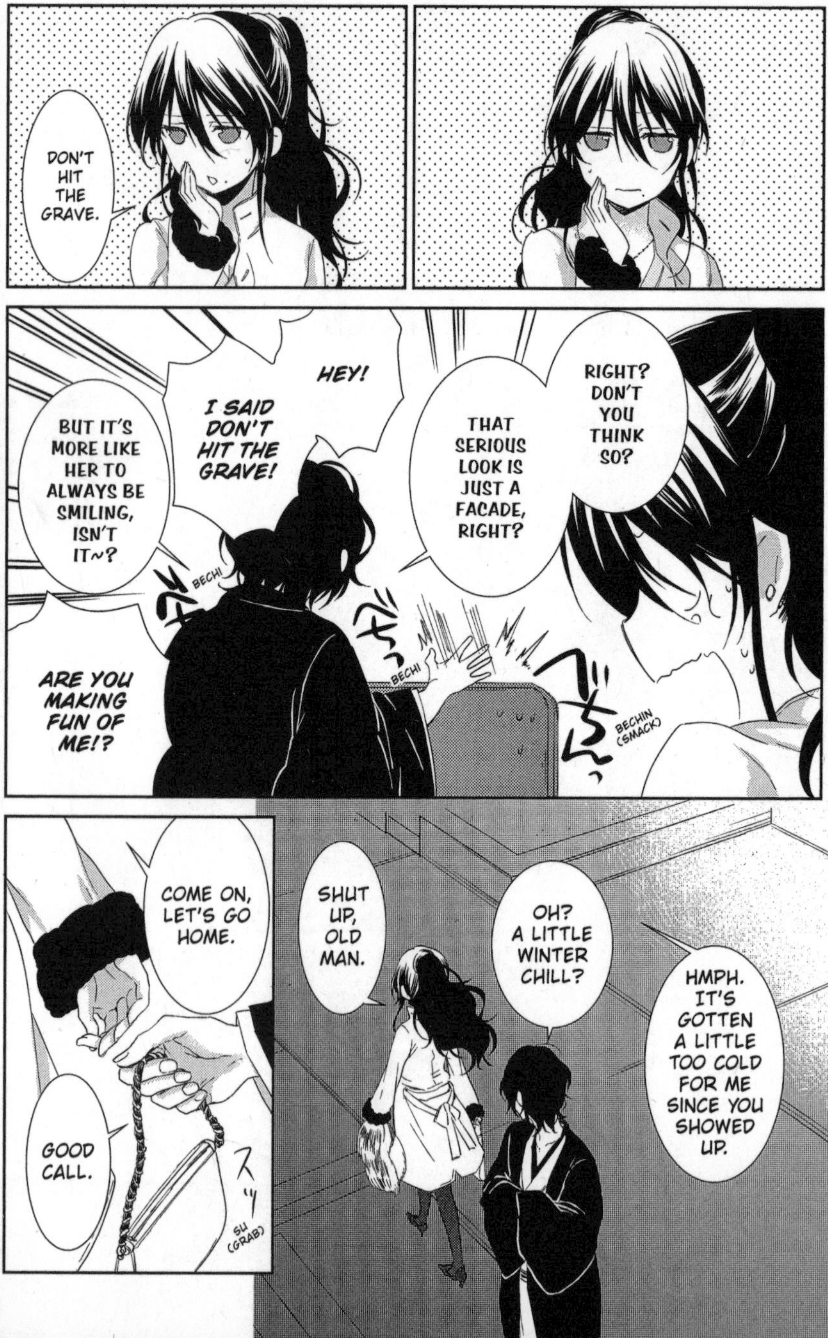
DON'T HIT THE GRAVE.
RIGHT? DON'T YOU THINK SO?
THAT SERIOUS LOOK IS JUST A FACADE, RIGHT?
HEY!
I SAID DON'T HIT THE GRAVE!
BUT IT'S MORE LIKE HER TO ALWAYS BE SMILING, ISN'T IT~?
BECHIN (SMACK)
BECHI
BECHI
ARE YOU MAKING FUN OF ME!?
HMPH. IT'S GOTTEN A LITTLE TOO COLD FOR ME SINCE YOU SHOWED UP.
OH? A LITTLE WINTER CHILL?
SHUT UP, OLD MAN.
COME ON, LET'S GO HOME.
GOOD CALL.
SU (GRAB)

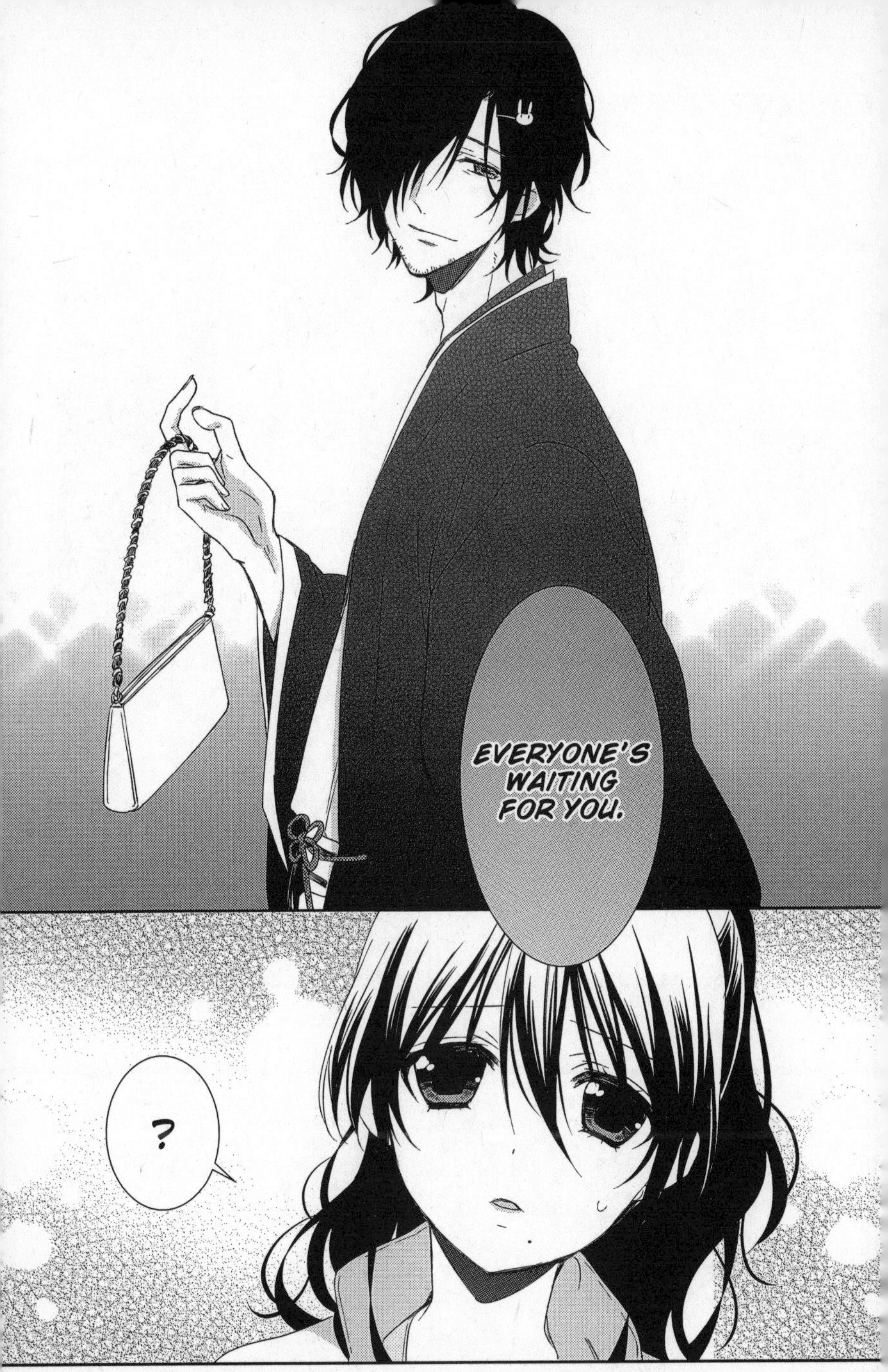
EVERYONE'S WAITING FOR YOU.
?

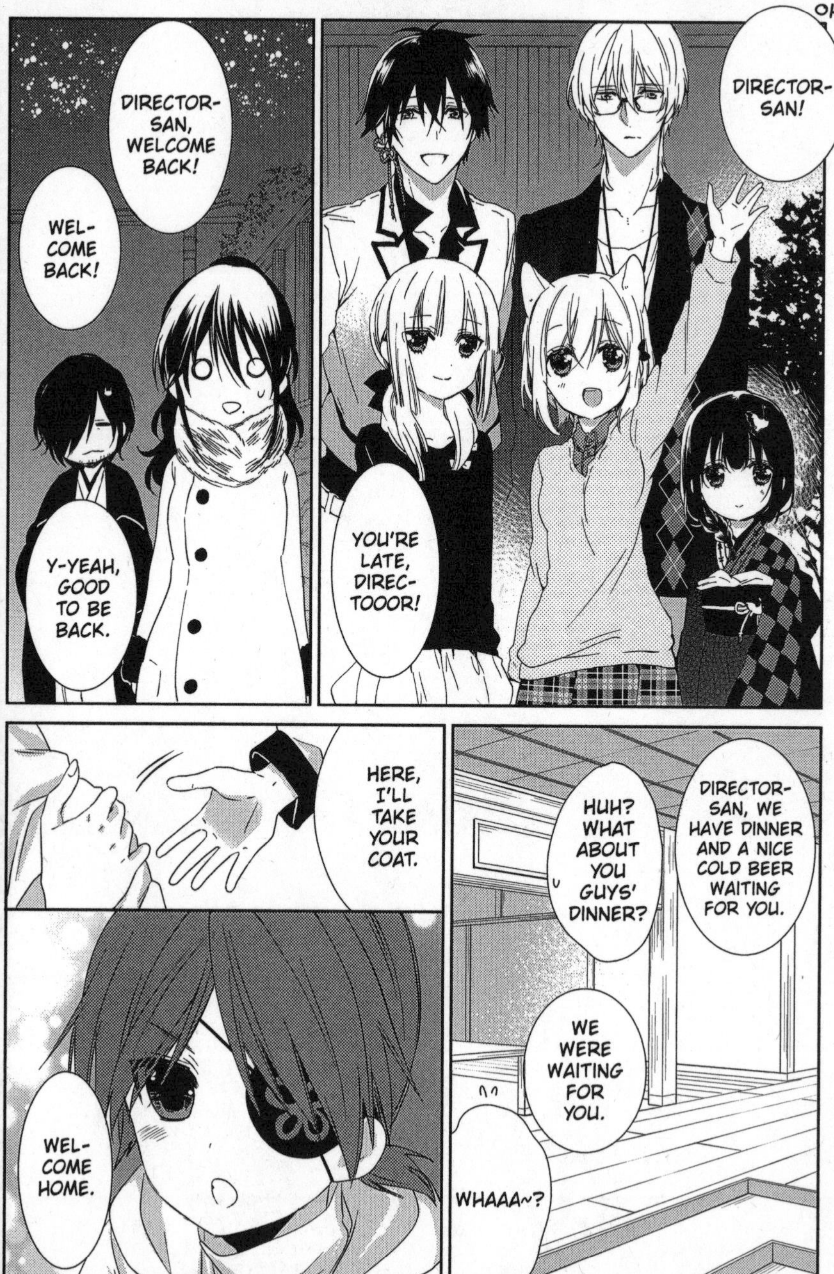
OH!
DIRECTOR-SAN!
YOU'RE LATE, DIRECTOOOR!
DIRECTOR-SAN, WELCOME BACK!
WELCOME BACK!
Y-YEAH, GOOD TO BE BACK.
DIRECTOR-SAN, WE HAVE DINNER AND A NICE COLD BEER WAITING FOR YOU.
HUH? WHAT ABOUT YOU GUYS' DINNER?
WE WERE WAITING FOR YOU.
WHAAA~?
HERE, I'LL TAKE YOUR COAT.
WELCOME HOME.

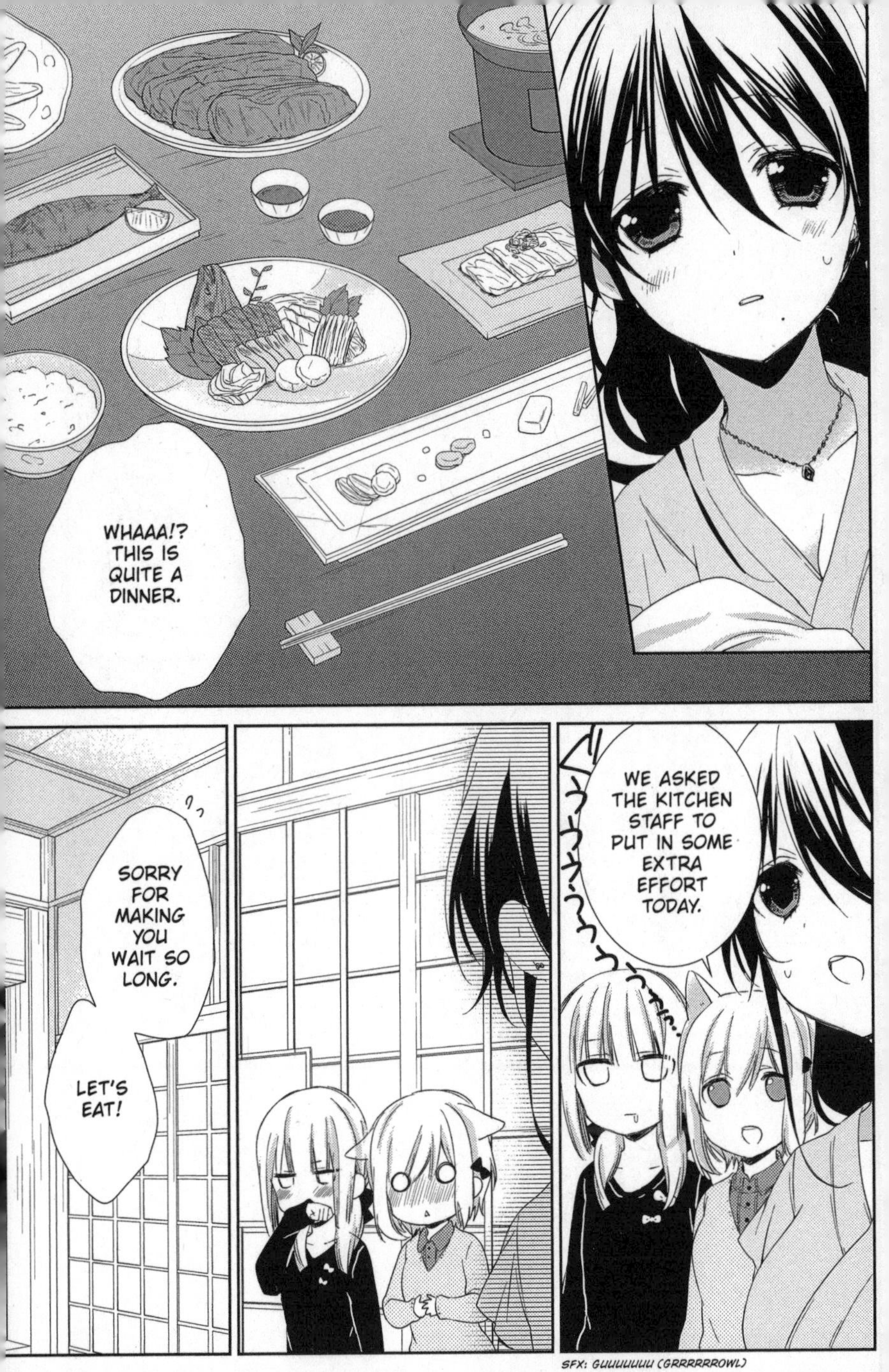
WHAAA!? THIS IS QUITE A DINNER.
WE ASKED THE KITCHEN STAFF TO PUT IN SOME EXTRA EFFORT TODAY.
SORRY FOR MAKING YOU WAIT SO LONG.
LET'S EAT!

SFX: GUUUUUUU (GRRRRRROWL)

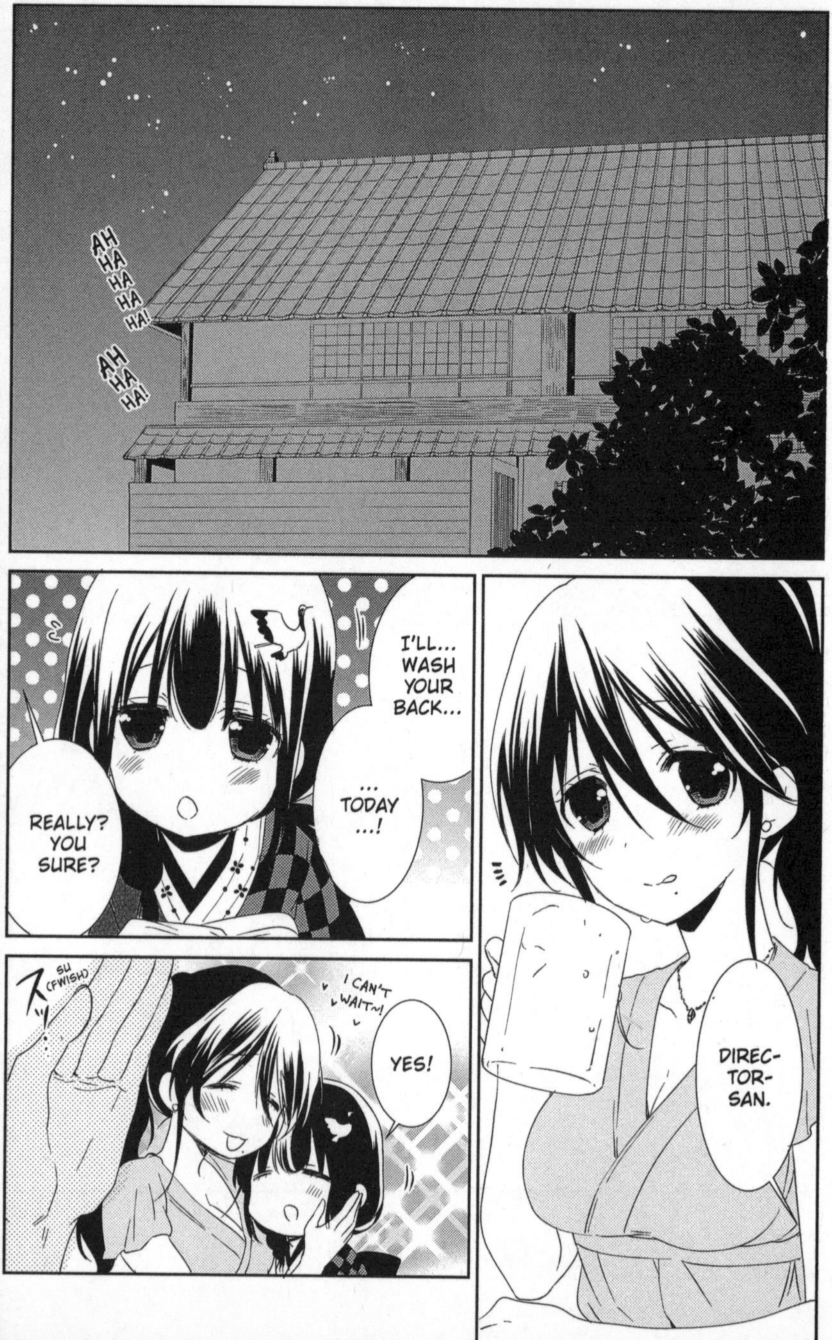
AH HA HA HA HA!
AH HA HA!
DIREC-TOR-SAN.
I'LL... WASH YOUR BACK...
... TODAY ...!
REALLY? YOU SURE?
I CAN'T WAIT~!
YES!
SU (FWISH)

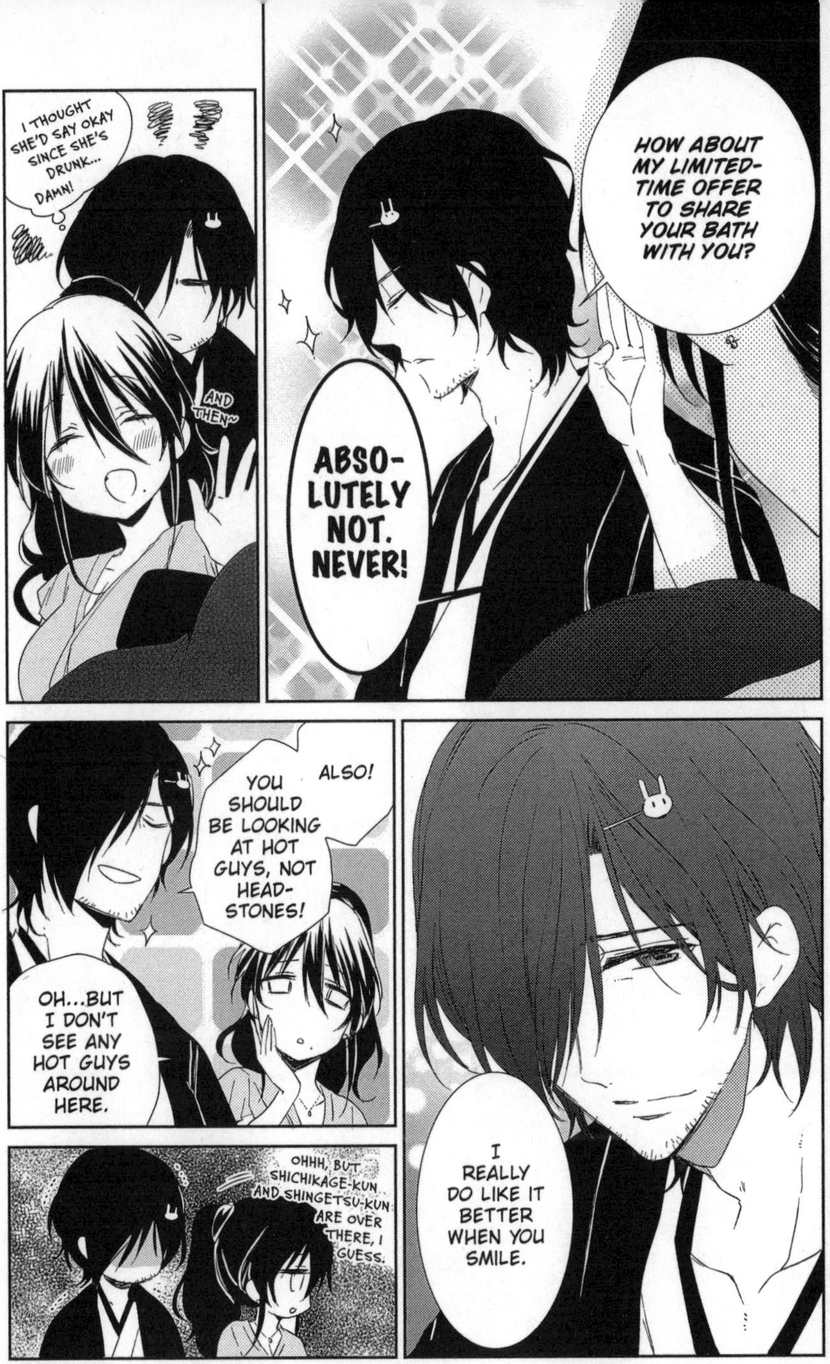
HOW ABOUT MY LIMITED-TIME OFFER TO SHARE YOUR BATH WITH YOU?
ABSO-LUTELY NOT. NEVER!
I THOUGHT SHE'D SAY OKAY SINCE SHE'S DRUNK... DAMN!
AND THEN~
I REALLY DO LIKE IT BETTER WHEN YOU SMILE.
ALSO!
YOU SHOULD BE LOOKING AT HOT GUYS, NOT HEAD-STONES!
OH...BUT I DON'T SEE ANY HOT GUYS AROUND HERE.
OHHH, BUT SHICHIKAGE-KUN AND SHINGETSU-KUN ARE OVER THERE, I GUESS.

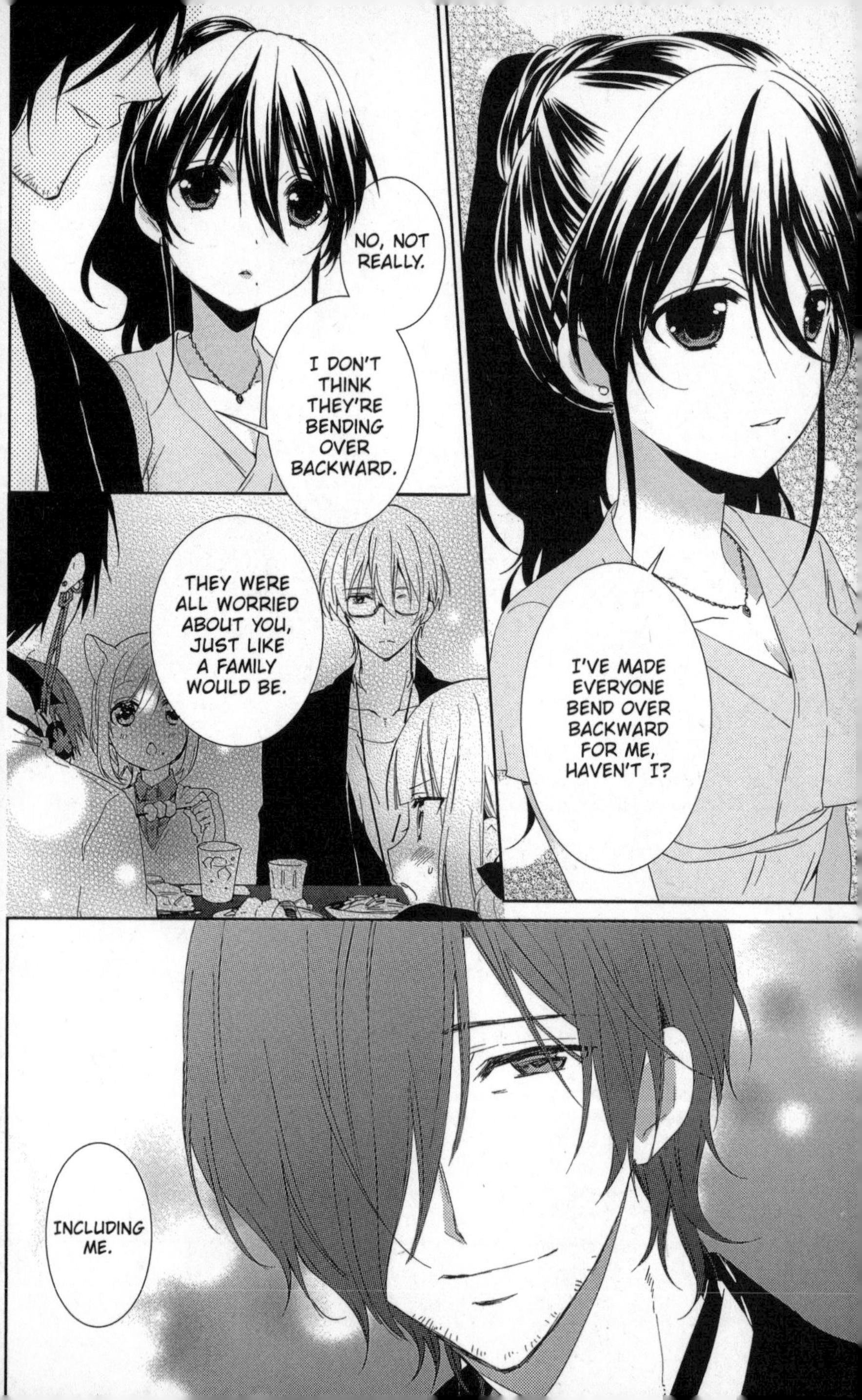
I'VE MADE EVERYONE BEND OVER BACKWARD FOR ME, HAVEN'T I?
NO, NOT REALLY.
I DON'T THINK THEY'RE BENDING OVER BACKWARD.
THEY WERE ALL WORRIED ABOUT YOU, JUST LIKE A FAMILY WOULD BE.
INCLUDING ME.

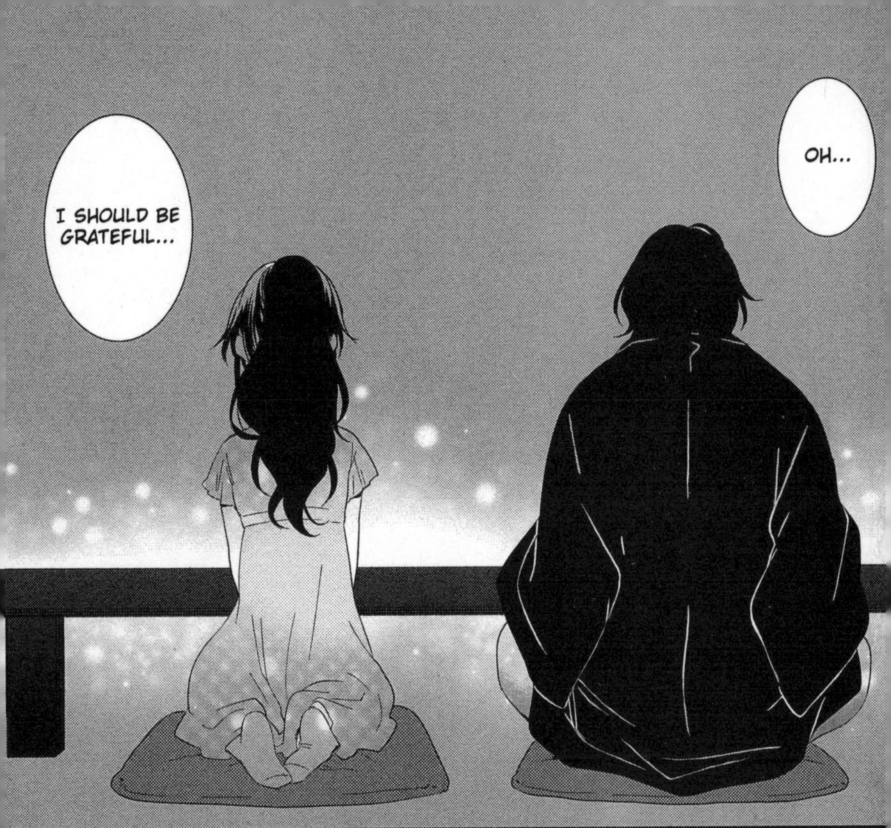
OH...
I SHOULD BE GRATEFUL...
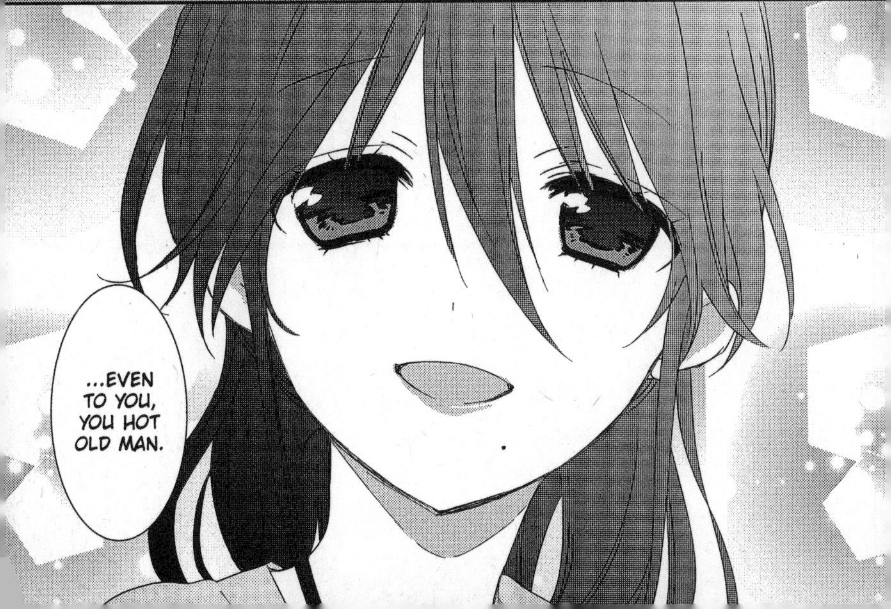
...EVEN TO YOU, YOU HOT OLD MAN.

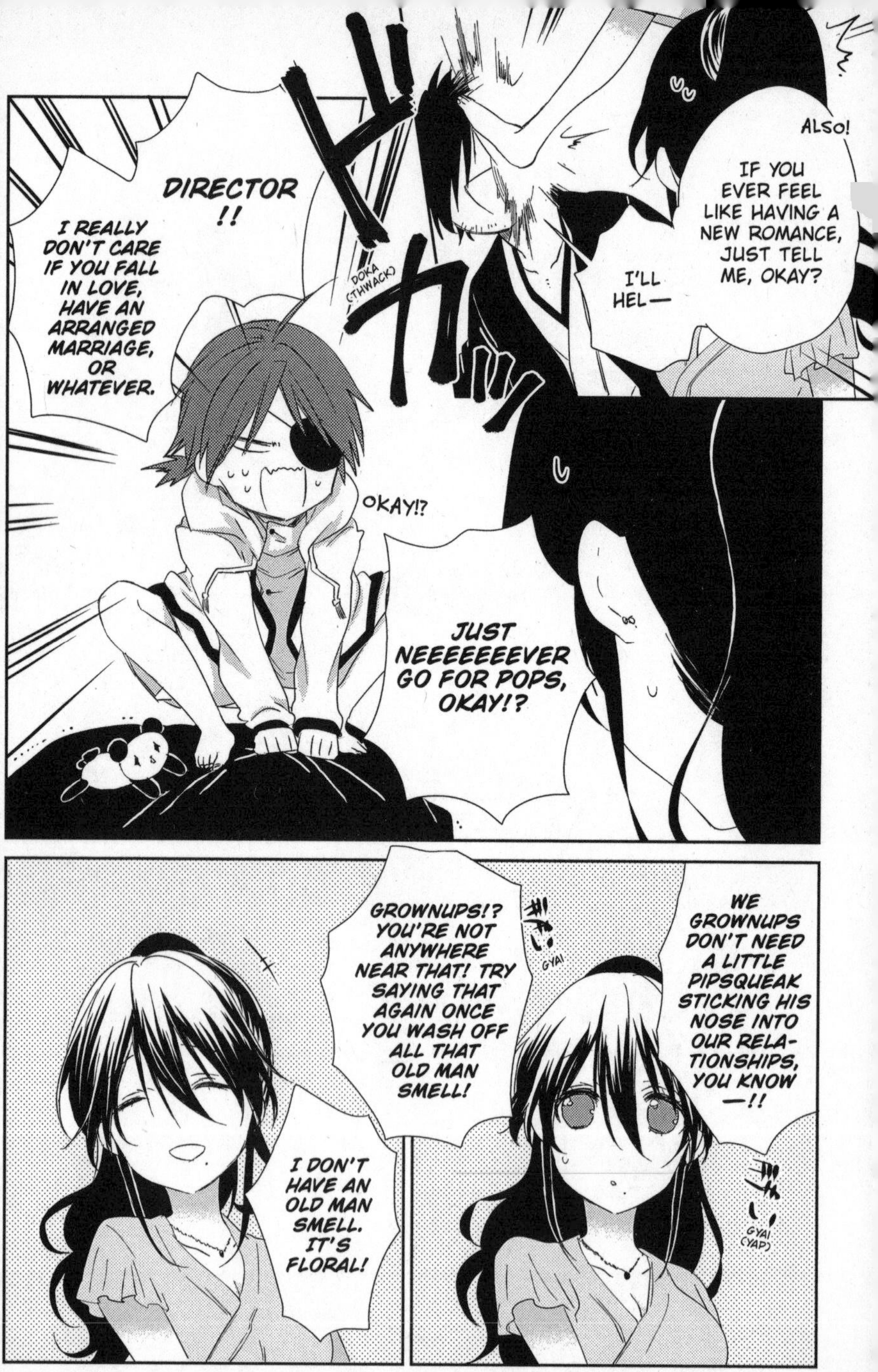

ALSO!
IF YOU EVER FEEL LIKE HAVING A NEW ROMANCE, JUST TELL ME, OKAY?
I'LL HEL—
DOKA (THWACK)
DIRECTOR!!
I REALLY DON'T CARE IF YOU FALL IN LOVE, HAVE AN ARRANGED MARRIAGE, OR WHATEVER.
OKAY!?
JUST NEEEEEEEEVER GO FOR POPS, OKAY!?
WE GROWNUPS DON'T NEED A LITTLE PIPSQUEAK STICKING HIS NOSE INTO OUR RELA-TIONSHIPS, YOU KNOW—!!
GYA! (YAP)
GROWNUPS!? YOU'RE NOT ANYWHERE NEAR THAT! TRY SAYING THAT AGAIN ONCE YOU WASH OFF ALL THAT OLD MAN SMELL!
GYA!
I DON'T HAVE AN OLD MAN SMELL. IT'S FLORAL!

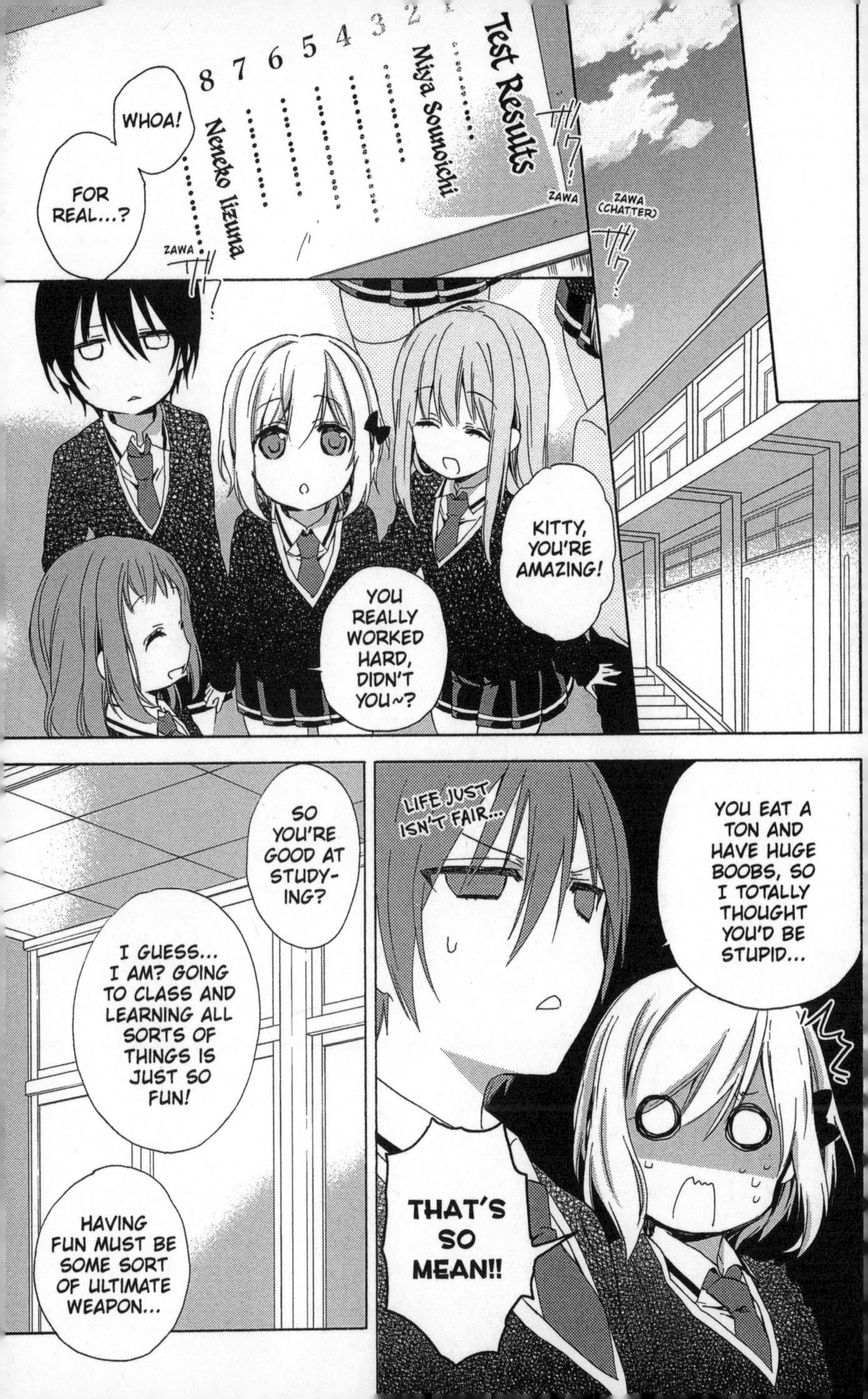

ZAWA
ZAWA (CHATTER)
Test Results
1
2 Miya Sounoichi
3
4
5
6
7
8 Neneko Iizuna
WHOA!
FOR REAL...?
ZAWA
KITTY, YOU'RE AMAZING!
YOU REALLY WORKED HARD, DIDN'T YOU~?
YOU EAT A TON AND HAVE HUGE BOOBS, SO I TOTALLY THOUGHT YOU'D BE STUPID...
LIFE JUST ISN'T FAIR...
THAT'S SO MEAN!!
SO YOU'RE GOOD AT STUDYING?
I GUESS... I AM? GOING TO CLASS AND LEARNING ALL SORTS OF THINGS IS JUST SO FUN!
HAVING FUN MUST BE SOME SORT OF ULTIMATE WEAPON...

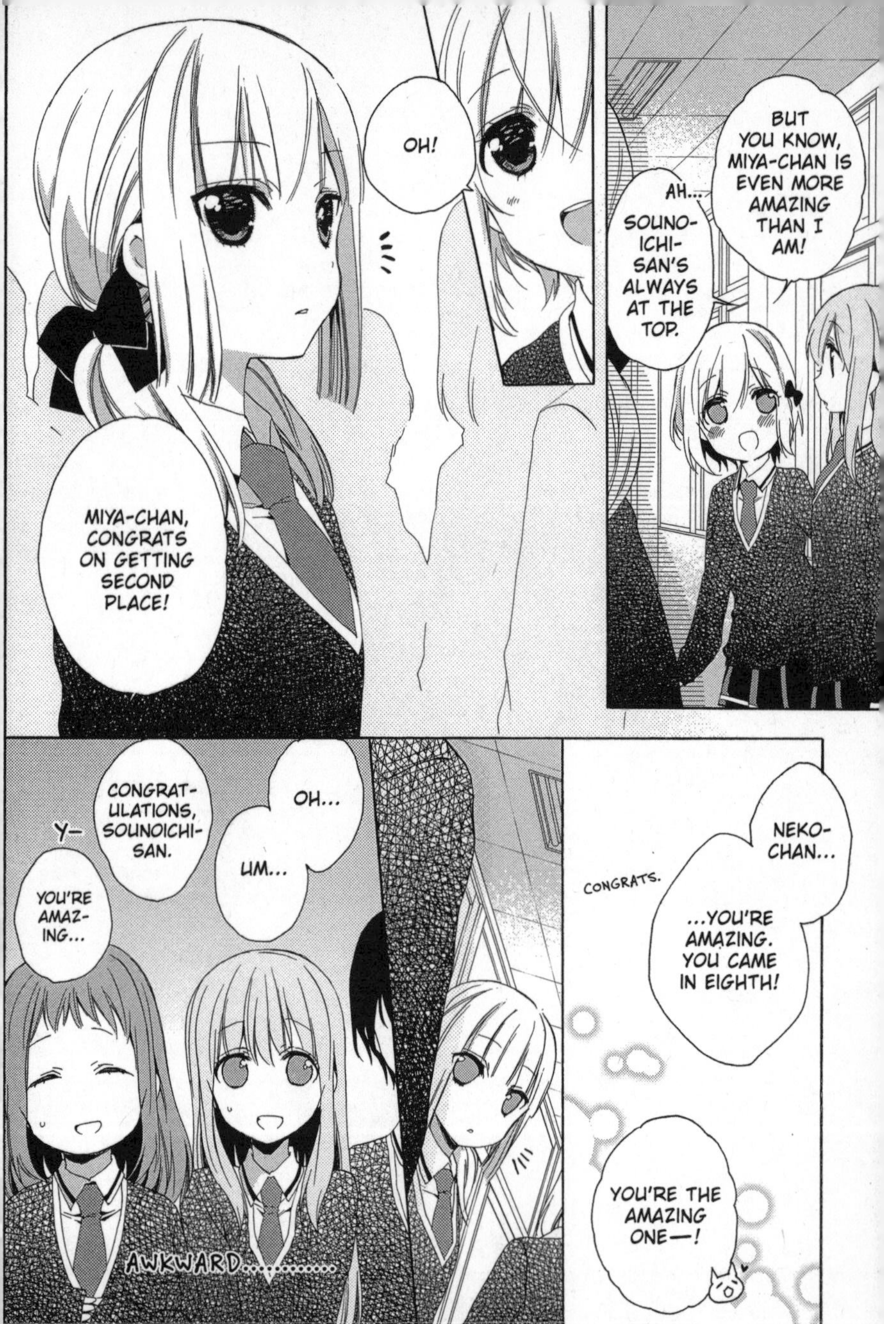
BUT YOU KNOW, MIYA-CHAN IS EVEN MORE AMAZING THAN I AM!
AH... SOUNOICHI-SAN'S ALWAYS AT THE TOP.
OH!
MIYA-CHAN, CONGRATS ON GETTING SECOND PLACE!
NEKO-CHAN...
CONGRATS.
...YOU'RE AMAZING. YOU CAME IN EIGHTH!
YOU'RE THE AMAZING ONE—!
OH...
UM...
CONGRATULATIONS, SOUNOICHI-SAN.
Y-
YOU'RE AMAZING...
AWKWARD.............

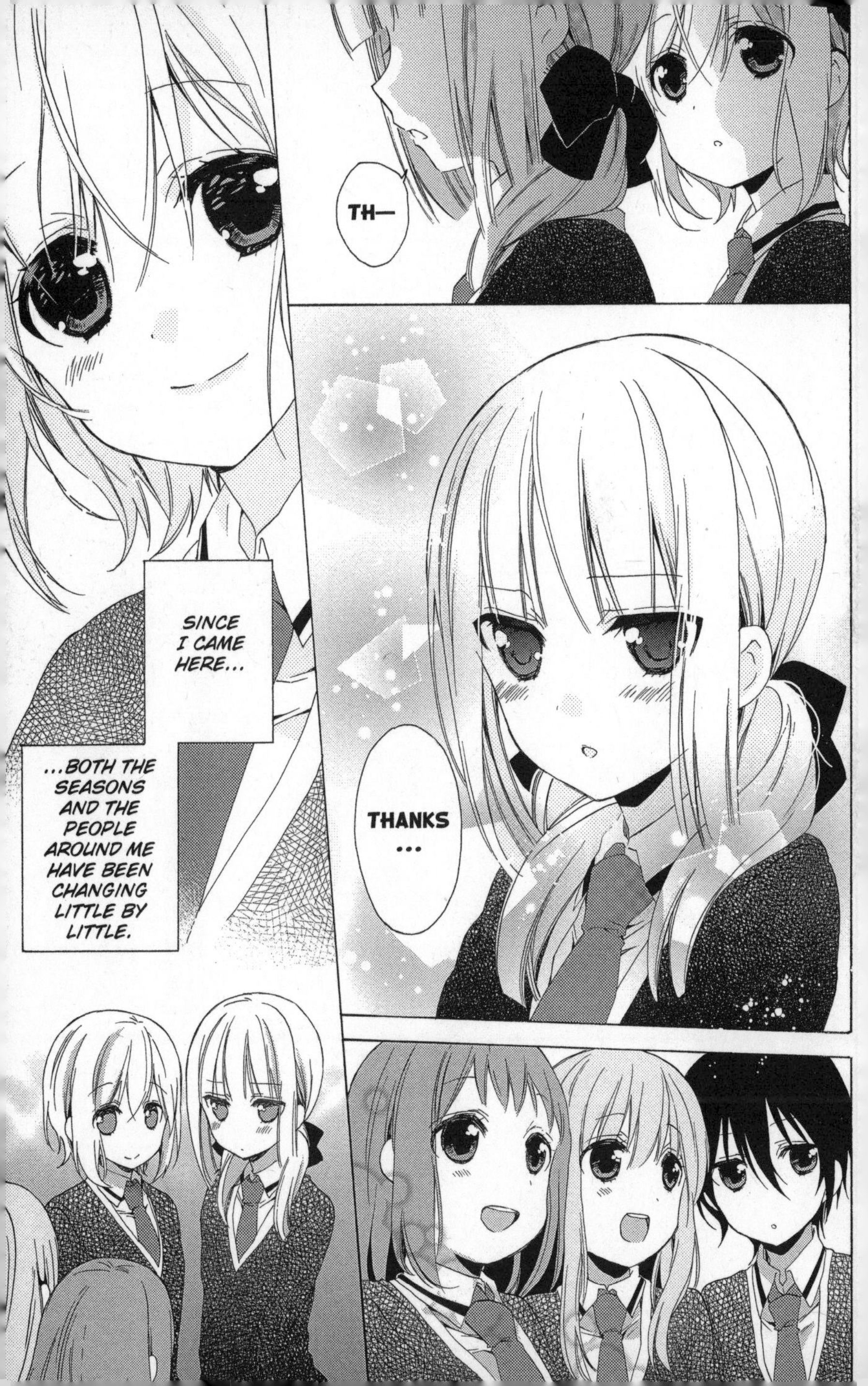
TH—
THANKS...
SINCE I CAME HERE...
...BOTH THE SEASONS AND THE PEOPLE AROUND ME HAVE BEEN CHANGING LITTLE BY LITTLE.

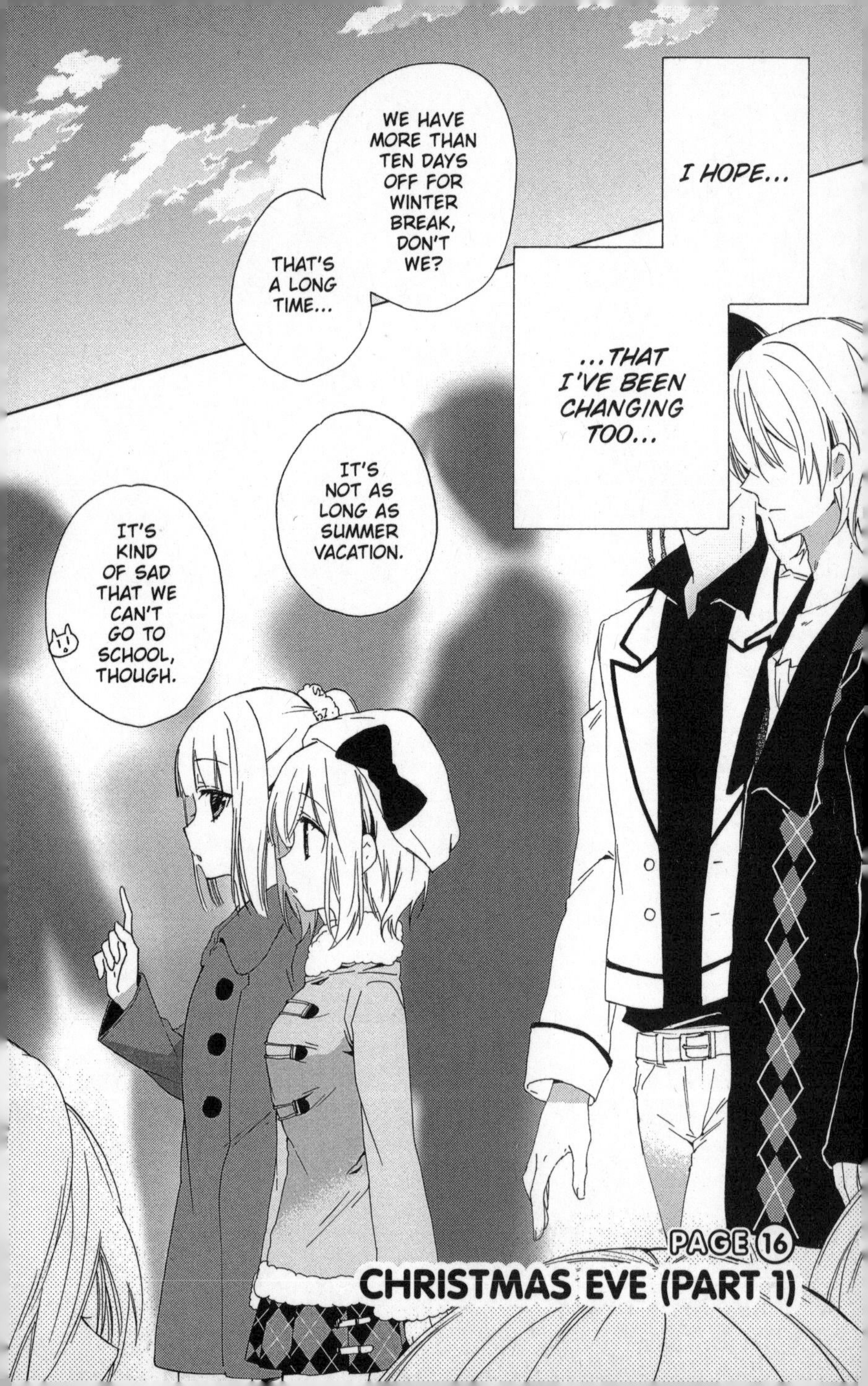
I HOPE...
...THAT I'VE BEEN CHANGING TOO...
WE HAVE MORE THAN TEN DAYS OFF FOR WINTER BREAK, DON'T WE?
THAT'S A LONG TIME...
IT'S NOT AS LONG AS SUMMER VACATION.
IT'S KIND OF SAD THAT WE CAN'T GO TO SCHOOL, THOUGH.
PAGE 16
CHRISTMAS EVE (PART 1)

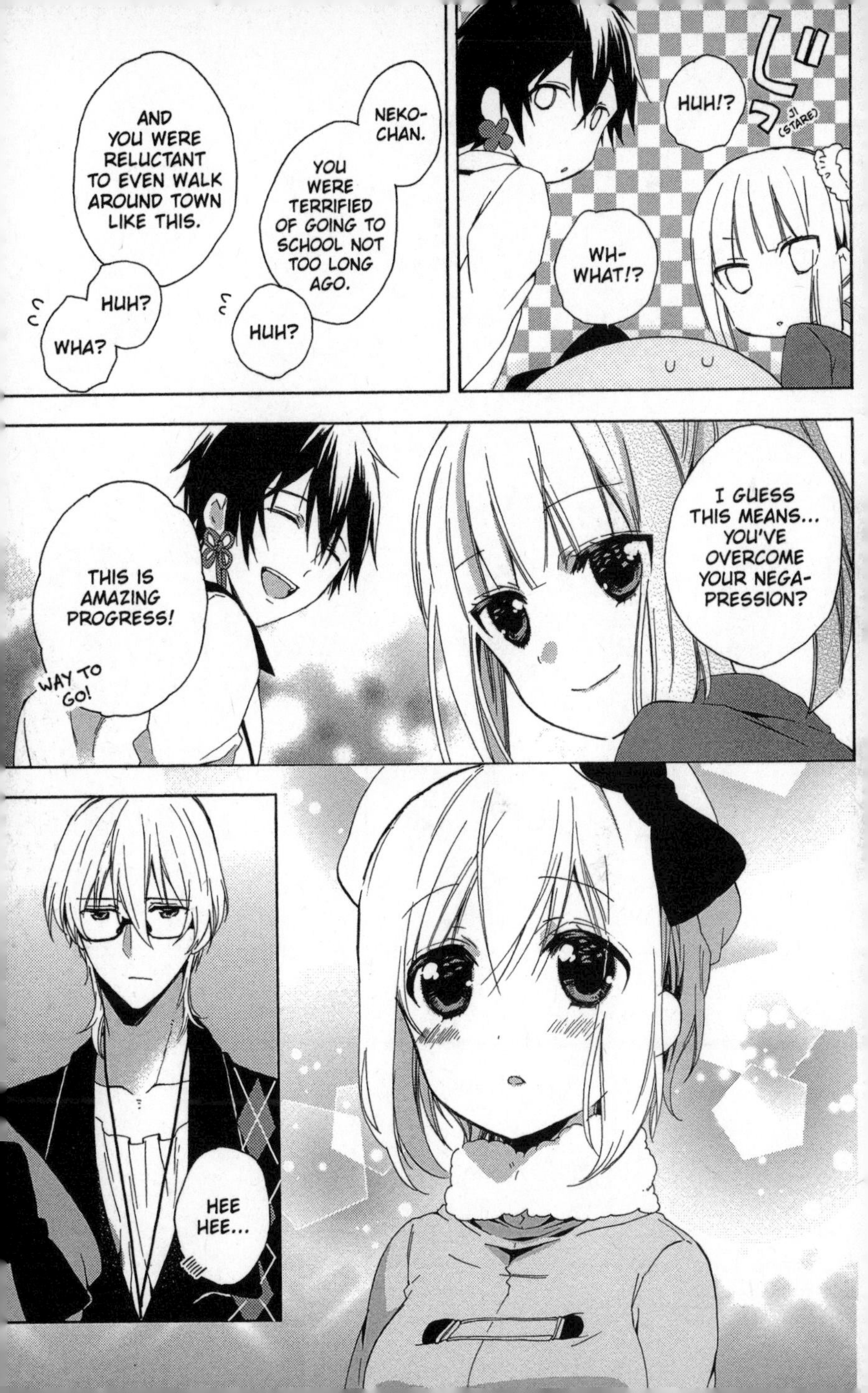
HUH!?
JI (STARE)
WH-WHAT!?
NEKO-CHAN.
YOU WERE TERRIFIED OF GOING TO SCHOOL NOT TOO LONG AGO.
AND YOU WERE RELUCTANT TO EVEN WALK AROUND TOWN LIKE THIS.
HUH?
HUH?
WHA?
I GUESS THIS MEANS... YOU'VE OVERCOME YOUR NEGA-PRESSION?
THIS IS AMAZING PROGRESS!
WAY TO GO!
HEE HEE...

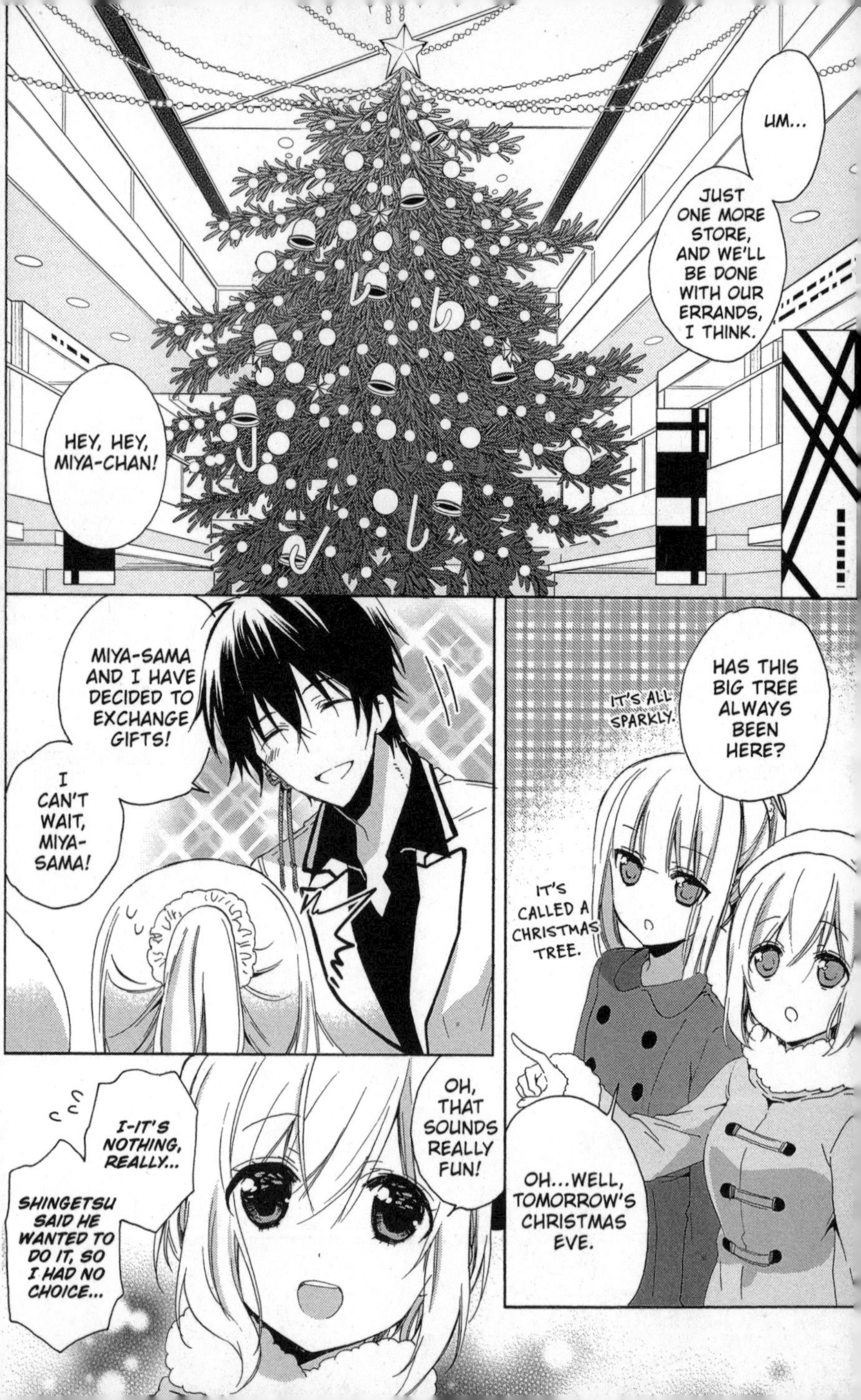
UM...
JUST ONE MORE STORE, AND WE'LL BE DONE WITH OUR ERRANDS, I THINK.
HEY, HEY, MIYA-CHAN!
HAS THIS BIG TREE ALWAYS BEEN HERE?
IT'S ALL SPARKLY.
IT'S CALLED A CHRISTMAS TREE.
OH...WELL, TOMORROW'S CHRISTMAS EVE.
MIYA-SAMA AND I HAVE DECIDED TO EXCHANGE GIFTS!
I CAN'T WAIT, MIYA-SAMA!
OH, THAT SOUNDS REALLY FUN!
I-IT'S NOTHING, REALLY...
SHINGETSU SAID HE WANTED TO DO IT, SO I HAD NO CHOICE...

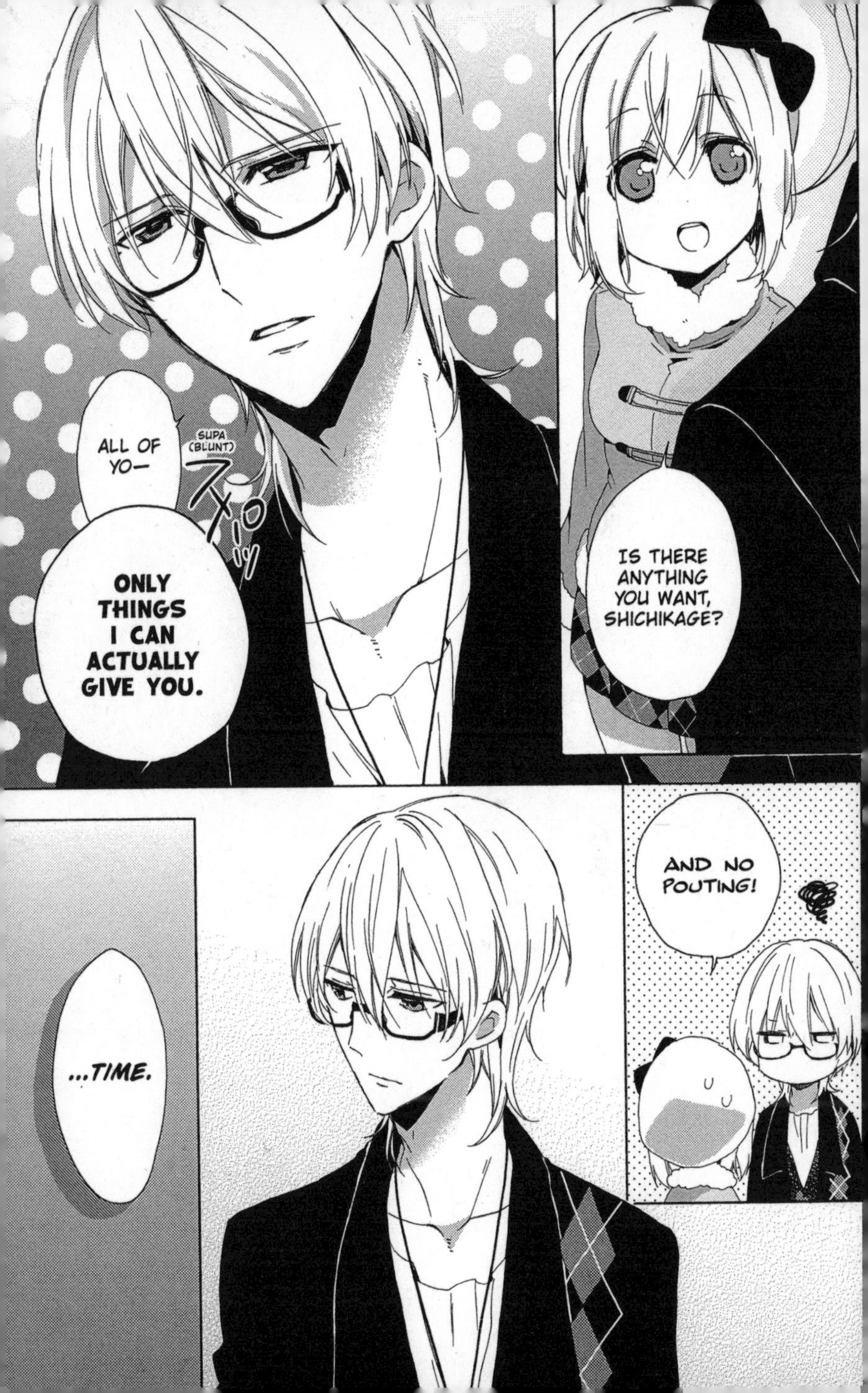
IS THERE ANYTHING YOU WANT, SHICHIKAGE?
ALL OF YO—
SUPA (BLUNT)
ONLY THINGS I CAN ACTUALLY GIVE YOU.
AND NO POUTING!
...TIME.

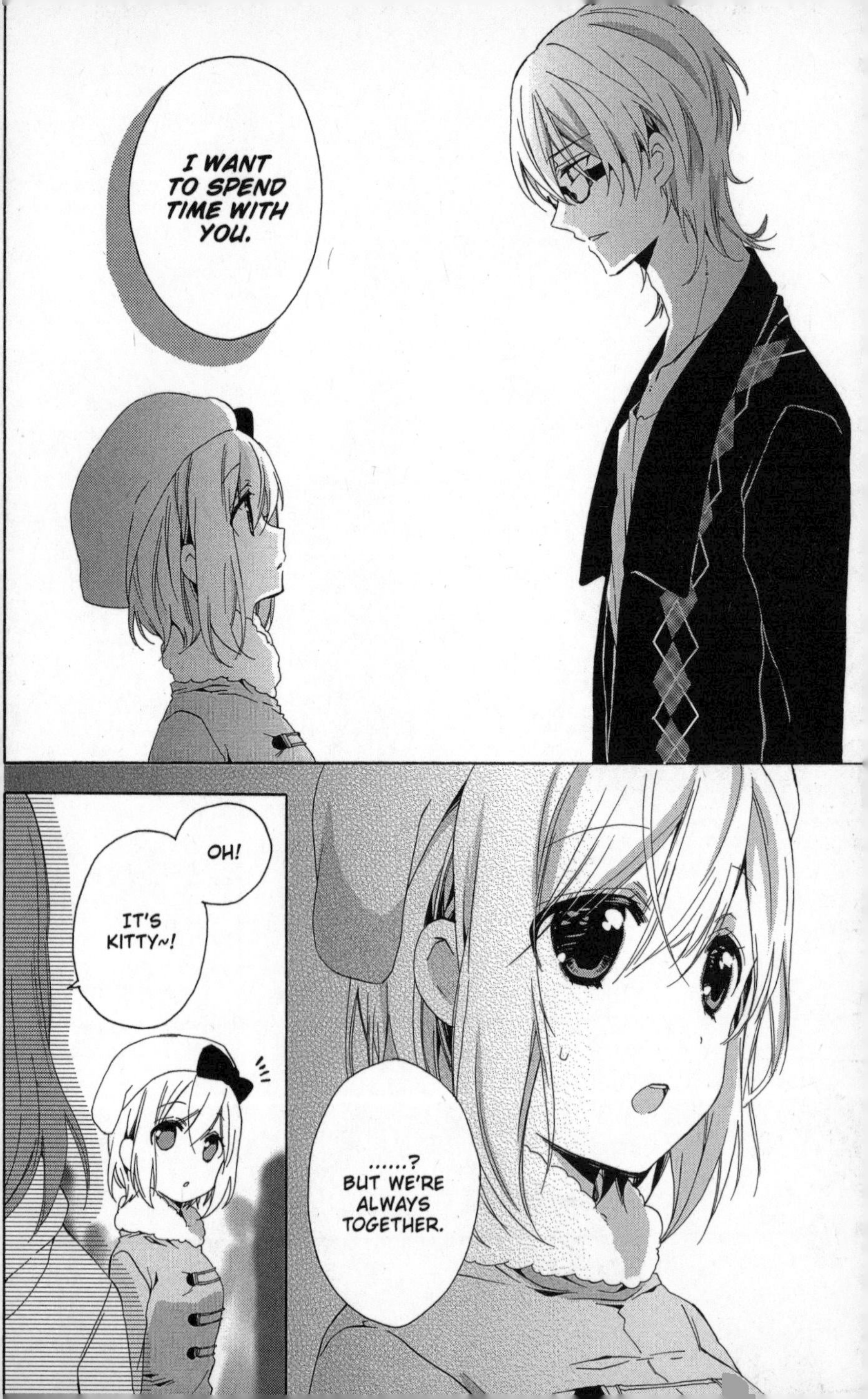
I WANT TO SPEND TIME WITH YOU.
......? BUT WE'RE ALWAYS TOGETHER.
OH!
IT'S KITTY~!

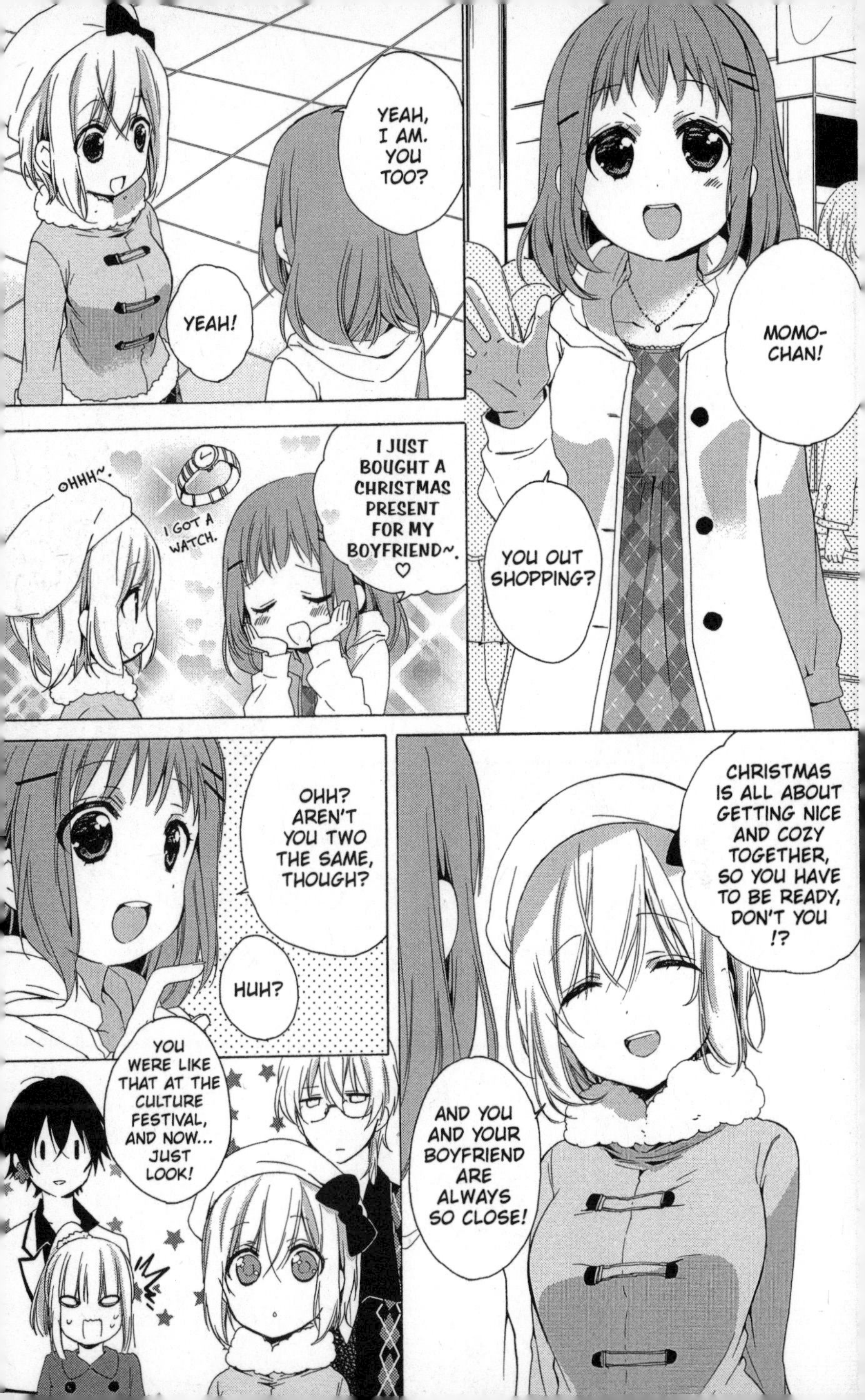
MOMO-CHAN!
YOU OUT SHOPPING?
YEAH, I AM. YOU TOO?
YEAH!
I JUST BOUGHT A CHRISTMAS PRESENT FOR MY BOYFRIEND~. ♡
I GOT A WATCH.
OHHH~.
CHRISTMAS IS ALL ABOUT GETTING NICE AND COZY TOGETHER, SO YOU HAVE TO BE READY, DON'T YOU !?
AND YOU AND YOUR BOYFRIEND ARE ALWAYS SO CLOSE!
OHH? AREN'T YOU TWO THE SAME, THOUGH?
HUH?
YOU WERE LIKE THAT AT THE CULTURE FESTIVAL, AND NOW... JUST LOOK!

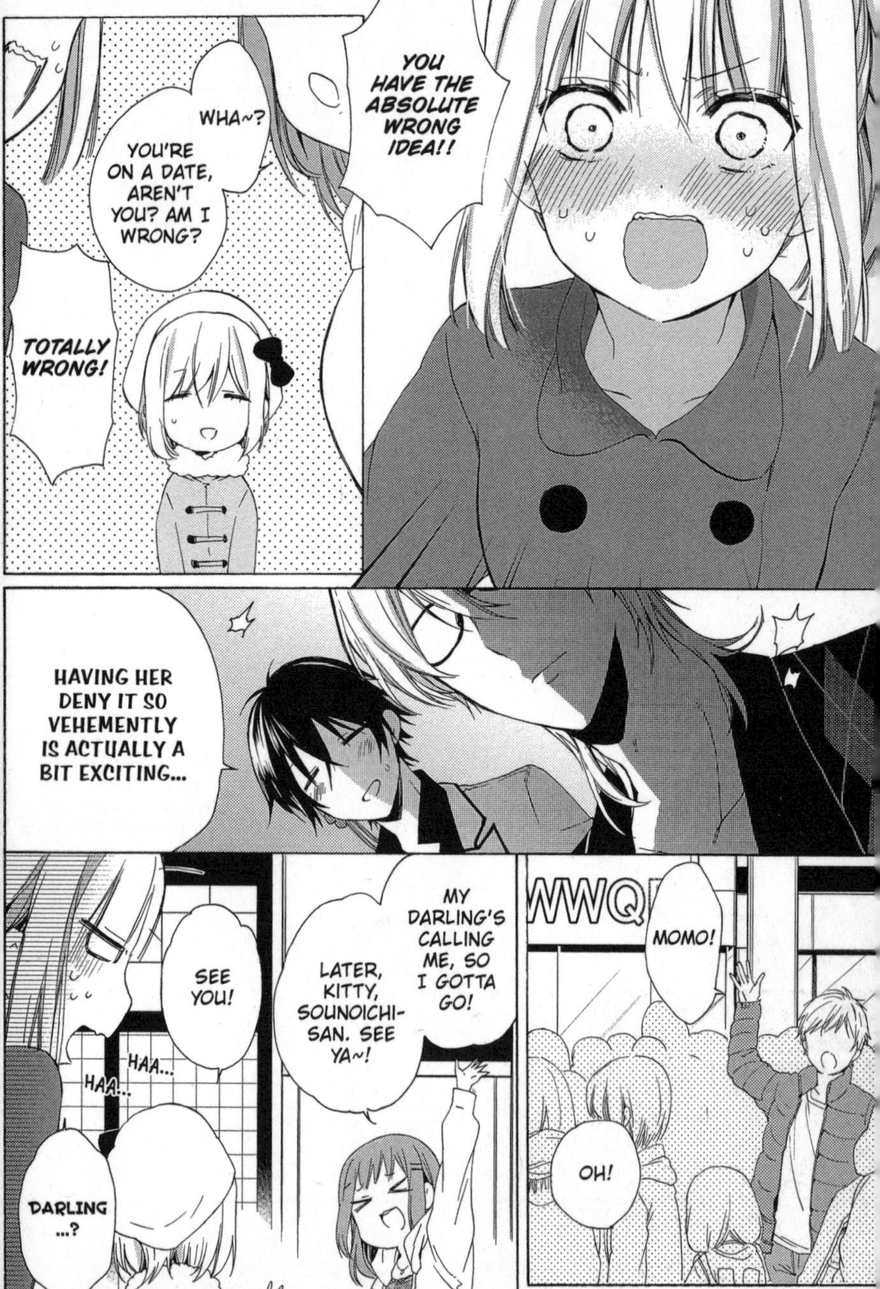
YOU HAVE THE ABSOLUTE WRONG IDEA!!
WHA~?
YOU'RE ON A DATE, AREN'T YOU? AM I WRONG?
TOTALLY WRONG!
HAVING HER DENY IT SO VEHEMENTLY IS ACTUALLY A BIT EXCITING...
MOMO!
OH!
MY DARLING'S CALLING ME, SO I GOTTA GO!
LATER, KITTY, SOUNOICHI-SAN. SEE YA~!
SEE YOU!
HAA... HAA...
DARLING ...?

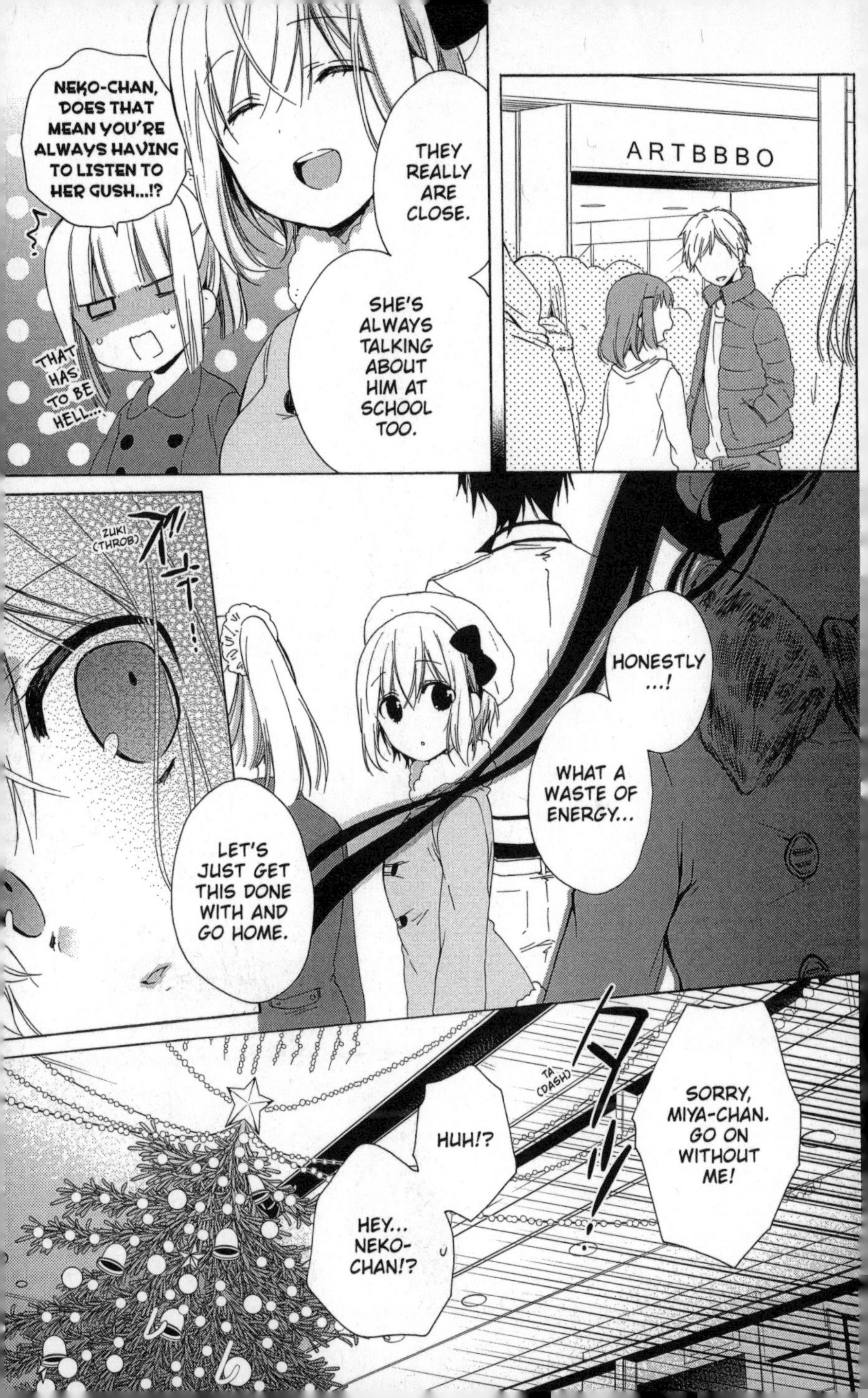
ARTBBBO
THEY REALLY ARE CLOSE.
SHE'S ALWAYS TALKING ABOUT HIM AT SCHOOL TOO.
NEKO-CHAN, DOES THAT MEAN YOU'RE ALWAYS HAVING TO LISTEN TO HER GUSH...!?
THAT HAS TO BE HELL...
HONESTLY...!
WHAT A WASTE OF ENERGY...
LET'S JUST GET THIS DONE WITH AND GO HOME.
ZUKI (THROB)
TA (DASH)
SORRY, MIYA-CHAN. GO ON WITHOUT ME!
HUH!?
HEY... NEKO-CHAN!?

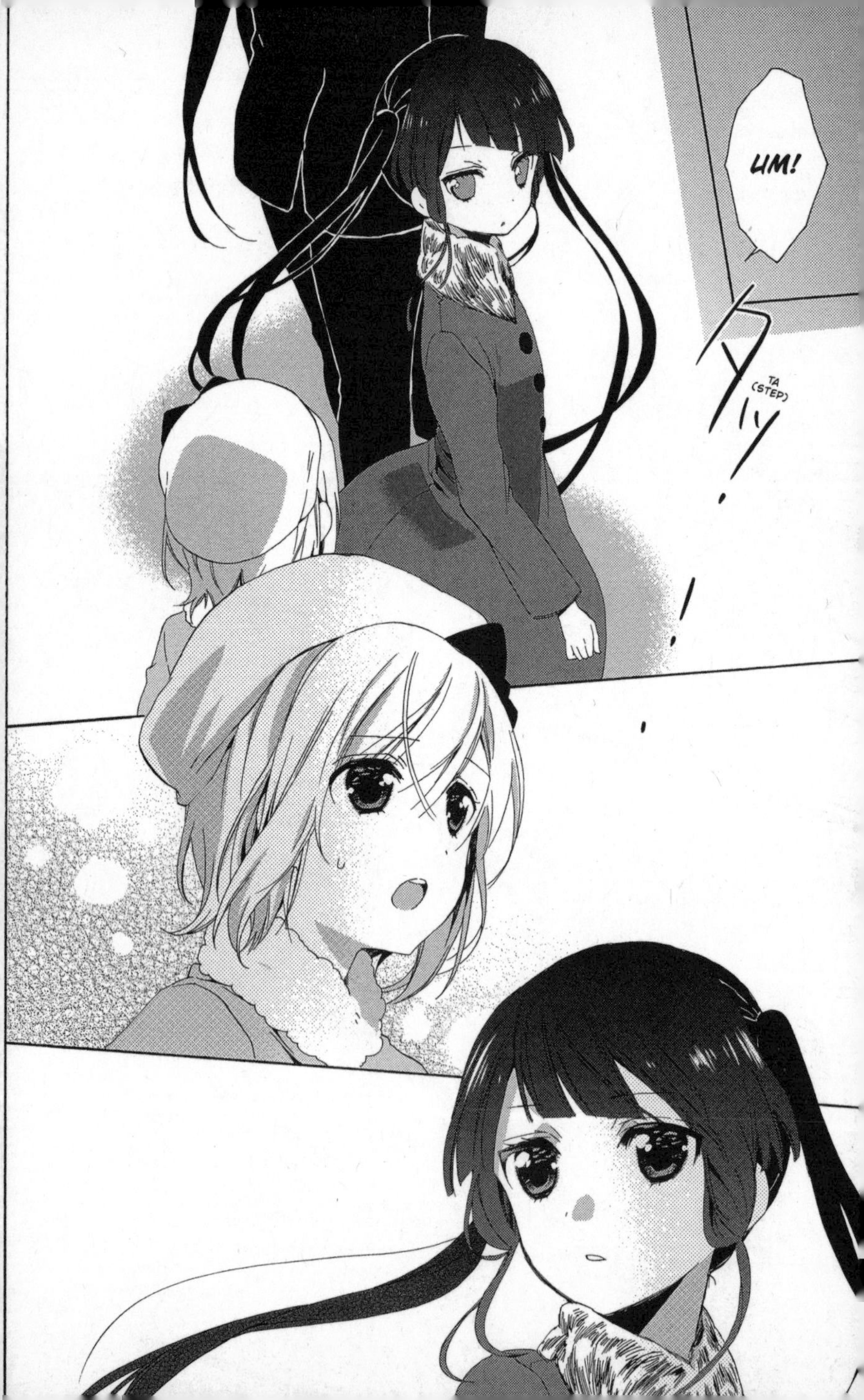
UM!
タッ
TA (STEP)

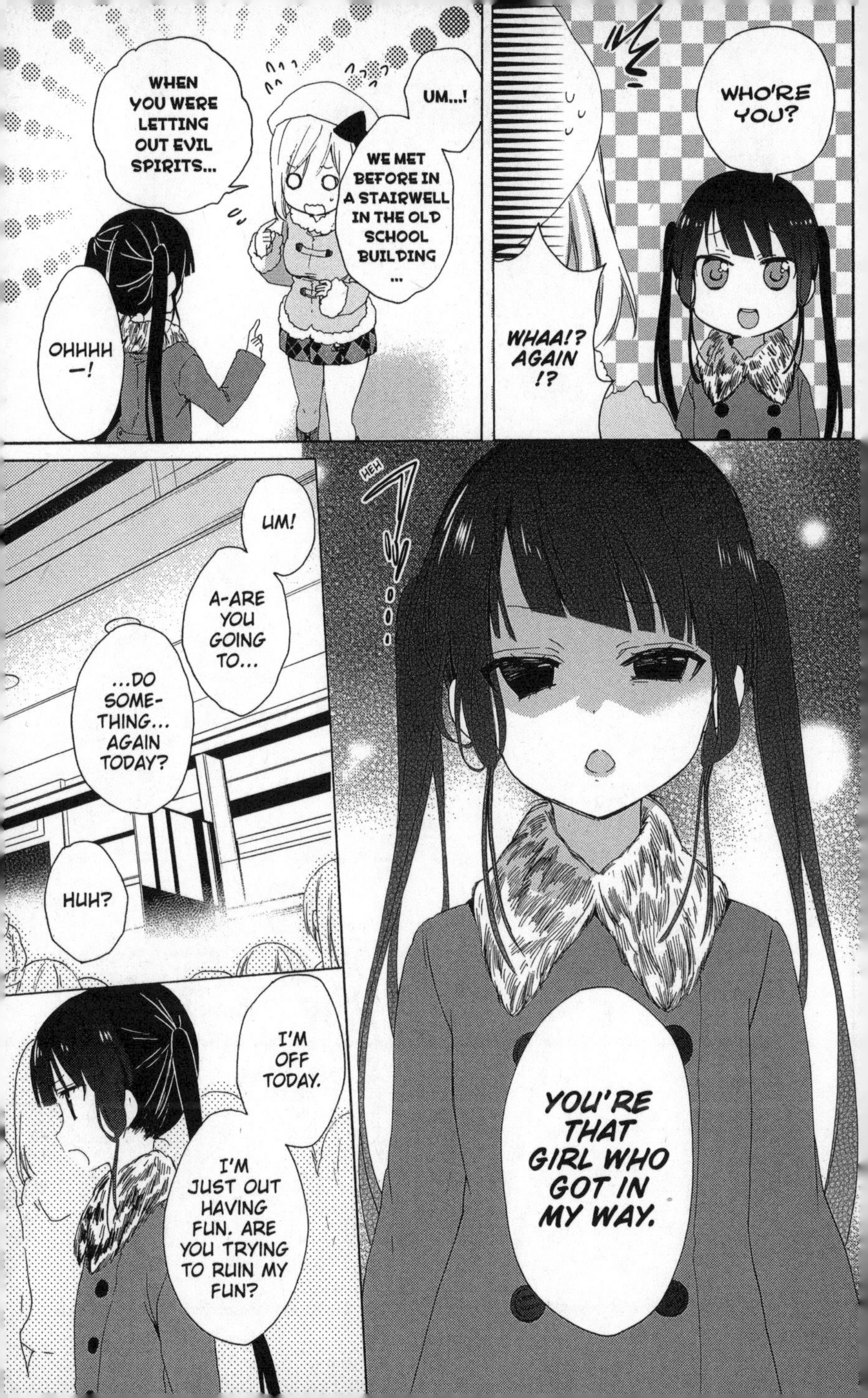
WHO'RE YOU?
WHAA!? AGAIN !?
UM...!
WE MET BEFORE IN A STAIRWELL IN THE OLD SCHOOL BUILDING ...
WHEN YOU WERE LETTING OUT EVIL SPIRITS...
OHHHH—!
HEH
YOU'RE THAT GIRL WHO GOT IN MY WAY.
UM!
A-ARE YOU GOING TO...
...DO SOME-THING... AGAIN TODAY?
HUH?
I'M OFF TODAY.
I'M JUST OUT HAVING FUN. ARE YOU TRYING TO RUIN MY FUN?

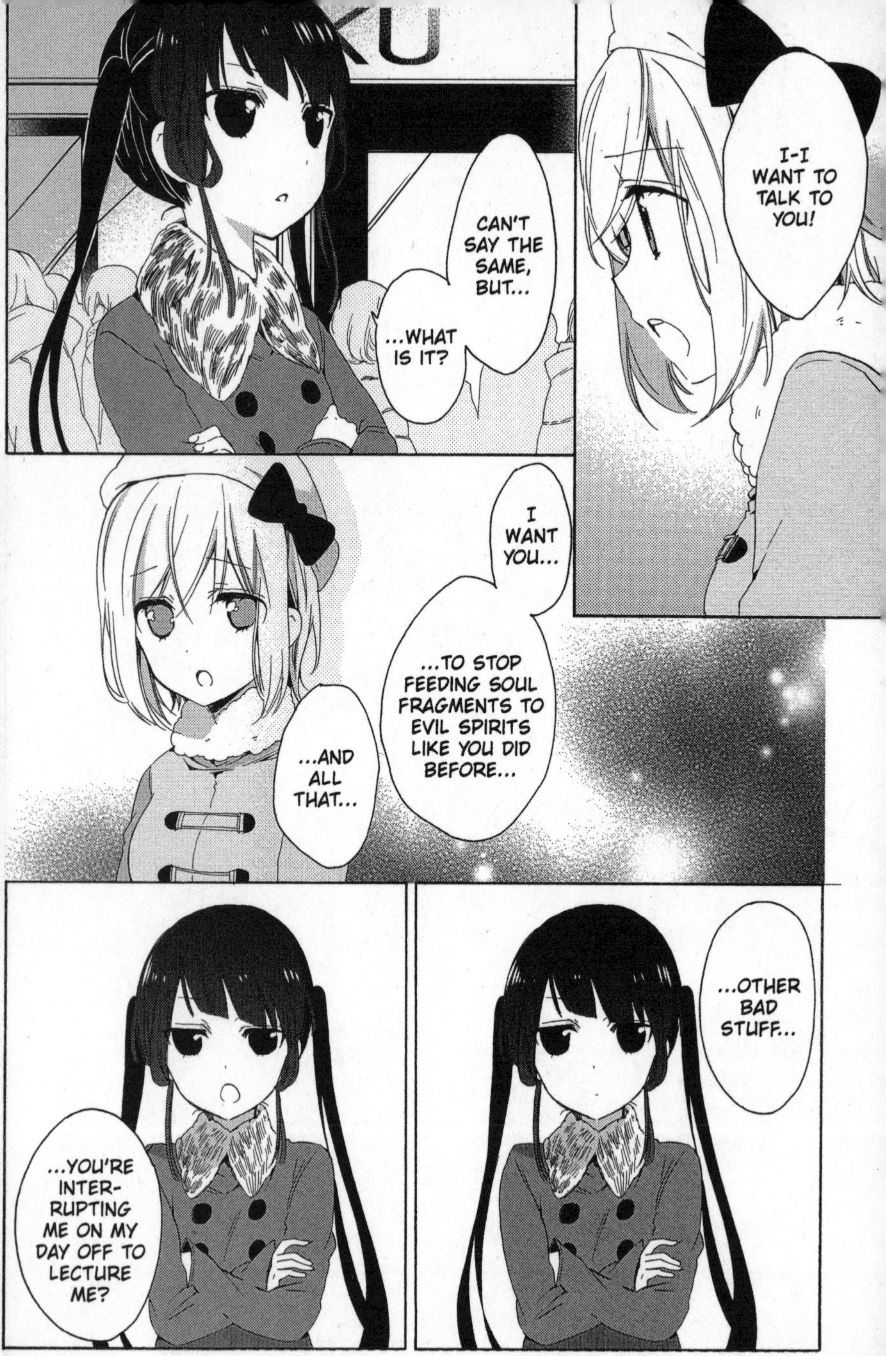
I-I WANT TO TALK TO YOU!
CAN'T SAY THE SAME, BUT...
...WHAT IS IT?
I WANT YOU...
...TO STOP FEEDING SOUL FRAGMENTS TO EVIL SPIRITS LIKE YOU DID BEFORE...
...AND ALL THAT...
...OTHER BAD STUFF...
...YOU'RE INTER-RUPTING ME ON MY DAY OFF TO LECTURE ME?

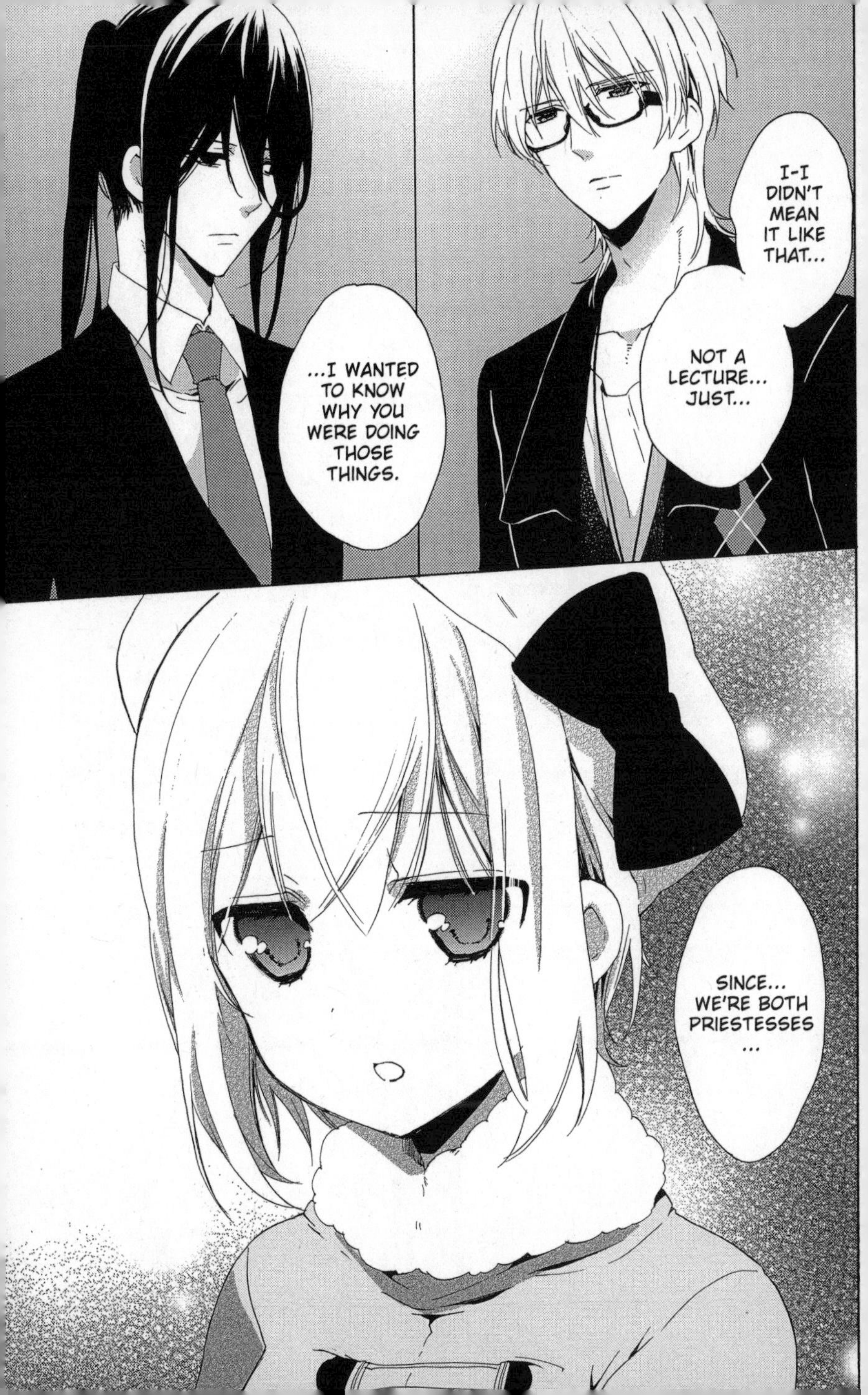
I-I DIDN'T MEAN IT LIKE THAT...
NOT A LECTURE... JUST...
...I WANTED TO KNOW WHY YOU WERE DOING THOSE THINGS.
SINCE... WE'RE BOTH PRIESTESSES ...

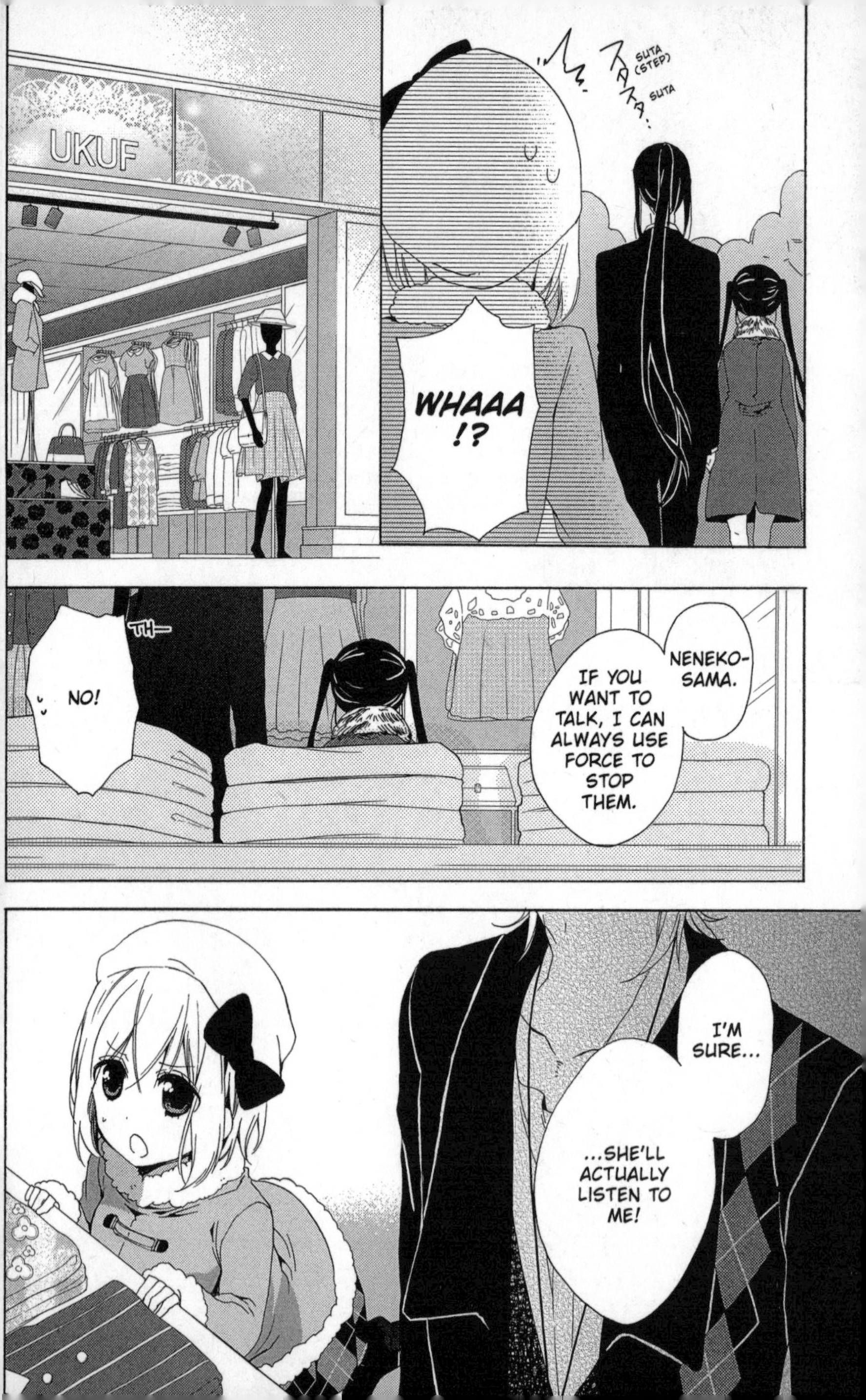

スタスタ
SUTA (STEP) SUTA
WHAAA !?
UKUF
NENEKO-SAMA.
IF YOU WANT TO TALK, I CAN ALWAYS USE FORCE TO STOP THEM.
TH—
NO!
I'M SURE...
...SHE'LL ACTUALLY LISTEN TO ME!

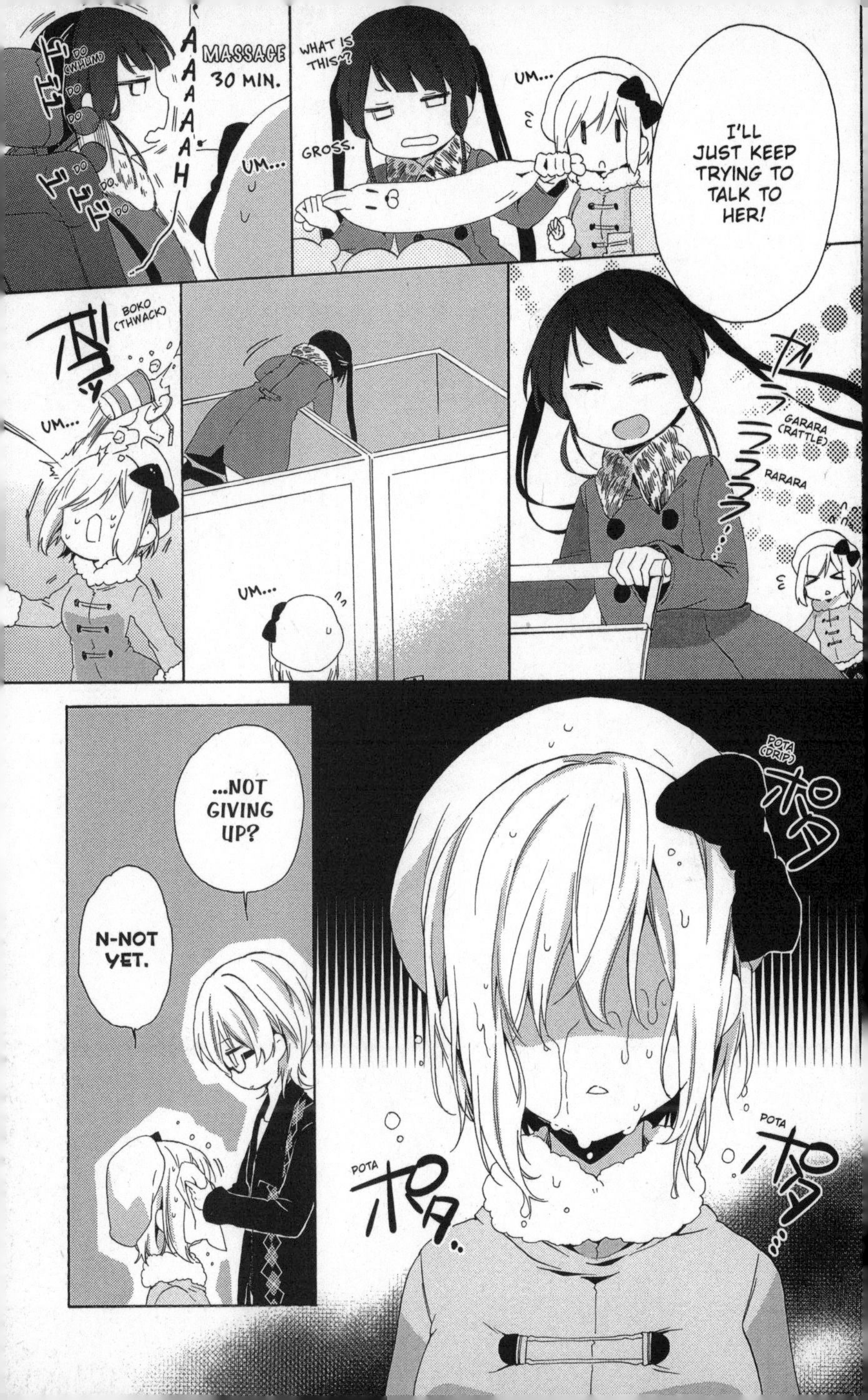
WHAT IS THIS~?
UM...
GROSS.
MASSAGE 30 MIN.
AAAAAAH
DO (WHUN) DO DO DO
UM...
DO DO DO
I'LL JUST KEEP TRYING TO TALK TO HER!
GARARA (RATTLE)
RARARA
UM...
BOKO (THWACK)
UM...
POTA (DRIP)
POTA
POTA
...NOT GIVING UP?
N-NOT YET.

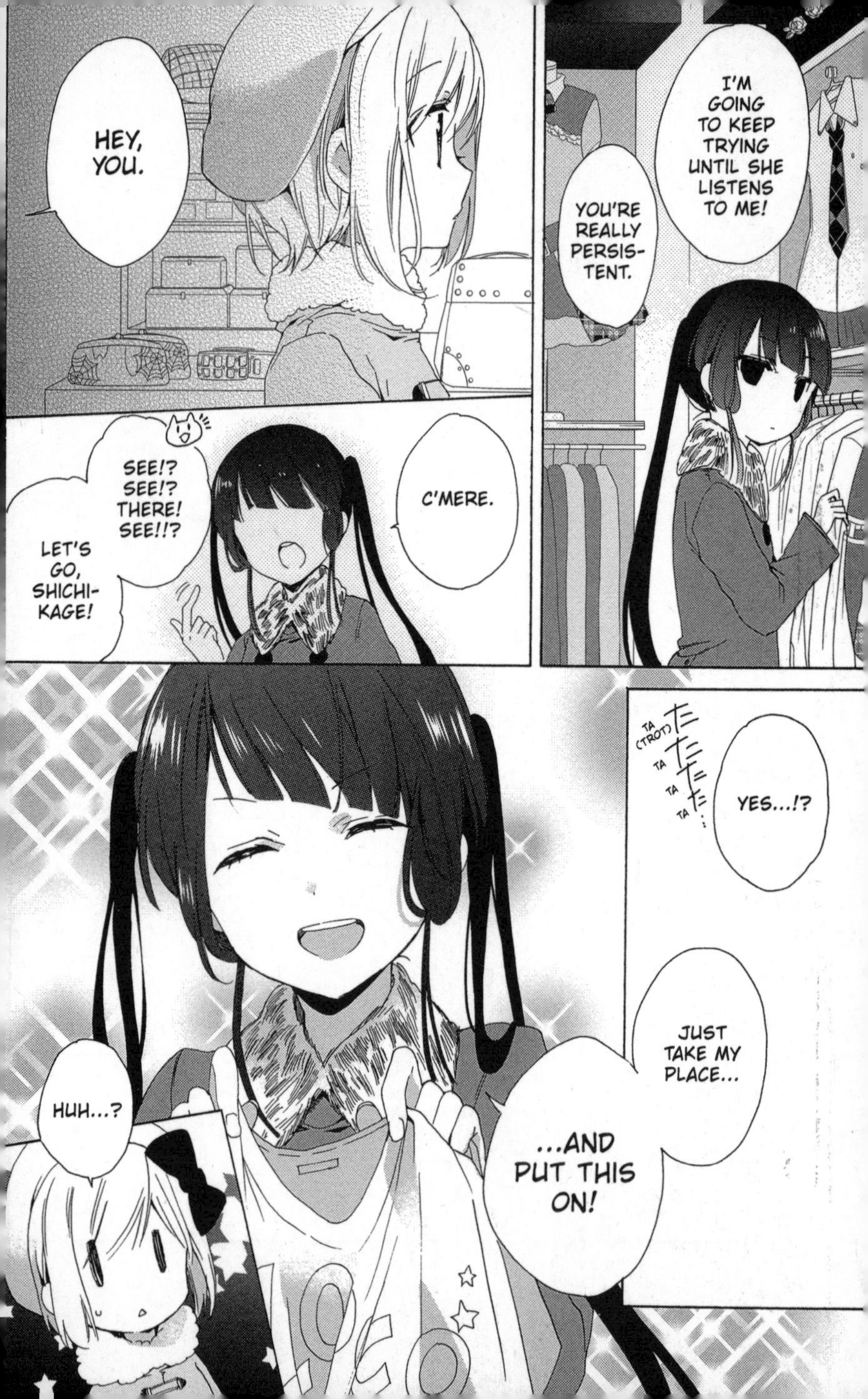
I'M GOING TO KEEP TRYING UNTIL SHE LISTENS TO ME!
YOU'RE REALLY PERSIS-TENT.
HEY, YOU.
C'MERE.
SEE!? SEE!? THERE! SEE!!?
LET'S GO, SHICHI-KAGE!
TA (TROT) TA TA TA
YES...!?
JUST TAKE MY PLACE...
...AND PUT THIS ON!
HUH...?

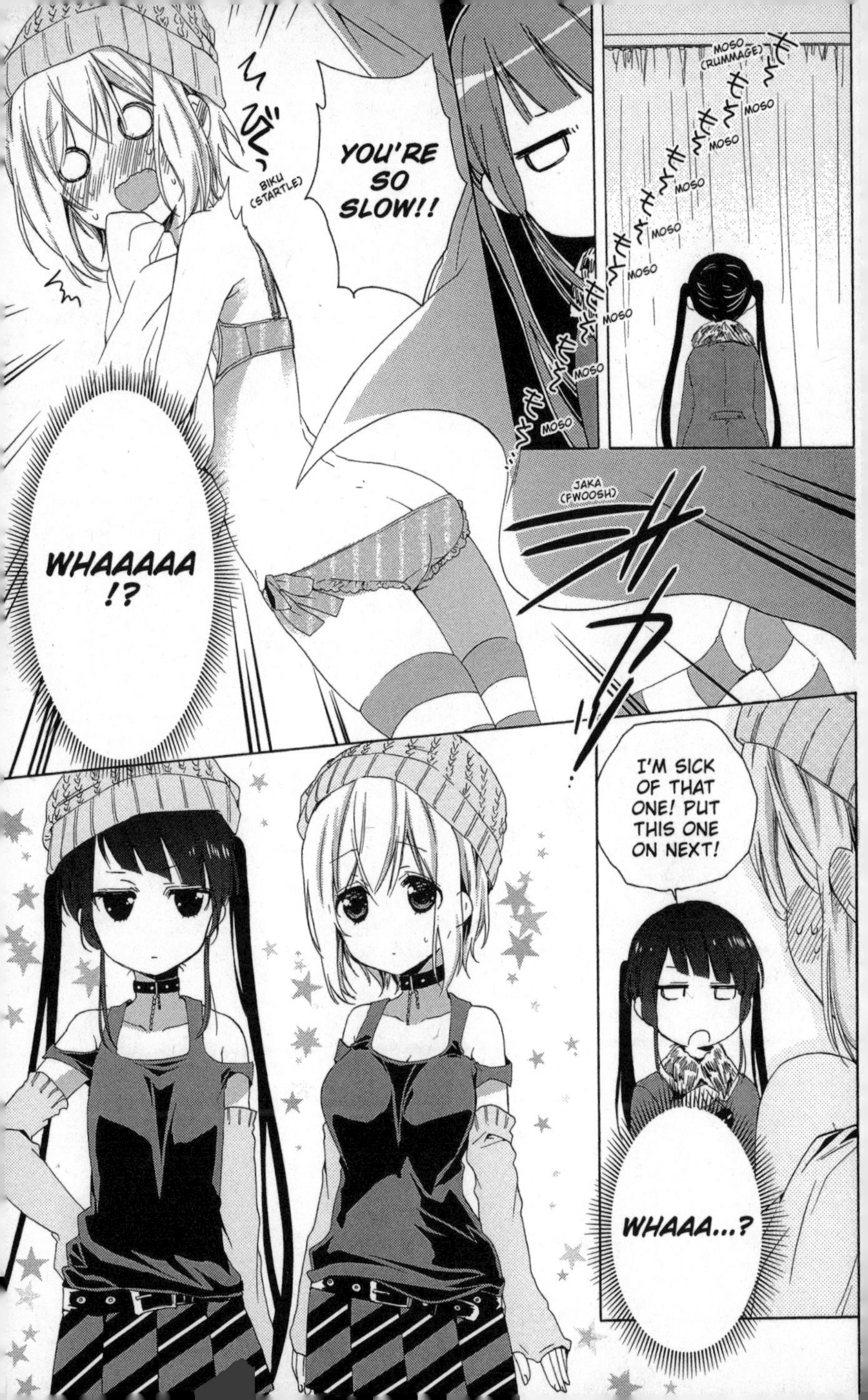

MOSO (RUMMAGE)
MOSO
MOSO
MOSO
MOSO
MOSO
MOSO
MOSO
MOSO
JAKA (FWOOSH)
BIKU (STARTLE)
YOU'RE SO SLOW!!
WHAAAAA !?
I'M SICK OF THAT ONE! PUT THIS ONE ON NEXT!
WHAAA...?

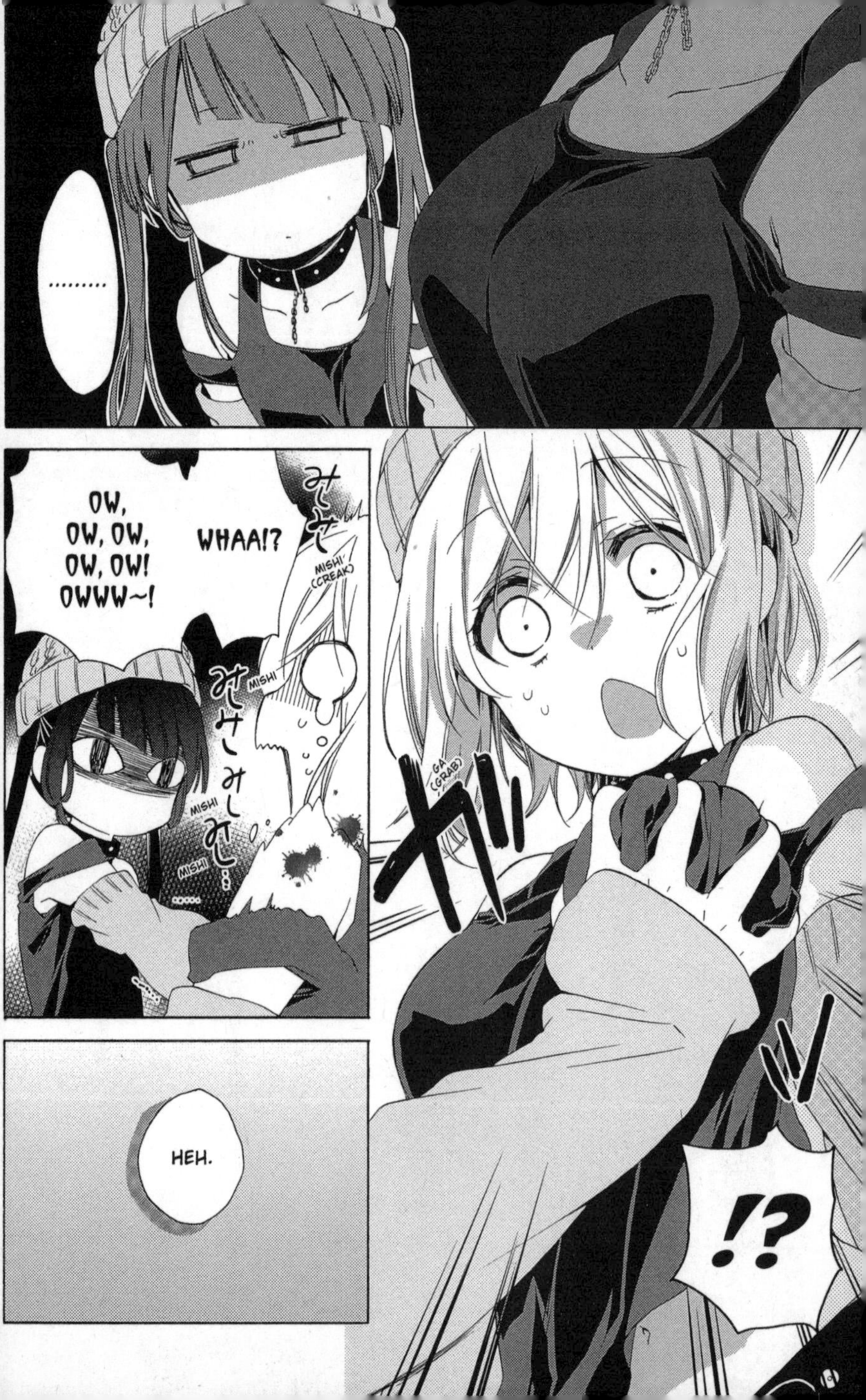

..........
GA (GRAB)
!?
みしみし
MISHI (CREAK)
WHAA!?
OW, OW, OW, OW, OW! OWWW~!
みしみしみしみし…
MISHI
MISHI
MISHI
HEH.

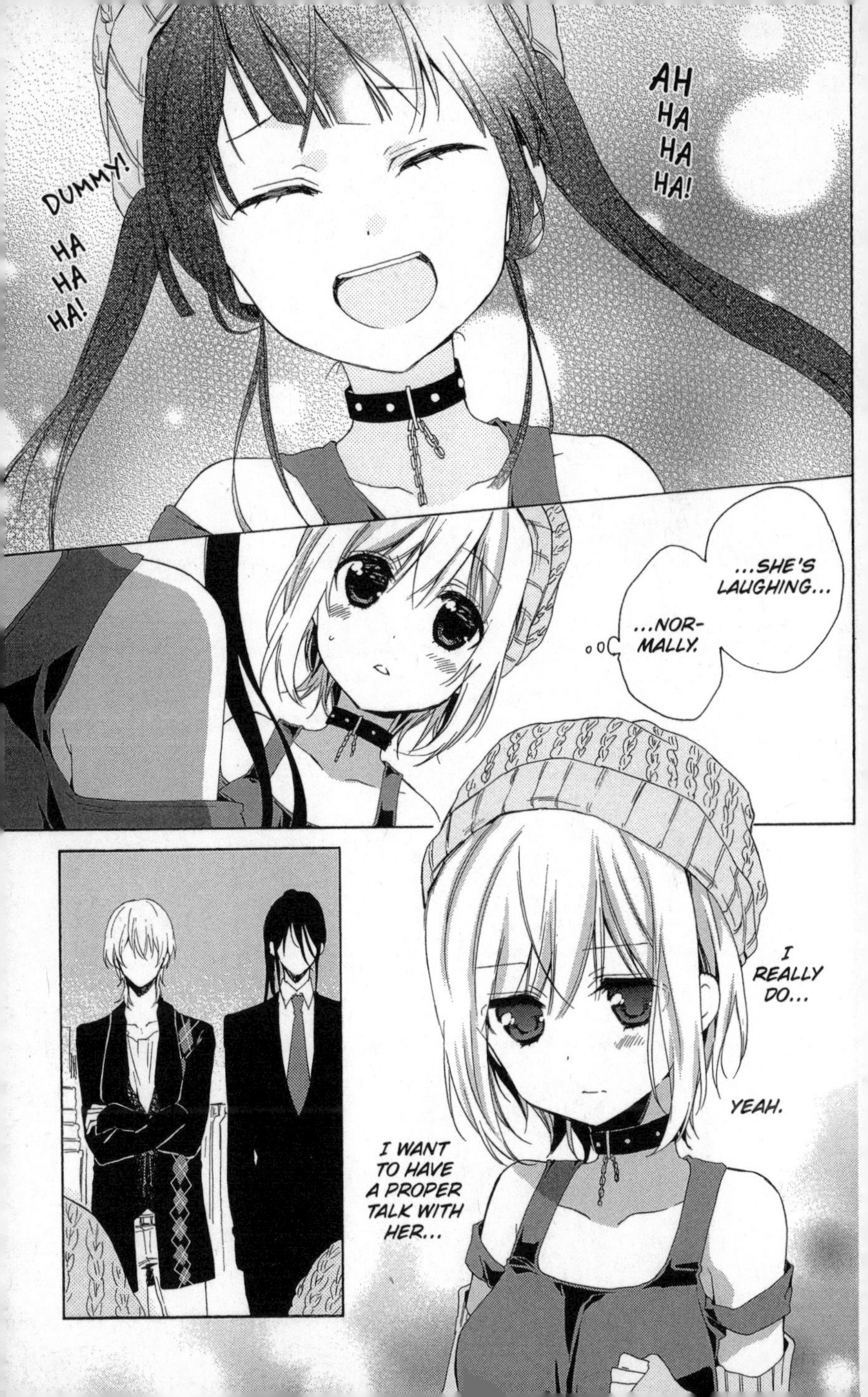
AH HA HA HA!
DUMMY!
HA HA HA!
...SHE'S LAUGHING...
...NOR-MALLY.
I REALLY DO...
YEAH.
I WANT TO HAVE A PROPER TALK WITH HER...

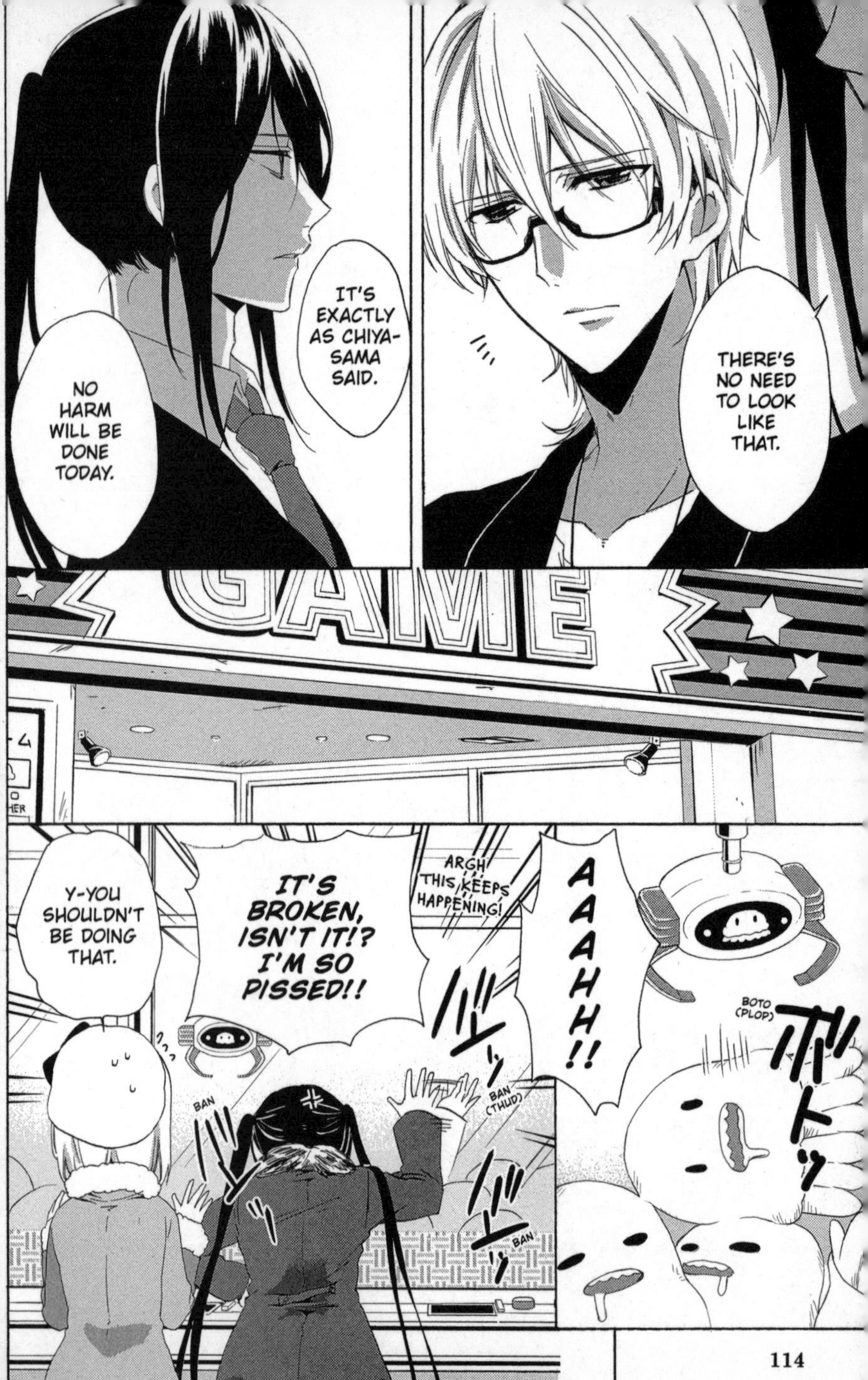
THERE'S NO NEED TO LOOK LIKE THAT.
IT'S EXACTLY AS CHIYA-SAMA SAID.
NO HARM WILL BE DONE TODAY.
GAME
AAAAHH!!
BOTO (PLOP)
ARGH THIS KEEPS HAPPENING!
IT'S BROKEN, ISN'T IT!? I'M SO PISSED!!
BAN (THUD)
BAN
Y-YOU SHOULDN'T BE DOING THAT.
BAN

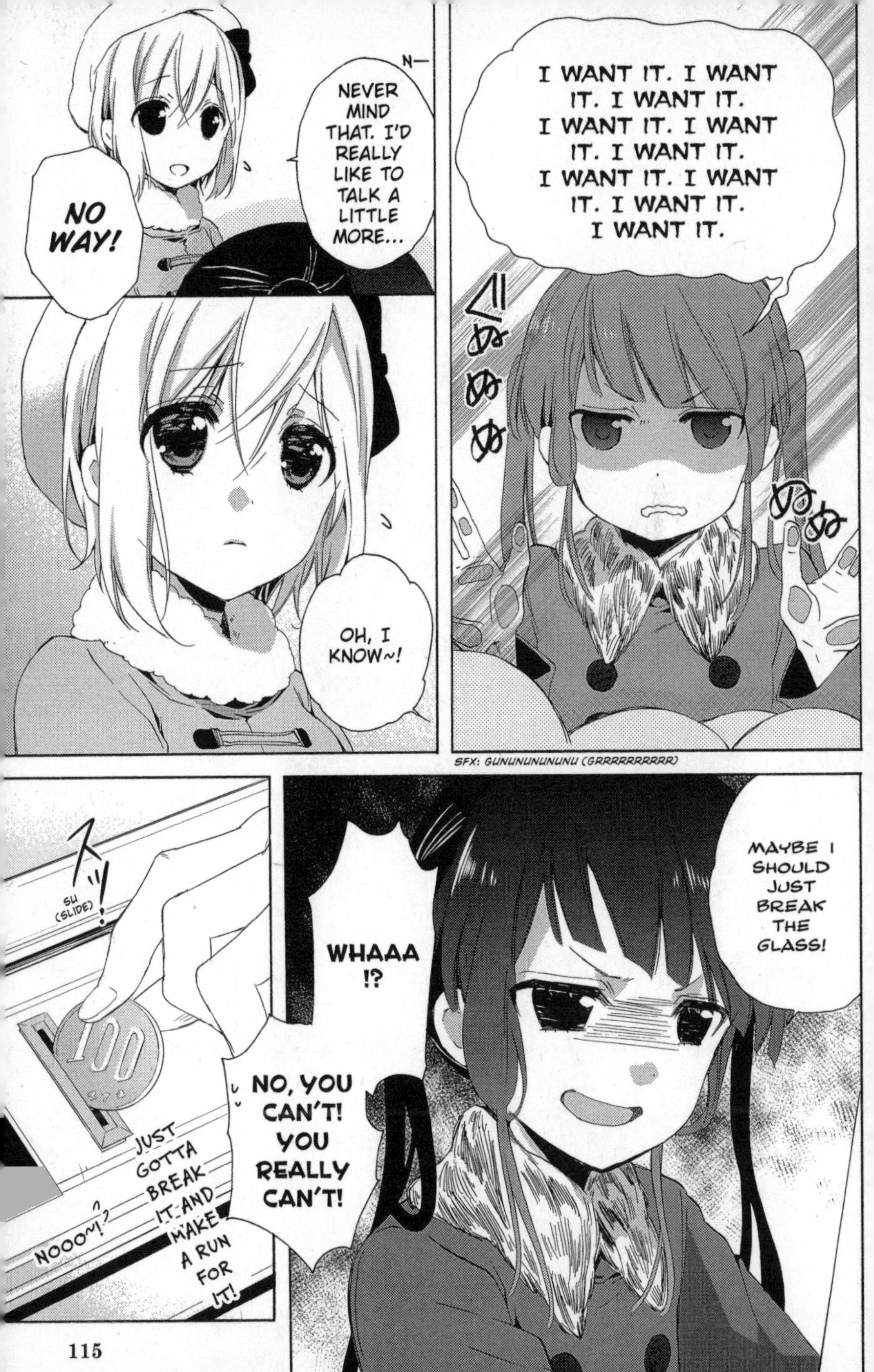

I WANT IT. I WANT IT. I WANT IT. I WANT IT. I WANT IT. I WANT IT. I WANT IT.
ぐぬぬぬぬ
ぬぬ
SFX: GUNUNUNUNUNU (GRRRRRRRRRR)
N—
NEVER MIND THAT. I'D REALLY LIKE TO TALK A LITTLE MORE...
NO WAY!
OH, I KNOW~!
MAYBE I SHOULD JUST BREAK THE GLASS!
WHAAA!?
NO, YOU CAN'T! YOU REALLY CAN'T!
SU (SLIDE)
JUST GOTTA BREAK IT AND MAKE A RUN FOR IT!
NOOO~!?

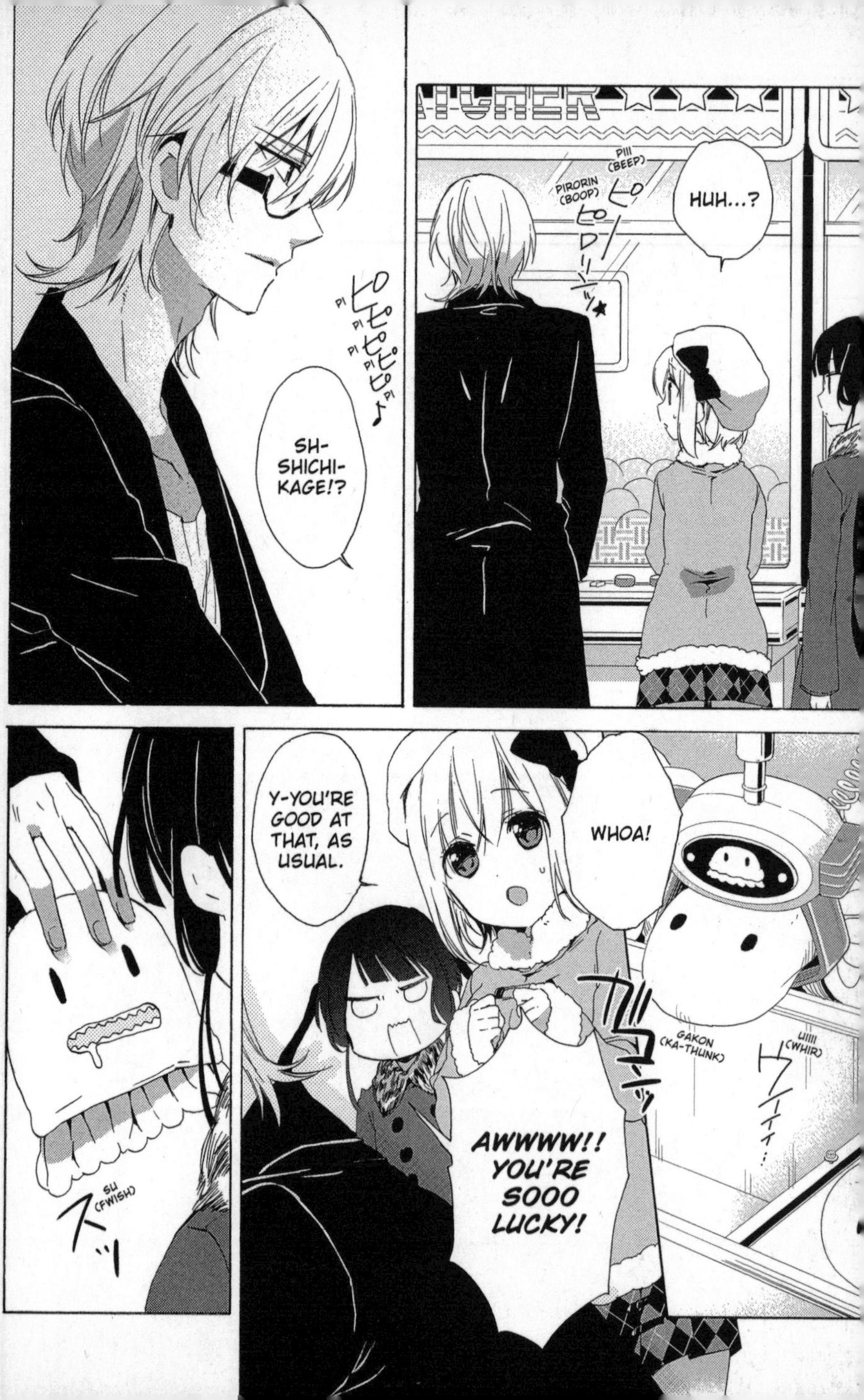
HUH...?
PIII (BEEP)
PIRORIN (BOOP)
PI PI PI PI PI
SH-SHICHIKAGE!?
WHOA!
UIII (WHIR)
GAKON (KA-THUNK)
Y-YOU'RE GOOD AT THAT, AS USUAL.
AWWWW!! YOU'RE SOOO LUCKY!
SU (FWISH)

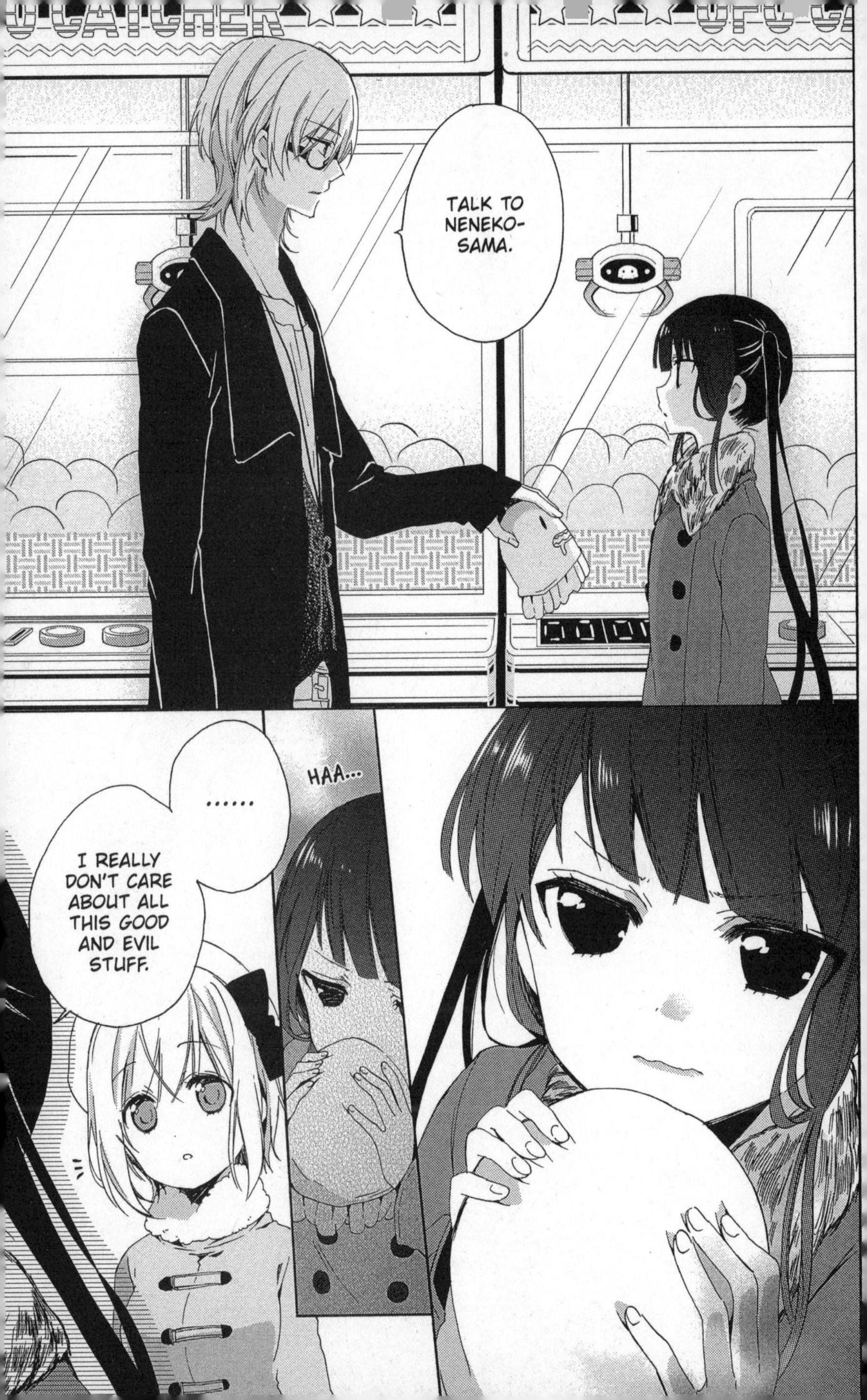
TALK TO NENEKO-SAMA.
HAA...
......
I REALLY DON'T CARE ABOUT ALL THIS GOOD AND EVIL STUFF.

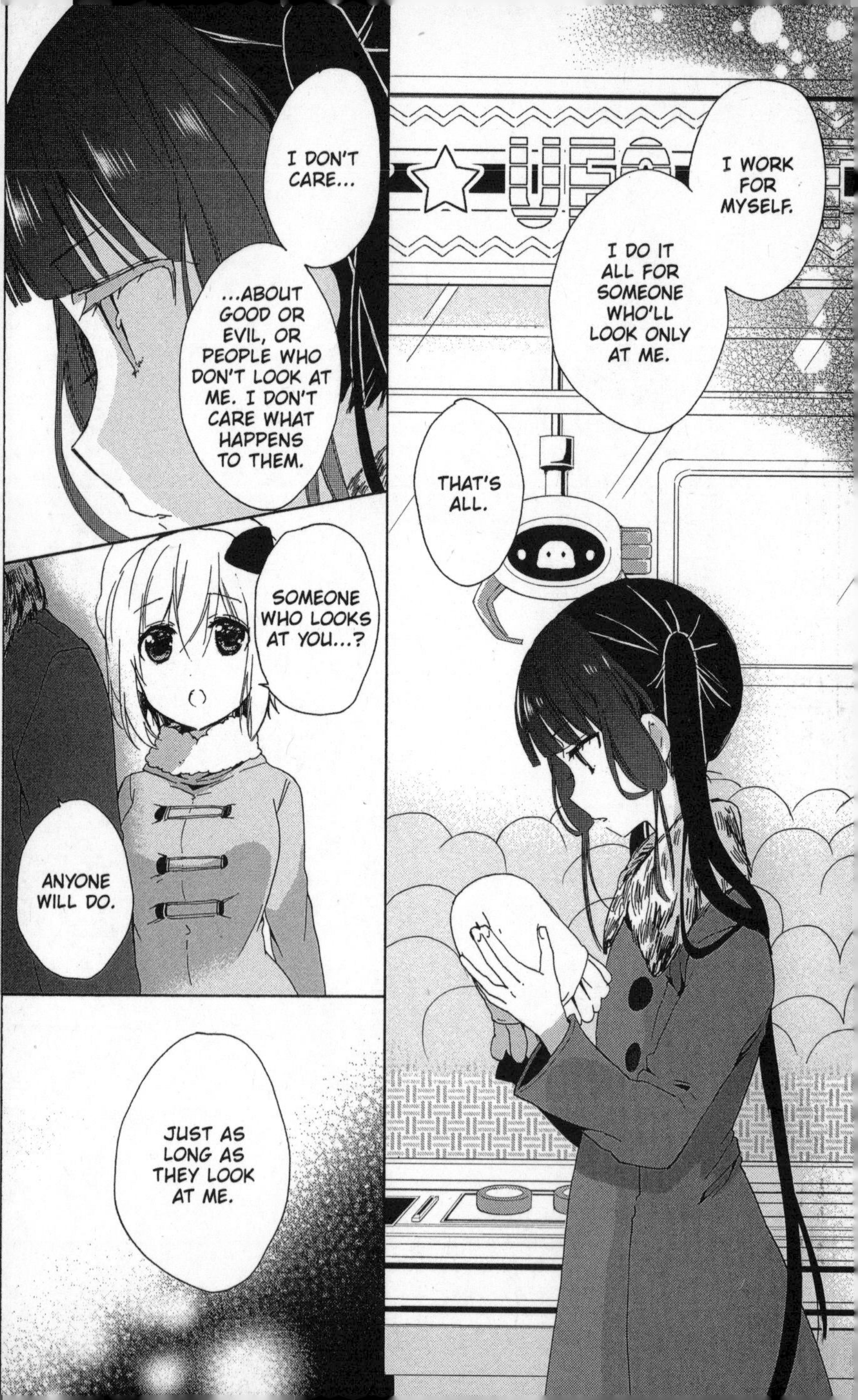
I WORK FOR MYSELF.
I DO IT ALL FOR SOMEONE WHO'LL LOOK ONLY AT ME.
THAT'S ALL.
I DON'T CARE...
...ABOUT GOOD OR EVIL, OR PEOPLE WHO DON'T LOOK AT ME. I DON'T CARE WHAT HAPPENS TO THEM.
SOMEONE WHO LOOKS AT YOU...?
ANYONE WILL DO.
JUST AS LONG AS THEY LOOK AT ME.

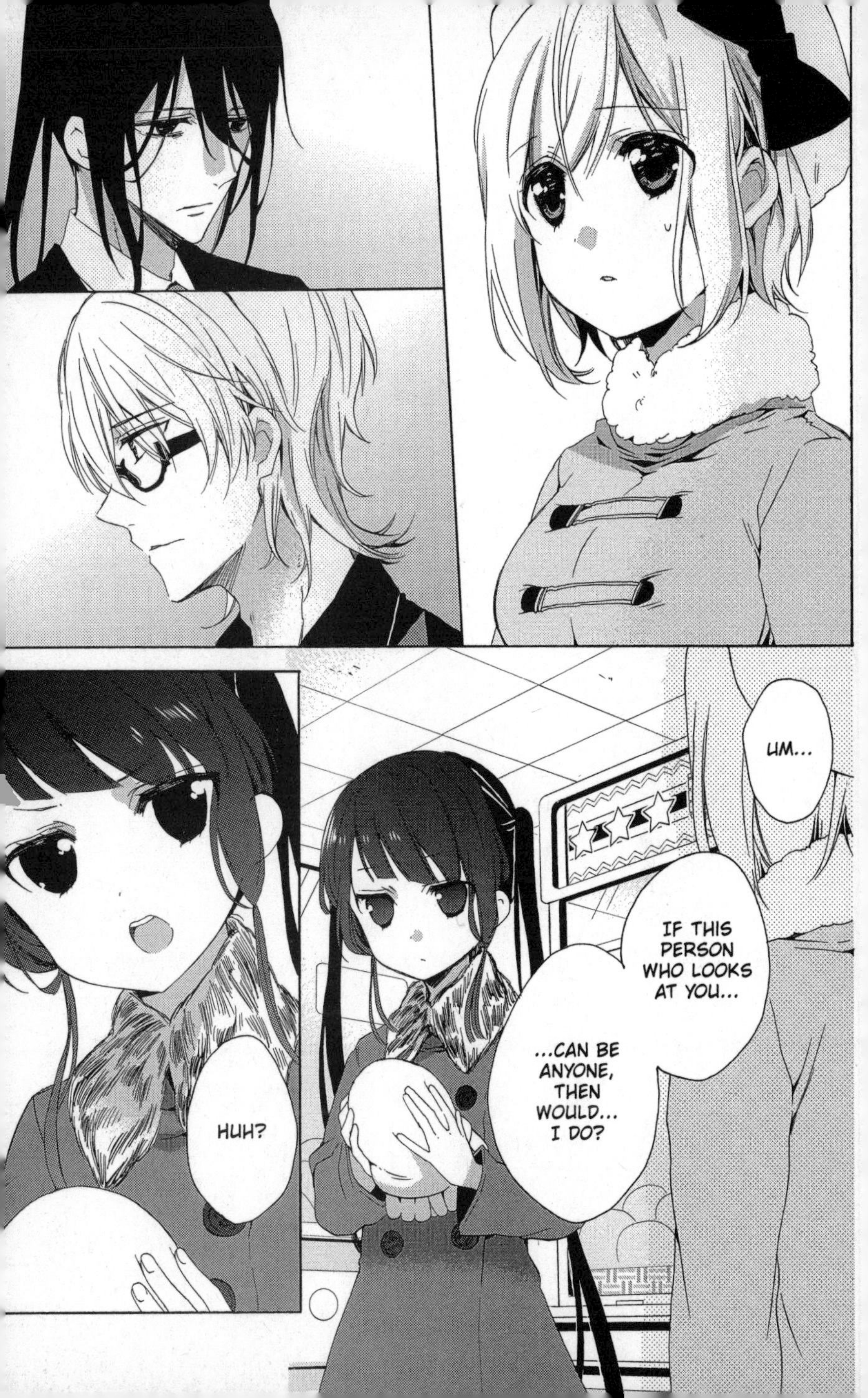
UM...
IF THIS PERSON WHO LOOKS AT YOU...
...CAN BE ANYONE, THEN WOULD... I DO?
HUH?

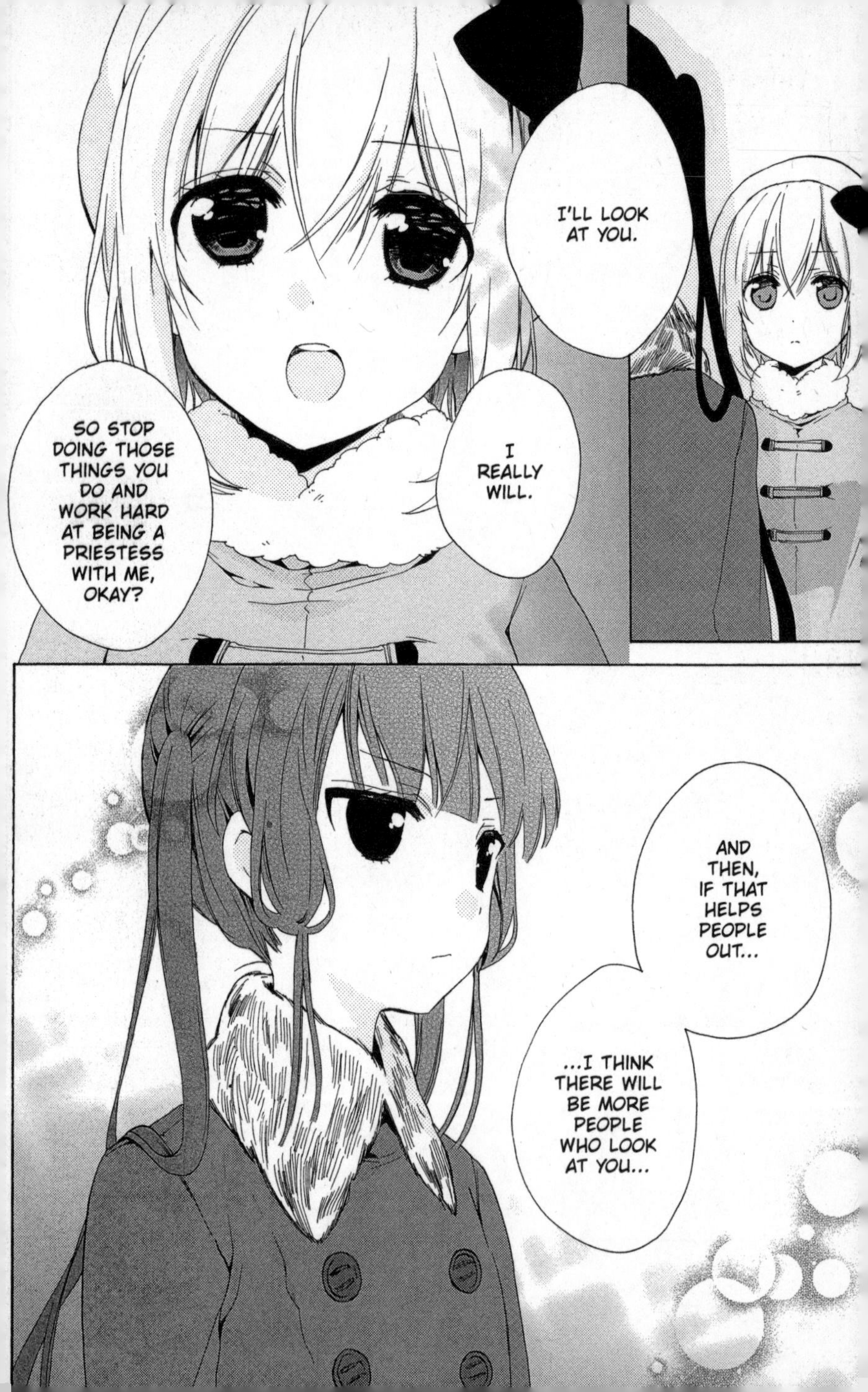
I'LL LOOK AT YOU.
I REALLY WILL.
SO STOP DOING THOSE THINGS YOU DO AND WORK HARD AT BEING A PRIESTESS WITH ME, OKAY?
AND THEN, IF THAT HELPS PEOPLE OUT...
...I THINK THERE WILL BE MORE PEOPLE WHO LOOK AT YOU...

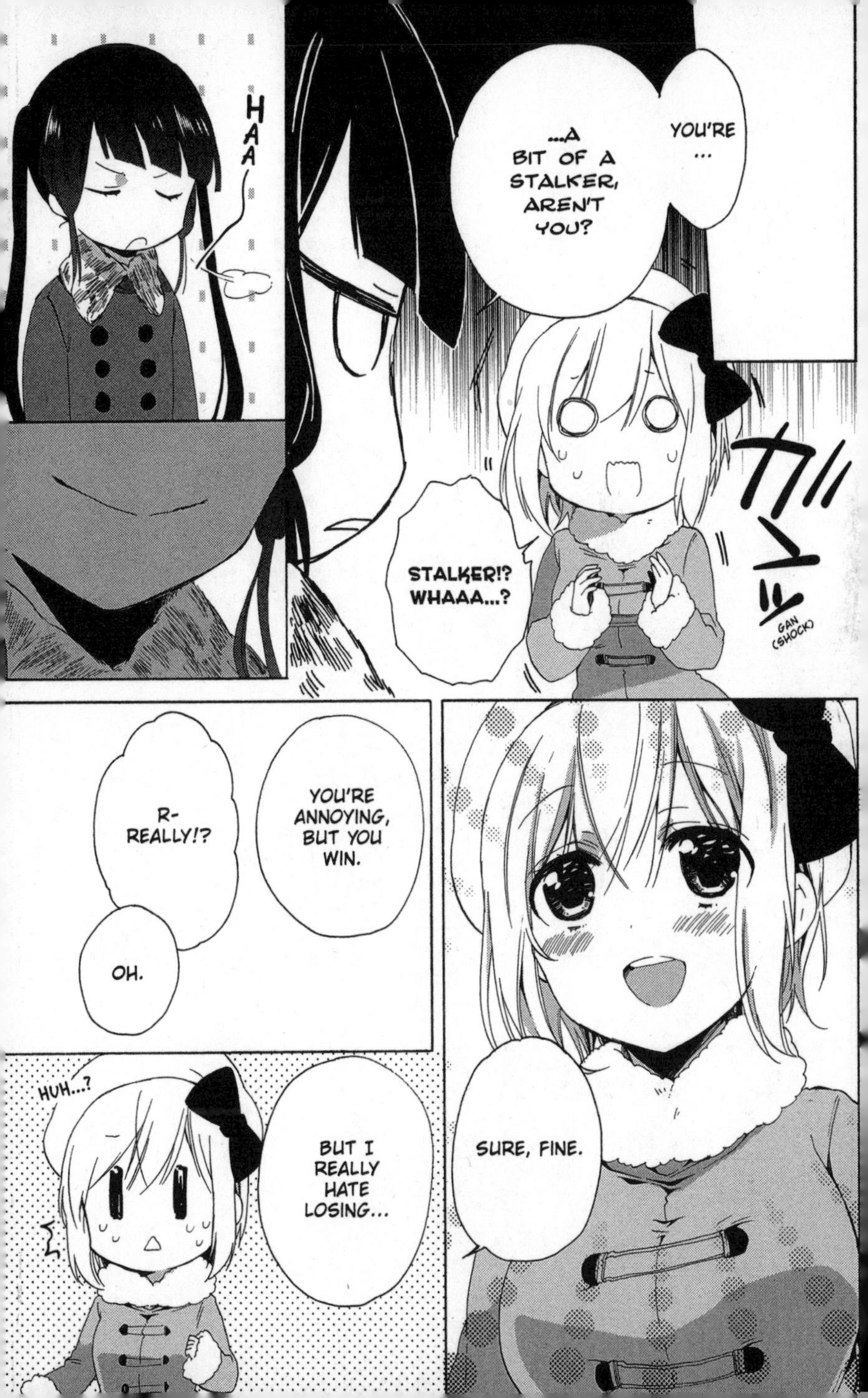
YOU'RE ...
...A BIT OF A STALKER, AREN'T YOU?
STALKER!? WHAAA...?
GAN (SHOCK)
HAA
SURE, FINE.
YOU'RE ANNOYING, BUT YOU WIN.
R-REALLY!?
OH.
BUT I REALLY HATE LOSING...
HUH...?

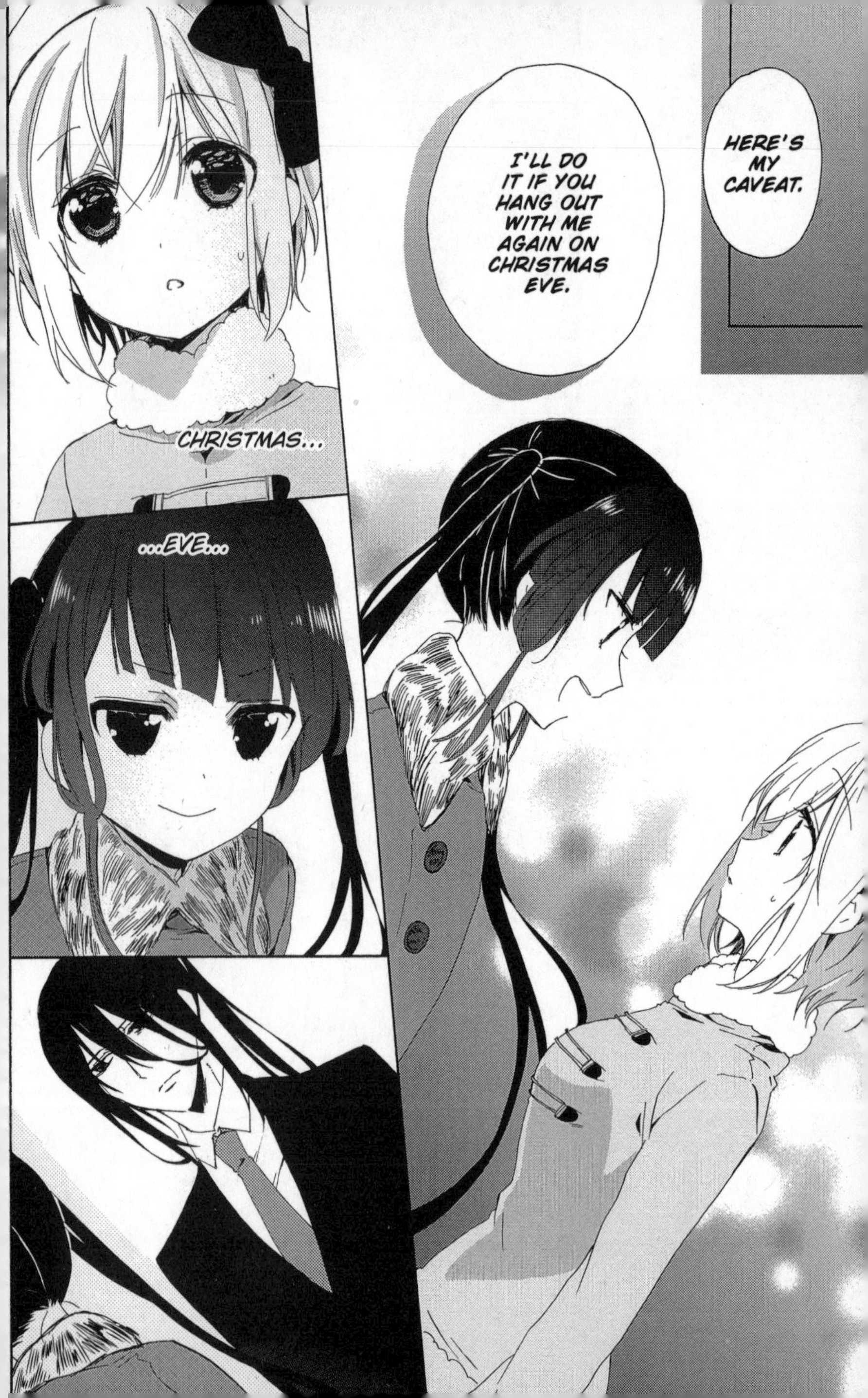
HERE'S MY CAVEAT.
I'LL DO IT IF YOU HANG OUT WITH ME AGAIN ON CHRISTMAS EVE.
CHRISTMAS...
...EVE...

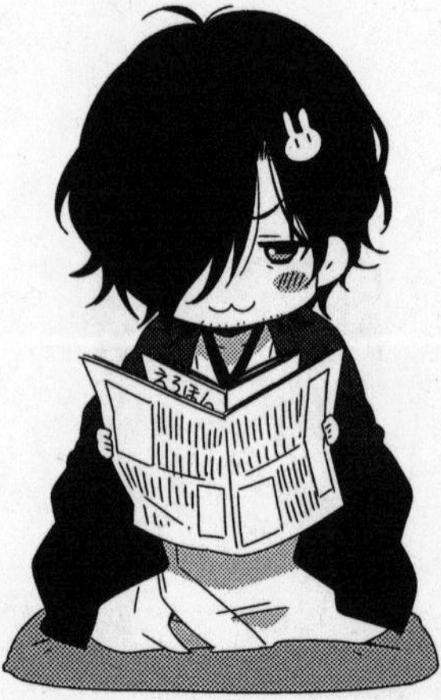
えろほん

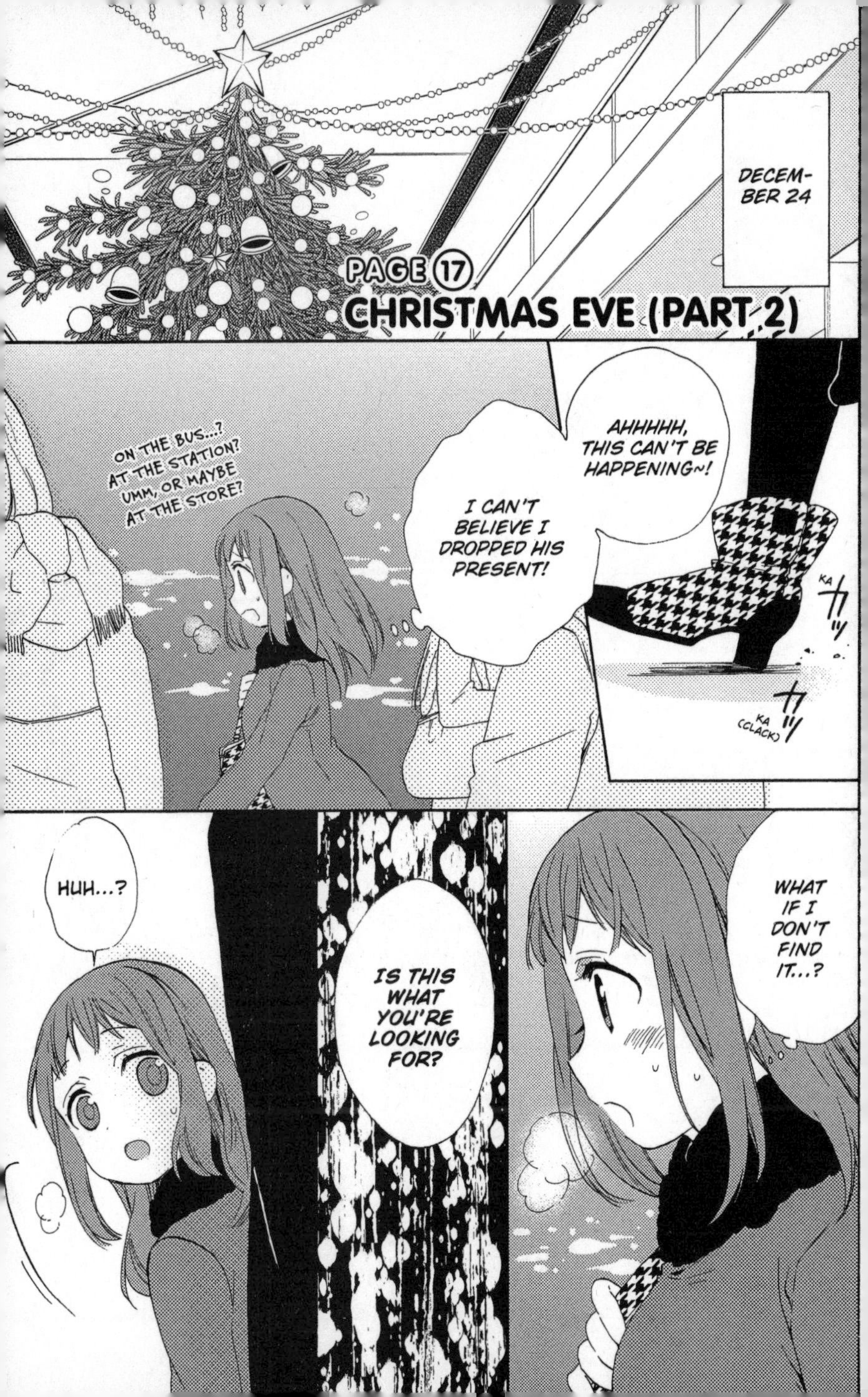
DECEMBER 24
PAGE 17
CHRISTMAS EVE (PART 2)
KA
KA (CLACK)
AHHHHH, THIS CAN'T BE HAPPENING~!
I CAN'T BELIEVE I DROPPED HIS PRESENT!
ON THE BUS...? AT THE STATION? UMM, OR MAYBE AT THE STORE?
WHAT IF I DON'T FIND IT...?
IS THIS WHAT YOU'RE LOOKING FOR?
HUH...?

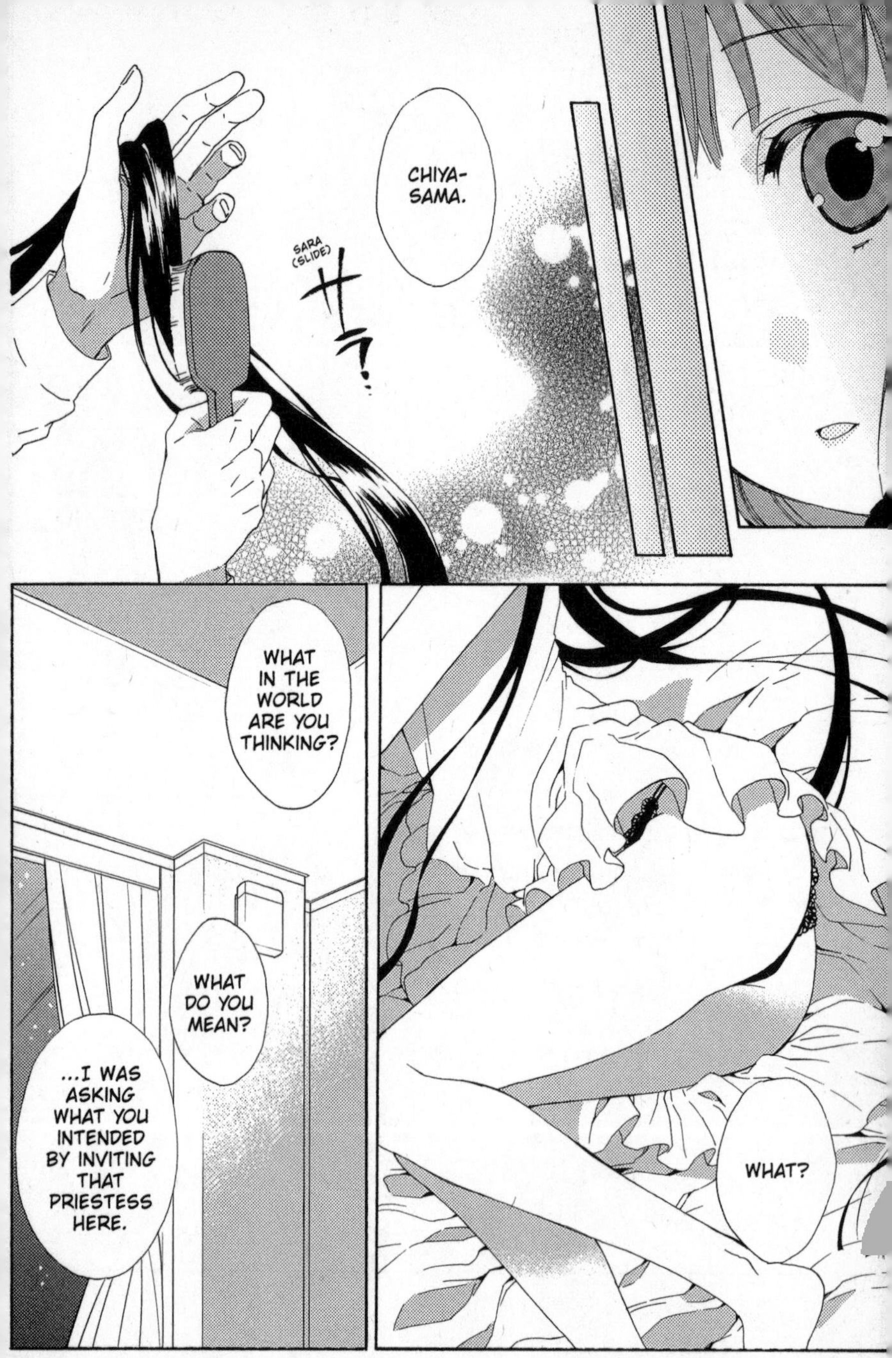
CHIYA-SAMA.
SARA (SLIDE)
WHAT?
WHAT IN THE WORLD ARE YOU THINKING?
WHAT DO YOU MEAN?
...I WAS ASKING WHAT YOU INTENDED BY INVITING THAT PRIESTESS HERE.

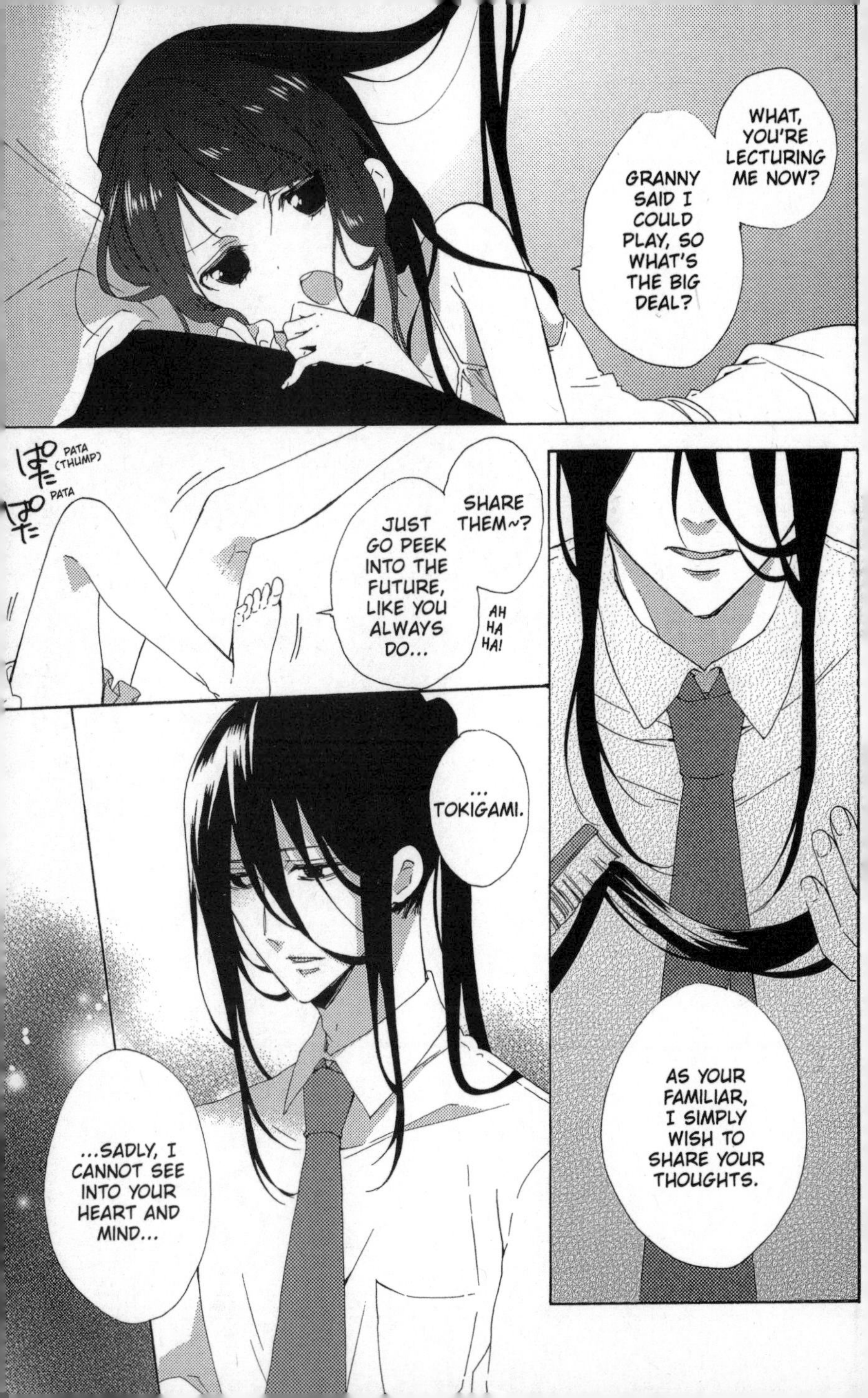
WHAT, YOU'RE LECTURING ME NOW?
GRANNY SAID I COULD PLAY, SO WHAT'S THE BIG DEAL?
AS YOUR FAMILIAR, I SIMPLY WISH TO SHARE YOUR THOUGHTS.
SHARE THEM~?
JUST GO PEEK INTO THE FUTURE, LIKE YOU ALWAYS DO...
AH HA HA!
ぱた PATA (THUMP)
ぱた PATA
...TOKIGAMI.
...SADLY, I CANNOT SEE INTO YOUR HEART AND MIND...

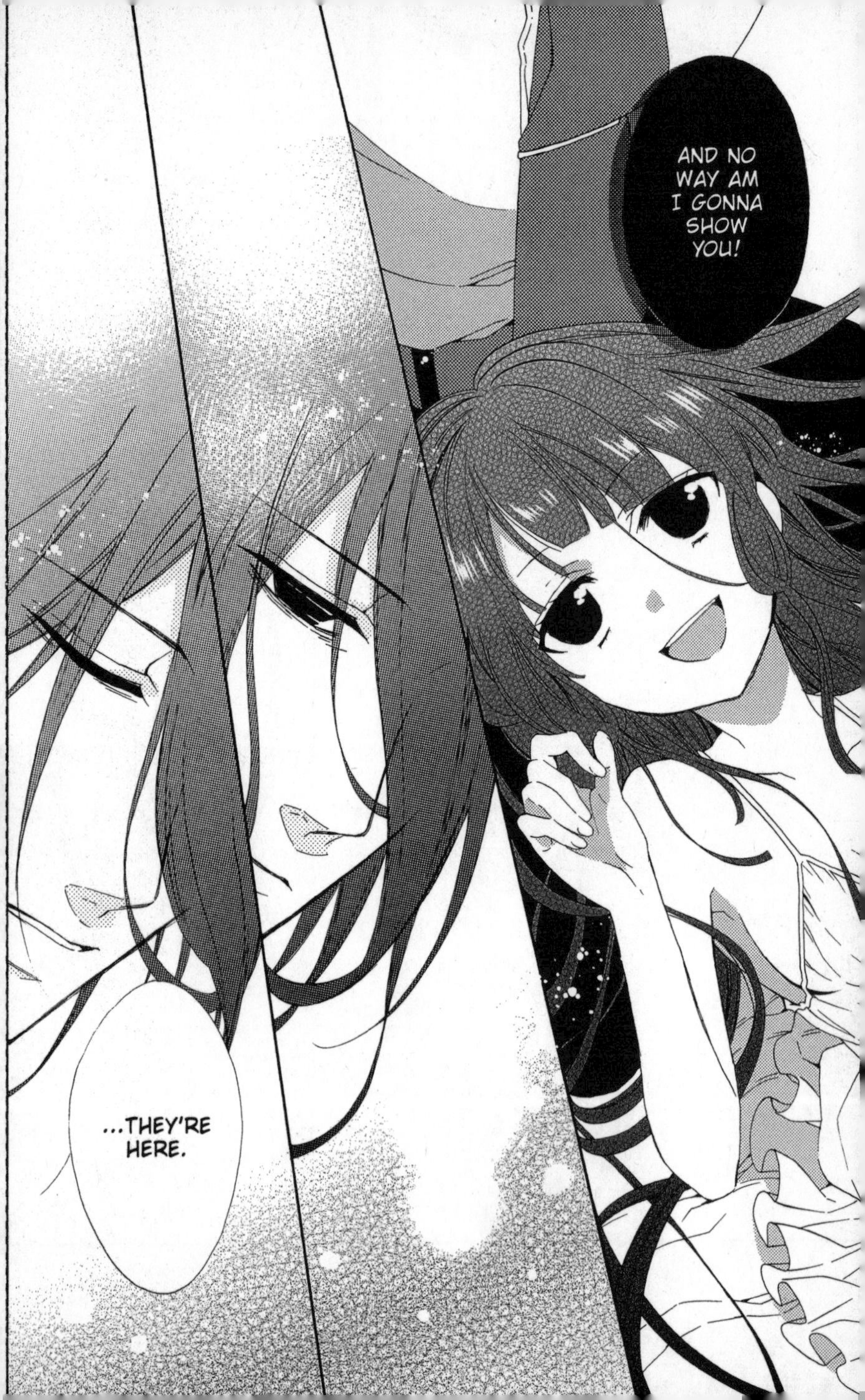
AND NO WAY AM I GONNA SHOW YOU!
...THEY'RE HERE.

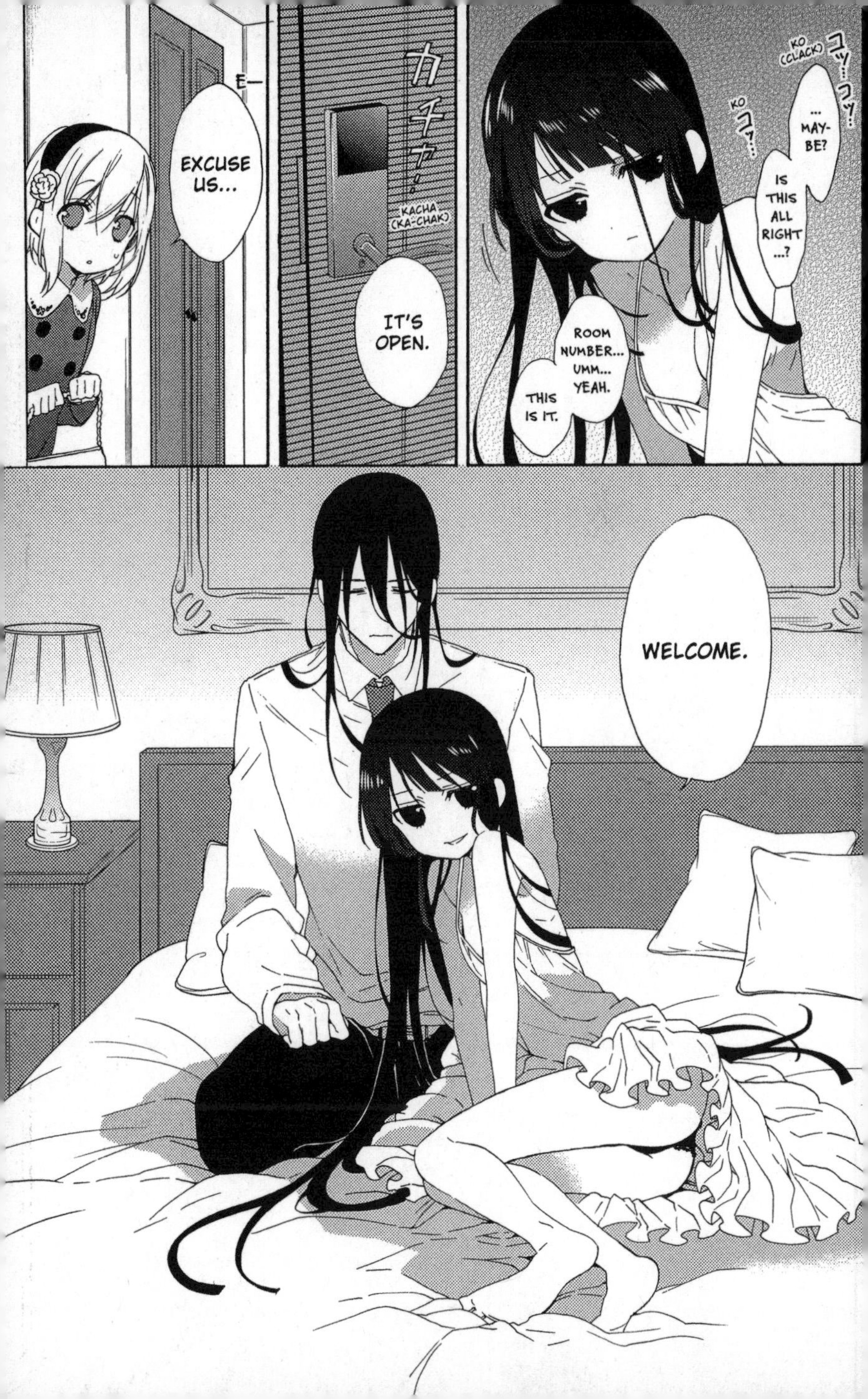
KO (CLACK) コツ…コツ…
KO コツ…
...MAY-BE?
IS THIS ALL RIGHT ...?
ROOM NUMBER... UMM... YEAH.
THIS IS IT.
カチャ!
KACHA (KA-CHAK)
IT'S OPEN.
E—
EXCUSE US...
WELCOME.

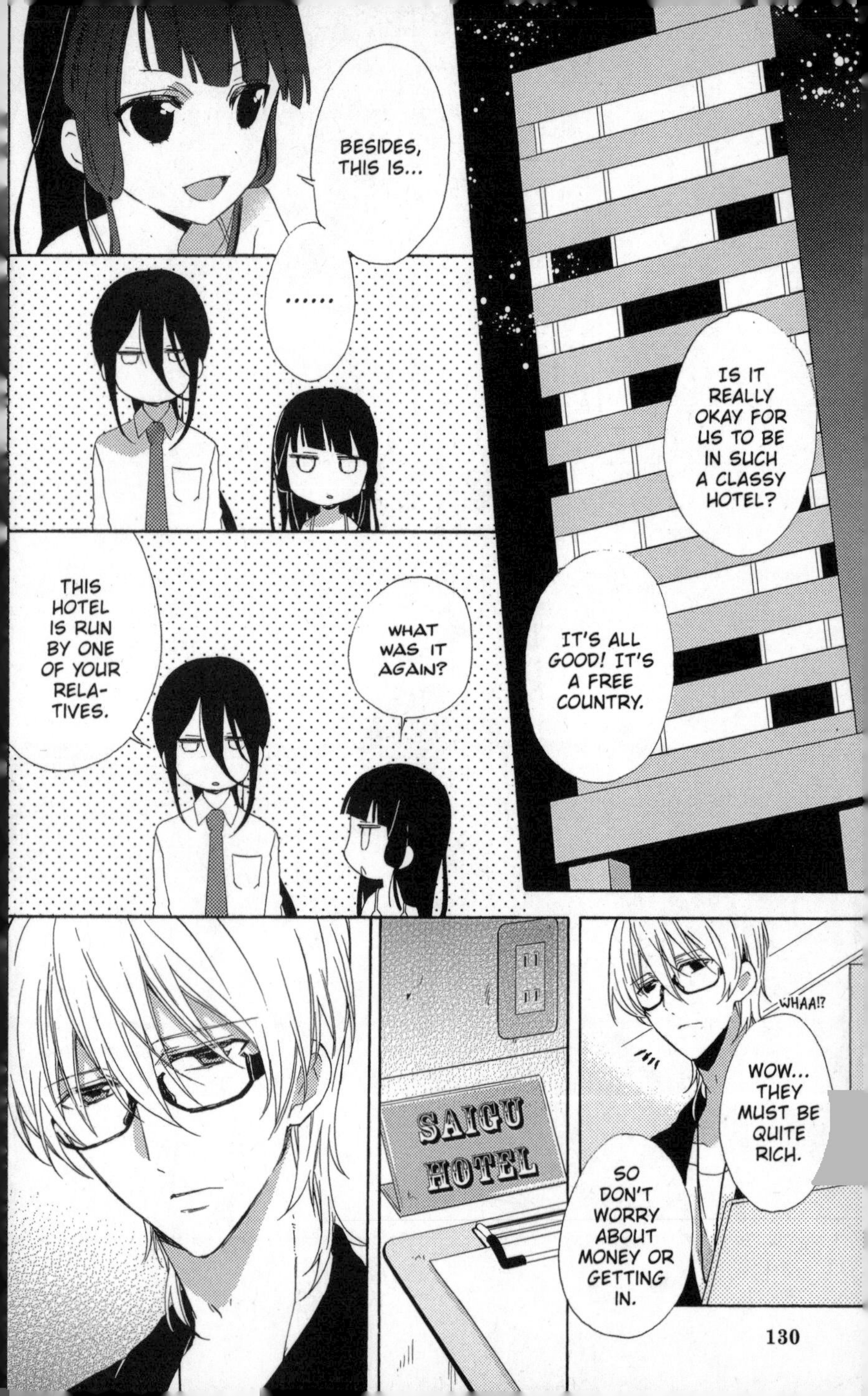
IS IT REALLY OKAY FOR US TO BE IN SUCH A CLASSY HOTEL?
IT'S ALL GOOD! IT'S A FREE COUNTRY.
BESIDES, THIS IS...
......
WHAT WAS IT AGAIN?
THIS HOTEL IS RUN BY ONE OF YOUR RELATIVES.
WHAA!?
WOW... THEY MUST BE QUITE RICH.
SO DON'T WORRY ABOUT MONEY OR GETTING IN.
SAIGU HOTEL

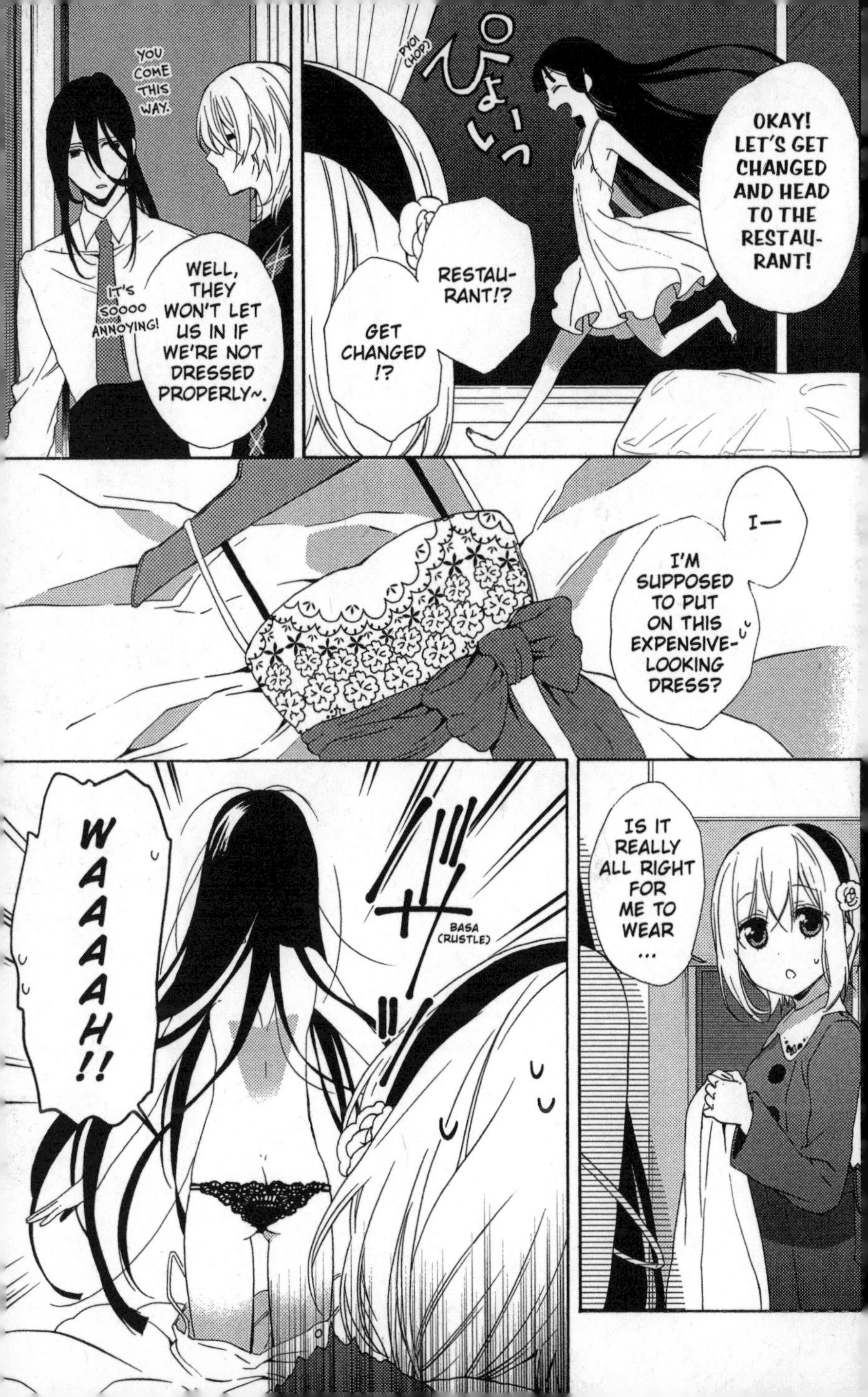

OKAY! LET'S GET CHANGED AND HEAD TO THE RESTAU-RANT!
ぴょいっ
PYOI (HOP)
RESTAU-RANT!?
GET CHANGED !?
YOU COME THIS WAY.
WELL, THEY WON'T LET US IN IF WE'RE NOT DRESSED PROPERLY~.
IT'S SOOOO ANNOYING!
I—
I'M SUPPOSED TO PUT ON THIS EXPENSIVE-LOOKING DRESS?
IS IT REALLY ALL RIGHT FOR ME TO WEAR ...
BASA (RUSTLE)
WAAAAAH!!

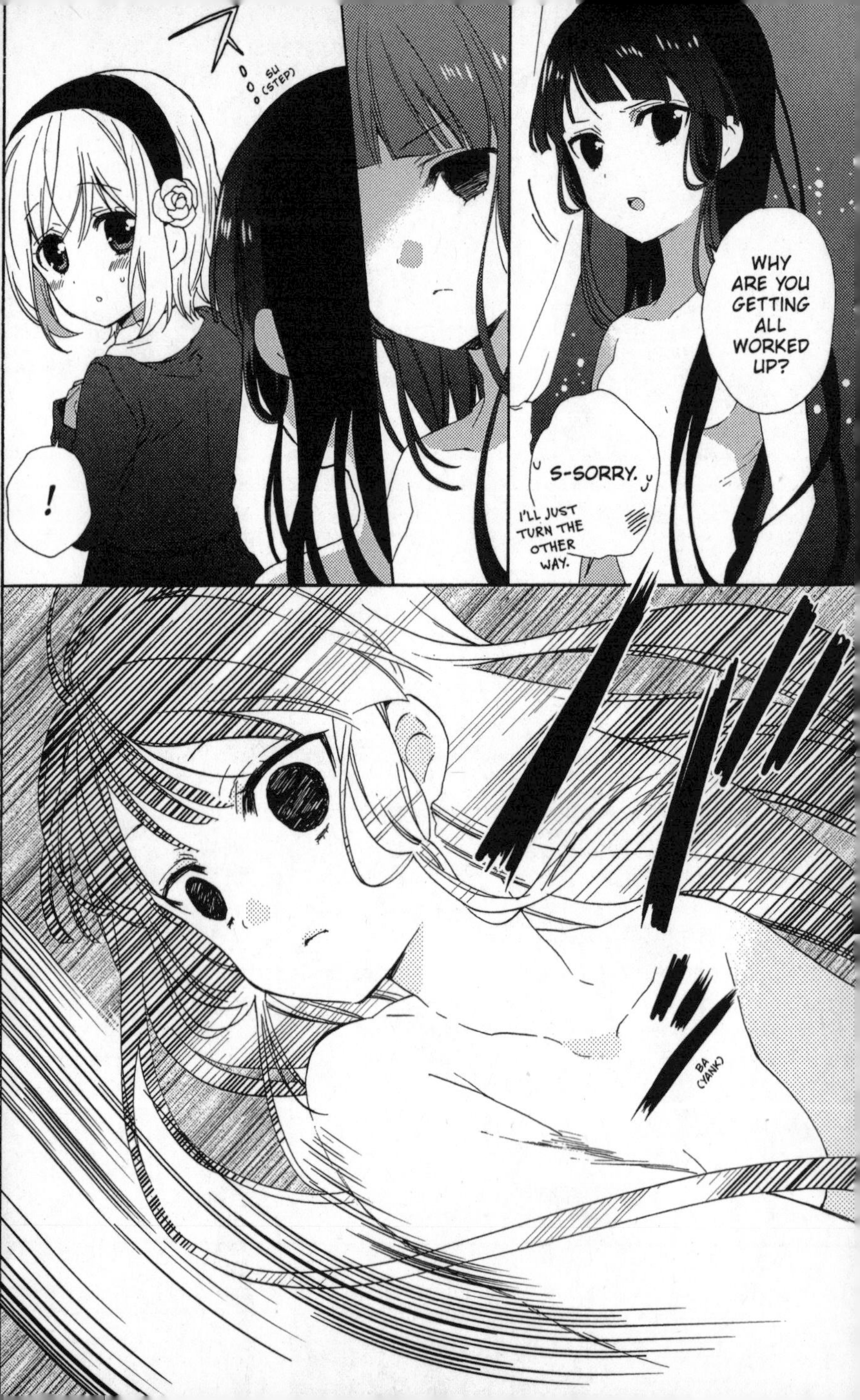
WHY ARE YOU GETTING ALL WORKED UP?
S-SORRY.
I'LL JUST TURN THE OTHER WAY.
SU (STEP)
!
BA (YANK)

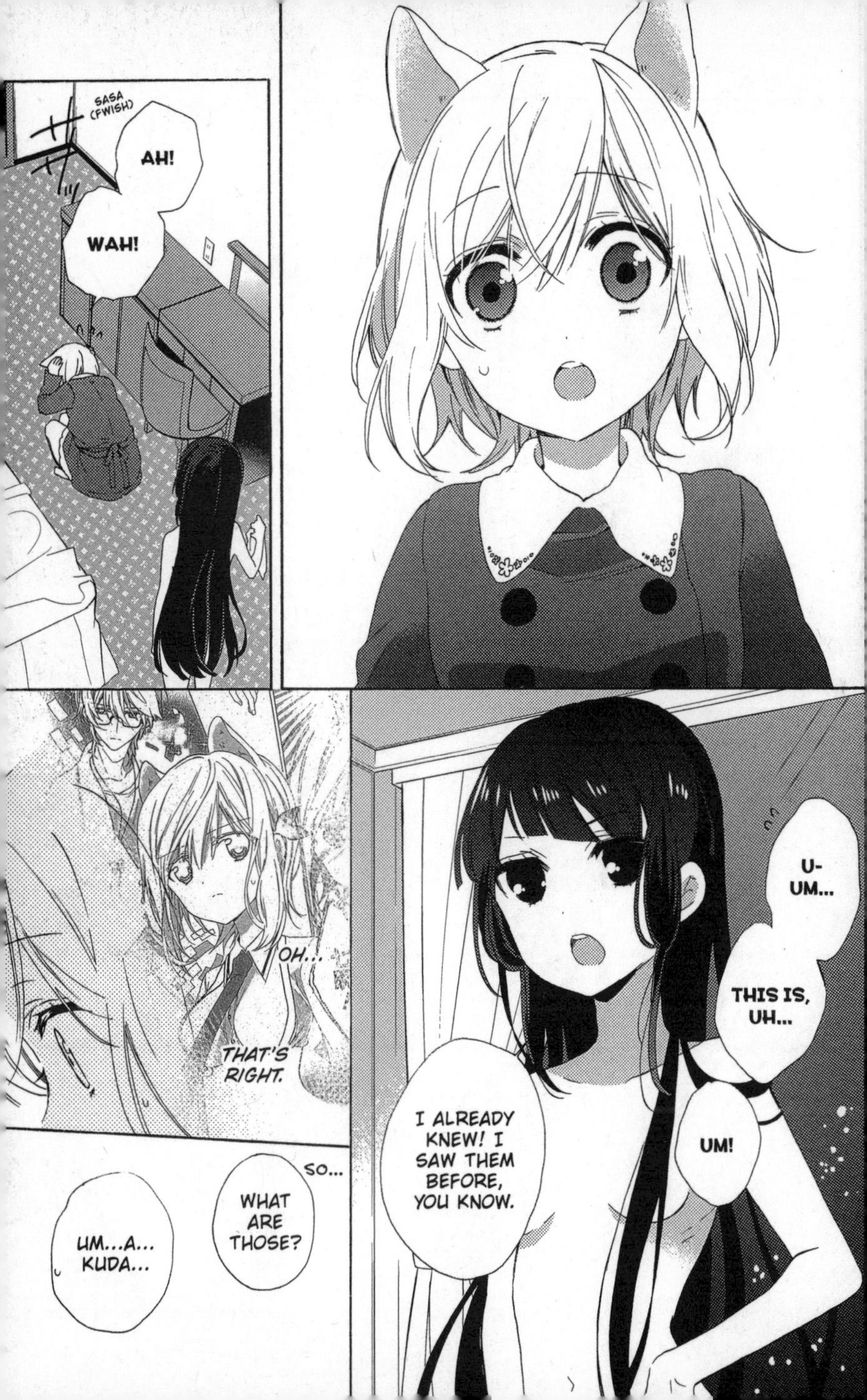
SASA (FWISH)
AH!
WAH!
U-UM...
THIS IS, UH...
UM!
I ALREADY KNEW! I SAW THEM BEFORE, YOU KNOW.
OH...
THAT'S RIGHT.
SO...
WHAT ARE THOSE?
UM...A... KUDA...

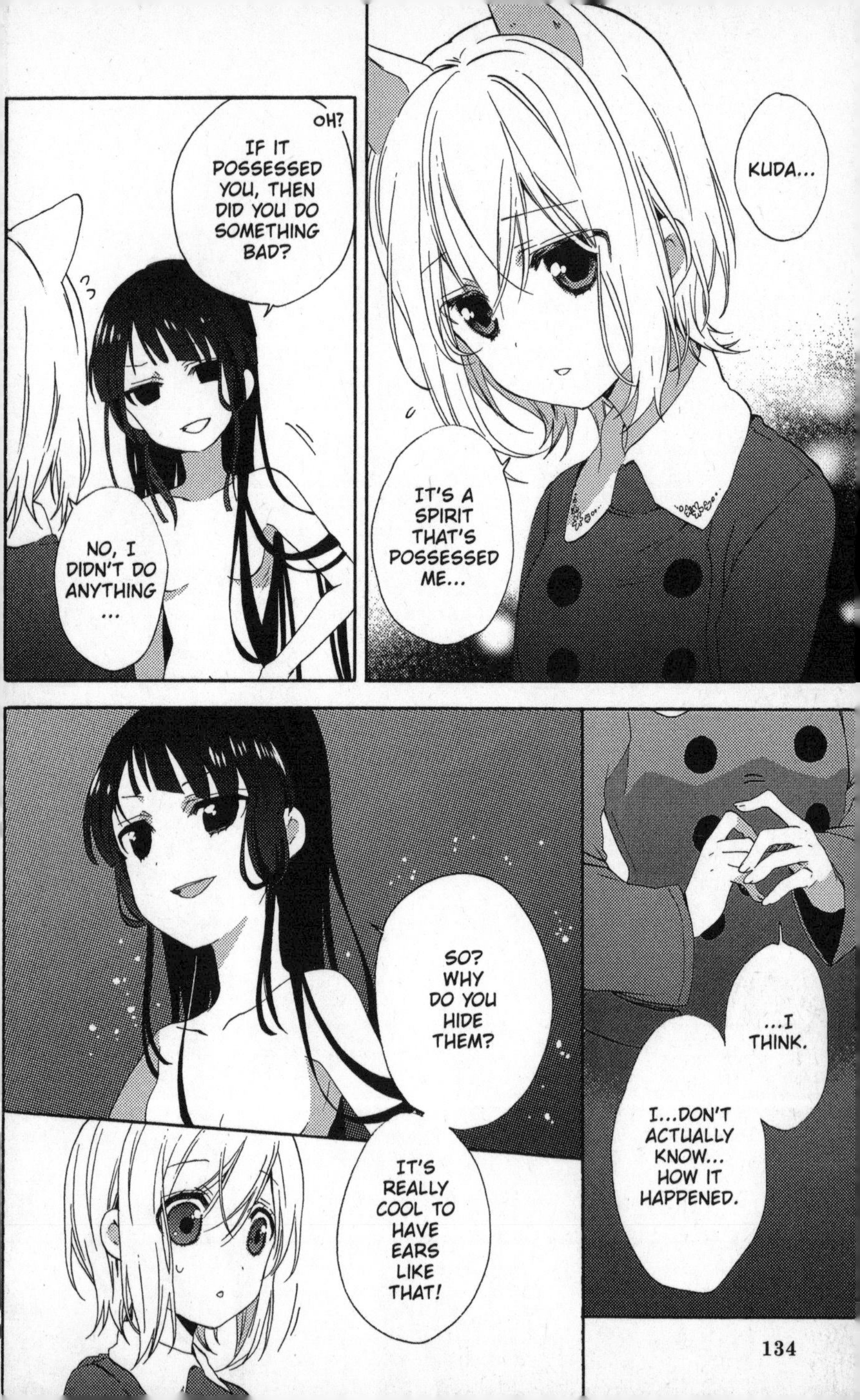
KUDA...
IT'S A SPIRIT THAT'S POSSESSED ME...
OH?
IF IT POSSESSED YOU, THEN DID YOU DO SOMETHING BAD?
NO, I DIDN'T DO ANYTHING...
...I THINK.
I...DON'T ACTUALLY KNOW... HOW IT HAPPENED.
SO? WHY DO YOU HIDE THEM?
IT'S REALLY COOL TO HAVE EARS LIKE THAT!

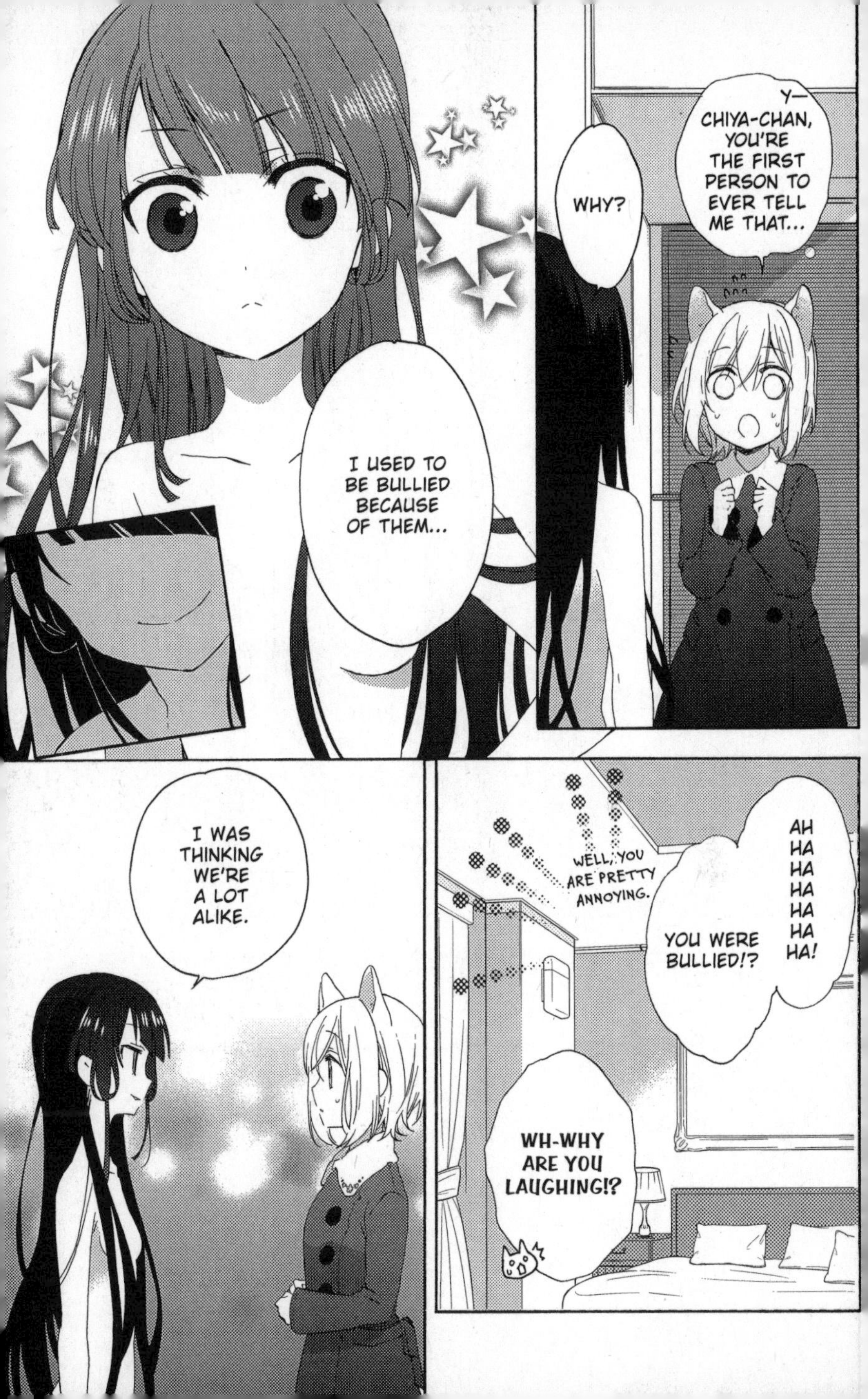

Y— CHIYA-CHAN, YOU'RE THE FIRST PERSON TO EVER TELL ME THAT...
WHY?
I USED TO BE BULLIED BECAUSE OF THEM...
YOU WERE BULLIED!?
AH HA HA HA HA HA HA!
WELL, YOU ARE PRETTY ANNOYING.
WH-WHY ARE YOU LAUGHING!?
I WAS THINKING WE'RE A LOT ALIKE.

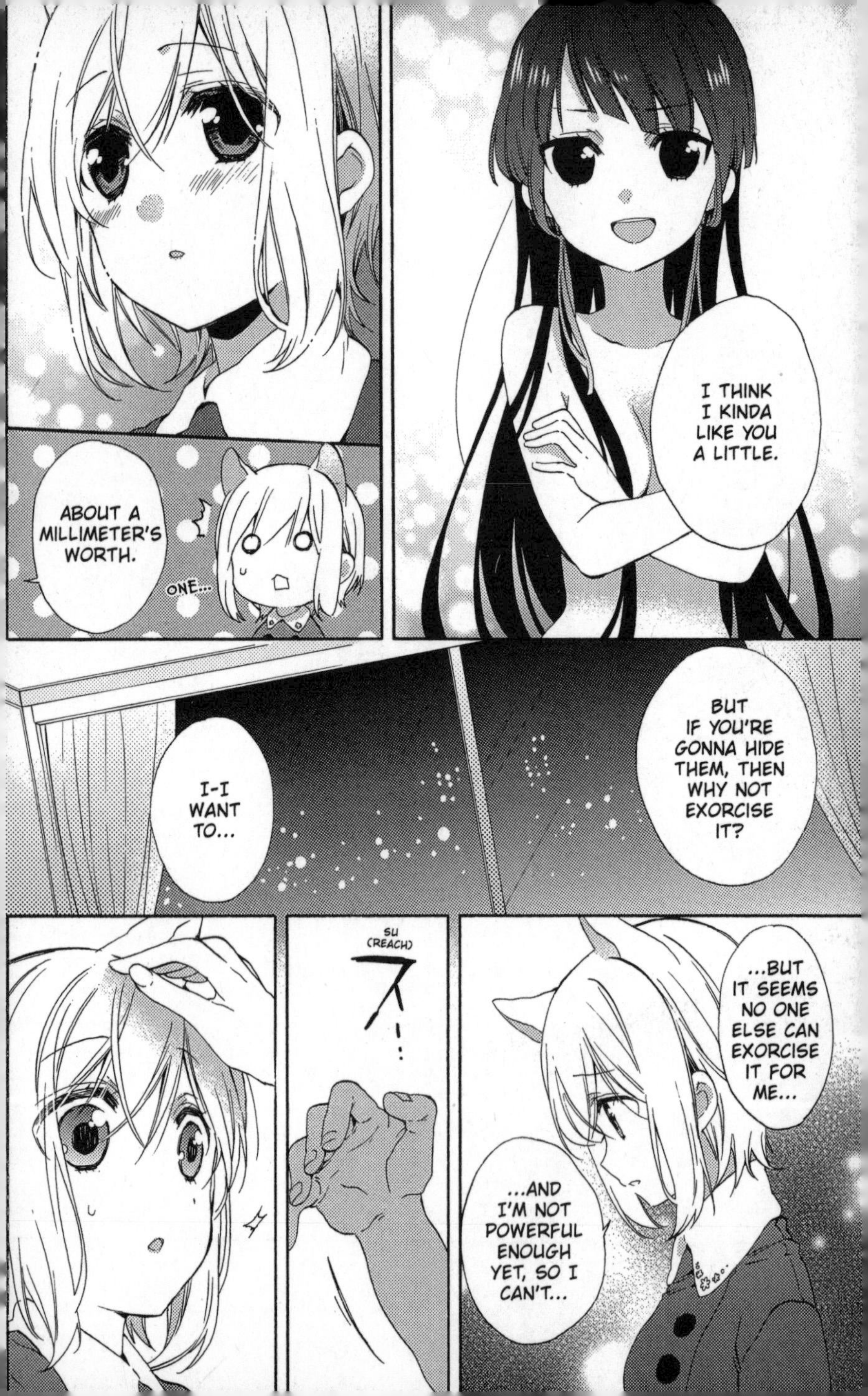
I THINK I KINDA LIKE YOU A LITTLE.
ABOUT A MILLIMETER'S WORTH.
ONE...
BUT IF YOU'RE GONNA HIDE THEM, THEN WHY NOT EXORCISE IT?
I-I WANT TO...
...BUT IT SEEMS NO ONE ELSE CAN EXORCISE IT FOR ME...
...AND I'M NOT POWERFUL ENOUGH YET, SO I CAN'T...
SU (REACH)

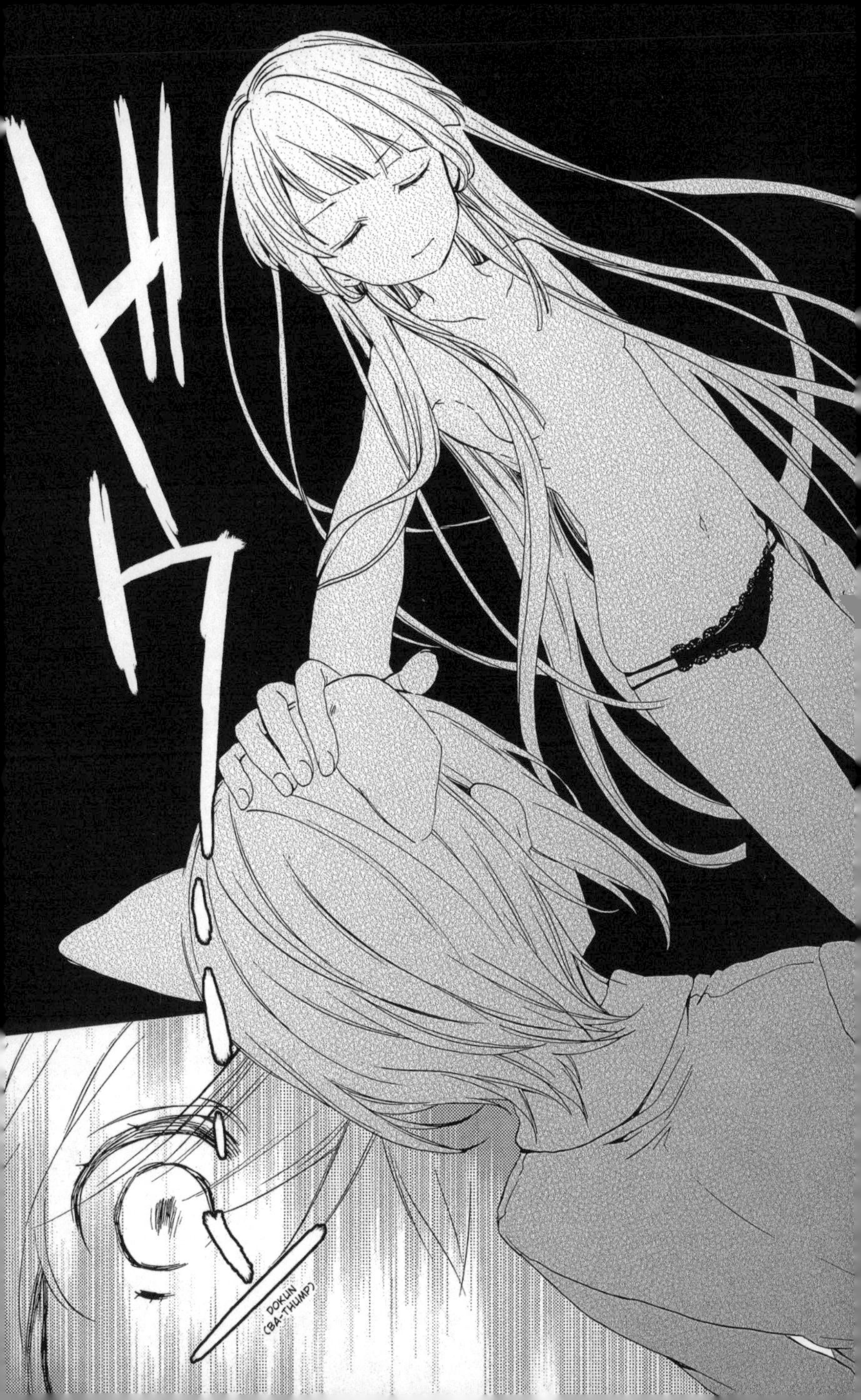
DOKUN (BA-THUMP)

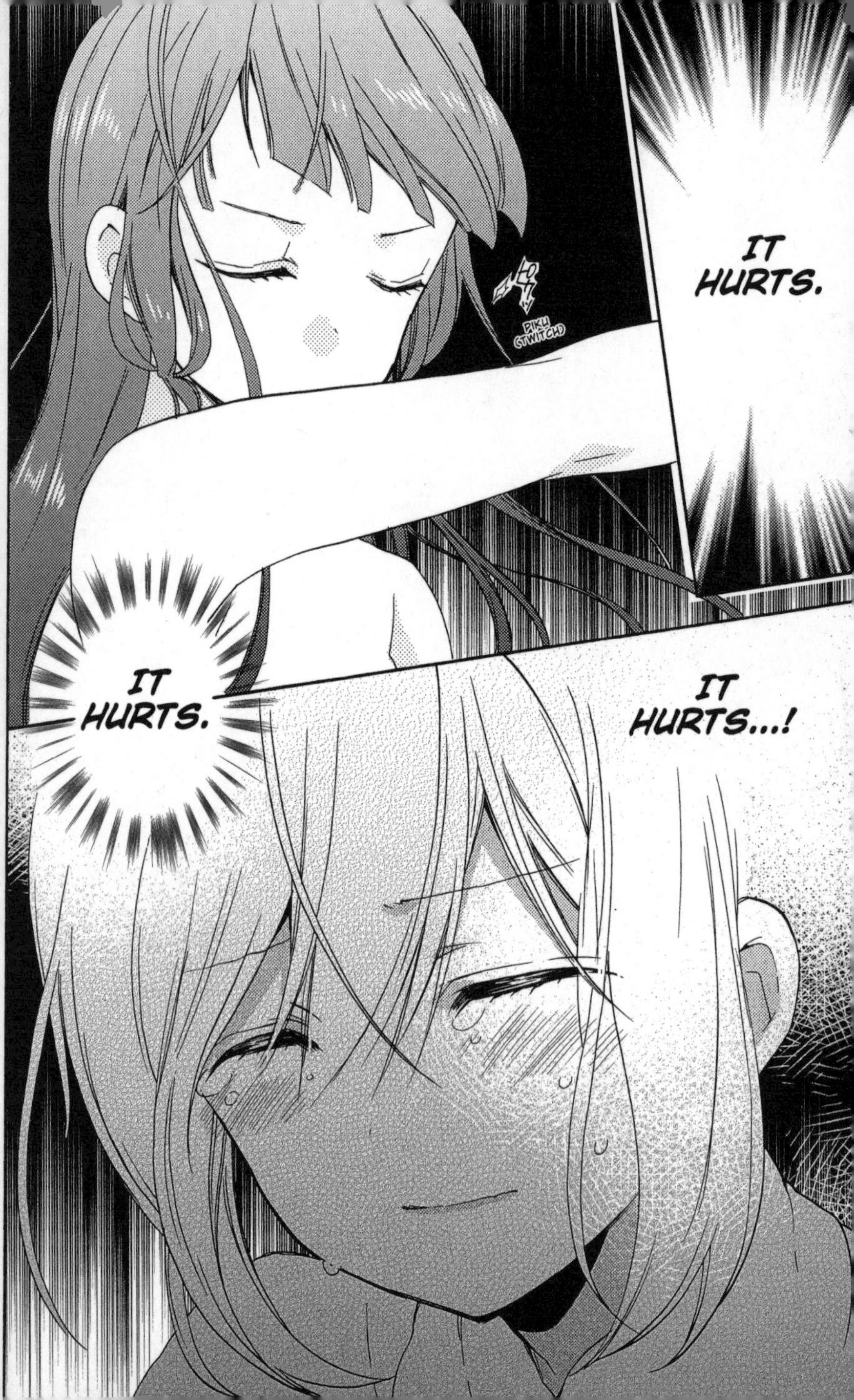
IT HURTS.
PIKU (TWITCH)
IT HURTS...!
IT HURTS.

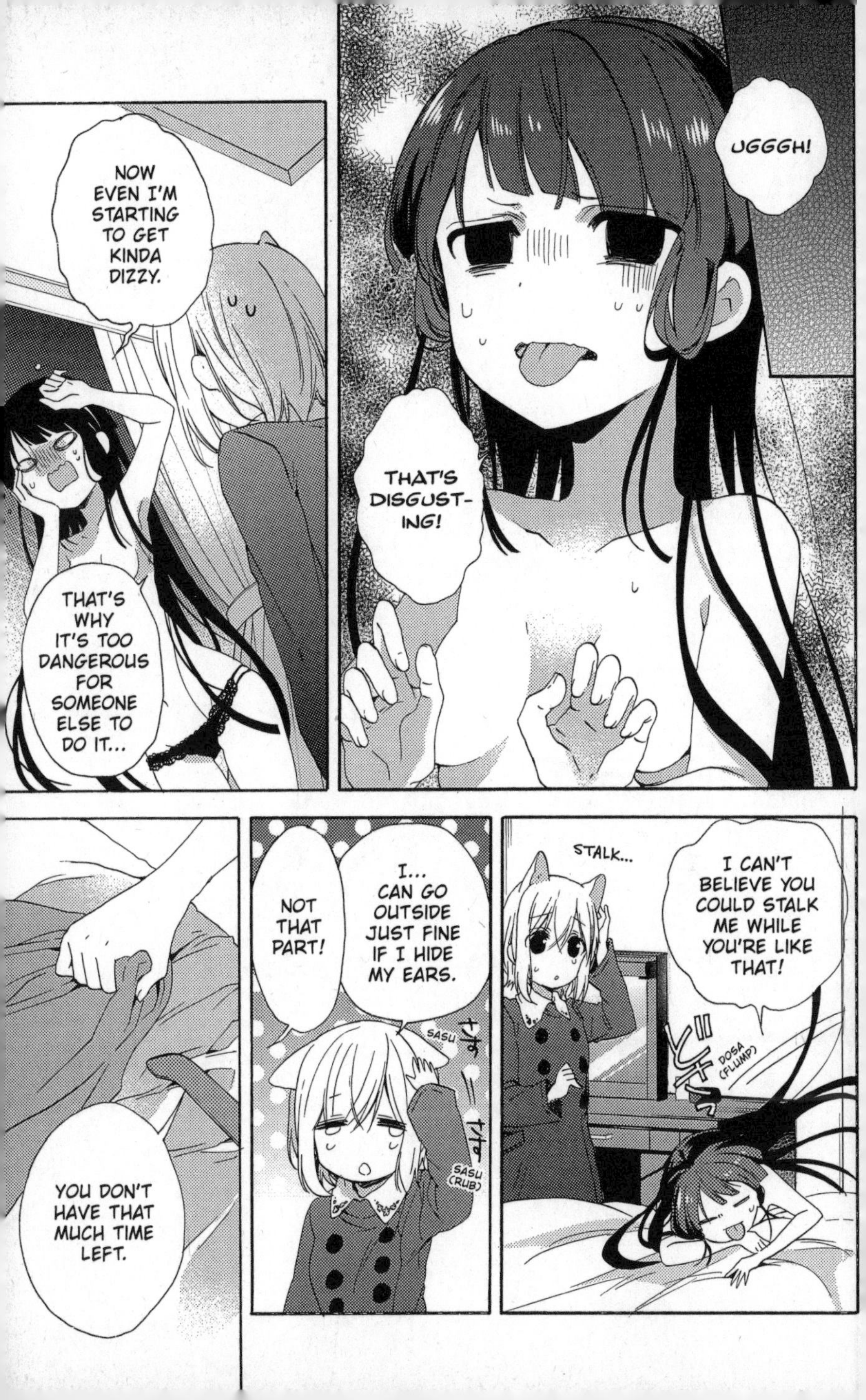
UGGGH!
THAT'S DISGUST-ING!
NOW EVEN I'M STARTING TO GET KINDA DIZZY.
THAT'S WHY IT'S TOO DANGEROUS FOR SOMEONE ELSE TO DO IT...
I CAN'T BELIEVE YOU COULD STALK ME WHILE YOU'RE LIKE THAT!
STALK...
DOSA (FLUMP)
I... CAN GO OUTSIDE JUST FINE IF I HIDE MY EARS.
NOT THAT PART!
SASU
SASU (RUB)
YOU DON'T HAVE THAT MUCH TIME LEFT.

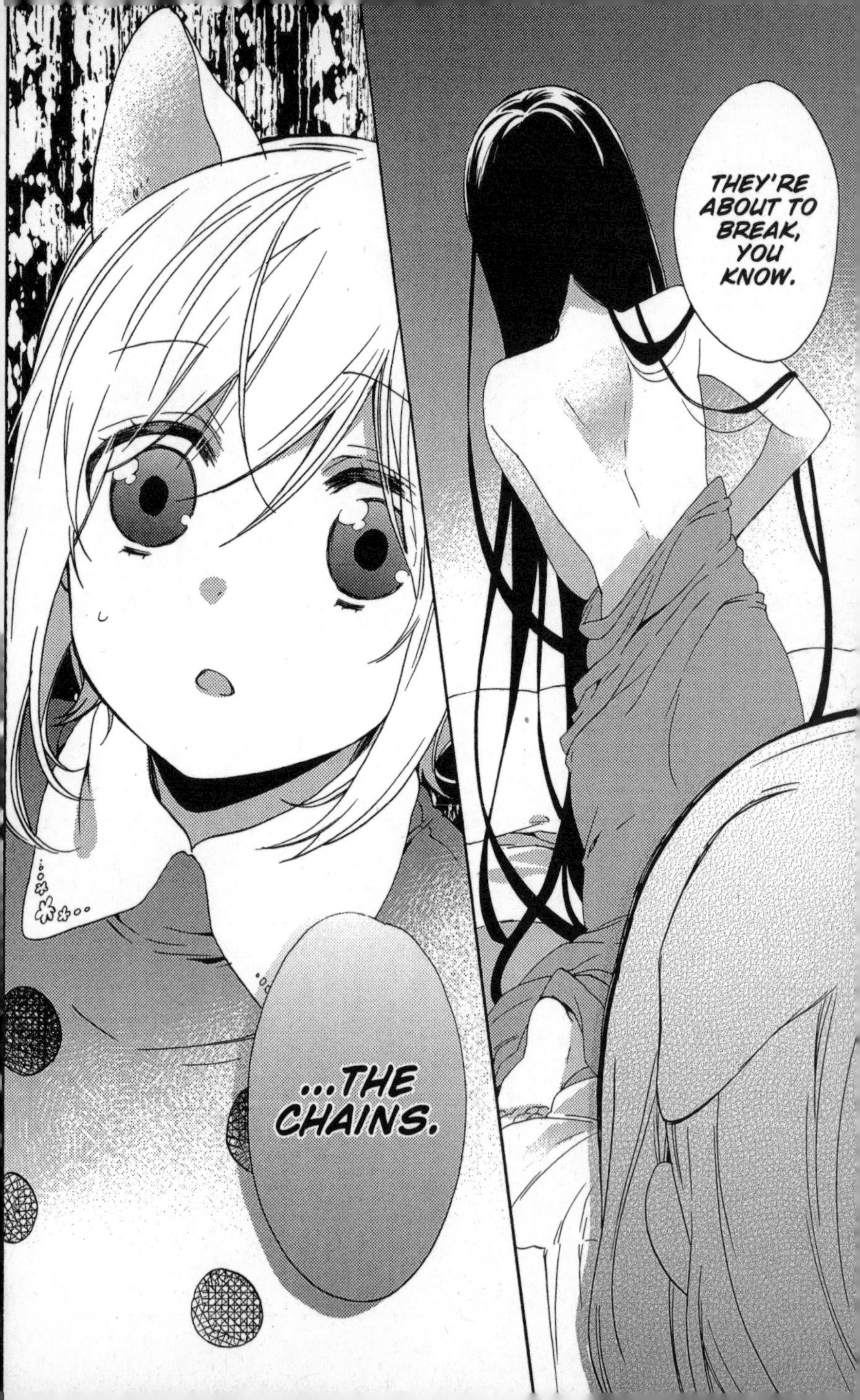
THEY'RE ABOUT TO BREAK, YOU KNOW.
...THE CHAINS.

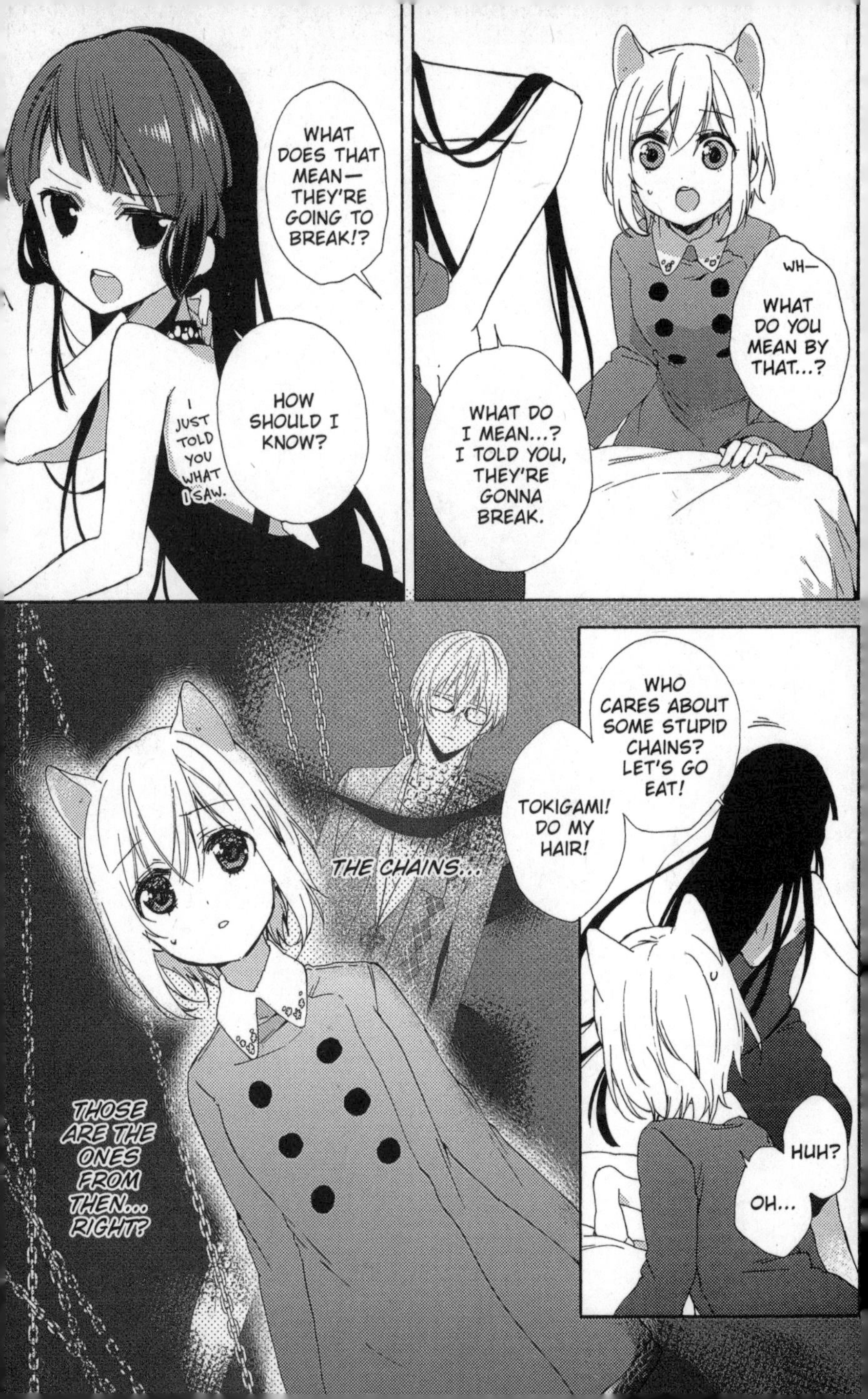
WH—
WHAT DO YOU MEAN BY THAT...?
WHAT DO I MEAN...? I TOLD YOU, THEY'RE GONNA BREAK.
WHAT DOES THAT MEAN—THEY'RE GOING TO BREAK!?
HOW SHOULD I KNOW?
I JUST TOLD YOU WHAT I SAW.
WHO CARES ABOUT SOME STUPID CHAINS? LET'S GO EAT!
TOKIGAMI! DO MY HAIR!
HUH?
OH...
THE CHAINS...
THOSE ARE THE ONES FROM THEN... RIGHT?

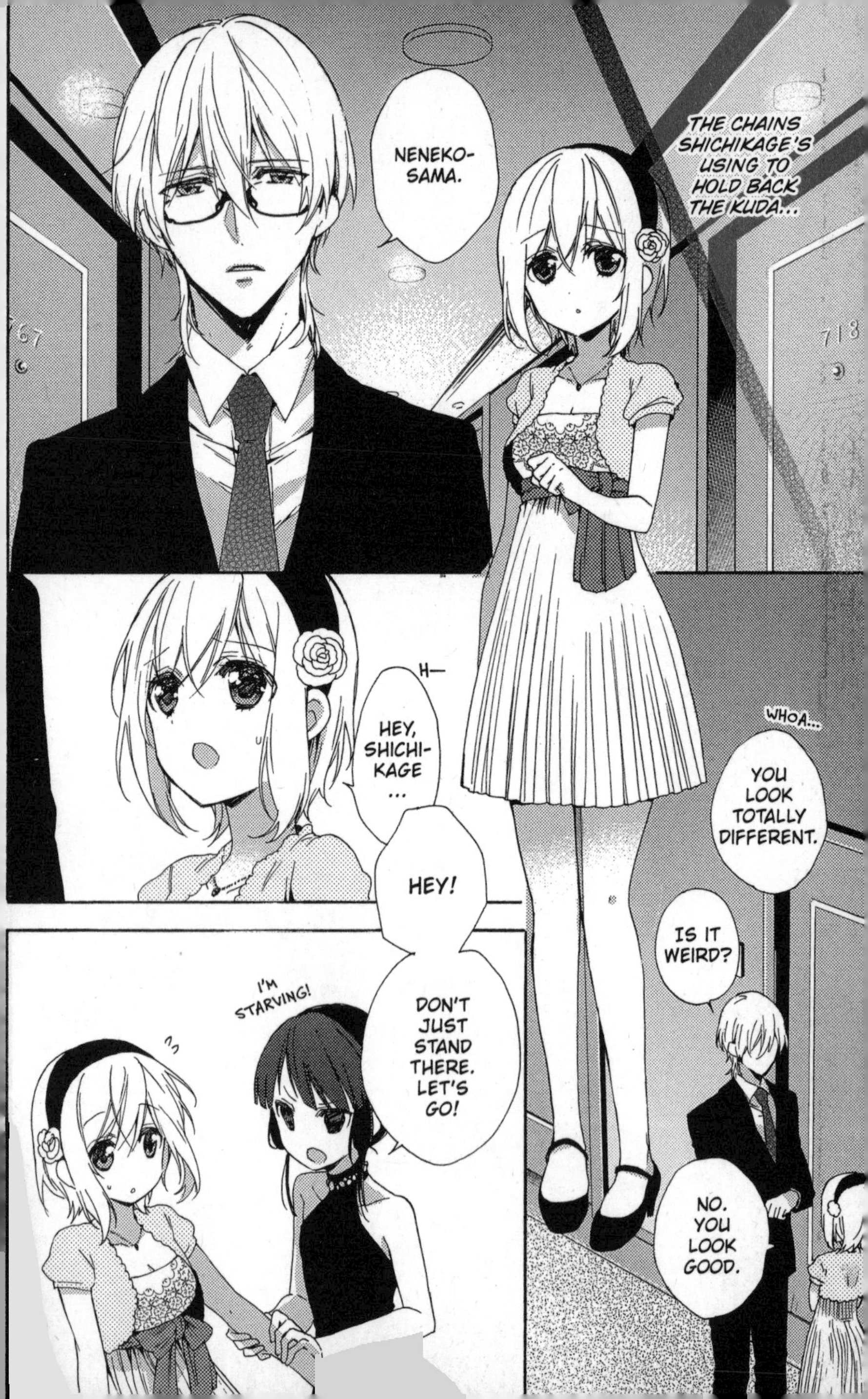
THE CHAINS SHICHIKAGE'S USING TO HOLD BACK THE KUDA...
NENEKO-SAMA.
WHOA...
YOU LOOK TOTALLY DIFFERENT.
IS IT WEIRD?
NO. YOU LOOK GOOD.
H—
HEY, SHICHIKAGE...
HEY!
DON'T JUST STAND THERE. LET'S GO!
I'M STARVING!

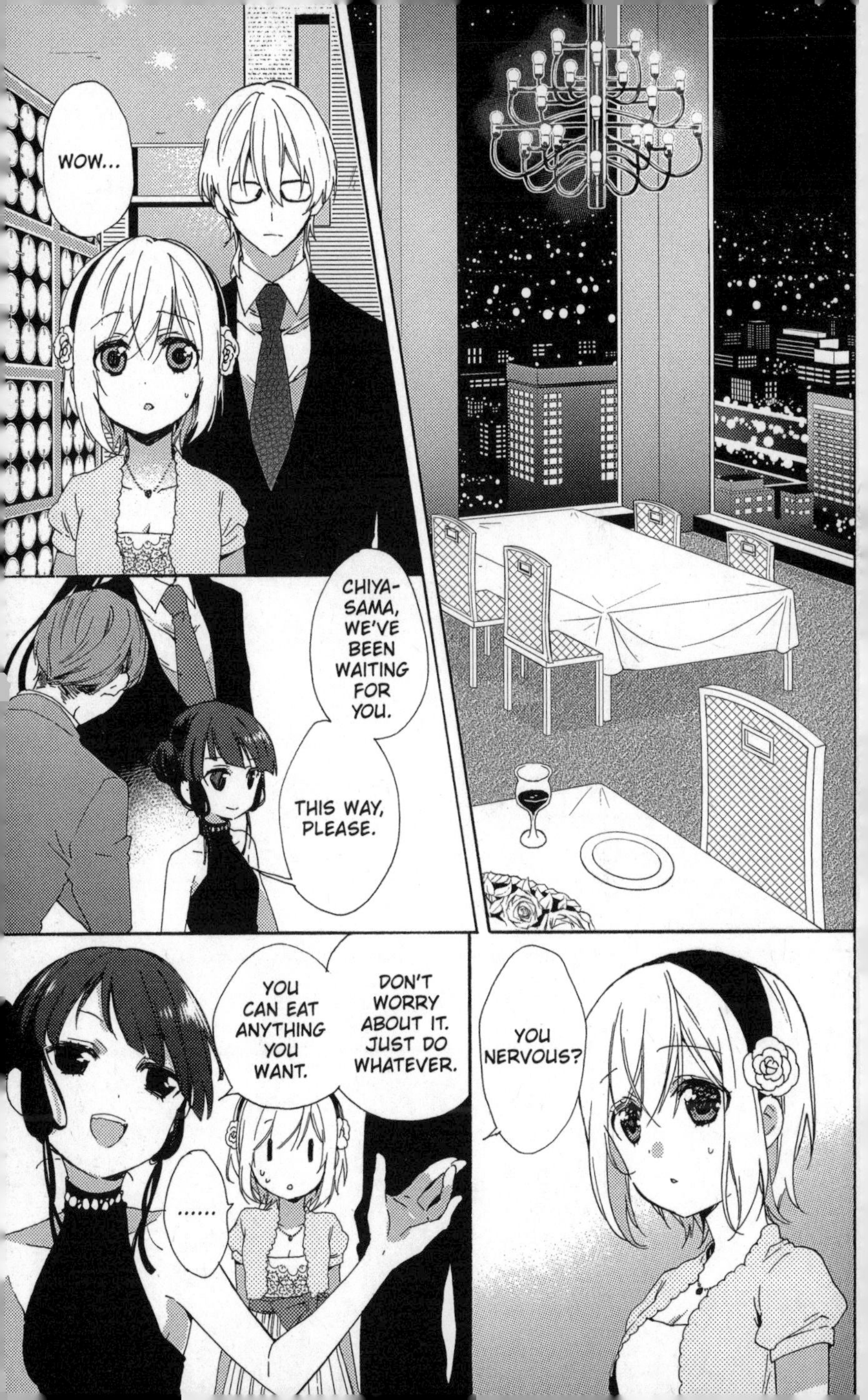
WOW...
CHIYA-SAMA, WE'VE BEEN WAITING FOR YOU.
THIS WAY, PLEASE.
YOU NERVOUS?
DON'T WORRY ABOUT IT. JUST DO WHATEVER.
YOU CAN EAT ANYTHING YOU WANT.
......

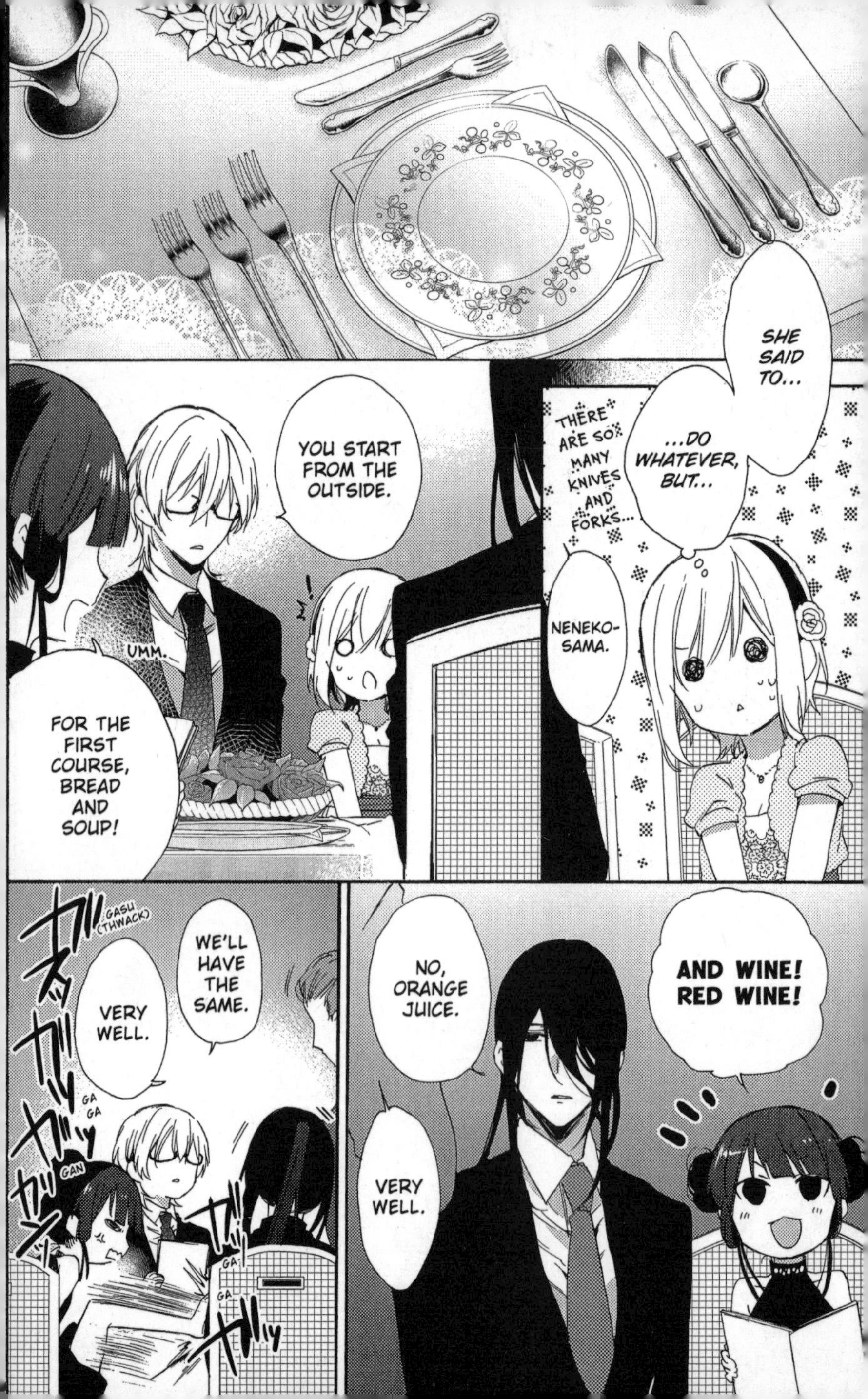
SHE SAID TO...
...DO WHATEVER, BUT...
THERE ARE SO MANY KNIVES AND FORKS...
NENEKO-SAMA.
YOU START FROM THE OUTSIDE.
UMM.
FOR THE FIRST COURSE, BREAD AND SOUP!
AND WINE! RED WINE!
NO, ORANGE JUICE.
VERY WELL.
WE'LL HAVE THE SAME.
VERY WELL.
GASU (THWACK)
GA GA
GAN
GA
GA

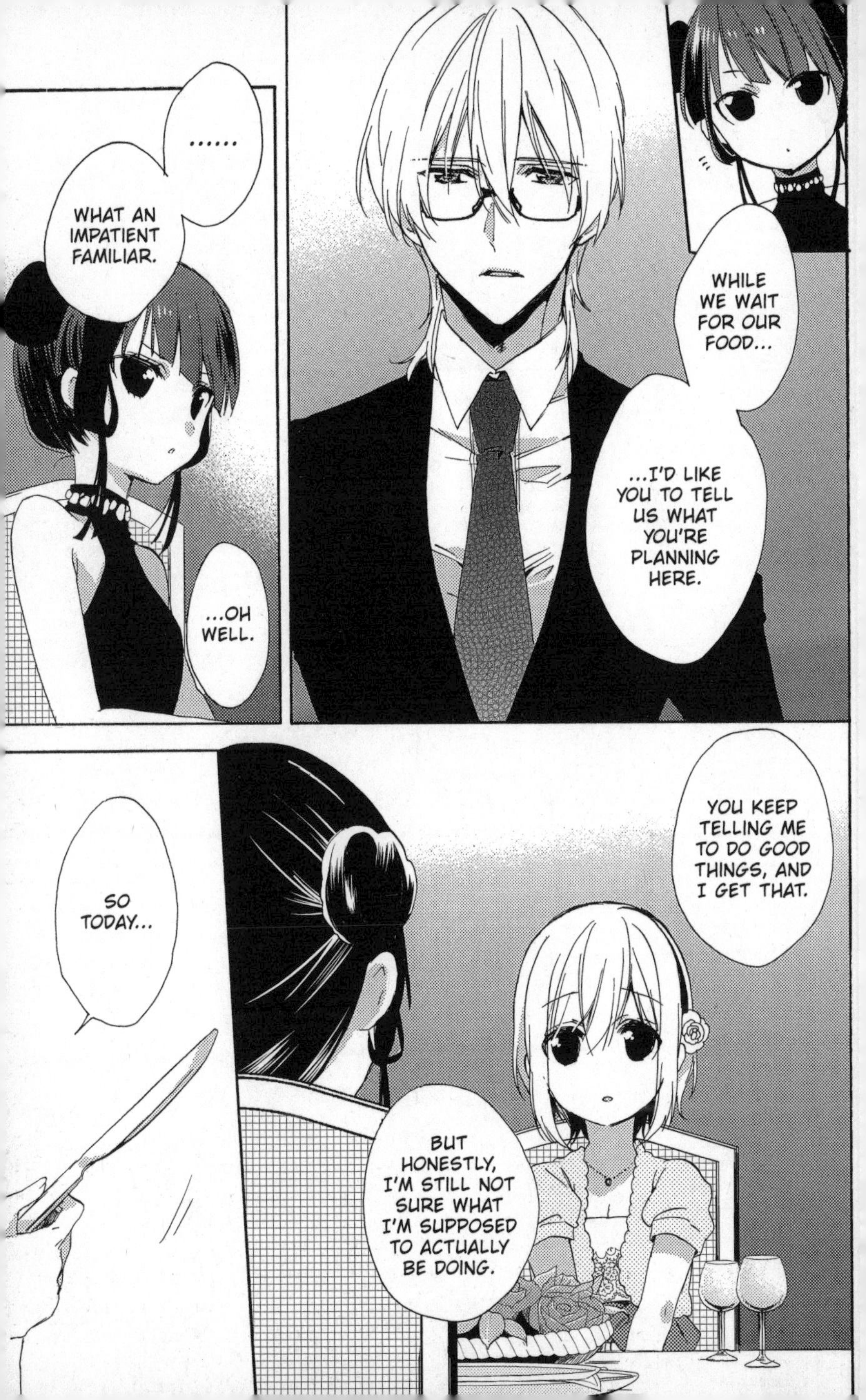
WHILE WE WAIT FOR OUR FOOD...
...I'D LIKE YOU TO TELL US WHAT YOU'RE PLANNING HERE.
......
WHAT AN IMPATIENT FAMILIAR.
...OH WELL.
YOU KEEP TELLING ME TO DO GOOD THINGS, AND I GET THAT.
BUT HONESTLY, I'M STILL NOT SURE WHAT I'M SUPPOSED TO ACTUALLY BE DOING.
SO TODAY...

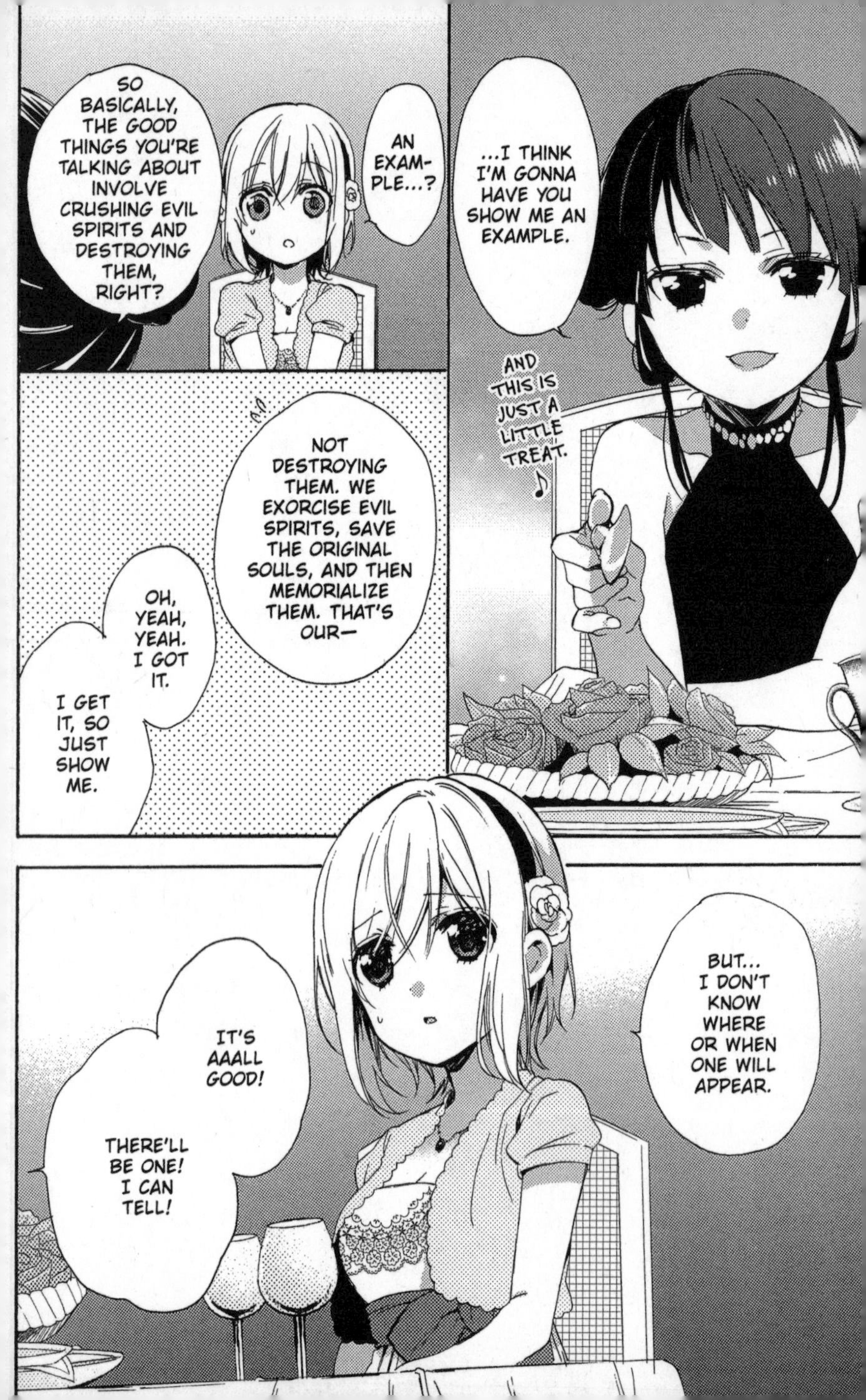
...I THINK I'M GONNA HAVE YOU SHOW ME AN EXAMPLE.
AND THIS IS JUST A LITTLE TREAT. ♪
AN EXAMPLE...?
SO BASICALLY, THE GOOD THINGS YOU'RE TALKING ABOUT INVOLVE CRUSHING EVIL SPIRITS AND DESTROYING THEM, RIGHT?
NOT DESTROYING THEM. WE EXORCISE EVIL SPIRITS, SAVE THE ORIGINAL SOULS, AND THEN MEMORIALIZE THEM. THAT'S OUR—
OH, YEAH, YEAH. I GOT IT.
I GET IT, SO JUST SHOW ME.
BUT... I DON'T KNOW WHERE OR WHEN ONE WILL APPEAR.
IT'S AAALL GOOD!
THERE'LL BE ONE! I CAN TELL!

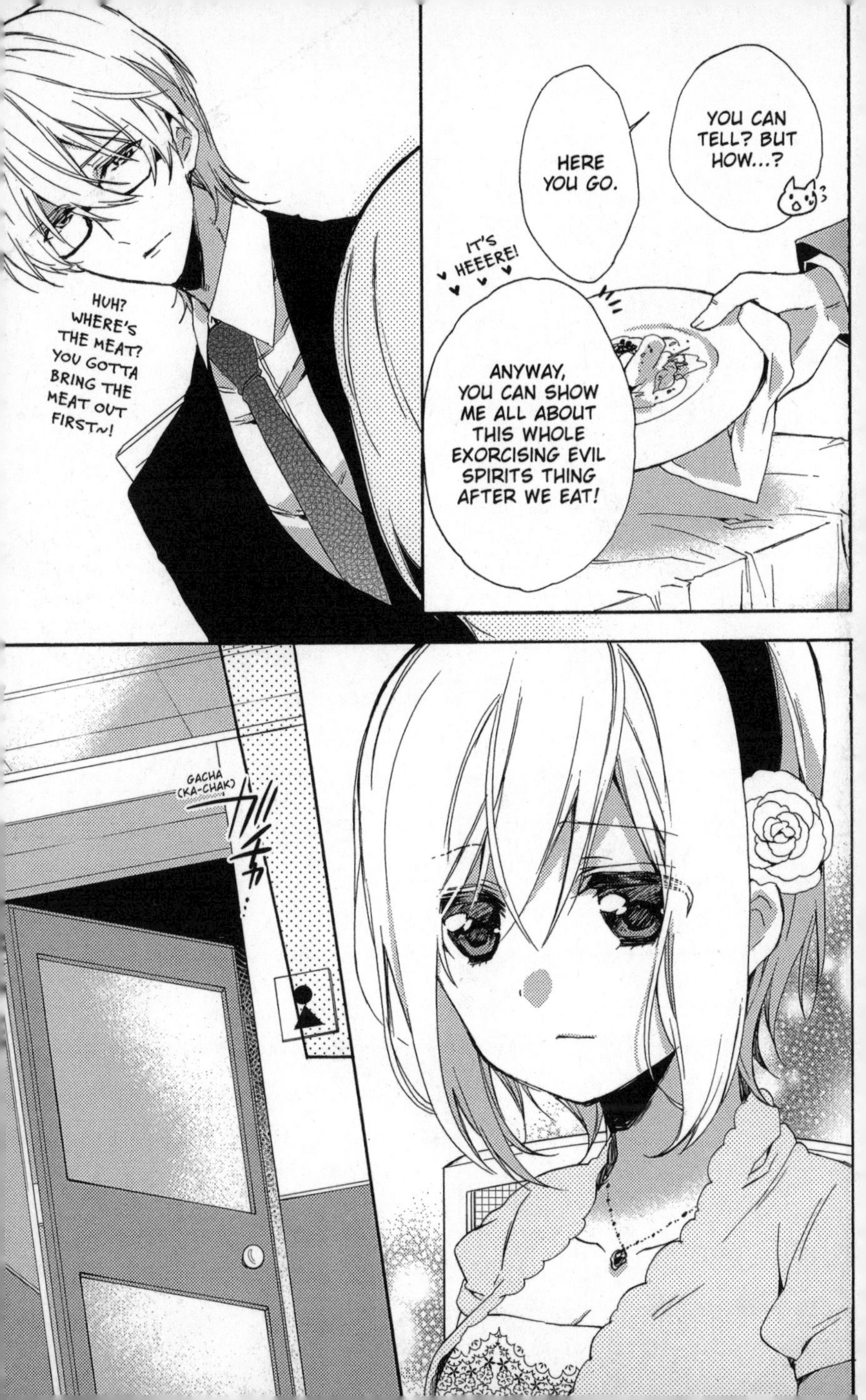
YOU CAN TELL? BUT HOW...?
HERE YOU GO.
IT'S HEEERE!
ANYWAY, YOU CAN SHOW ME ALL ABOUT THIS WHOLE EXORCISING EVIL SPIRITS THING AFTER WE EAT!
HUH? WHERE'S THE MEAT? YOU GOTTA BRING THE MEAT OUT FIRST~!
GACHA (KA-CHAK)

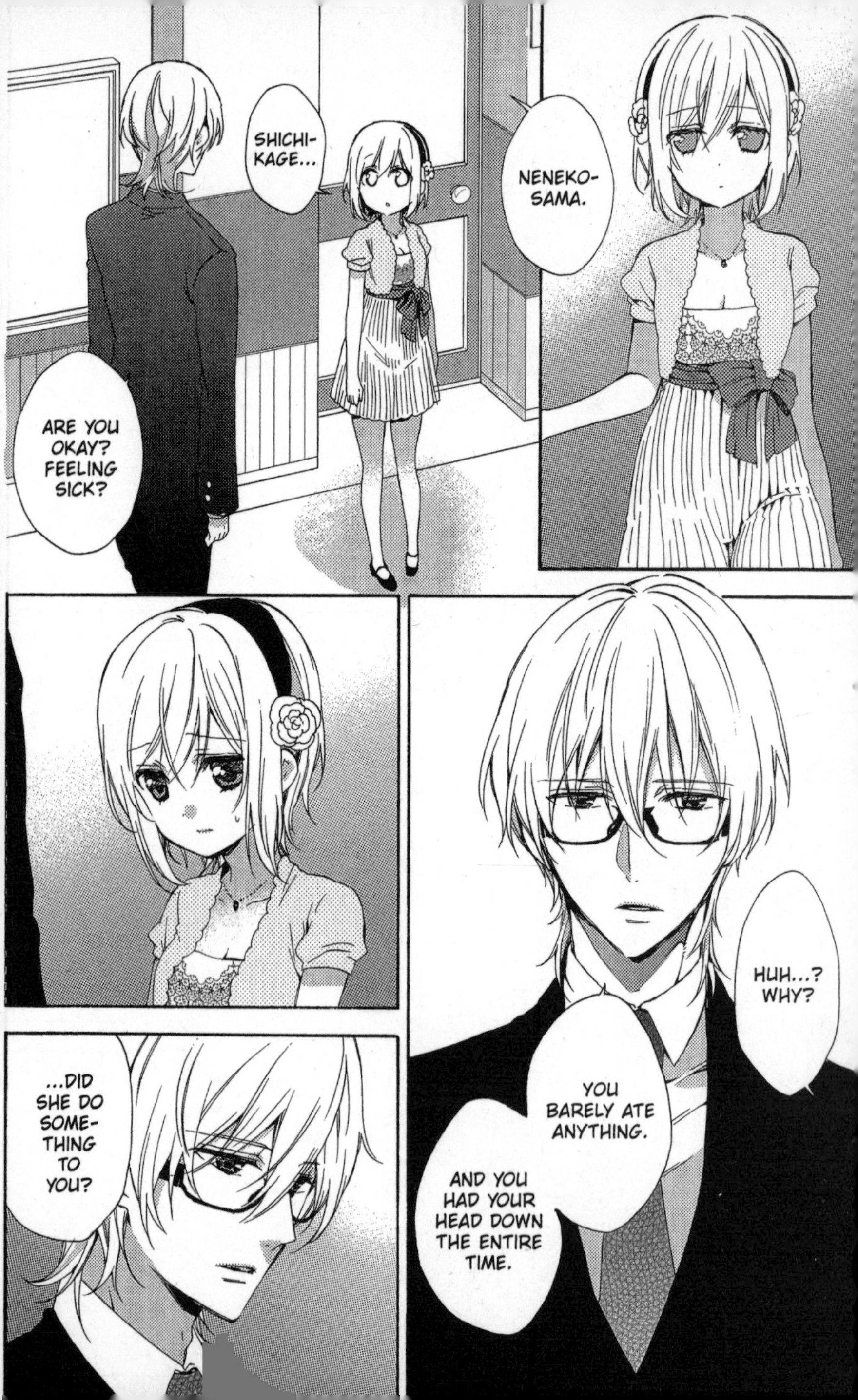
NENEKO-SAMA.
SHICHI-KAGE...
ARE YOU OKAY? FEELING SICK?
HUH...? WHY?
YOU BARELY ATE ANYTHING.
AND YOU HAD YOUR HEAD DOWN THE ENTIRE TIME.
...DID SHE DO SOME-THING TO YOU?

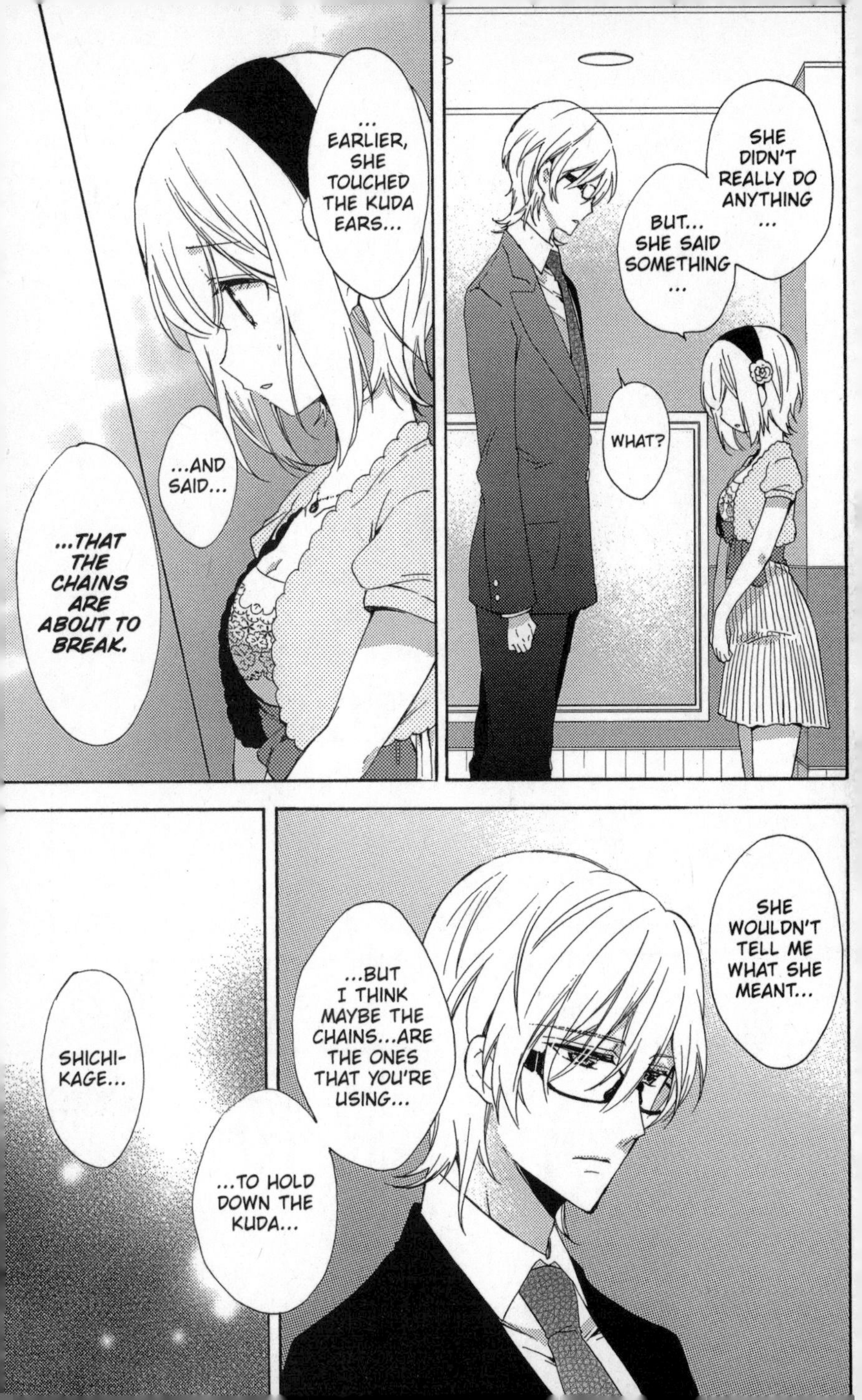
SHE DIDN'T REALLY DO ANYTHING...
BUT... SHE SAID SOMETHING...
WHAT?
...EARLIER, SHE TOUCHED THE KUDA EARS...
...AND SAID...
...THAT THE CHAINS ARE ABOUT TO BREAK.
SHE WOULDN'T TELL ME WHAT SHE MEANT...
...BUT I THINK MAYBE THE CHAINS...ARE THE ONES THAT YOU'RE USING...
...TO HOLD DOWN THE KUDA...
SHICHI-KAGE...

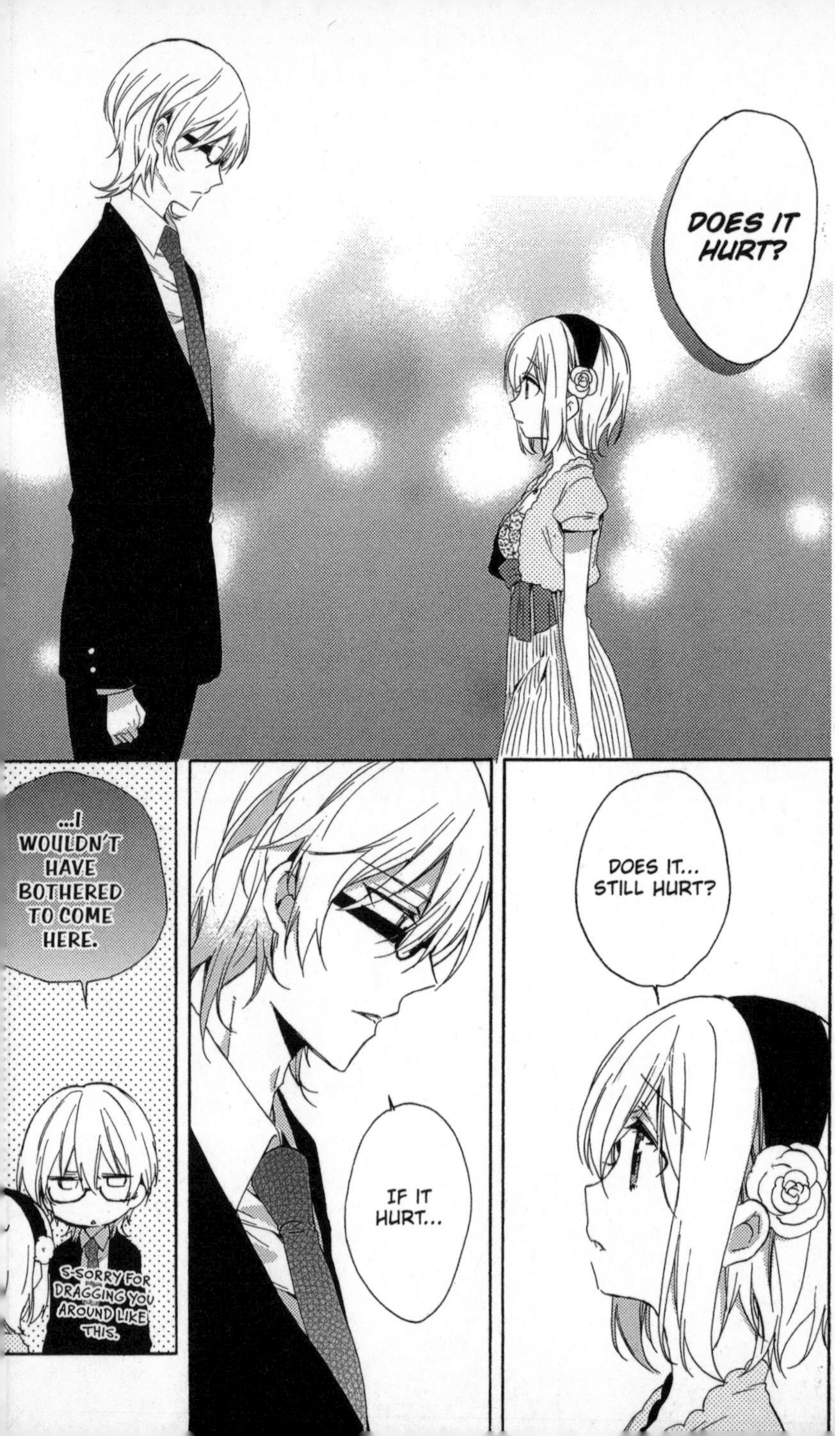
DOES IT HURT?
DOES IT... STILL HURT?
IF IT HURT...
...I WOULDN'T HAVE BOTHERED TO COME HERE.
S-SORRY FOR DRAGGING YOU AROUND LIKE THIS.

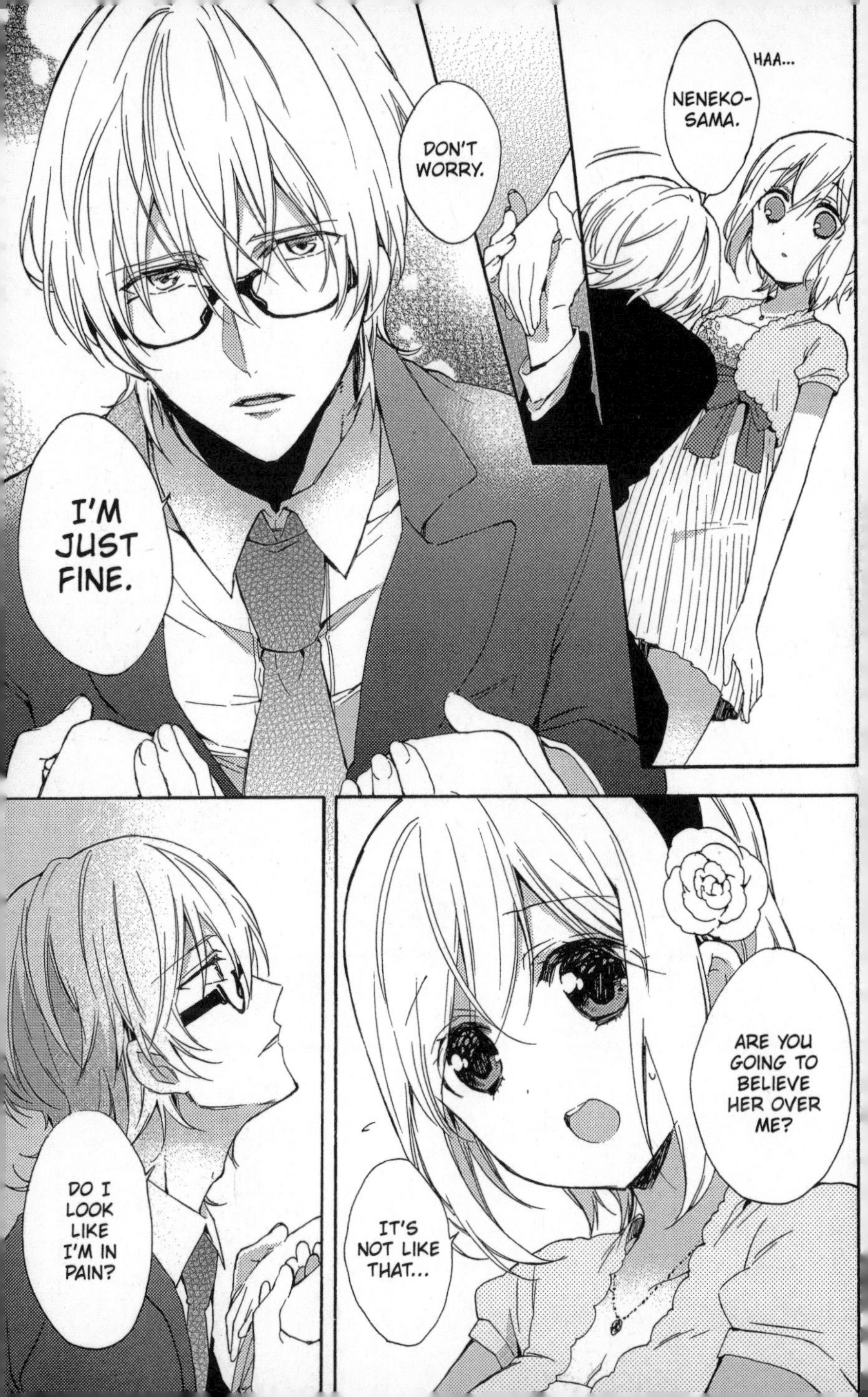
HAA...
NENEKO-SAMA.
DON'T WORRY.
I'M JUST FINE.
ARE YOU GOING TO BELIEVE HER OVER ME?
IT'S NOT LIKE THAT...
DO I LOOK LIKE I'M IN PAIN?

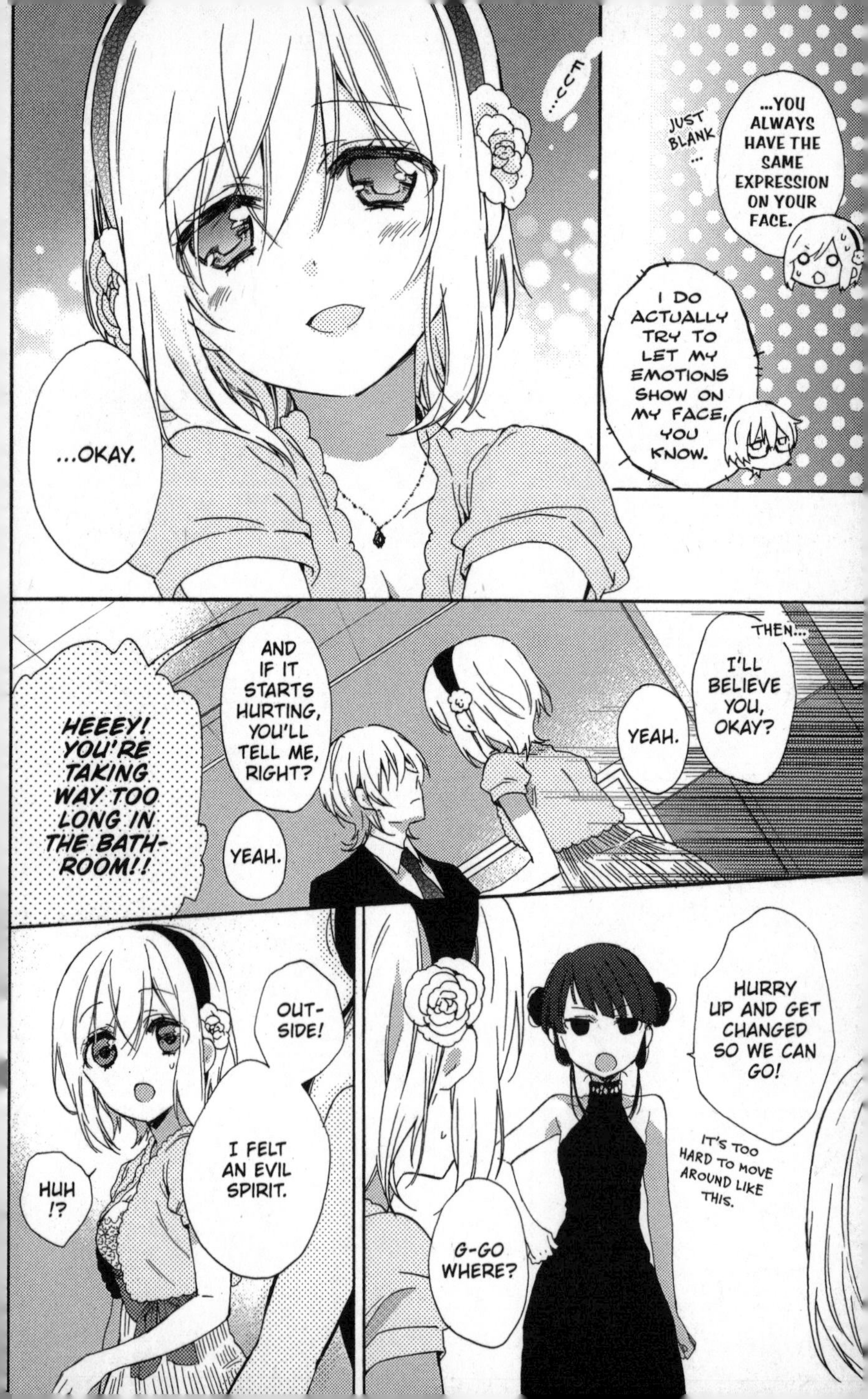
...YOU ALWAYS HAVE THE SAME EXPRESSION ON YOUR FACE.
JUST BLANK...
I DO ACTUALLY TRY TO LET MY EMOTIONS SHOW ON MY FACE, YOU KNOW.
...CCT
...OKAY.
THEN...
I'LL BELIEVE YOU, OKAY?
YEAH.
AND IF IT STARTS HURTING, YOU'LL TELL ME, RIGHT?
YEAH.
HEEEY! YOU'RE TAKING WAY TOO LONG IN THE BATH-ROOM!!
HURRY UP AND GET CHANGED SO WE CAN GO!
IT'S TOO HARD TO MOVE AROUND LIKE THIS.
G-GO WHERE?
OUT-SIDE!
I FELT AN EVIL SPIRIT.
HUH!?

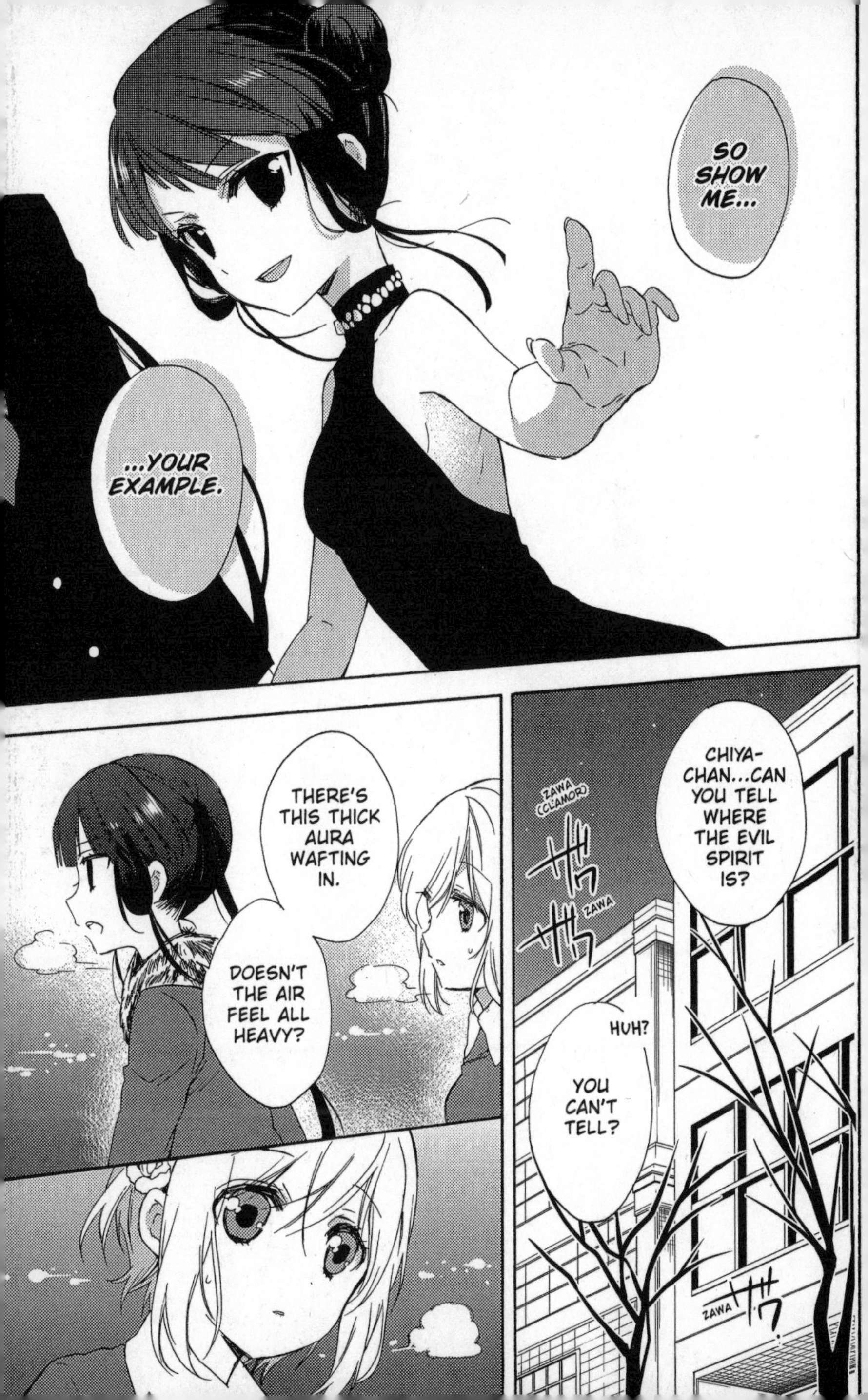
SO SHOW ME...
...YOUR EXAMPLE.
CHIYA-CHAN...CAN YOU TELL WHERE THE EVIL SPIRIT IS?
ZAWA (CLAMOR)
ZAWA
HUH?
YOU CAN'T TELL?
ZAWA
THERE'S THIS THICK AURA WAFTING IN.
DOESN'T THE AIR FEEL ALL HEAVY?

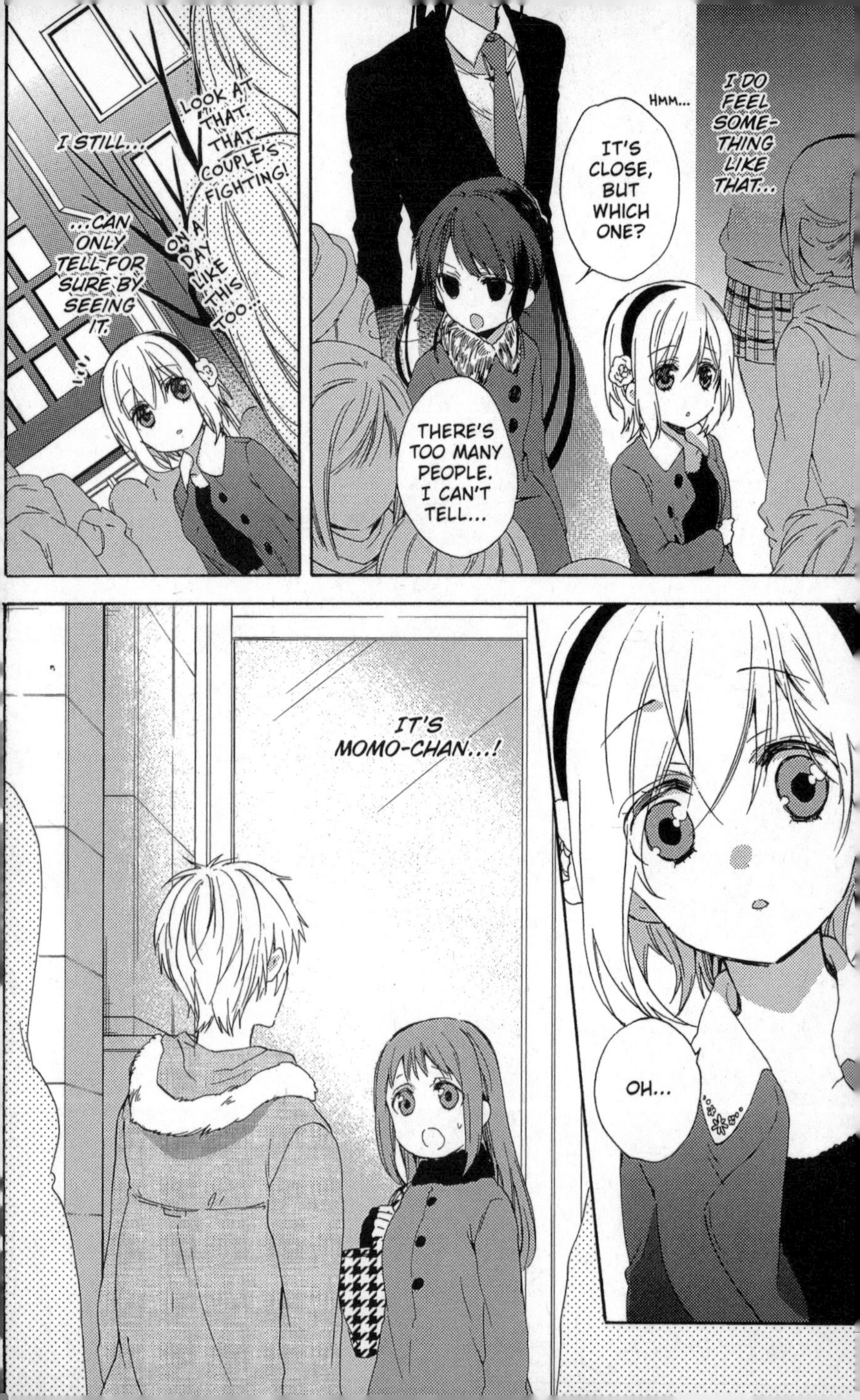
I DO FEEL SOMETHING LIKE THAT...
HMM...
IT'S CLOSE, BUT WHICH ONE?
THERE'S TOO MANY PEOPLE. I CAN'T TELL...
LOOK AT THAT. THAT COUPLE'S FIGHTING!
ON A DAY LIKE THIS TOO...
I STILL...
...CAN ONLY TELL FOR SURE BY SEEING IT.
OH...
IT'S MOMO-CHAN...!

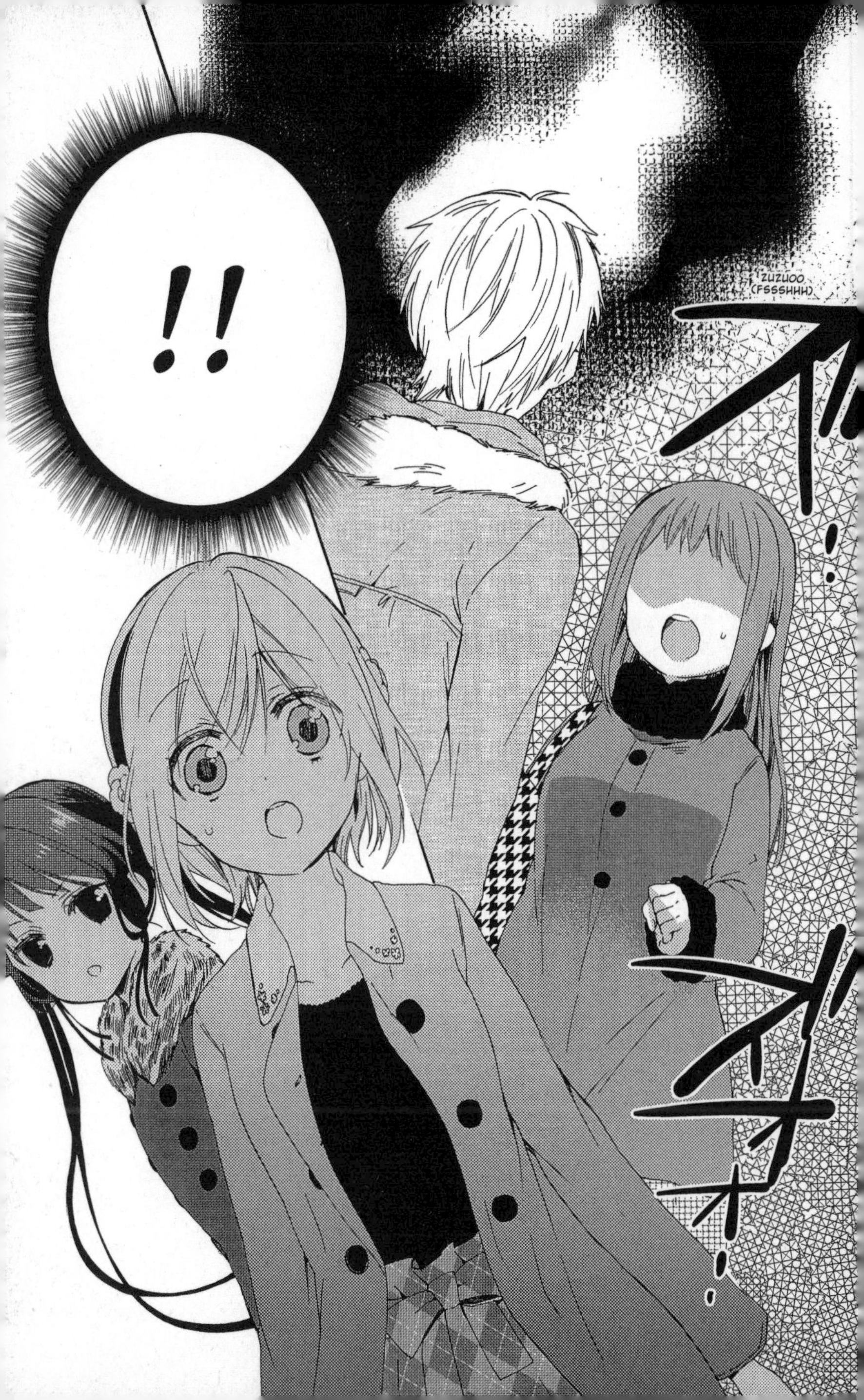
!!
ZUZUOO
(FSSSHHH)

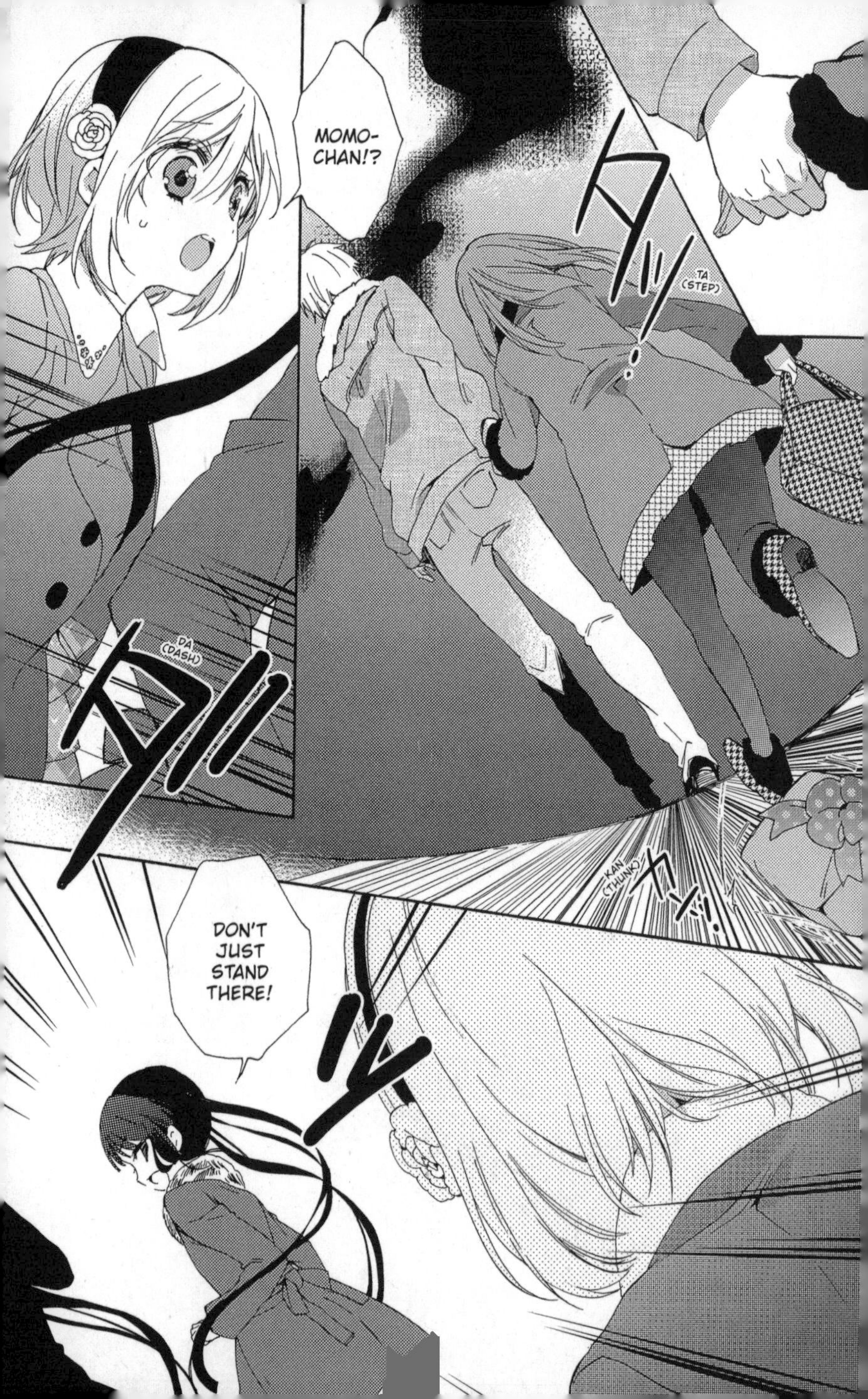
MOMO-CHAN!?
TA (STEP)
KAN (THUNK)
DA (DASH)
DON'T JUST STAND THERE!

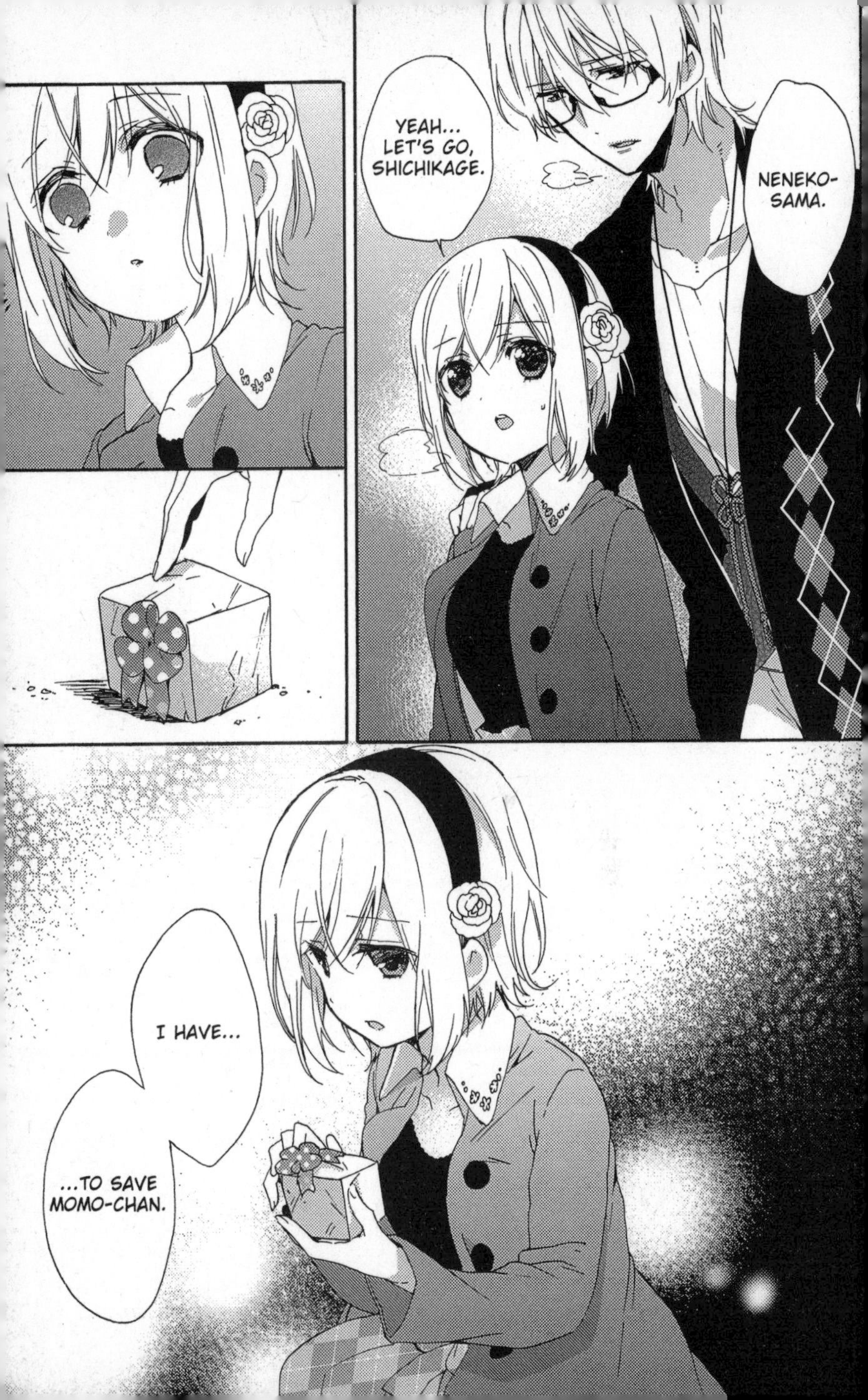
NENEKO-SAMA.
YEAH... LET'S GO, SHICHIKAGE.
I HAVE...
...TO SAVE MOMO-CHAN.

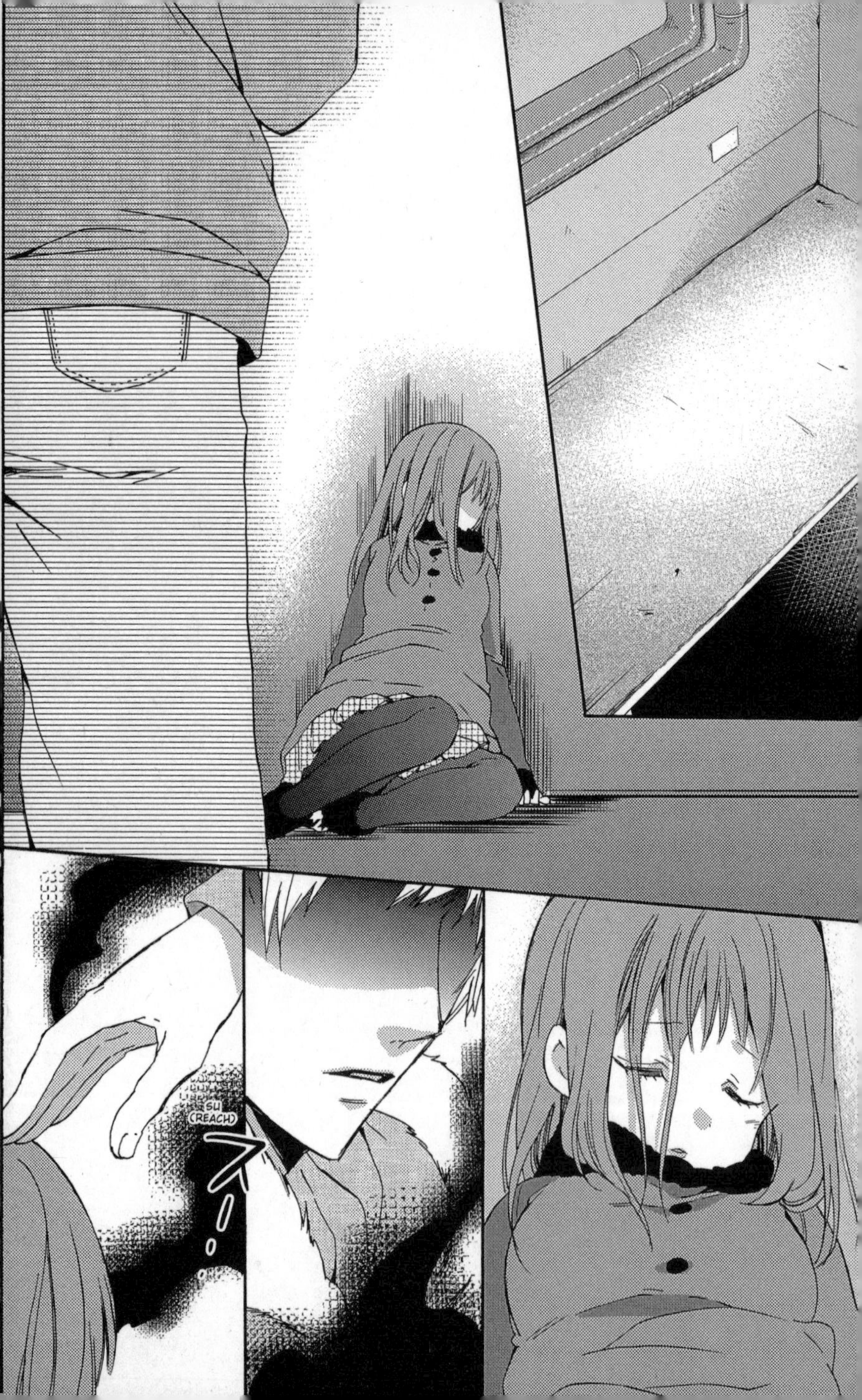
SU
(REACH)

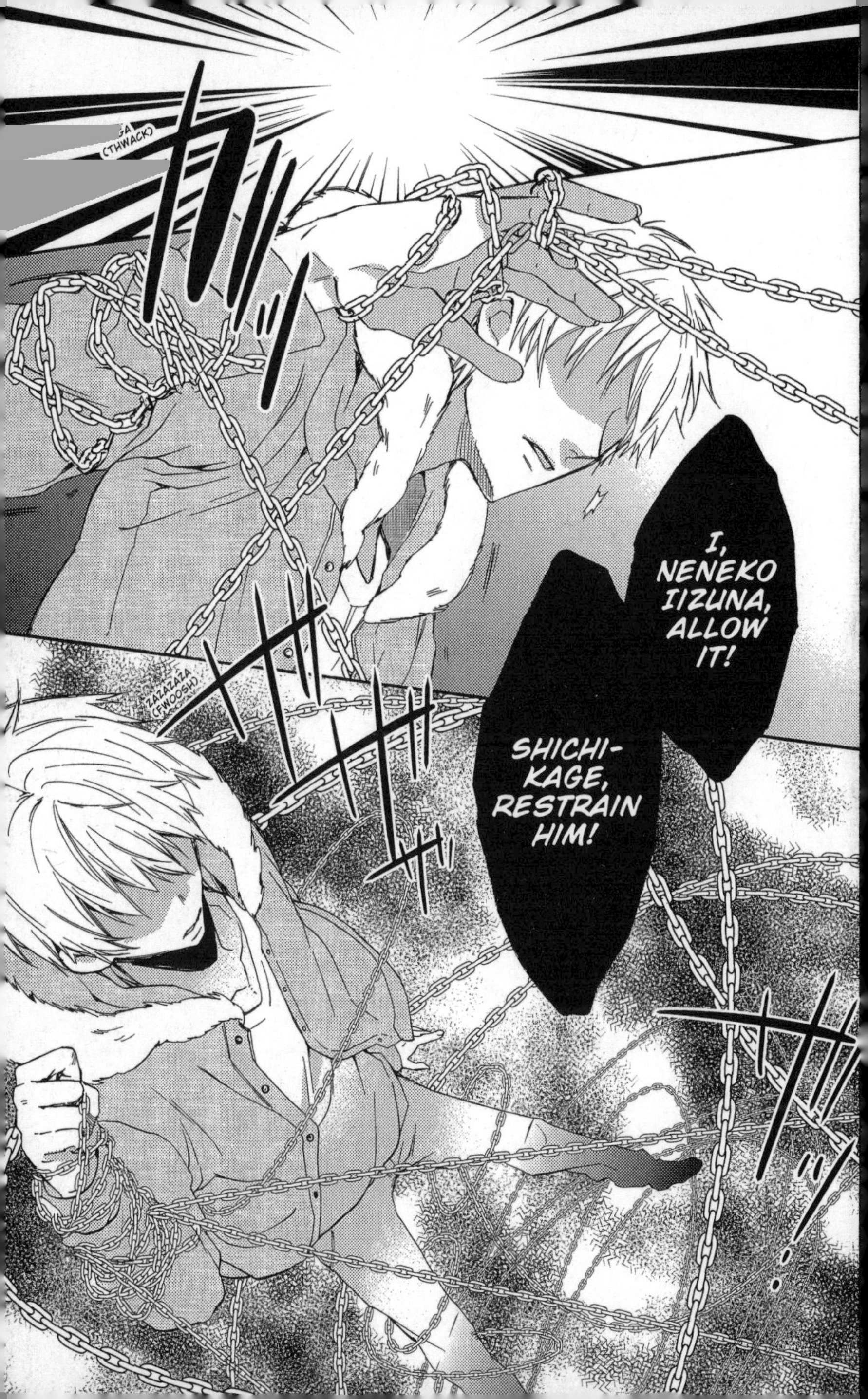
GA (THWACK)
I, NENEKO IIZUNA, ALLOW IT!
SHICHI-KAGE, RESTRAIN HIM!
ZAZAZAZA (FWOOSH)

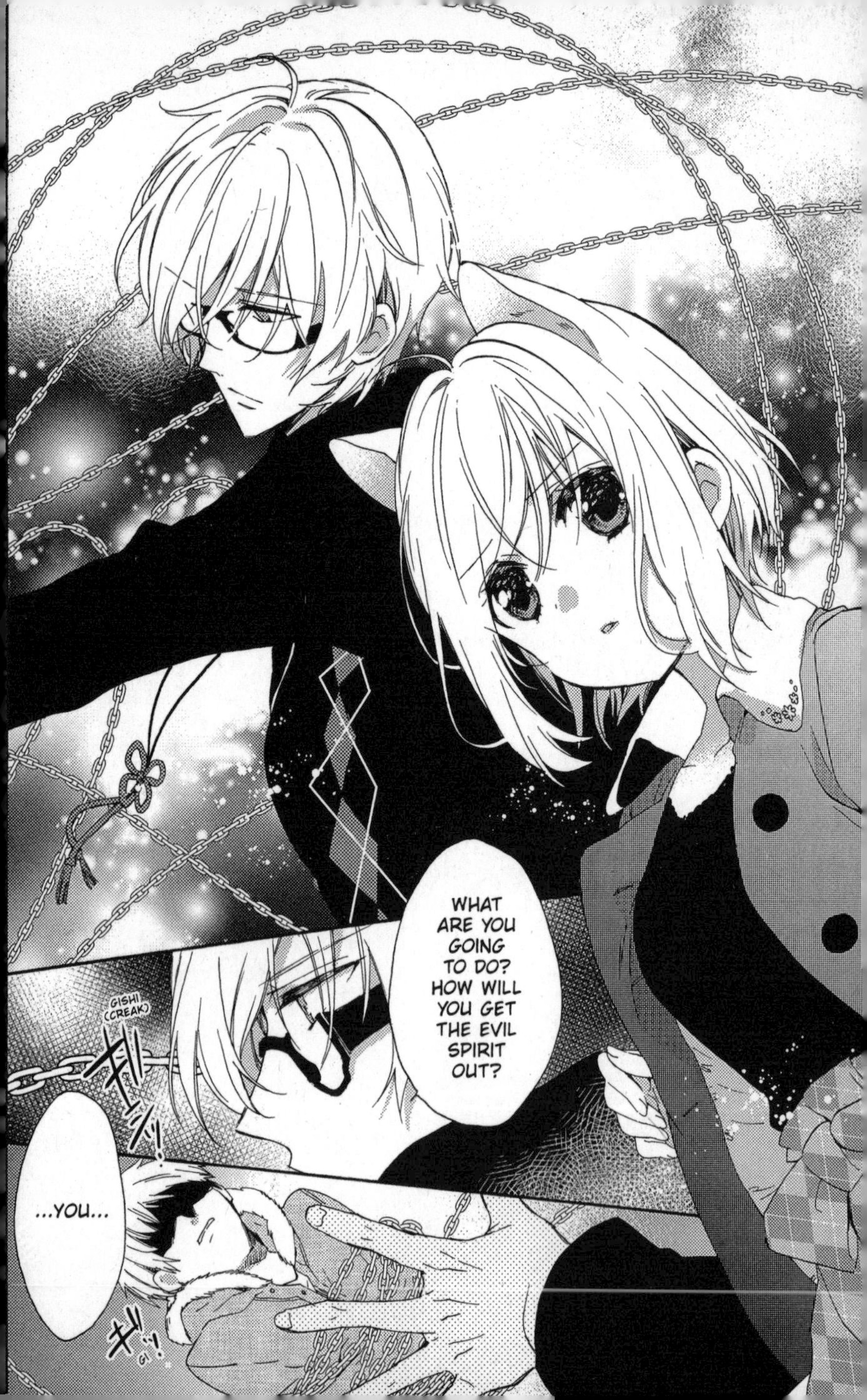
WHAT ARE YOU GOING TO DO? HOW WILL YOU GET THE EVIL SPIRIT OUT?
GISHI (CREAK)
...YOU...
GI

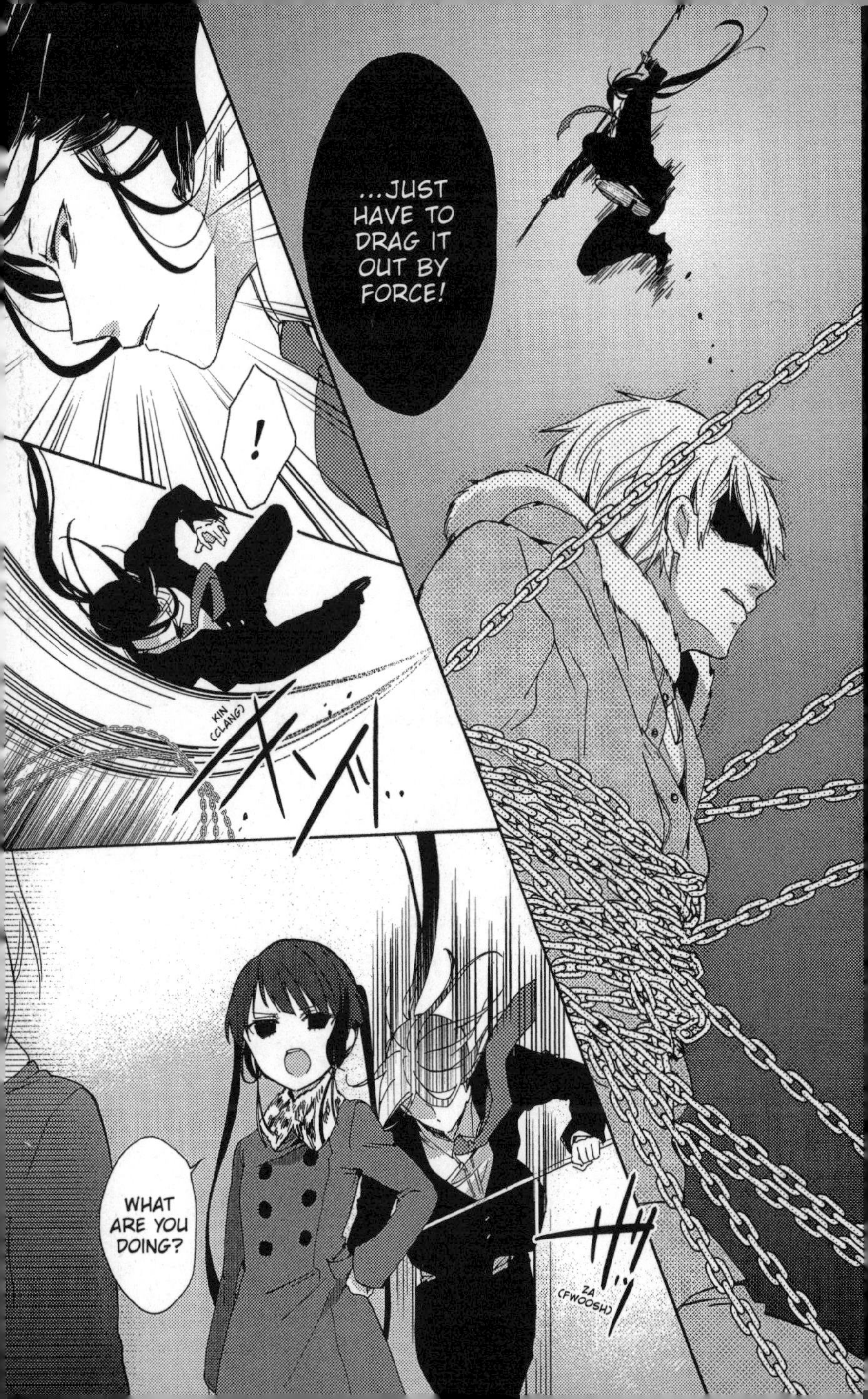
...JUST HAVE TO DRAG IT OUT BY FORCE!
!
KIN (CLANG)
WHAT ARE YOU DOING?
ZA (FWOOSH)

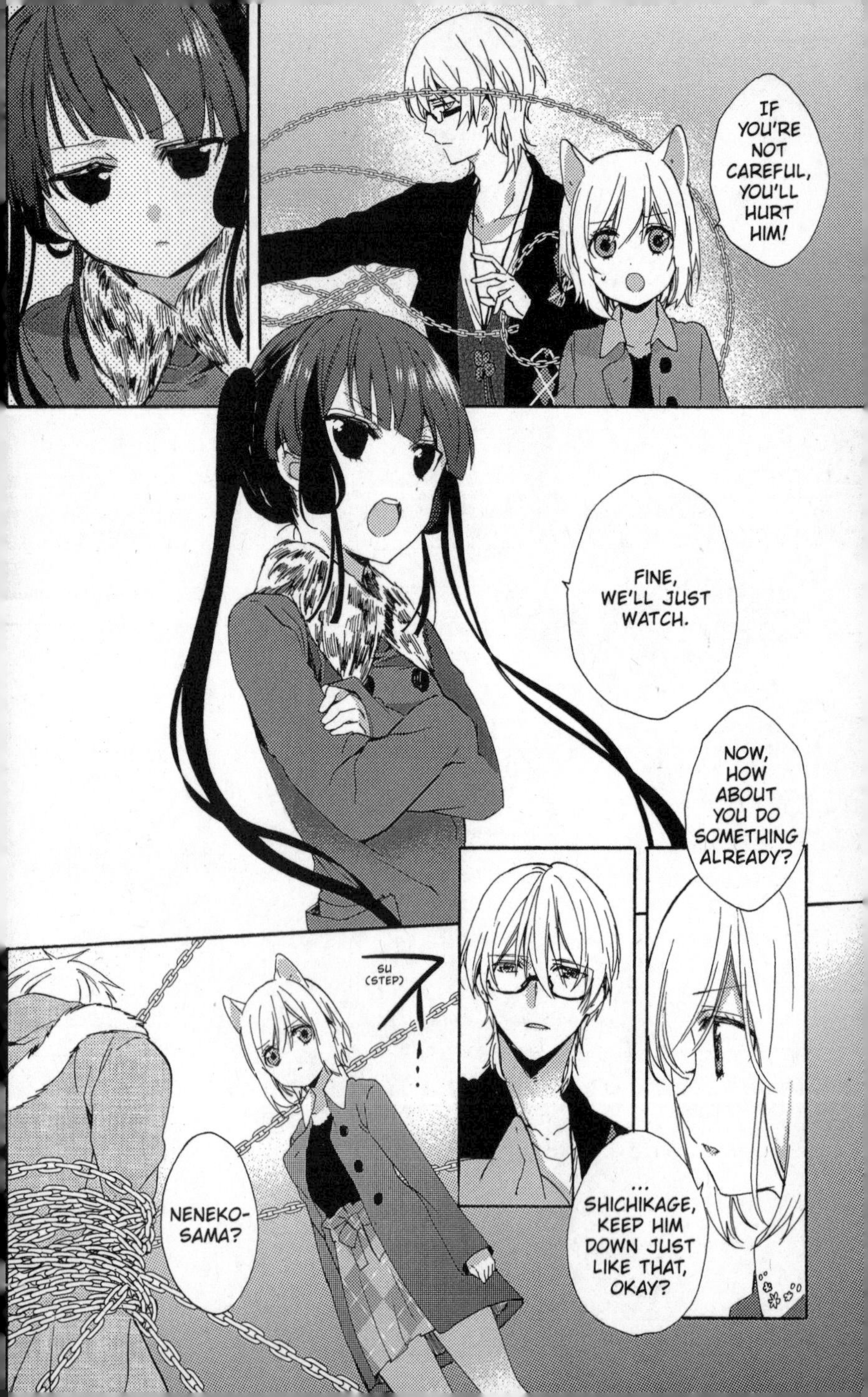
IF YOU'RE NOT CAREFUL, YOU'LL HURT HIM!
FINE, WE'LL JUST WATCH.
NOW, HOW ABOUT YOU DO SOMETHING ALREADY?
... SHICHIKAGE, KEEP HIM DOWN JUST LIKE THAT, OKAY?
SU (STEP)
NENEKO-SAMA?

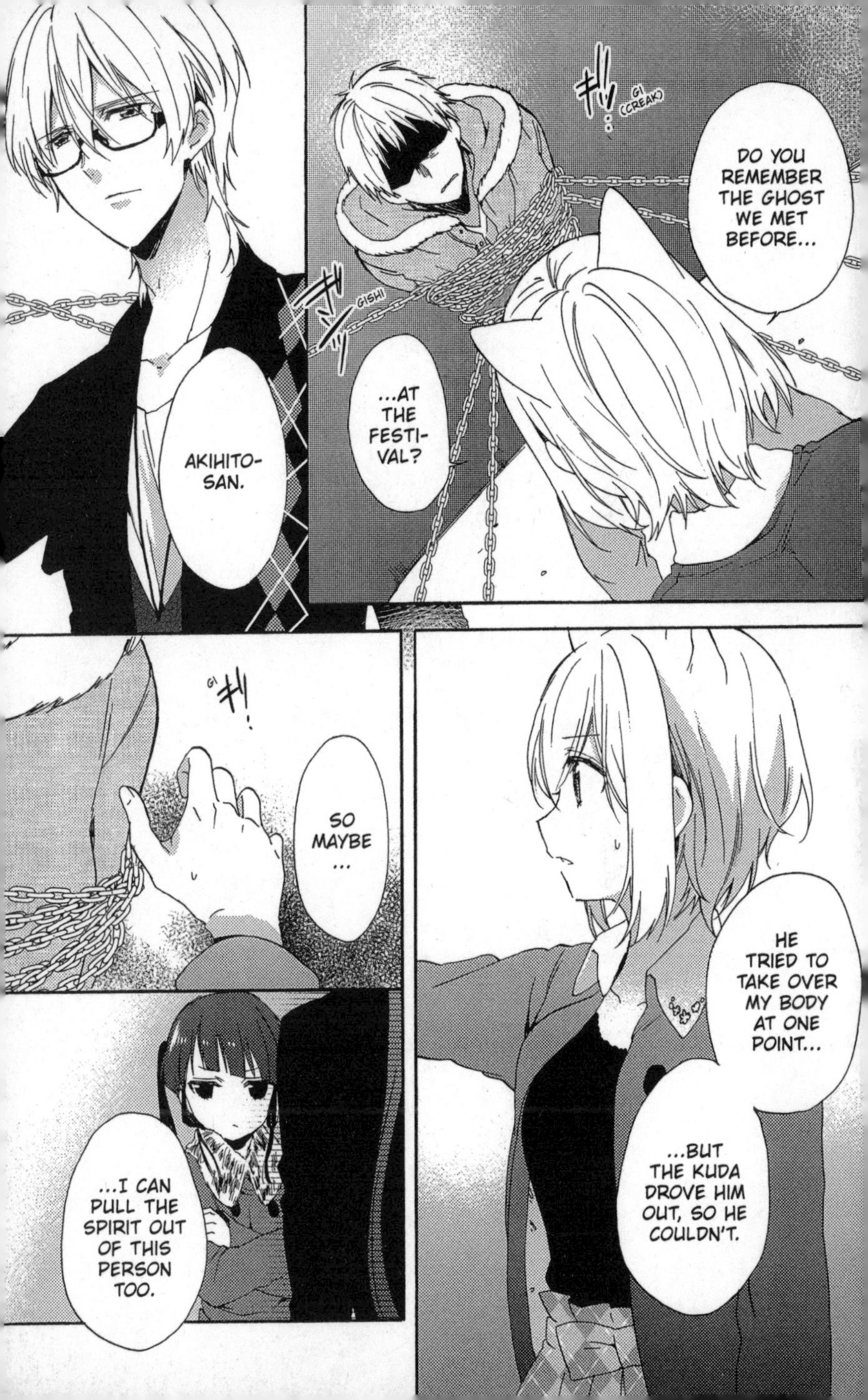
GI (CREAK)
DO YOU REMEMBER THE GHOST WE MET BEFORE...
GISHI
...AT THE FESTIVAL?
AKIHITO-SAN.
HE TRIED TO TAKE OVER MY BODY AT ONE POINT...
...BUT THE KUDA DROVE HIM OUT, SO HE COULDN'T.
GI
SO MAYBE ...
...I CAN PULL THE SPIRIT OUT OF THIS PERSON TOO.

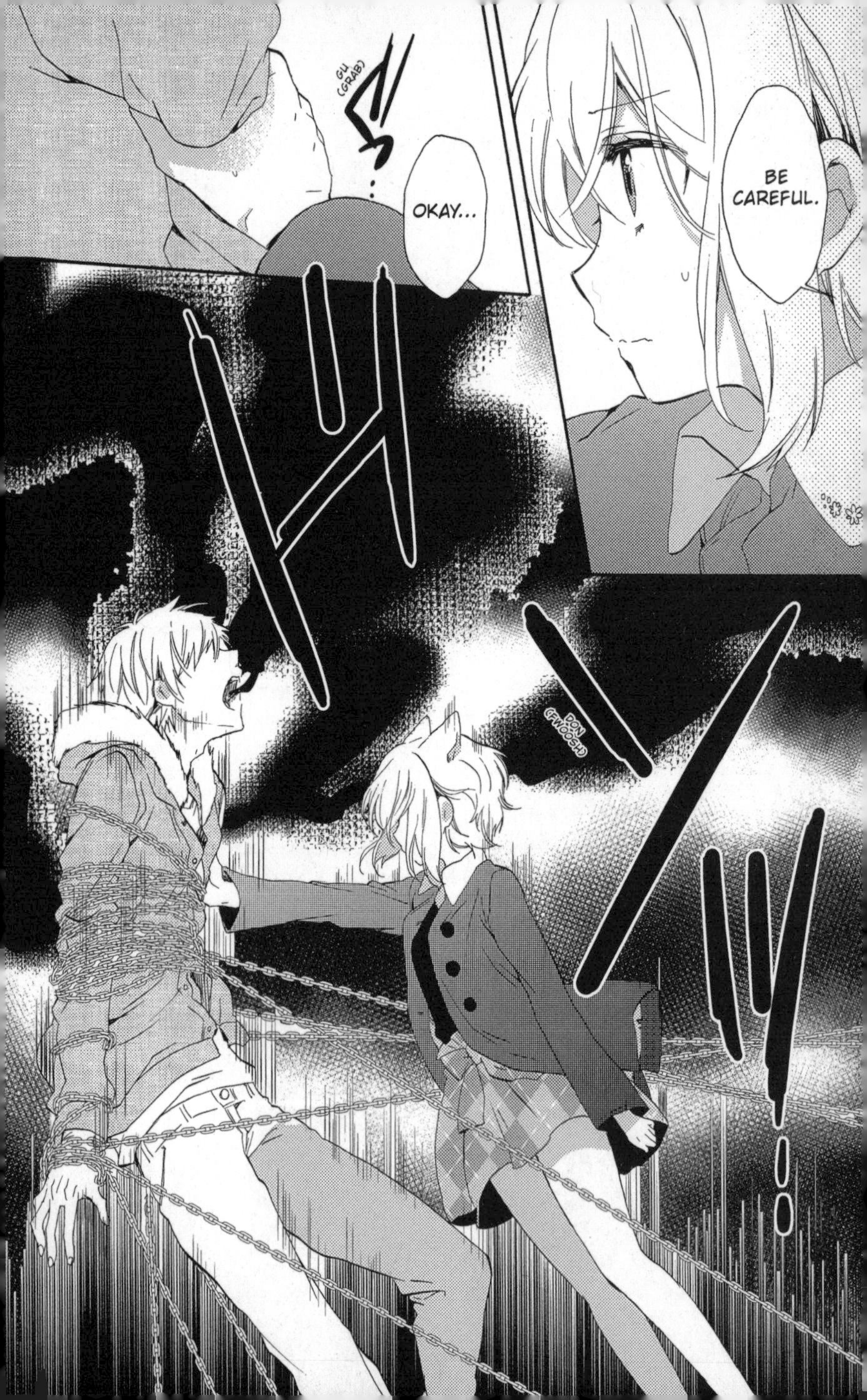
BE CAREFUL.
GU (GRAB)
OKAY...
DON (FWOOSH)

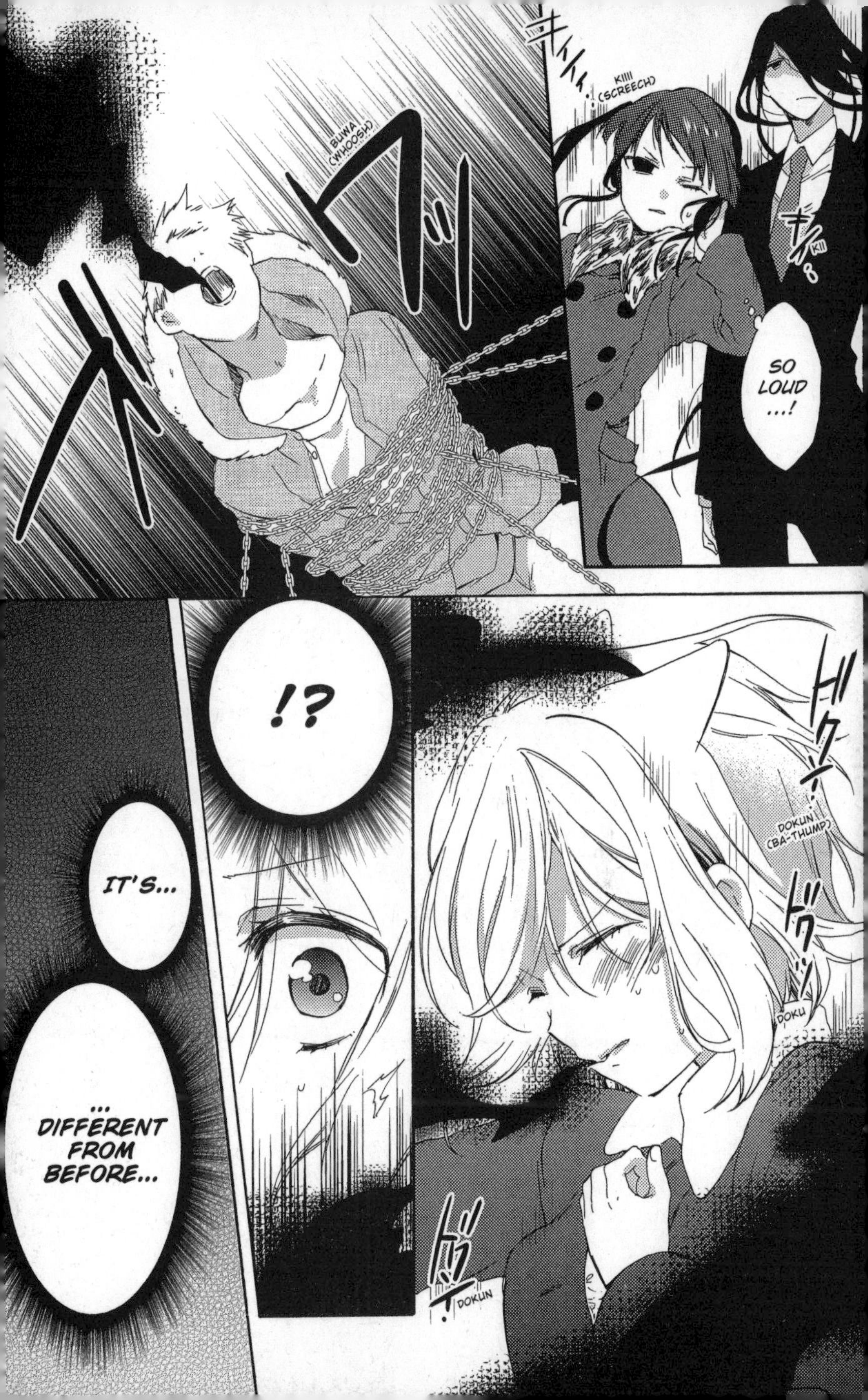
KIIII (SCREECH)
KII
SO LOUD ...!
BUWA (WHOOSH)
DOKUN (BA-THUMP)
DOKU
DOKUN
!?
IT'S...
... DIFFERENT FROM BEFORE...

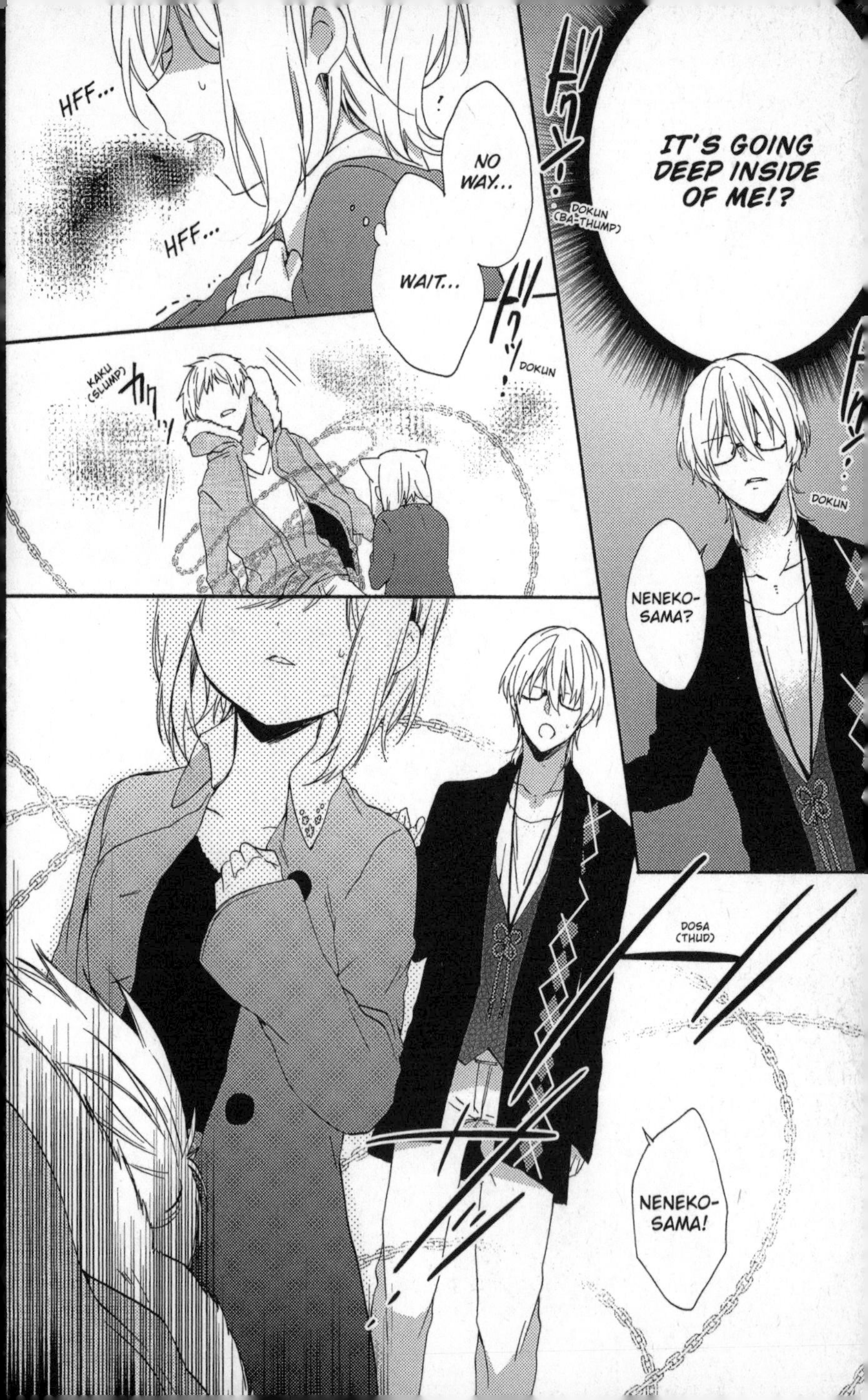
IT'S GOING DEEP INSIDE OF ME!?
DOKUN (BA-THUMP)
DOKUN
NENEKO-SAMA?
NO WAY...
WAIT...
HFF...
HFF...
DOKUN
KAKU (SLUMP)
NENEKO-SAMA!
DOSA (THUD)

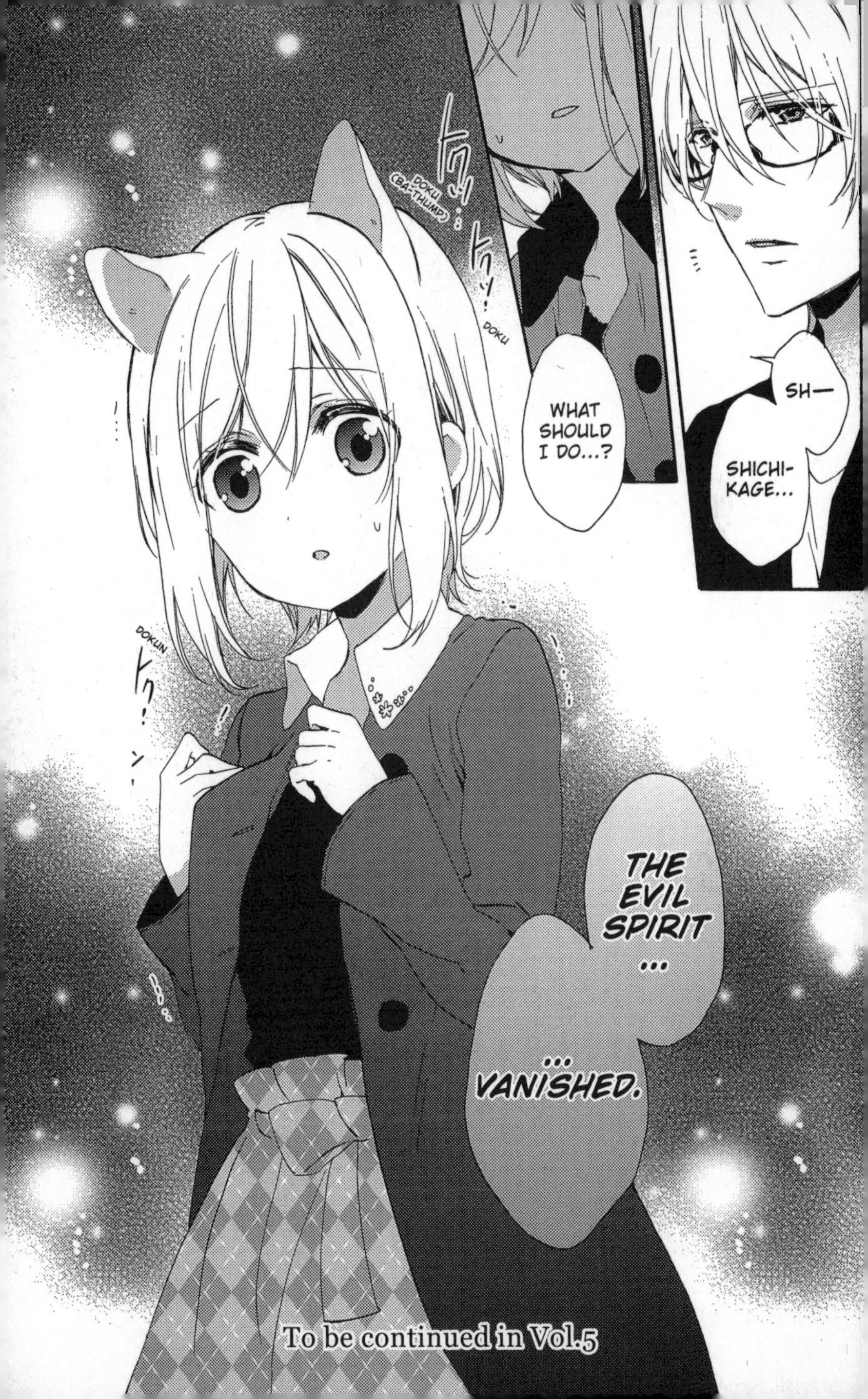
SH—
SHICHIKAGE...
DOKU (BA-THUMP)
DOKU
WHAT SHOULD I DO...?
DOKUN
THE EVIL SPIRIT ...
... VANISHED.
To be continued in Vol.5

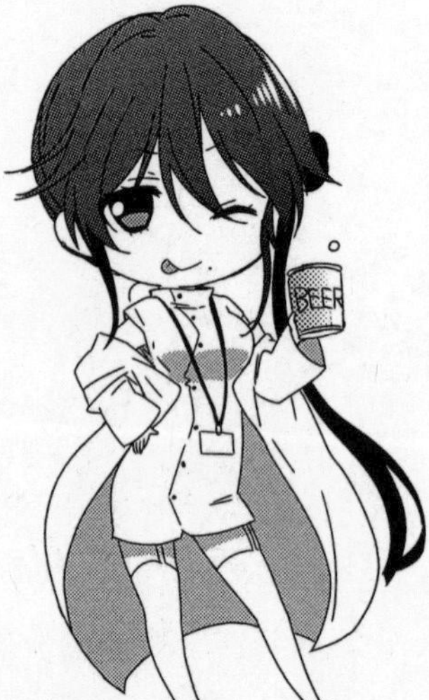
BEER

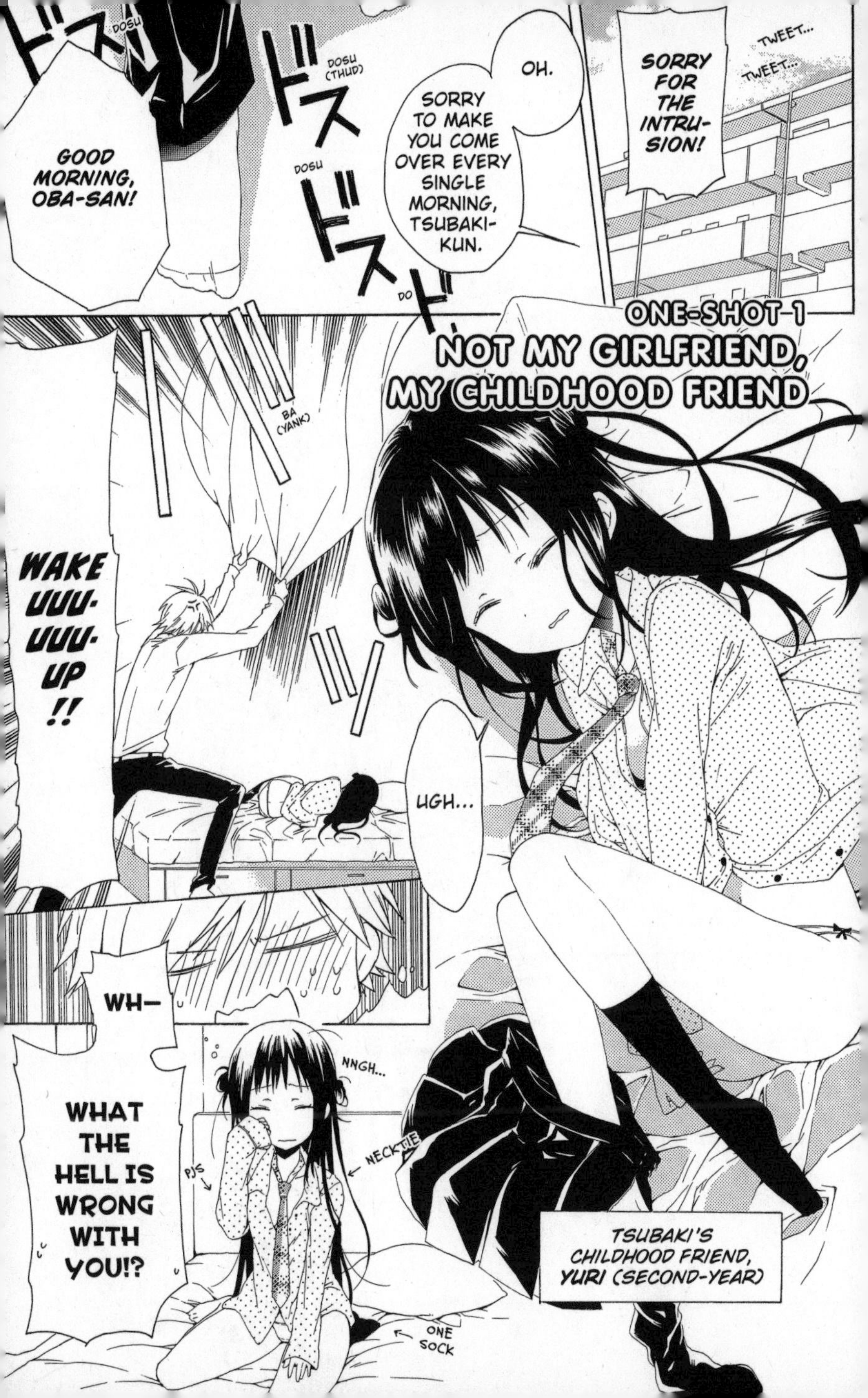
TWEET...
TWEET...
SORRY FOR THE INTRUSION!
OH.
SORRY TO MAKE YOU COME OVER EVERY SINGLE MORNING, TSUBAKI-KUN.
DOSU (THUD)
DOSU
DO
DOSU
GOOD MORNING, OBA-SAN!
ONE-SHOT 1
NOT MY GIRLFRIEND, MY CHILDHOOD FRIEND
BA (YANK)
UGH...
WAKE UUUU-UUU-UP !!
WH—
TSUBAKI'S CHILDHOOD FRIEND, YURI (SECOND-YEAR)
NNGH...
NECKTIE
PJS
ONE SOCK
WHAT THE HELL IS WRONG WITH YOU!?

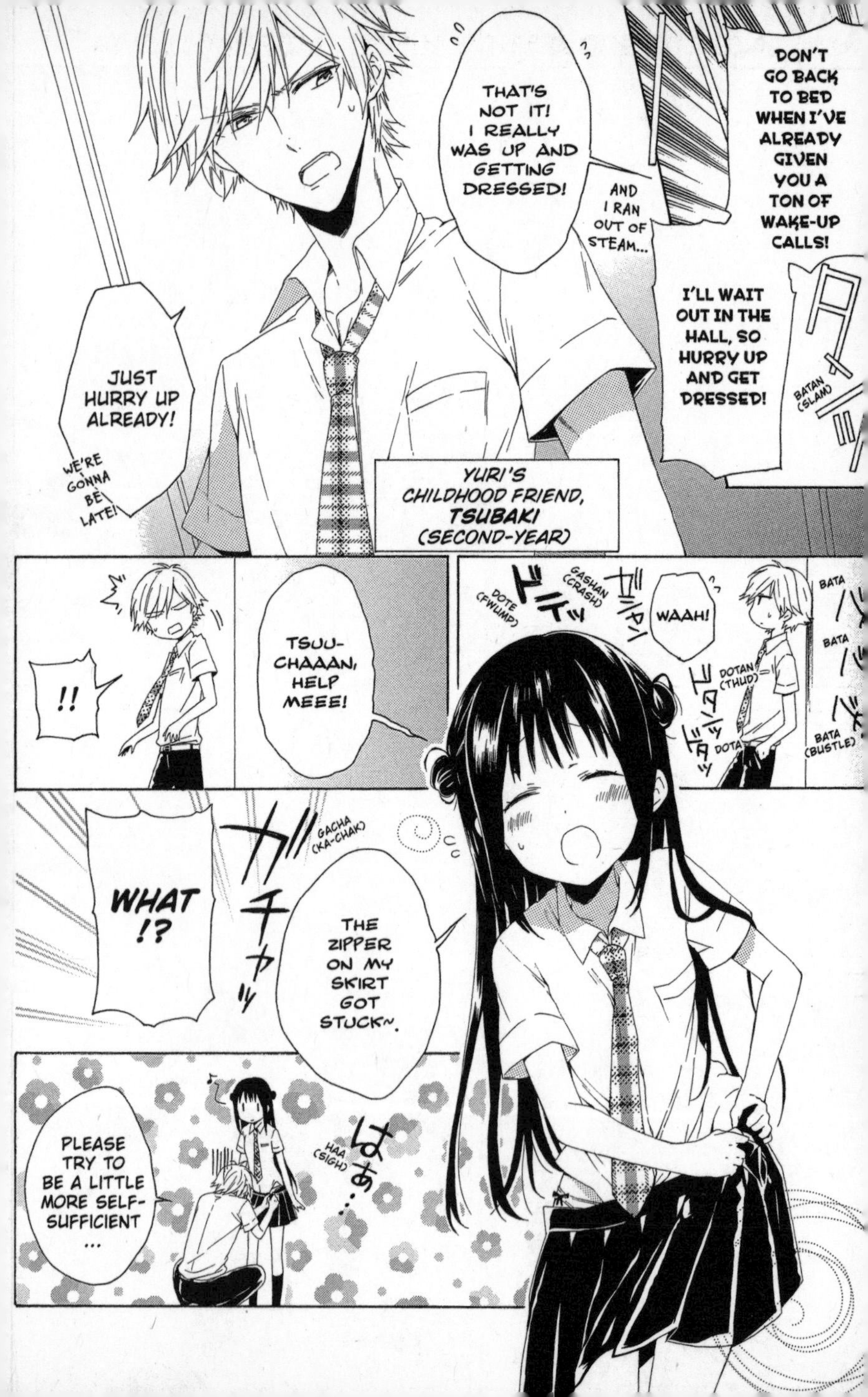
DON'T GO BACK TO BED WHEN I'VE ALREADY GIVEN YOU A TON OF WAKE-UP CALLS!
I'LL WAIT OUT IN THE HALL, SO HURRY UP AND GET DRESSED!
BATAN (SLAM)
THAT'S NOT IT! I REALLY WAS UP AND GETTING DRESSED!
AND I RAN OUT OF STEAM...
JUST HURRY UP ALREADY!
WE'RE GONNA BE LATE!
YURI'S CHILDHOOD FRIEND, TSUBAKI (SECOND-YEAR)
BATA
BATA
BATA (BUSTLE)
WAAH!
GASHAN (CRASH)
DOTE (FWUMP)
DOTAN (THUD)
DOTA
TSUU-CHAAAN, HELP MEEE!
!!
THE ZIPPER ON MY SKIRT GOT STUCK~.
GACHA (KA-CHAK)
WHAT!?
HAA (SIGH)
PLEASE TRY TO BE A LITTLE MORE SELF-SUFFICIENT...

# A CHILDHOOD FRIEND'S LUNCH MADE WITH LOVE

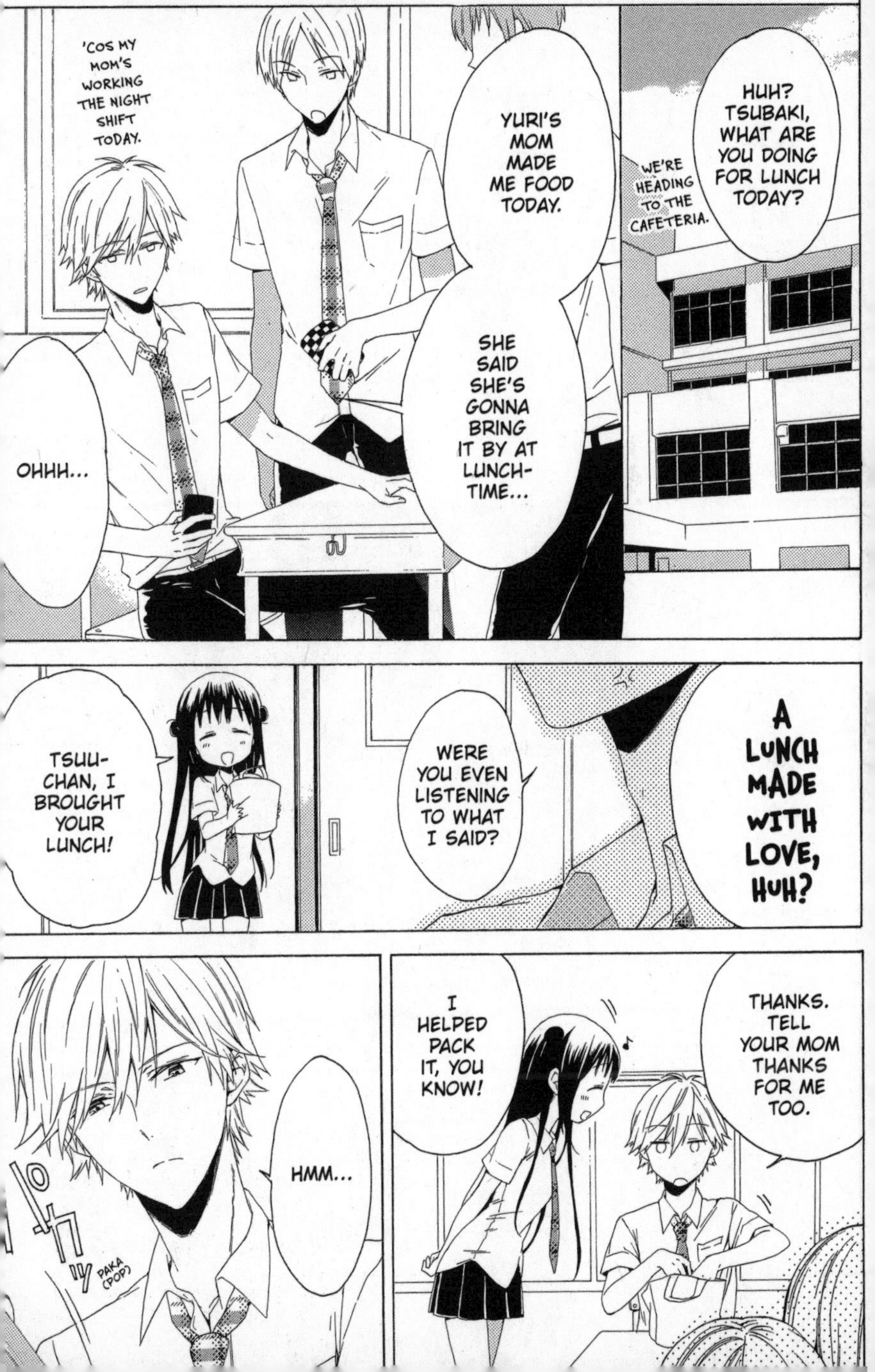
HUH? TSUBAKI, WHAT ARE YOU DOING FOR LUNCH TODAY?
WE'RE HEADING TO THE CAFETERIA.
YURI'S MOM MADE ME FOOD TODAY.
SHE SAID SHE'S GONNA BRING IT BY AT LUNCH-TIME...
'COS MY MOM'S WORKING THE NIGHT SHIFT TODAY.
OHHH...
A LUNCH MADE WITH LOVE, HUH?
WERE YOU EVEN LISTENING TO WHAT I SAID?
TSUU-CHAN, I BROUGHT YOUR LUNCH!
THANKS. TELL YOUR MOM THANKS FOR ME TOO.
I HELPED PACK IT, YOU KNOW!
HMM...
PAKA (POP)

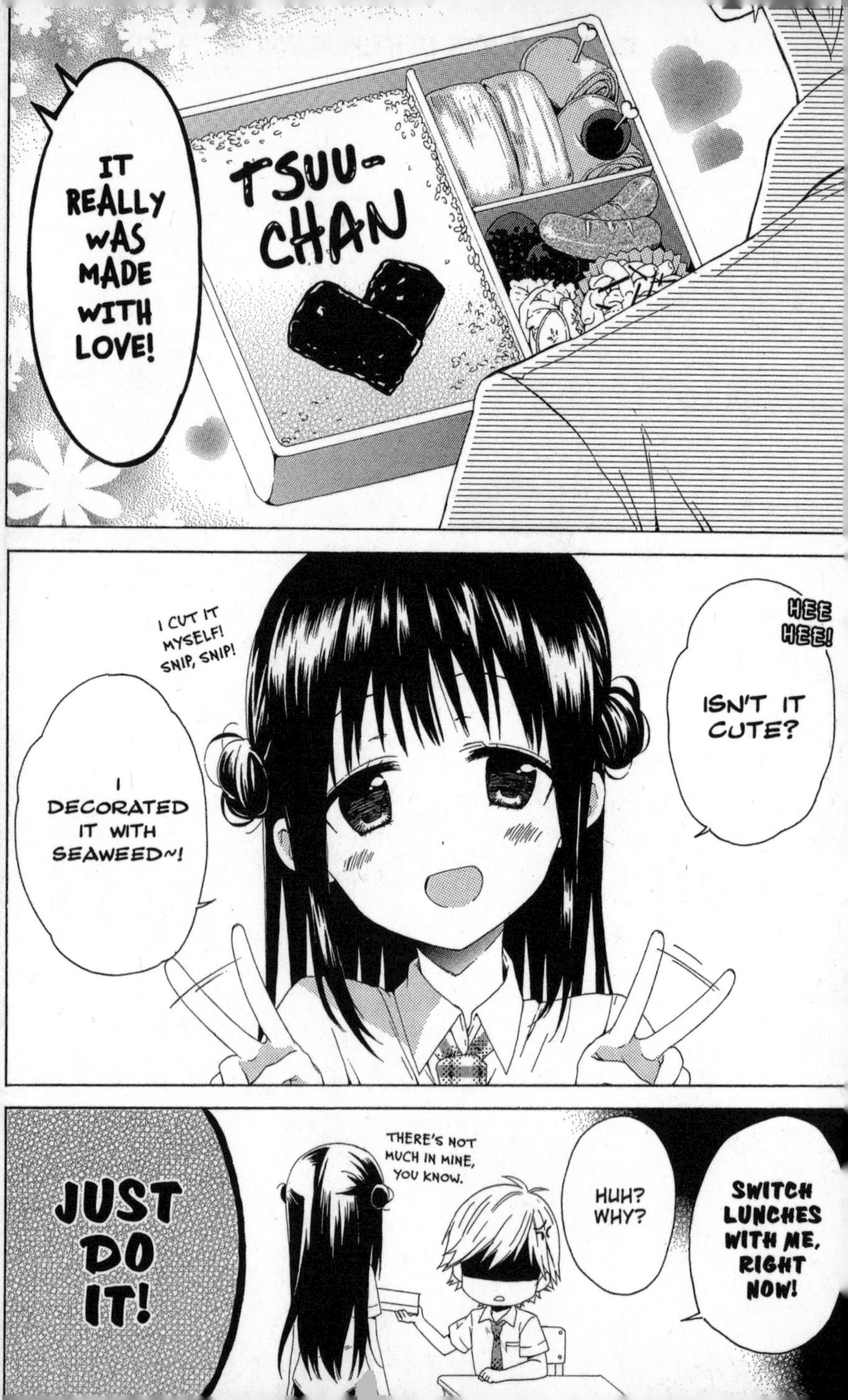
IT REALLY WAS MADE WITH LOVE!
TSUU-CHAN
HEE HEE!
ISN'T IT CUTE?
I CUT IT MYSELF! SNIP, SNIP!
I DECORATED IT WITH SEAWEED~!
SWITCH LUNCHES WITH ME, RIGHT NOW!
HUH? WHY?
THERE'S NOT MUCH IN MINE, YOU KNOW.
JUST DO IT!

# INSISTENT ON BEING FRIENDS

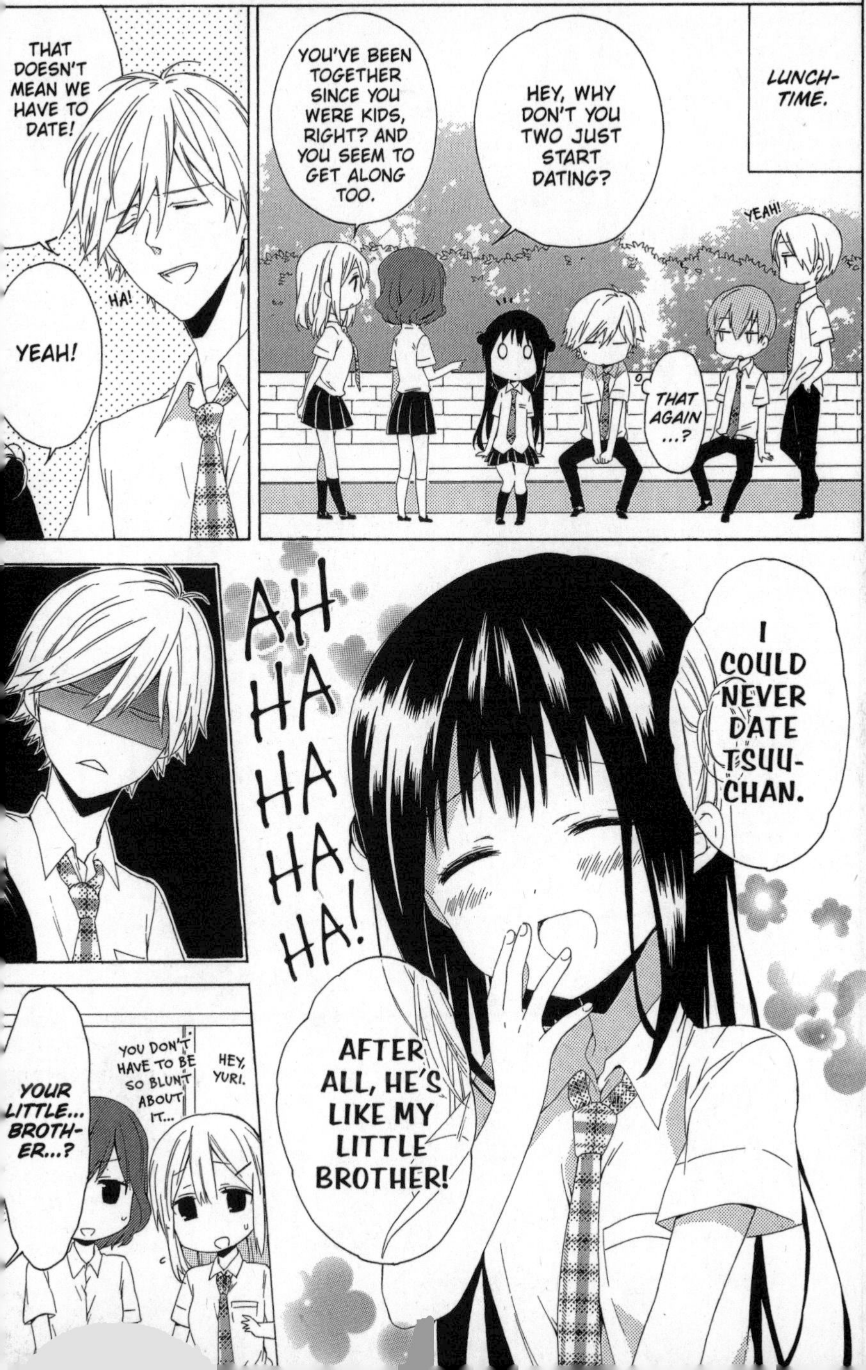
LUNCH-TIME.
HEY, WHY DON'T YOU TWO JUST START DATING?
YOU'VE BEEN TOGETHER SINCE YOU WERE KIDS, RIGHT? AND YOU SEEM TO GET ALONG TOO.
YEAH!
THAT AGAIN ...?
THAT DOESN'T MEAN WE HAVE TO DATE!
HA!
YEAH!
I COULD NEVER DATE TSUU-CHAN.
AH HA HA HA HA HA!
AFTER ALL, HE'S LIKE MY LITTLE BROTHER!
HEY, YURI.
YOU DON'T HAVE TO BE SO BLUNT ABOUT IT...
YOUR LITTLE... BROTHER...?

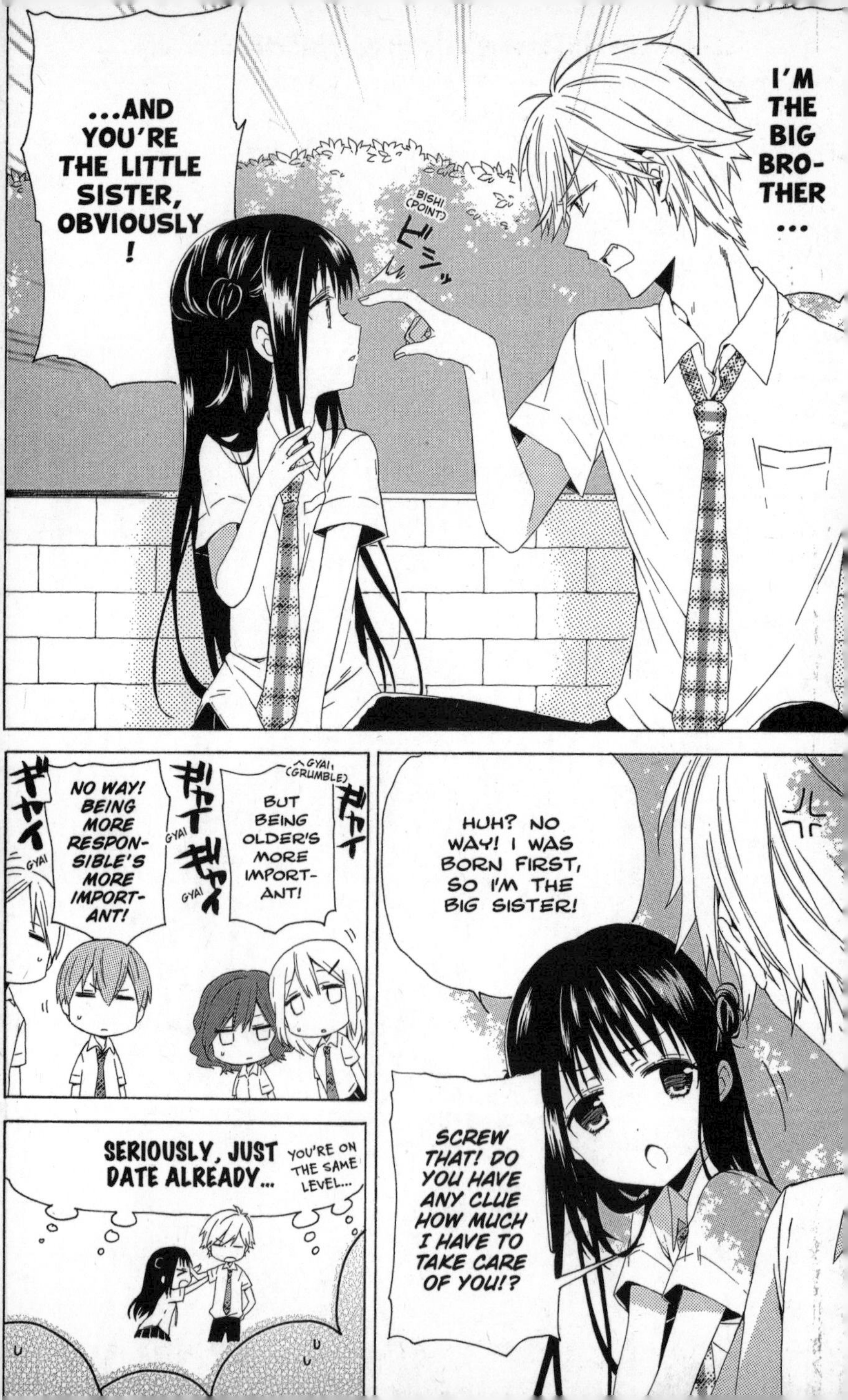
I'M THE BIG BRO-THER...
BISHI (POINT)
ビシッ
...AND YOU'RE THE LITTLE SISTER, OBVIOUSLY!
HUH? NO WAY! I WAS BORN FIRST, SO I'M THE BIG SISTER!
SCREW THAT! DO YOU HAVE ANY CLUE HOW MUCH I HAVE TO TAKE CARE OF YOU!?
ギャイ
GYAI, (GRUMBLE)
BUT BEING OLDER'S MORE IMPORTANT!
ギャイ
GYAI
ギャイ
GYAI
NO WAY! BEING MORE RESPON-SIBLE'S MORE IMPORT-ANT!
ギャイ
GYAI
YOU'RE ON THE SAME LEVEL...
SERIOUSLY, JUST DATE ALREADY...

# HOW TO DEAL WITH A CHILDHOOD FRIEND

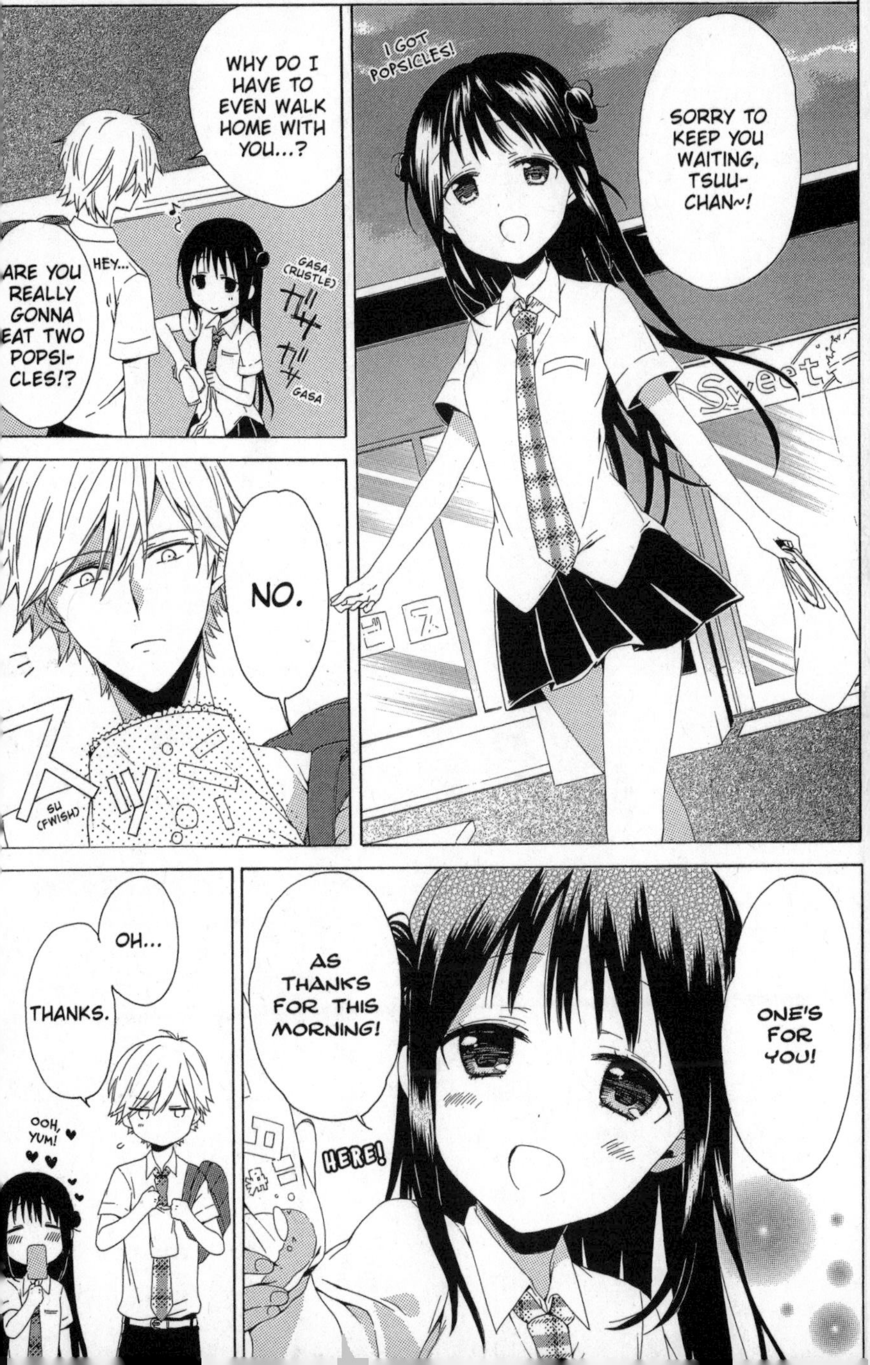
I GOT POPSICLES!
SORRY TO KEEP YOU WAITING, TSUU-CHAN~!
WHY DO I HAVE TO EVEN WALK HOME WITH YOU...?
GASA (RUSTLE)
GASA
HEY...
ARE YOU REALLY GONNA EAT TWO POPSICLES!?
NO.
SU (FWISH)
ONE'S FOR YOU!
AS THANKS FOR THIS MORNING!
HERE!
OH...
THANKS.
OOH, YUM!

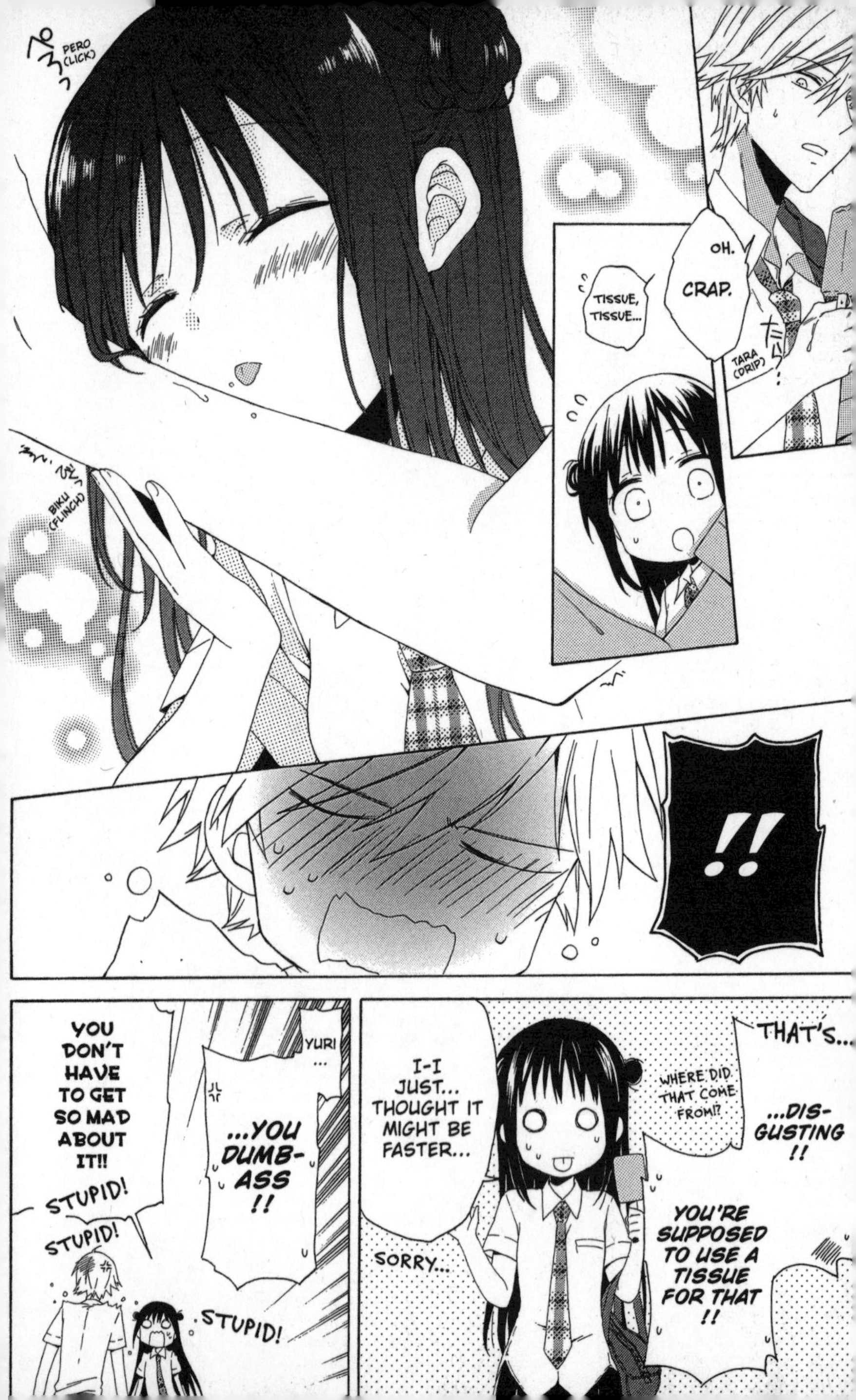
OH.
CRAP.
TARA (DRIP)
TISSUE, TISSUE...
PERO (LICK)
BIKU (FLINCH)
!!
THAT'S...
WHERE DID THAT COME FROM!?
...DIS-GUSTING !!
YOU'RE SUPPOSED TO USE A TISSUE FOR THAT !!
I-I JUST... THOUGHT IT MIGHT BE FASTER...
SORRY...
YURI ...
...YOU DUMB-ASS !!
YOU DON'T HAVE TO GET SO MAD ABOUT IT!!
STUPID!
STUPID!
STUPID!

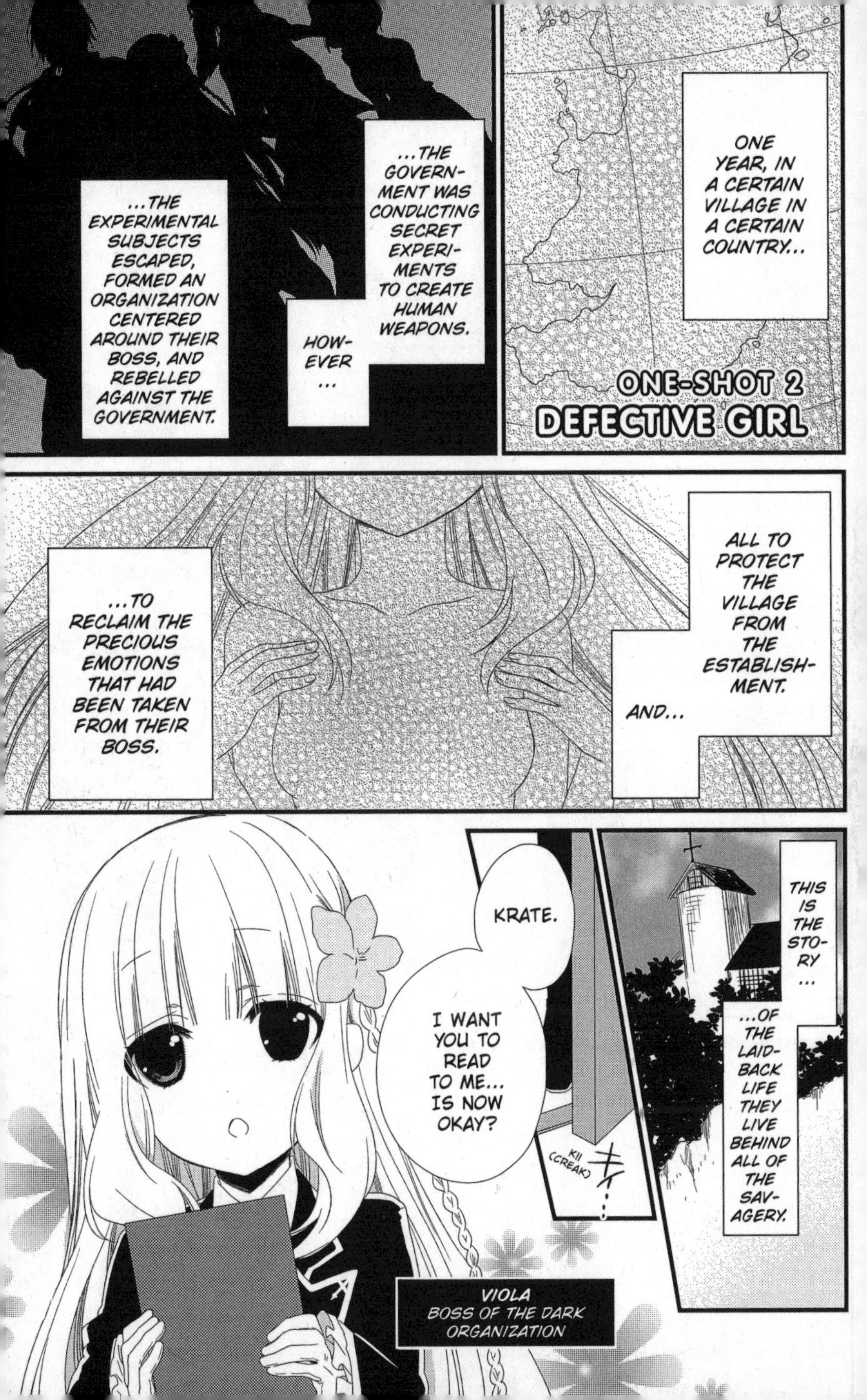
ONE YEAR, IN A CERTAIN VILLAGE IN A CERTAIN COUNTRY...
ONE-SHOT 2
DEFECTIVE GIRL
...THE GOVERNMENT WAS CONDUCTING SECRET EXPERIMENTS TO CREATE HUMAN WEAPONS.
HOWEVER...
...THE EXPERIMENTAL SUBJECTS ESCAPED, FORMED AN ORGANIZATION CENTERED AROUND THEIR BOSS, AND REBELLED AGAINST THE GOVERNMENT.
ALL TO PROTECT THE VILLAGE FROM THE ESTABLISHMENT.
AND...
...TO RECLAIM THE PRECIOUS EMOTIONS THAT HAD BEEN TAKEN FROM THEIR BOSS.
THIS IS THE STORY...
...OF THE LAID-BACK LIFE THEY LIVE BEHIND ALL OF THE SAVAGERY.
KII (CREAK)
KRATE.
I WANT YOU TO READ TO ME... IS NOW OKAY?
VIOLA
BOSS OF THE DARK ORGANIZATION

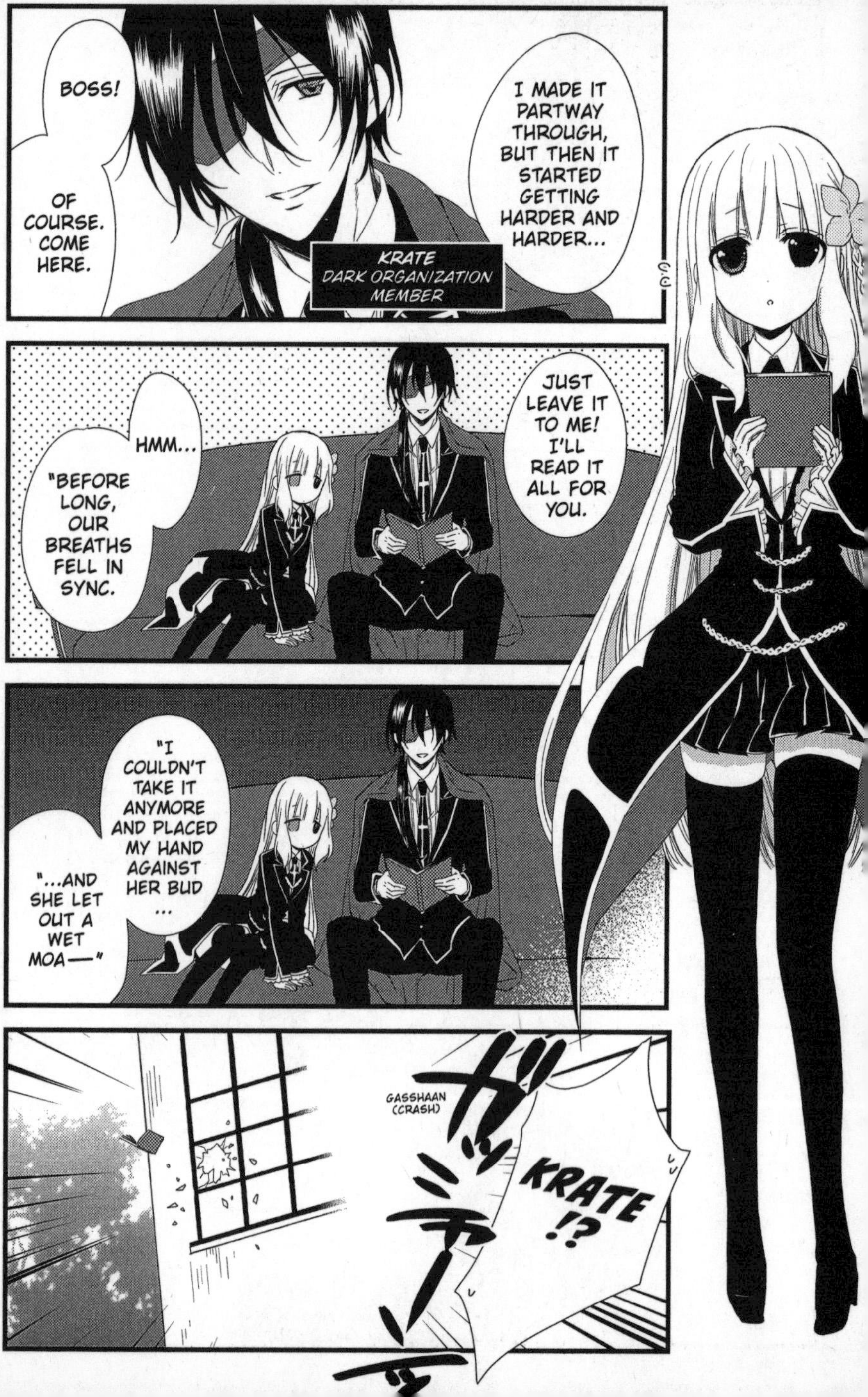
I MADE IT PARTWAY THROUGH, BUT THEN IT STARTED GETTING HARDER AND HARDER...
KRATE
DARK ORGANIZATION MEMBER
BOSS!
OF COURSE. COME HERE.
JUST LEAVE IT TO ME! I'LL READ IT ALL FOR YOU.
HMM...
"BEFORE LONG, OUR BREATHS FELL IN SYNC.
"I COULDN'T TAKE IT ANYMORE AND PLACED MY HAND AGAINST HER BUD ...
"...AND SHE LET OUT A WET MOA—"
KRATE !?
GASSHAAN (CRASH)

# YOU SAID YOU'D TELL ME...

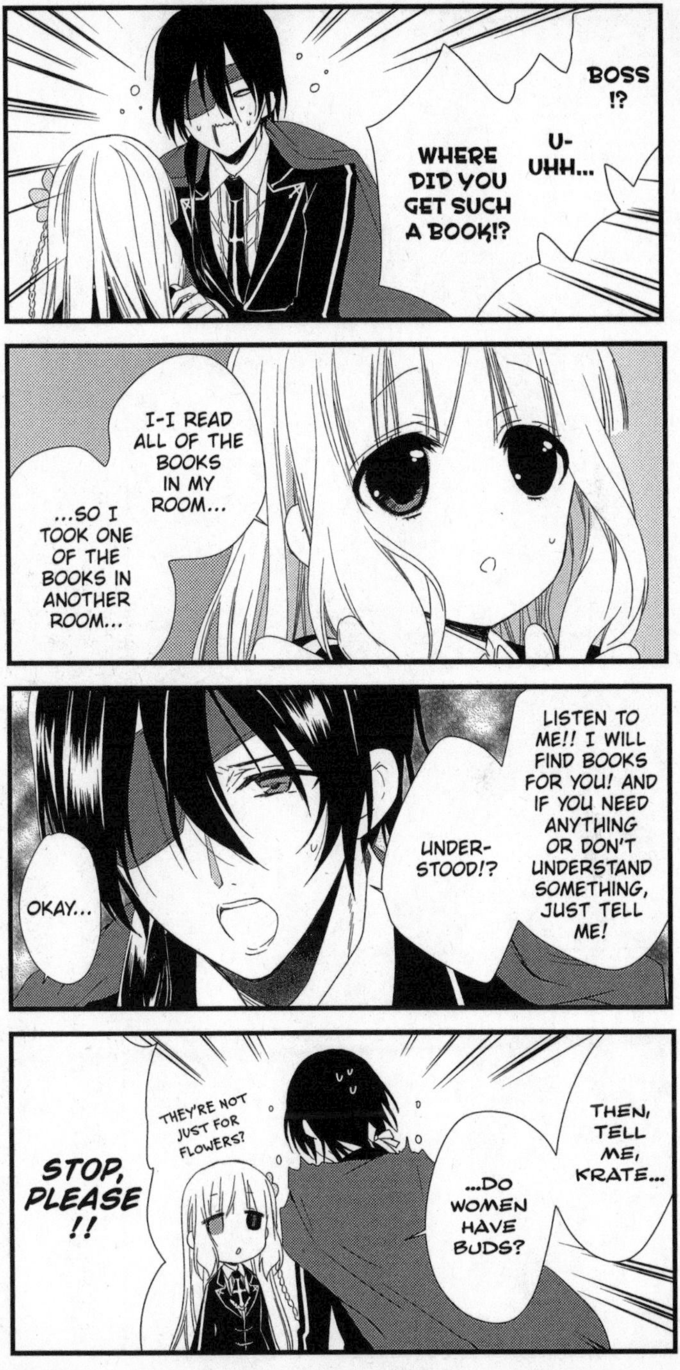
BOSS !?
U- UHH...
WHERE DID YOU GET SUCH A BOOK!?
I-I READ ALL OF THE BOOKS IN MY ROOM...
...SO I TOOK ONE OF THE BOOKS IN ANOTHER ROOM...
LISTEN TO ME!! I WILL FIND BOOKS FOR YOU! AND IF YOU NEED ANYTHING OR DON'T UNDERSTAND SOMETHING, JUST TELL ME!
UNDER- STOOD!?
OKAY...
THEN, TELL ME, KRATE...
...DO WOMEN HAVE BUDS?
THEY'RE NOT JUST FOR FLOWERS?
STOP, PLEASE !!

# STEP BY STEP

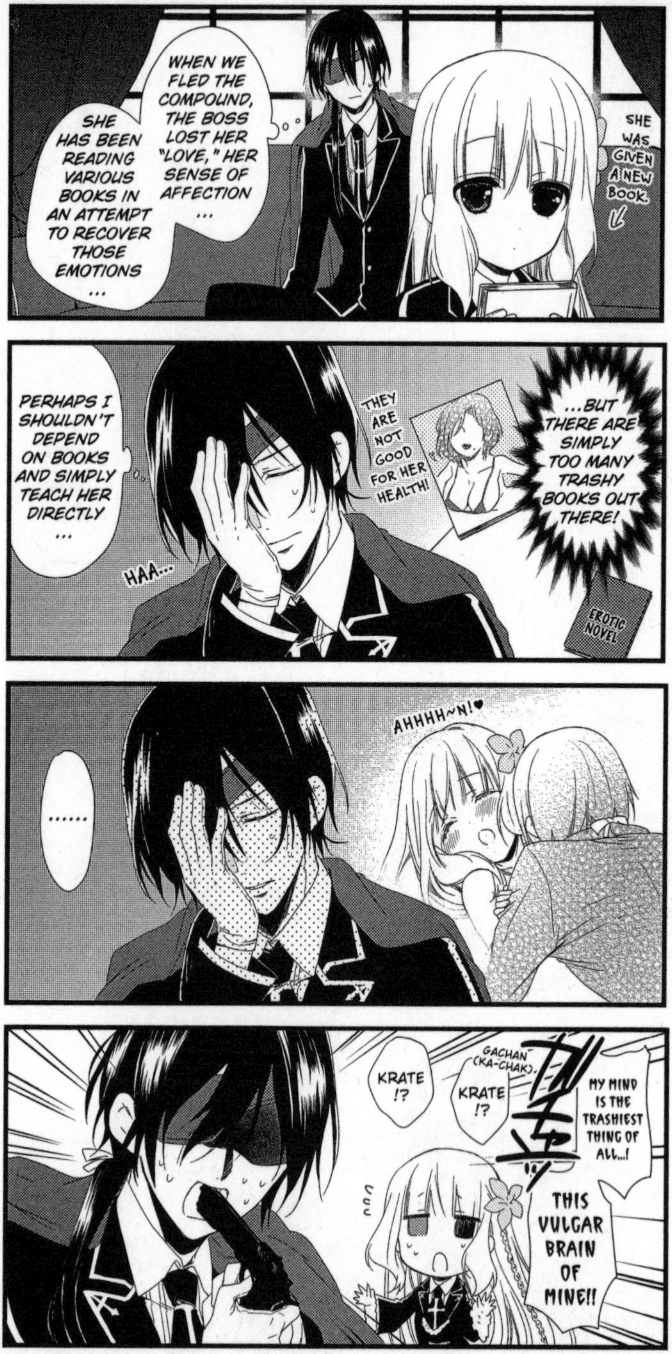
SHE WAS GIVEN A NEW BOOK.
WHEN WE FLED THE COMPOUND, THE BOSS LOST HER "LOVE," HER SENSE OF AFFECTION ...
SHE HAS BEEN READING VARIOUS BOOKS IN AN ATTEMPT TO RECOVER THOSE EMOTIONS ...
...BUT THERE ARE SIMPLY TOO MANY TRASHY BOOKS OUT THERE!
THEY ARE NOT GOOD FOR HER HEALTH!
EROTIC NOVEL
PERHAPS I SHOULDN'T DEPEND ON BOOKS AND SIMPLY TEACH HER DIRECTLY ...
HAA...
AHHHH~N!♥
......
MY MIND IS THE TRASHIEST THING OF ALL...!
THIS VULGAR BRAIN OF MINE!!
GACHAN (KA-CHAK)
KRATE !?
KRATE !?

# PERFECT

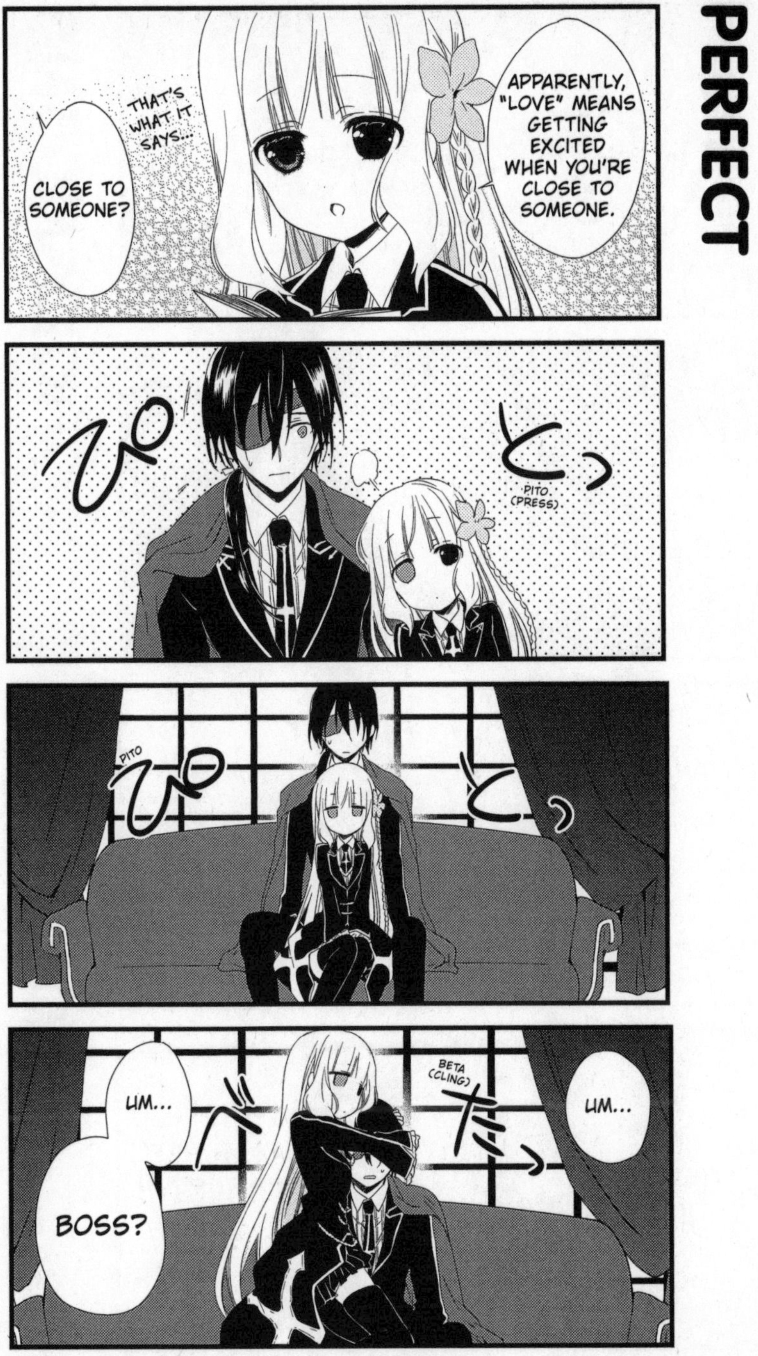
APPARENTLY, "LOVE" MEANS GETTING EXCITED WHEN YOU'RE CLOSE TO SOMEONE.
THAT'S WHAT IT SAYS...
CLOSE TO SOMEONE?
ぴとっ
PITO (PRESS)
ぴとっ
PITO
UM...
BETA (CLING)
べたっ
UM...
BOSS?

UNCONSCIOUSLY...

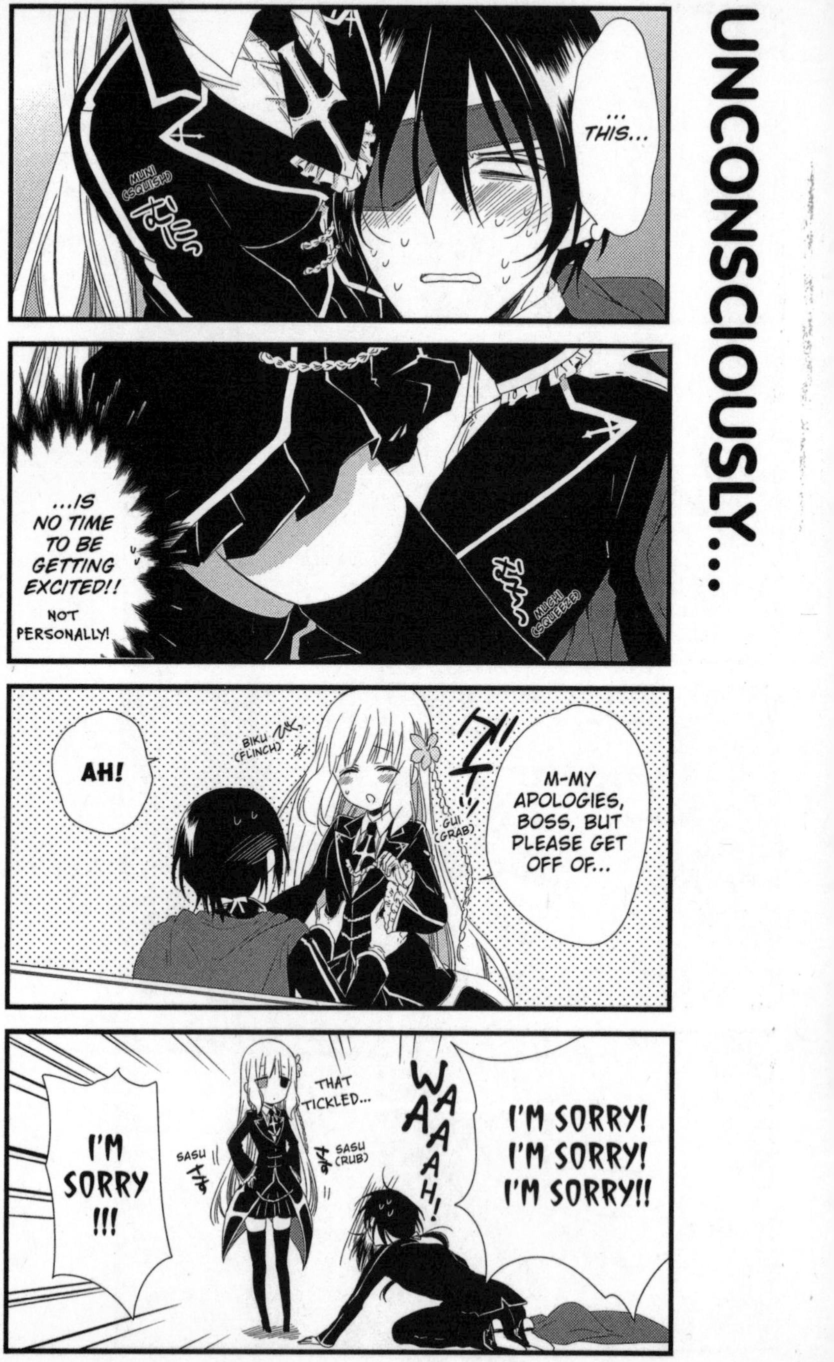
... THIS...
MUNI (SQUISH)
MUCHI (SQUEEZE)
...IS NO TIME TO BE GETTING EXCITED!!
NOT PERSONALLY!
M-MY APOLOGIES, BOSS, BUT PLEASE GET OFF OF...
GUI (GRAB)
BIKU (FLINCH)
AH!
I'M SORRY! I'M SORRY! I'M SORRY!!
WAAAAAH!
SASU (RUB)
THAT TICKLED...
SASU
I'M SORRY !!!

# EXCITED AND TREMBLING

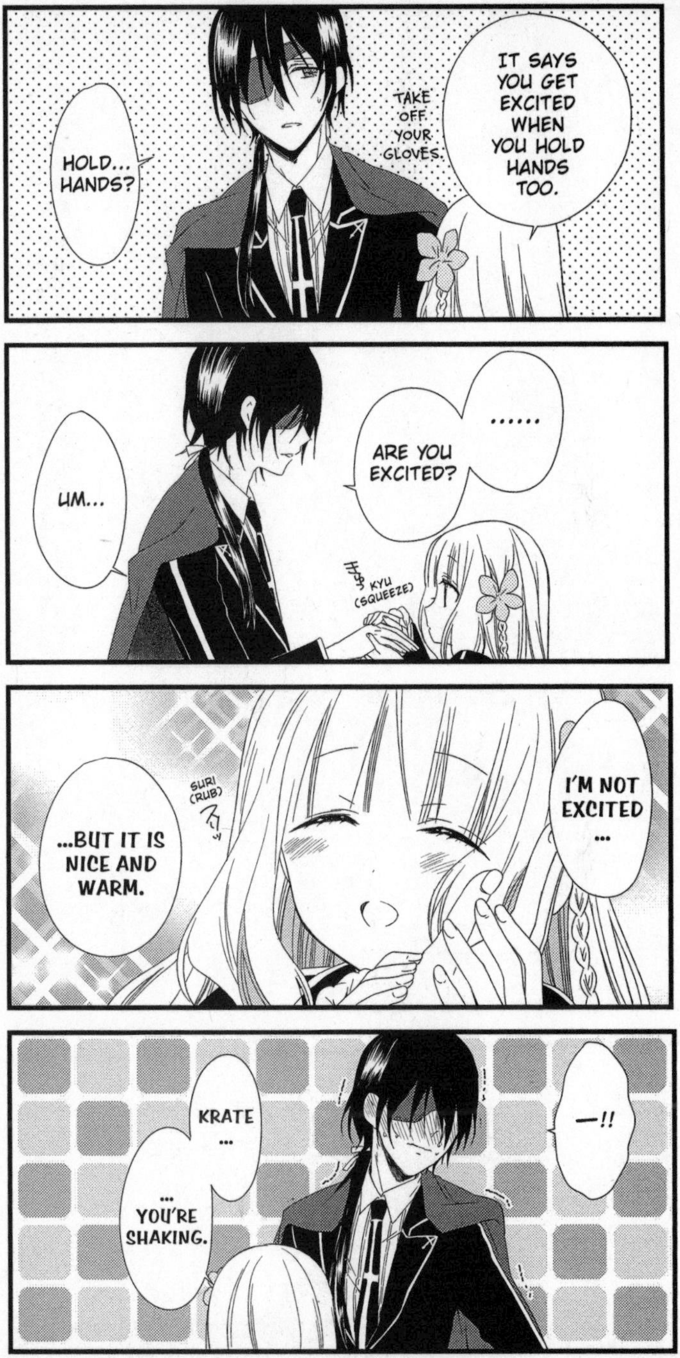
IT SAYS YOU GET EXCITED WHEN YOU HOLD HANDS TOO.
TAKE OFF YOUR GLOVES.
HOLD... HANDS?
......
ARE YOU EXCITED?
KYU (SQUEEZE)
UM...
I'M NOT EXCITED ...
SURI (RUB)
...BUT IT IS NICE AND WARM.
—!!
KRATE ...
... YOU'RE SHAKING.

# COMPATIBLE PARTNER

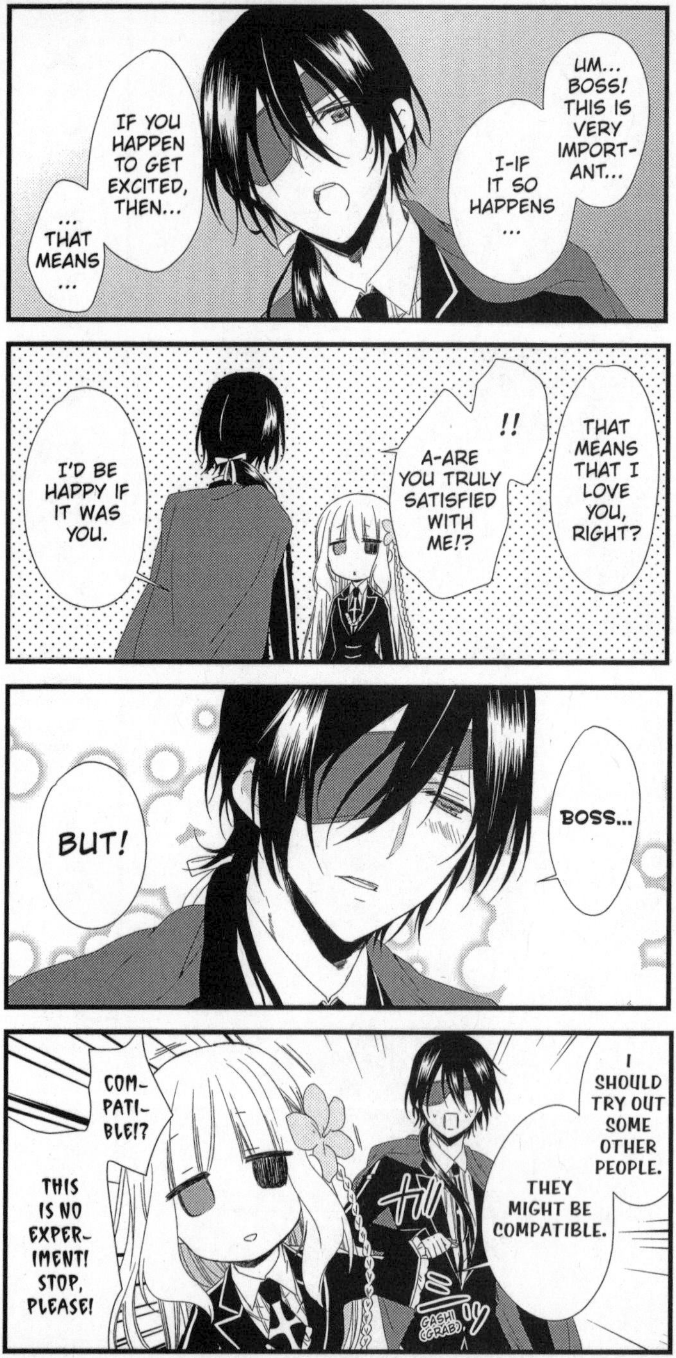
UM... BOSS! THIS IS VERY IMPORT-ANT...
I-IF IT SO HAPPENS ...
IF YOU HAPPEN TO GET EXCITED, THEN...
... THAT MEANS ...
THAT MEANS THAT I LOVE YOU, RIGHT?
!!
A-ARE YOU TRULY SATISFIED WITH ME!?
I'D BE HAPPY IF IT WAS YOU.
BOSS...
BUT!
I SHOULD TRY OUT SOME OTHER PEOPLE.
THEY MIGHT BE COMPATIBLE.
COM-PATI-BLE!?
GASH! (GRAB)
THIS IS NO EXPER-IMENT! STOP, PLEASE!

Hello, I'm Miyuki Nakayama.

Thank you so much for picking up *Spirits* Volume 4! Anyway, this is the afterword, but as I mentioned in Volume 3, I think I'm going to talk about the drama CD.

### ■ NENEKO   Mikako Komatsu-san

I first heard of her as a singer, and I listened to a lot of her CDs while working on my manuscripts. I especially love *ABC* and *Searchlight*. I still listen to those ones on repeat now. In one particular anime, she plays a cheerful girl who can sometimes get a bit gloomy, and I thought that her voice during those times was perfect for Neneko. Right after I found myself thinking, "Oh, this voice would be so cute for her," they approached me about the drama CD, so I accepted gladly! (She really was the perfect voice for Neneko. It sounded so adorable, it made me want to restrain her myself! (LOL))

### ■ SHICHIKAGE   Takahiro Sakurai-san

For some reason, ever since Volume 1 came out, my friends and other acquaintances have been saying, "He has Sakurai-san's voice" about Shichikage. (LOL) To be honest, I think he's the most difficult character to put a voice to, so I was so glad to find the absolute perfect voice for him! He's so cool! It makes me want to let everything slide, even when he's pushing it.

### ■ MIYA   Yuka Iguchi-san

I saw her play a cool and collected character in this one game, so I asked if she could handle the role of Miya. She usually plays cheerful characters, so the gap between those and Miya is just too good. Just as I expected, she went from cool to affectionate toward Neneko, embarrassed toward Shingetsu, and finally, a little standoffish. Each and every little shift is just too cute!

### ■ SHINGETSU   Kenichi Suzumura-san

Suzumura-san's sweet, kind voice is just perfect for the way Shingetsu is always smiling and a little bit spacey. It's so cute! But even when going a little crazy, as well as when he whispers to Miya sweetly with a touch of cruelty mixed in, his voice is just so amazing! It even made me start to have a thing for Shingetsu myself. (LOL)

### ■ MEME   Yui Ogura-san

When it comes to adorable little girls who make you want to protect them, I just couldn't think of anyone but Ogura-san. She really is an angel! She agreed to swear a little bit for me, but even that was just too cute!

### ■ ENISHI   Shinichiro Miki-san

Once again, I couldn't think of anyone for Enishi but Miki-san, and that was the strongest image I had out of all the characters. It's the perfect voice for a pervy yet adorable old man character you just can't hate. He truly was Enishi! His voice when he was talking with Ogura-san was so gentle, like a father talking to his child. It was downright soothing.

MIKAKOSHI, MIKAKOSHI, THIS ISN'T "GIVE UP," IT'S "CHAIN UP."

WHY THAT ALL OF SUDDEN!?

!?

HUH!?

**NOTE:** Sakurai-san suddenly explained how to read a character in the middle of the recording. Their exchange was adorable.

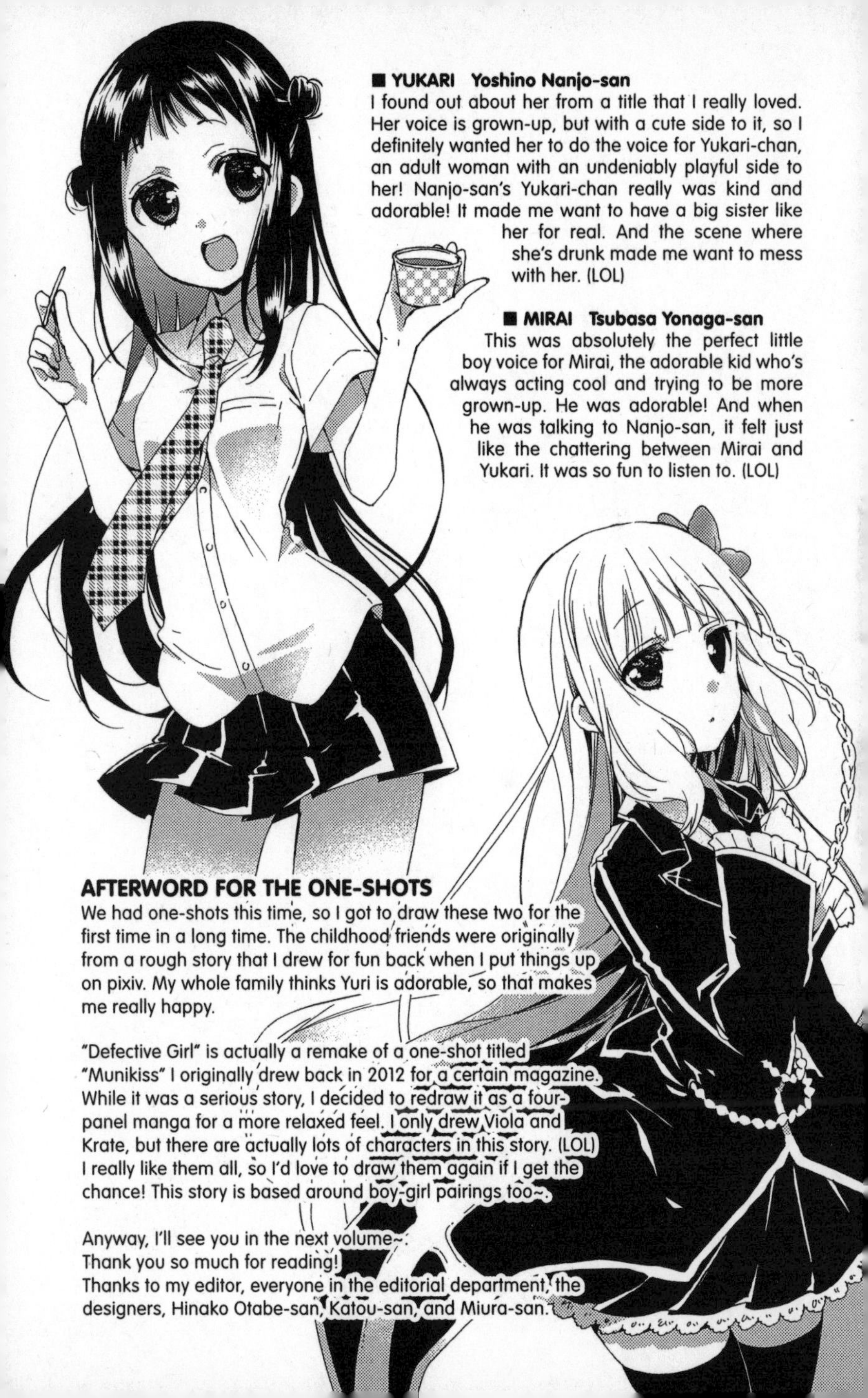

**■ YUKARI Yoshino Nanjo-san**
I found out about her from a title that I really loved. Her voice is grown-up, but with a cute side to it, so I definitely wanted her to do the voice for Yukari-chan, an adult woman with an undeniably playful side to her! Nanjo-san's Yukari-chan really was kind and adorable! It made me want to have a big sister like her for real. And the scene where she's drunk made me want to mess with her. (LOL)

**■ MIRAI Tsubasa Yonaga-san**
This was absolutely the perfect little boy voice for Mirai, the adorable kid who's always acting cool and trying to be more grown-up. He was adorable! And when he was talking to Nanjo-san, it felt just like the chattering between Mirai and Yukari. It was so fun to listen to. (LOL)

## AFTERWORD FOR THE ONE-SHOTS

We had one-shots this time, so I got to draw these two for the first time in a long time. The childhood friends were originally from a rough story that I drew for fun back when I put things up on pixiv. My whole family thinks Yuri is adorable, so that makes me really happy.

"Defective Girl" is actually a remake of a one-shot titled "Munikiss" I originally drew back in 2012 for a certain magazine. While it was a serious story, I decided to redraw it as a four-panel manga for a more relaxed feel. I only drew Viola and Krate, but there are actually lots of characters in this story. (LOL) I really like them all, so I'd love to draw them again if I get the chance! This story is based around boy-girl pairings too~.

Anyway, I'll see you in the next volume~.
Thank you so much for reading!
Thanks to my editor, everyone in the editorial department, the designers, Hinako Otabe-san, Katou-san, and Miura-san.

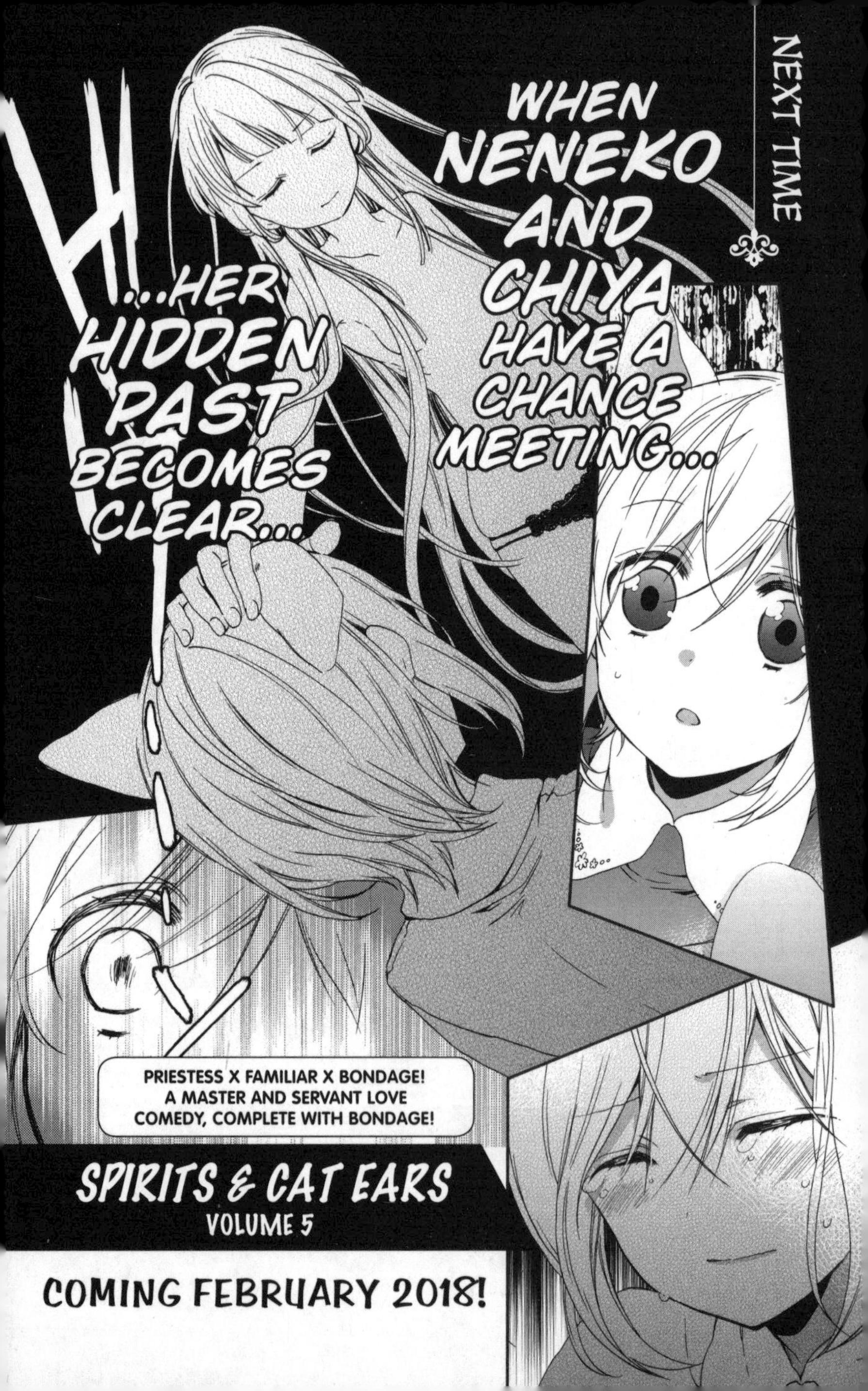
NEXT TIME
WHEN NENEKO AND CHIYA HAVE A CHANCE MEETING...
...HER HIDDEN PAST BECOMES CLEAR...
PRIESTESS X FAMILIAR X BONDAGE! A MASTER AND SERVANT LOVE COMEDY, COMPLETE WITH BONDAGE!
SPIRITS & CAT EARS
VOLUME 5
COMING FEBRUARY 2018!

# Spirits & Cat Ears

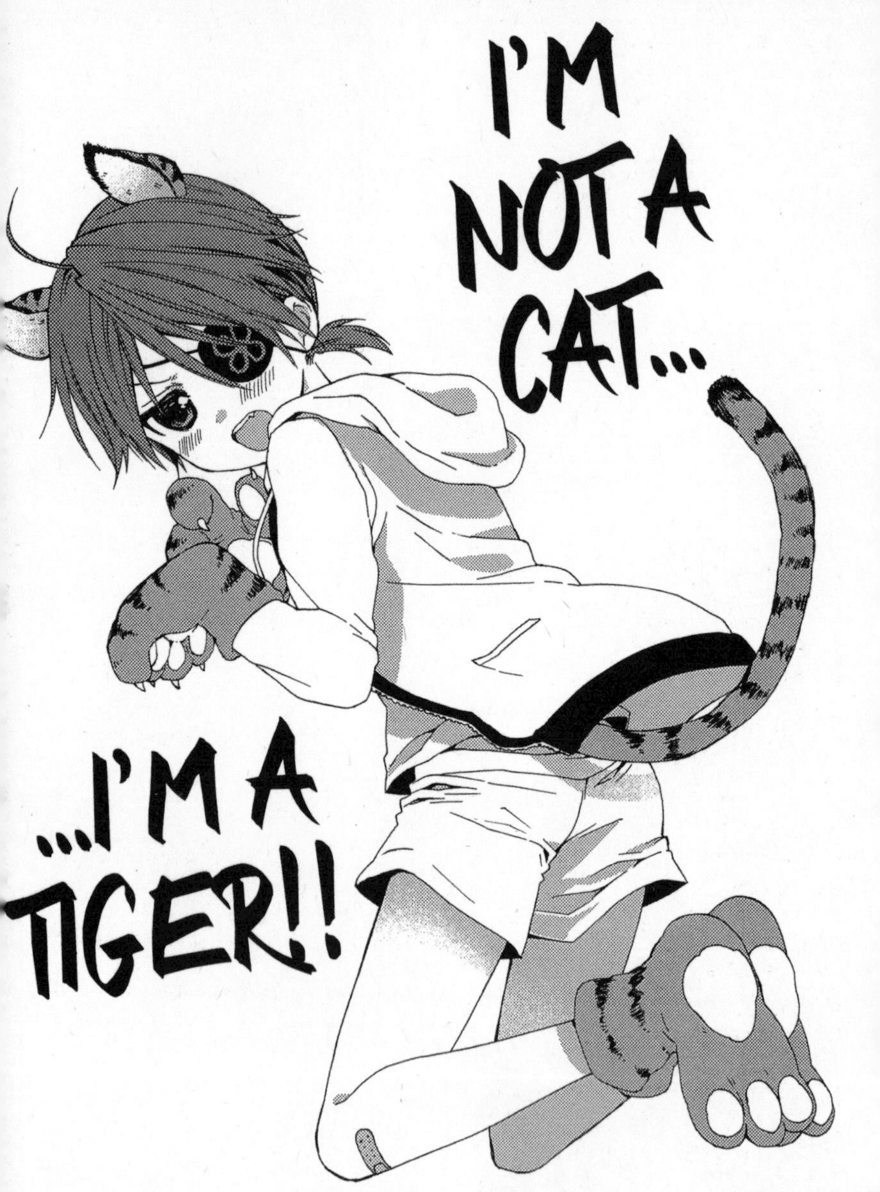
I'M NOT A CAT...
...I'M A TIGER!!

IF THE TWO ON THE COVER SWAPPED SIZES...

*SEE "ADULT TRANSFORMATION" IN VOLUME 3

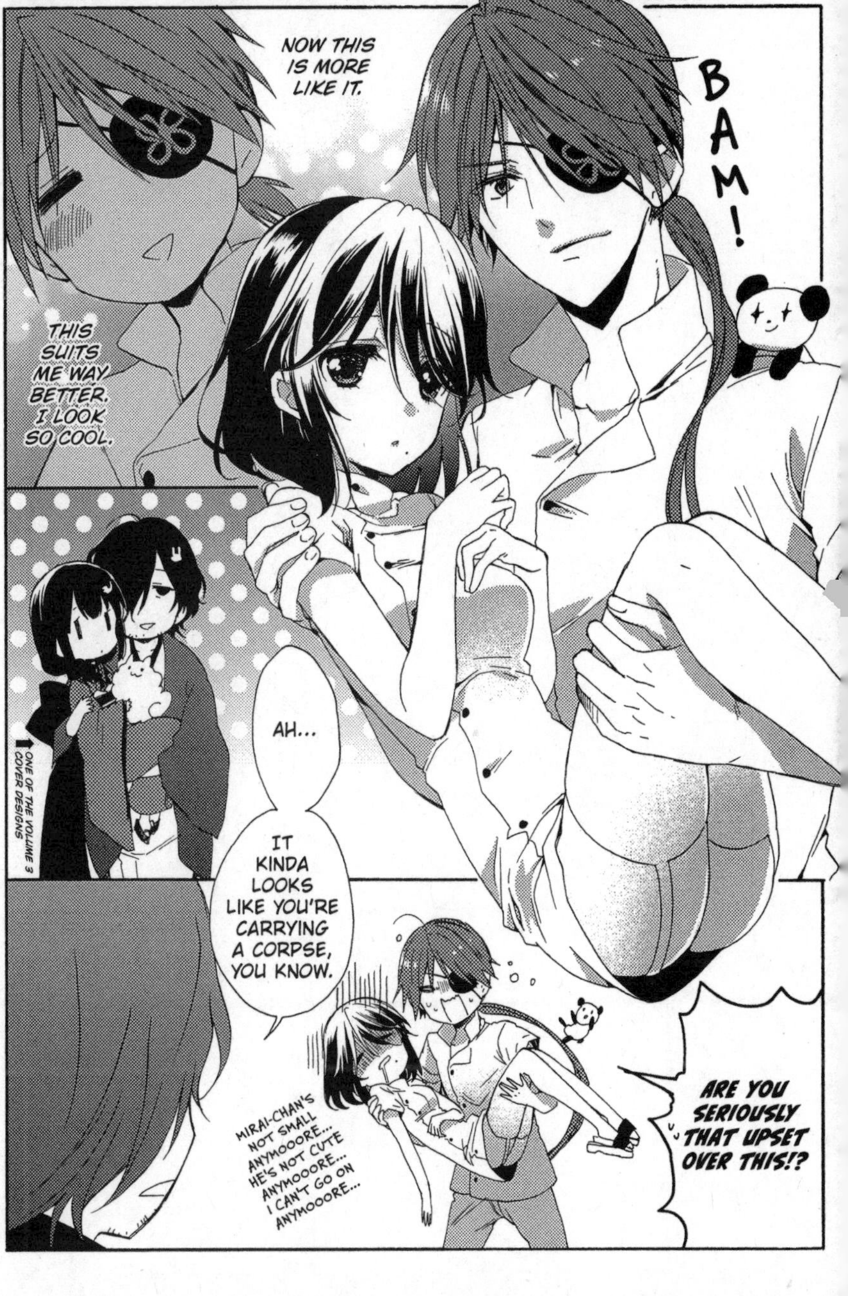
BAM!
NOW THIS IS MORE LIKE IT.
THIS SUITS ME WAY BETTER. I LOOK SO COOL.
AH...
IT KINDA LOOKS LIKE YOU'RE CARRYING A CORPSE, YOU KNOW.
ONE OF THE VOLUME 3 COVER DESIGNS
ARE YOU SERIOUSLY THAT UPSET OVER THIS!?
MIRAI-CHAN'S NOT SMALL ANYMOOORE... HE'S NOT CUTE ANYMOOORE... I CAN'T GO ON ANYMOOORE...

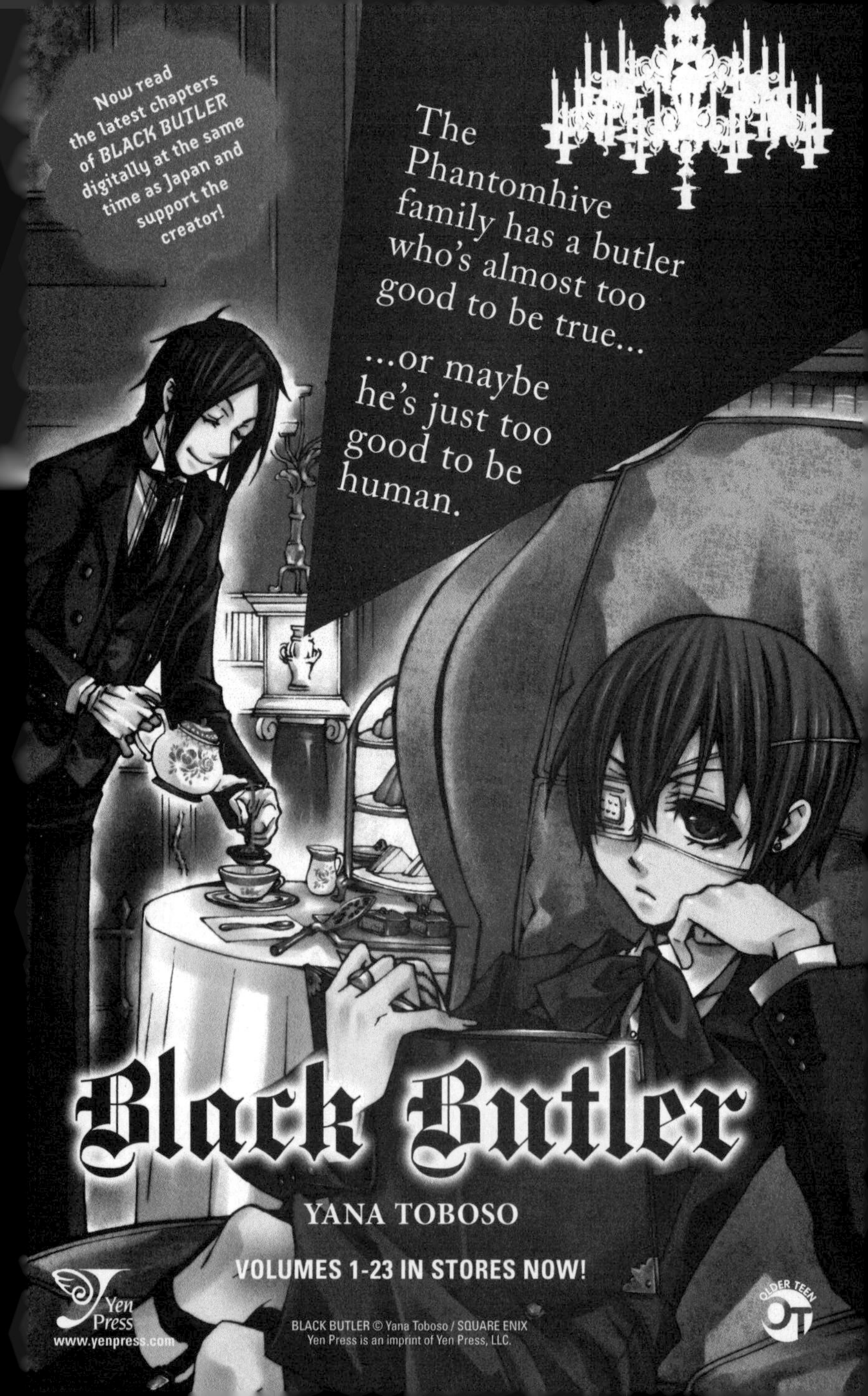
Now read the latest chapters of BLACK BUTLER digitally at the same time as Japan and support the creator!
The Phantomhive family has a butler who's almost too good to be true...
...or maybe he's just too good to be human.
Black Butler
YANA TOBOSO
VOLUMES 1-23 IN STORES NOW!
Yen Press
www.yenpress.com
BLACK BUTLER © Yana Toboso / SQUARE ENIX
Yen Press is an imprint of Yen Press, LLC.
OLDER TEEN
OT

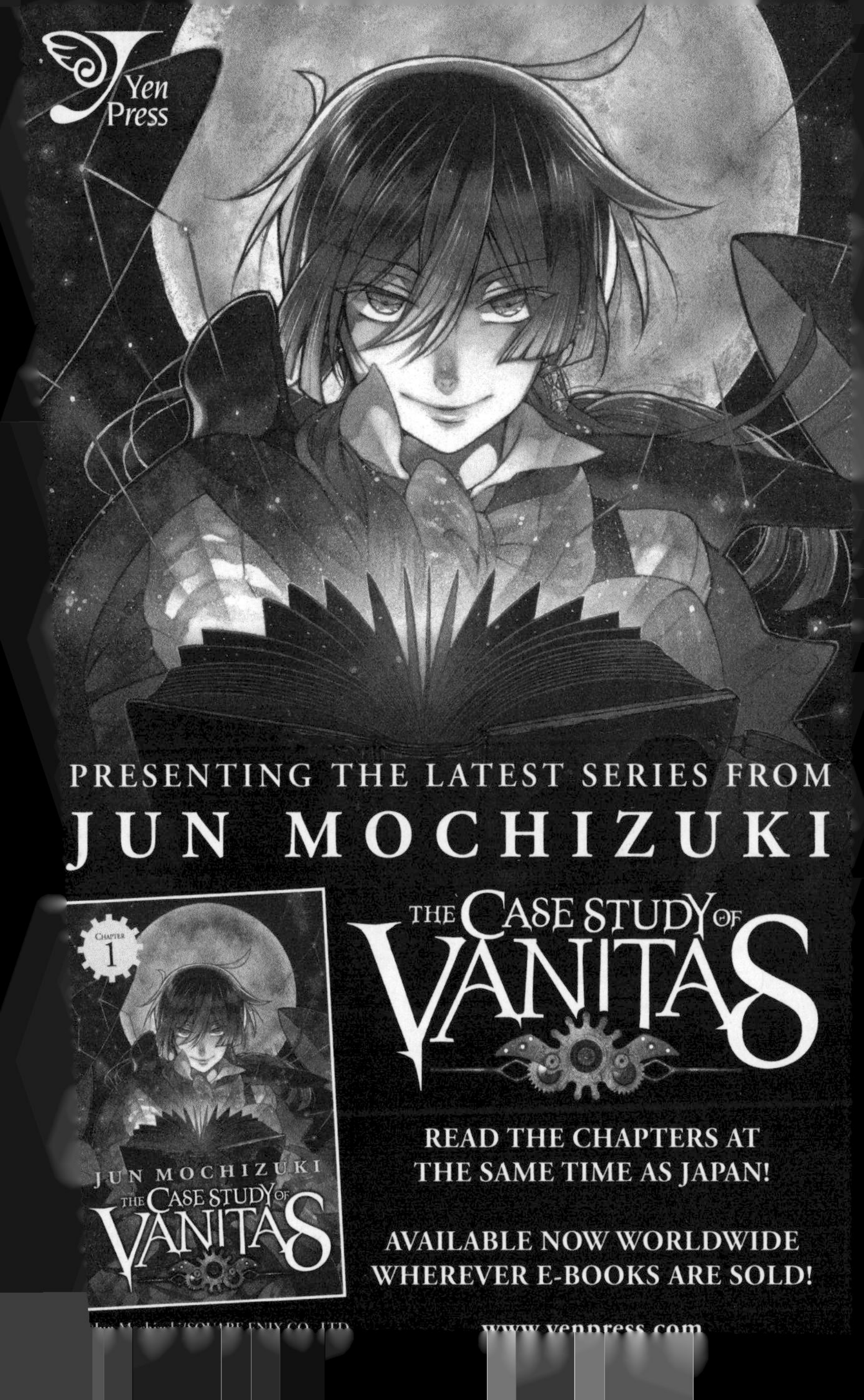
Yen Press
PRESENTING THE LATEST SERIES FROM
JUN MOCHIZUKI
CHAPTER 1
JUN MOCHIZUKI
THE CASE STUDY OF VANITAS
THE CASE STUDY OF VANITAS
READ THE CHAPTERS AT THE SAME TIME AS JAPAN!
AVAILABLE NOW WORLDWIDE WHEREVER E-BOOKS ARE SOLD!
www.yenpress.com

# *Two girls, a new school, and the beginning of a beautiful friendship.*

Volumes 1-3 available now

## *Kiss & White Lily for My Dearest Girl*

In middle school, Ayaka Shiramine was the perfect student: hard-working, with excellent grades and a great personality to match. As Ayaka enters high school she expects to still be on top, but one thing she didn't account for is her new classmate, the lazy yet genuine genius Yurine Kurosawa. What's in store for Ayaka and Yurine as they go through high school...together?

Kiss and White Lily For My Dearest Girl © Canno / KADOKAWA CORPORATION

**Karino Takatsu, creator of SERVANT × SERVICE, presents:**

# My Monster Girl's Too Cool For You

**Burning adoration melts her heart...literally!**

In a world where *youkai* and humans attend school together, a boy named Atsushi Fukuzumi falls for snow *youkai* Muku Shiroishi. Fukuzumi's passionate feelings melt Muku's heart...and the rest of her?! The first volume of an interspecies romantic comedy you're sure to fall head over heels for is now available!!

Yen Press

YenPress.com

© Karino Takatsu/SQUARE ENIX CO., LTD.

**Read new installments of this series every month at the same time as Japan!**

CHAPTERS AVAILABLE NOW AT E-TAILERS EVERYWHERE!

**TWO CHILDREN. TWO WOLVES.**

**TWO LIVES. ONE CHOICE.**

Mamoru Hosoda, creator of *Summer Wars* and *The Boy and the Beast*, tells a tale of growing up and growing out, of roads taken and abandoned, and of the complicated bonds between a mother and her children. With Ame and Yuki's wolf father dead, Hana must raise her two children alone. But they are both human and wolf. How will they survive in a world with no place for them? Artist Yu brings Hosoda's film to manga form in a book YALSA called one of its top ten graphic novels of 2015!

**Available at bookstores everywhere!**

Yen Press

© 2012 "WOLF CHILDREN" FILM PARTNERS © Yu 2012, 2013

YenPress.com

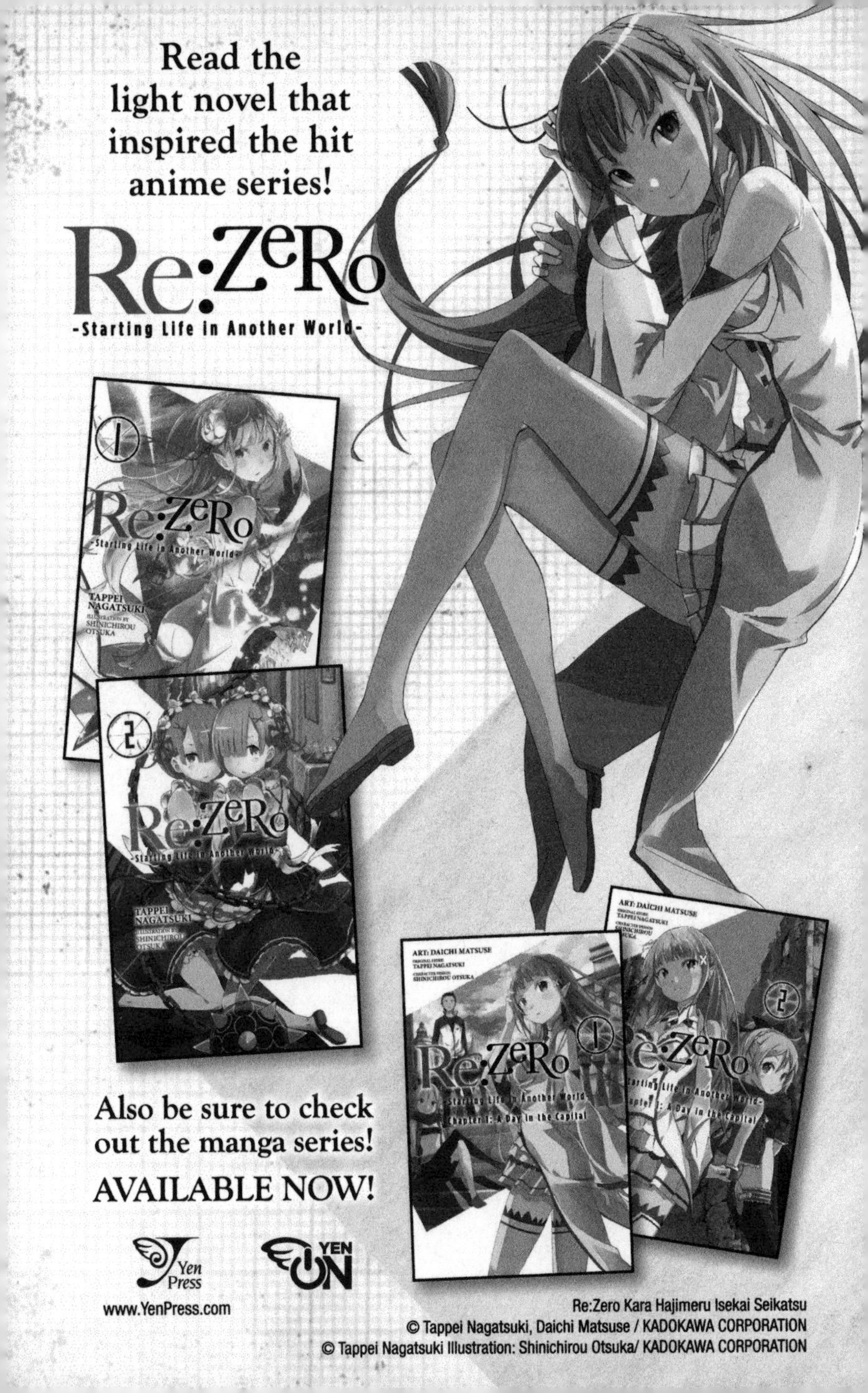

Read the light novel that inspired the hit anime series!
Re:ZeRo
-Starting Life in Another World-
Also be sure to check out the manga series!
AVAILABLE NOW!
Yen Press
YEN ON
www.YenPress.com
Re:Zero Kara Hajimeru Isekai Seikatsu
© Tappei Nagatsuki, Daichi Matsuse / KADOKAWA CORPORATION
© Tappei Nagatsuki Illustration: Shinichirou Otsuka/ KADOKAWA CORPORATION

zrac

# Spirits & Cat Ears 4

Miyuki
Nakayama

**Translation: Leighann Harvey**

**Lettering: Rochelle Gancio**

This book is a work of fiction. Names, characters, places, and incidents are the product of the author's imagination or are used fictitiously. Any resemblance to actual events, locales, or persons, living or dead, is coincidental.

KUDAMIMI NO NEKO Vol. 4
©Miyuki Nakayama 2015
First published in Japan in 2015 by KADOKAWA CORPORATION, Tokyo. English translation rights arranged with KADOKAWA CORPORATION, Tokyo through TUTTLE-MORI AGENCY, INC., Tokyo.

English translation © 2017
by Yen Press, LLC

Yen Press, LLC supports the right to free expression and the value of copyright. The purpose of copyright is to encourage writers and artists to produce the creative works that enrich our culture.

The scanning, uploading, and distribution of this book without permission is a theft of the author's intellectual property. If you would like permission to use material from the book (other than for review purposes), please contact the publisher. Thank you for your support of the author's rights.

Yen Press
1290 Avenue of the Americas
New York, NY 10104

Visit us at yenpress.com
facebook.com/yenpress
twitter.com/yenpress
yenpress.tumblr.com
instagram.com/yenpress

First Yen Press Edition: November 2017

Yen Press is an imprint of Yen Press, LLC. The Yen Press name and logo are trademarks of Yen Press, LLC.

The publisher is not responsible for websites (or their content) that are not owned by the publisher.

Library of Congress Control Number: 2016958578

ISBNs:
978-0-316-47060-5 (paperback)
978-0-316-47061-2 (ebook)

10 9 8 7 6 5 4 3 2 1

BVG

Printed in the United States of America

MAR – 1 – 2018